INTERNATIONAL RELATIONS—
STILL AN AMERICAN
SOCIAL SCIENCE?

SUNY series in Global Politics
James N. Rosenau, editor

INTERNATIONAL RELATIONS— STILL AN AMERICAN SOCIAL SCIENCE?

Toward Diversity in International Thought

edited by

ROBERT M. A. CRAWFORD
and
DARRYL S. L. JARVIS

State University
of New York
Press

Published by
State University of New York Press, Albany

© 2001 State University of New York

Production by Susan Geraghty
Marketing by Patrick Durocher

Printed in the United States of America

For information, address State University of New York Press,
90 State Street, Suite 700, Albany, NY 12207

Library of Congress Cataloging-in-Publication Data

International relations—still an American social science? : toward diversity in
international thought / edited by Robert M.A. Crawford, Darryl S.L. Jarvis.
    p. cm. — (SUNY series in global politics)
  Includes bibliographical references and index.
  ISBN 0-7914-4703-0 (alk. paper) — ISBN 0-7914-4704-9 (pbk. : alk. paper)
    1. International relations—Philosophy. 2. International relations—Social aspects. I.
Crawford, Robert M.A. II. Jarvis, Darryl S.L., 1963– III. Series.

JZ1242 .I579 2000
327—dc21
                                                                    99-088338

10 9 8 7 6 5 4 3 2 1

CONTENTS

TABLES AND FIGURES

PREFACE

The earliest inspiration for this volume was a seemingly innocent comment made during the course of cafeteria banter between graduate students of International Relations (IR) at the University of British Columbia. Signaling an intention to get back to work, one of our several American colleagues arose and said, "Well, as they say south of the border, *mañana!*" It was instantly, if somewhat brusquely, pointed out that it was unlikely that residents of Washington state (south of the *Canadian* border) said anything of the sort. It was a harmless enough oversight that might simply have reflected a personal failing like poor geography. Ignorance and parochialism can be difficult to distinguish. Several years and similar comments later, however, my co-editor and I began to wonder if there was not something peculiarly self-referential and parochial about American IR students and, thus, the discipline that they dominate. The anecdotal and impressionistic evidence for such a supposition has become overwhelming, including the immeasurably insensitive, absurd, and now infamous decision of the International Studies Association (ISA, the flagship organization of American IR) to treat Canadian money as a foreign currency while hosting its 1997 meetings in Toronto. Ironically, the Toronto meetings functioned as a testing ground for several of the essays below, and several of the authors remark the symbolism and significance of the ISA's decision. This volume is not offered as an exploration of parochialism per se, however, since this is an unavoidable occupational hazard in social and humane studies. Rather, it is comprised of essays that explore the implications of so nearly an exclusive American hegemony in international theory that Stanley Hoffmann describes it as an American social science. With the discipline of IR thus ordained, and scarcely a dissenting view in sight, how could IR programs at Canadian, Australian, British, French, Japanese, or other non-American universities be viewed as anything other than intellectual branch-plants for the home office of the American discipline? Is it really the case that a subject as explicitly global as IR has become an American social science, or has an American version of social science monopolized and colonized the study of IR? The most striking aspect of these searching questions is that they have only just begun to be raised, and have yet to receive sustained and serious attention.

The purpose of this volume is to begin the process of filling this gap. It is not a celebration of diversity for its own sake, is not based on denying or eradicating the existence of a peculiarly American conception of IR, and makes no pretense to speak for much more than the very limited range of research communities its authors represent. The latter is a reality of the field's existing composition more than it is a weakness. After all, if IR were a genuinely global subject the rationale for this book would disappear. Diversity as it is explored in this volume pertains largely to a process of finding, or creating, space for alternative nationally, transnationally or culturally derived conceptions of international relations as a subject worthy of interest, whether or not these conceptions are expressed in the question-begging language of "IR theory" or "*the* Discipline." Most of the essays below resist the "who-else-is-doing-what-we-do" standard of measurement that underpins prior evaluations of the field's aptitude toward American or Anglo-American hegemony. Rather, our contributors ask: whose doing what? where and how are they doing it? to what end? are there modes of exploration that the dominant conception of "the discipline" might lead us to overlook, either within or outside its traditionally Anglo-American core? These issues are framed not in the "question everything" mentality that has become the modus operandi advocated in much discussion of late, but in the conviction that the present sense of disarray and drift in the field is at least partly attributable to its chronic failure to articulate, let alone explore, its basic presuppositions. All the while that it is understood as an American monoscience, the health and progress of IR cannot be measured by the global diffusion of its techniques or replication of its institutional infrastructure. If IR is an American social science, we ask, what are we to make of intellectual activity directed at gaining some sort of purchase on what might broadly be called international studies, but falls outside the discipline's self-defined (or self-*un*defined) boundaries? At present, the insularity that tends to inhabit and fuel the logic of the American discipline leads to the assumption that the only relevant standard of theory is its own. Everything outside this rendering becomes a sort of theoretical *terra incognita* not because it is unAmerican, but because it is unrecognizable as IR. What may simply be different ways of thinking about international relations become theoretical absences or voids that make American IR hegemonic by default, not design. This book offers only a preliminary foray into the largely unexplored expanses of international theory outside the well charted terrain of American IR and, in the spirit of D. H. Lawrence invoked below by Martin Griffiths and Terry O'Callaghan, reminds the reader of the sorts of expeditionary hazards that can befall them when "the map appears . . . more real than the land."

We take great pleasure in acknowledging the contributions of others to the development of this volume. We are particularly grateful to our contributors for the high caliber of their essays, their professional and timely response to our and the reviewer's suggestion for revision, and, above all, their patience. Particular thanks are in order to those individuals who provided insightful commentary and feedback on individual essays and the project generally, including Kal Holsti, Robert Jackson, David Long, Steve Smith, Chris Brown, Martin Griffiths, Terry O'Callaghan, Molly Cochran, Kim Richard Nossal, Jan Pettman, Roger Spegele, Michael Banks and A. P. Rana. We are also very pleased to thank the anonymous reviewers whose thoughtful and balanced criticisms were much appreciated, and instrumental in improving the volume. Thanks also to the editorial staff at SUNY Press for their assistance and support throughout the project. Special thanks to Priscilla Ross and to the series editor, Professor James N. Rosenau, whose early enthusiasm and support for the project has nevered faultered through a sometimes difficult review process. We are particularly indebted to you, Jim, for your open-mindedness. Less courageous presses and editors might have found it easy to walk away from so controversial a project. Finally, our profound gratitude to our families.

Robert M. A. Crawford
The University of British Columbia

Darryl S. L. Jarvis
The University of Sydney

INTRODUCTION

International Relations as an Academic Discipline: If It's Good for America, Is It Good for the World?

Robert M. A. Crawford

While hardly subjects of sustained study or interest, the sociology and geography of knowledge in the discipline of International Relations (IR) have periodically engaged its more theoretically inclined students. The consensus to date is that IR is "international" only in subject matter and name, and pretty much a North Atlantic, disproportionately Anglo-American, preoccupation. This anomaly has generated occasional curiosity but generally failed to excite concern. National representation, it might be supposed, ought to play no role in assessing the health or viability of any scientific enterprise. At no point in the human struggle against disease, for example, do we feel compelled to ask whether our epidemiologists are from Bulgaria, Finland, or Tanzania. Why ought our equally pressing, and related, concerns with war, peace, dislocation, famine, wealth, poverty, genocide, environmental degradation, and so on, require the least bit of attention to nationality? Nationality, culture, location, and the myriad other constitutive elements of individual and group identities offer no prophylactic assurance against AIDS, no hedge against hyperinflation, and no shelter from radioactive fallout. This at least is something like the attitude that tends to dominate the mainstream conception of IR.

It is by no means clear, however, that the roster of items on the IR menu, or the means to their investigation, involve choices that transcend ideology. The only thing more remarkable than the persistent Anglo-American domination of the field is the apparently widespread willingness to ignore or downplay it. That the markedly parochial nature of the subject is candidly acknowledged has done little to moderate its clear pretension to theoretical universalism. It is seldom asked whether the mainstream conception of IR is itself a reflection of values, attitudes, and predispositions forged in the cauldron of particular historical, cultural, and national experiences and circumstances, or whether, indeed, there is something distinctively cultural about the idea that IR can or should be conceived as a discipline in the first place. The compulsion to rise above the fray of contending ideologies, in other words, may itself originate, consciously or unconsciously, in an ideological enterprise that, by definition and design, is rendered invisible by its universalist, homogenizing propensities. While supranational forces today seem everywhere in ascendance, cosmopolitanism can have a peculiarly national flavor. The much-heralded declining fortunes of the state aside, the nation remains, in the words of Hans Morgenthau, "the ultimate point of reference for political loyalties and actions" (Morgenthau 1948, 273). It seems a reasonable conjecture that nationality might also constitute an important, if not ultimate, point of reference for IR theorists. In light of the above considerations, the fact that this often appears not to be the case makes closer investigation all the more interesting and worthwhile.

And yet there is a clear tendency for international relations research to foster different interests, methods, and disciplinary attitudes across the few national settings in which it can be said to constitute a subject of sustained interest. The evidence for parochialism is everywhere and not confined to what Stanley Hoffmann described famously (and parochially!) as its American heartland (Hoffmann, 1977 and reprinted in this volume). Ironically, such parochialism is only magnified by the ostensibly ecumenical objectives behind the growing attempt to identify non-American centers of discussion. Consider, for example, the practice of describing European international relations theory as "continental," as though there were no other continent to which this designation could refer, and no distinctions within this category worth noting; or the common depiction of *the* discipline as Anglo-American despite strong evidence of a distinctively British approach; or the usually implicit assumption that settings like Canada, Australia, and New Zealand have no indigenous theoretical tradition, and merely consume ideas produced in the nationally based centers of the field; in still other countries activity commensurate with international relations theorizing may be noted, but is defined in terms of its consumption, replication, or imitation of what counts as theoretical activity elsewhere. In short, international relations scholars even seem fated to be parochial about their parochialism.

The lack of disciplinary credentials for the study of international relations in the vast bulk of countries whose interactions collectively form its traditional subject matter suggests a number of possibilities, the exploration and implications of which constitute the principal activity of this collection. There are no clear answers to this problem, and not even any consensus that parochialism is a problem, since it is just as likely to be an unavoidable occupational hazard as the product of a conscious and deliberate practice. Even so, like other occupational hazards, precautions should be taken to minimize its dangers, with examples of the latter including homogeneity in the guise of universalism, mutual antipathy, disdain, and lack of respect, or a general unwillingness to find value in the positions of others. "Better to jaw jaw, than to war war," said Winston Churchill, and the same applies to intellectual life in general, and in the particular case of what we might call (for the sake of not begging the question) international studies, especially since "war war" is an increasingly common feature of its literary and other sites of exchange (when and where there is exchange).

The rationale for this volume is to explore generally the implications of a propensity toward parochialism in international relations theory and, more particularly, the persistence of an assimilationist logic exemplified, and bound up with, a distinctly American conception of disciplinarity, science, and progress. Paradoxically, perhaps even perversely, the reaction thus far to this well-known problem seems to have done little to yield alternative conceptions of discipline, theory, international relations, and so forth, because it has failed to recognize that its own reaction is in large measure defined by the very assimilationist logic to which it stands opposed. The term "diversity"—no less than discipline, theory, or social science—is too often assumed to be part of a shared vocabulary, leaving us with an incomplete picture of the differences, divisions, and distinctions that presumably are at stake. Left unarticulated, there is a natural propensity for dominant conceptions of diversity and sameness to stand-in. Thus, for example, diversity could easily describe the plurality of methodological approaches and normative orientations that have been used to describe theory within what Hoffmann calls the American discipline of IR, despite its recent preoccupation with things neorealist and neoliberal. Diversity in this case, however, seems to refer only to variations on a central rationalist-empiricist theme that is not itself opened to question. The thrust of much recent activity—largely outside the "official" boundaries of IR it must be noted—is, by contrast, aimed at transcending diversity in this self-limiting sense. But to what extent is this possible without altogether rejecting the discipline of IR, since its claims to legitimacy are based on universally valid precepts that can allow nothing more than tinkering, assimilation, or the mere replacement of one planetary dogma with another? Consider, for example, Charles Taylor's discussion of the "politics of recognition" in the intellectual life of a multicultural world:

> the last thing one wants at this stage from Eurocentered intellectuals is positive judgments of the worth of cultures that they have not intensively studied. For real judgments of worth suppose a fused horizon of standards. . . . The peremptory demand for favorable judgments of worth is paradoxically . . . homogenizing. For it implies that we already have the standards to make such judgments . . . those of North Atlantic civilization. And so the judgments implicitly and consciously will cram the others into our categories. For instance, we will think of their "artists" as creating "works," which we then can include in our canon. By implicitly invoking our standards to judge all civilizations and cultures, the politics of difference can end up making everyone the same. (Taylor, 1994, 70–71)

Taylor's characterization is no less relevant to the study of international relations or, at least, would be if the latter came close to constituting a multicultural enterprise. It is multinational to be sure, but outside its American and Anglo-European cores consists of little more than foreign policy analyses, and what counts as a theory or discipline is in *all* places measured by the yardstick of what is endorsed officially as such in the United States. When it is suggested, for example, that a distinctive British, Canadian, Australian, or Indian approach to international relations exists, the burden of proof for such a claim falls squarely on those who make it, and the only admissible standards of evidence are degrees of conformity to the conception of discipline which alone need not authenticate its claims, or bother with a national prefix.

What then should be done as regards the problem of American intellectual hegemony in international relations theory? The essays in this volume reflect a wide range of responses and it would be ironic in the extreme if a collection aimed at the exploration of diversity tried to distill its findings into anything resembling a unitary creed. The only thing resembling an undisputed reality in international studies is that whatever ultimate destination awaits it is a very long way off. In this context of uncertainty answers are less interesting than questions. It would require a disdain of monumental proportions to foreclose the possibility that new and important insights might yet come (or might already be awaiting discovery) from beyond the present intellectual, geographical, and cultural boundaries of the field (see Taylor, 1994, 72–73). The point is not that there is anything intrinsically valuable in the multiplicity of national, ethnic, cultural, gendered, sexed, linguistic, religious, moral, historical, individual, and countless other viewpoints that comprise international society, but that we may never be in a position to make judgments of worth among them, not least because we fail to take them seriously. This said, however, it is impossible to imagine anything other than chaos if international relations is to be approached as anything we want it to be, with its "theories" purely individualized series of reflections constituting a sort of performance art. What distinguishes the approaches below from the solipsistic excesses of the more extreme modes of postmodernism that (quite rightly) inspire suspicion is their commitment to the idea that international relations is composed of culturally defined groups which create meaningful lives for large numbers of people, albeit meanings that may clash with those held in other collectivities. There is no presumption in this volume that the traditional, problem-solving, substantive orientation of international relations theory should be jettisoned. On the contrary, it can only be augmented by a wider exploration of what these problems are, wider at least than what is presently offered in mainstream (largely American) IR.

Some of these points have been made before, often by theorists whose works, however unwittingly, have contributed to narrowing the field's conception of scientific endeavor, and fostering its Americanization. Hans Morgenthau's depiction of the inherent ambiguity of international politics, for example, his often skeptical attitude toward the simplistic "solutions" of science, and his keen awareness of the extent to which reality is socially constructed, sits uneasily beside his perceived status as "founding father" of the American science of IR (Morgenthau, 1948, 19). And Stanley Hoffmann's identification of a permanent and reciprocal relationship between scientific/empirical and philosophical/normative theory promised to point the new American discipline down an admirably broad intellectual pathway, but has since been belied by his failure to explore anything other than a scientific foundation for the subject (Hoffmann, 1965, 18–21). The point, then, is that the discipline has moved in a distinctly different, narrowly scientific, intellectually parochial and American direction than these immigrant theorists first envisioned. Thus, if some of the more strident critics of the American discipline are guilty of overlooking its intellectually diverse origins, the sin of their forgetfulness is at least partly absolved by the stunted development of a discipline that has made such things hard to remember.

This said it is no part of our intention to deride, belittle, or trivialize the accomplishments of American IR scholarship. Rather, just as Hoffmann suggests that Morgenthau served as a "goad and a foil" to creative scholarship, Hoffmann's essay "An American Social Science: International Relations" is put to similar use in this volume, to which end it is reprinted in its original form. As Hoffmann also suggests, "sound and fury are good for creative scholarship," and it is in this spirit that the energetic, wide-ranging, and provocative essays offered below are crafted. It must be stated at the outset, however, that this volume offers no consensus on how "American intellectual hegemony" should be conceptualized, measured, and defined, nor do our contributors agree on the degree to which nationality in any guise ultimately matters. This is a diverse collection with a range of responses. It must also be noted that some of the essays below do not explicitly and directly address the issues raised in Hoffmann's article. It is included here for a couple of reasons, neither of which is essential to our ultimate objectives. First, despite its richly deserved status as a "classic," it is not the most readily available work. Including it here makes it more widely accessible. The Hoffmann essay is so central to our theme that failing to cite it is in any case difficult, and the decision to include it obvious. Second, it adds the voice of a deeply respected and influential American (though not American-born) contributor to an otherwise largely non-American set of reflections. Its inclusion should help to remind a largely American audience of the centrality of the question of national experience in international relations theory and praxis. But it is no part of our intention to offer this volume as a sort of Hoffmann *festschrift*.[1] Hoffmann provides the first, rather than last, word on the problem of IR as an American social science, and his article is included not as a set of authoritative pronouncements to which our contributors feel compelled to respond, but as an intellectual stimulant for readers and contributors alike.

PARADOXES AND IRONIES

There are two primary dangers with asserting one's difference in the face of an enterprise driven by an unrelenting desire for universally applicable principles, laws, and maxims: (1) nobody will notice; (2) somebody will notice. With apologies to Oscar Wilde, the proponents of diversity in international thought might do well to accept that "the only thing worse than *not* being talked about is *being* talked about." There is an apparent tendency in American IR, for example, or any hegemonic enterprise for that matter, to turn today's alien or heretical construct into tomorrow's paradigm. Consider, for example, the fate of the "English School" of international relations, a distinct perspective that went largely unnoticed in mainstream IR debates until American scholars "discovered" the problem of interstate cooperation, international society, and "regimes." Once noticed—if noticed—the "English School" was assumed merely to complement regime analyses rather than the other way around (Buzan, 1993; Crawford, 1996, 1–7). And despite the knee-jerk reaction occasioned by postmodernist inspired critiques aimed explicitly at deconstructing the discipline, it is not unusual these days to hear seemingly traditional, empirically oriented scholars describe themselves as "liberal postmodernists," a moniker inspired by the American social philosopher Richard Rorty (see Diebert, 1997). As Molly Cochran suggests in this volume, synthesizing maneuvers of this sort are performed not in the name of hegemony but science: "progress in the discipline is more likely when its players agree to meet on the same playing field." One question implicit in this volume, however, is what happens when the location of the playing field, the rules of the game, whose keeping score, and what counts as victory have already been decided?

It is the above paradox that Chris Brown has in mind when he suggests that "American International Relations . . . are not parochial enough." Though there is a tendency in general usage to regard the term pejoratively, it may well be that parochialism is an inevitable function of living in different locales, be they sovereign or subnational states, provinces, territories, municipalities, counties, tribal homelands, cities, towns, villages, and so forth. In Canada, for example, its largely Ontario and Quebec–based opinion-leaders are fond of distilling the variety of interests and aspirations manifest in the rest of the country into monolithic packages called "the regions." Similarly, while residents in "the West" or "the prairies" complain about the parochialism of "the East" they tend to engage in a parochialism of their own, though of a double nature, the first part of which is simply a western version of regional stereotyping, and the second a failure to notice that Ontario and Quebec are not actually in eastern Canada! Complaints of this sort are heard the world over and may be expressed as grievances by rural inhabitants against suburban, suburban against urban, the "south" against the "north" (an opposition that echoes tragically in the United States or bemuses visitors to England today), islander against mainlander, downtowner against east-sider, outbacker against coastliner, and so forth. Who has not heard or made complaints of this sort? If these differences can excite passions between inhabitants of the same political communities, it takes little effort to imagine how convictions more deeply held can impact disputes within and, more fundamentally for international relations, between sovereign states. The propensity for American IR to be "wedded to the universal," as Brown puts it, may thus deny a fundamentally ineradicable part of what it means to be human, and impose a false conformity on a world that is morally, intellectually, and culturally fragmented. It is thus no more incumbent on scholars to transcend their parochialisms than to recognize that the perceived need to do so may itself derive from a parochial viewpoint with universal pretensions.

A second paradox, encountered directly by the editors when inviting submissions to this volume, is the propensity for investigation of this sort to generate roughly equal degrees of enthusiasm and disdain. Among the latter, reaction ranged from a mild interest tainted with indifference and resignation to the issue of American dominance, to a suspicion that the volume would merely be complicit in the project of intellectual hegemony it purports to question. In short, for some, questions of this sort are not worth asking or go too far while, for others, they do not go far enough. Reactions of this sort now typify international relations theory, which finds itself caught between the mutually contradictory postures of a seemingly open-ended perspectivism bent on the destruction of all pretenses to discipline, and the ostrich-like denial that there is anything fundamentally wrong. It is our hope that this volume can steer a middle course between these equally dogmatic intellectual hazards of navigation, and we would be disposed to regard critical attention from either camp as one indication of success. More importantly, however, the very existence of this collection indicates that a substantial number of international relations scholars remain committed to exposing theoretical authoritarianism in all its guises. To what extent this has been done is up to the reader to judge.

There is also an irony here that needs to be noted, especially as it might be perceived as a point of major vulnerability: the authorship of this volume on diversity does not seem very diverse. The volume also tends to reflect issues of concern to British, Canadian, and Australian-based scholars. The reasons for this are varied, but reducible largely to contingency factors. Every attempt was made, for example, to cover as much of the globe as possible but the very parochialism that inspired this collection helped to conspire against its objective of greater inclusiveness. In a number of cases potential contributors had to decline or withdraw for reasons related entirely to workload, other logistical considerations and, in one instance, failing health. As noted above, others declined for what might charitably be described as ideological objections sometimes to the project, but more often to the disciplinary construction of IR itself. What is left might not seem especially representative but this is largely an illusion since, once we get outside the American core of IR scholarship, there are few national research communities that can be said to treat the subject in an organized, and sustained manner, and fewer still that constitute genuinely indigenous sites of theory in the normal, albeit restrictive, IR sense. If this situation seems regrettable it is none the less real, though this collection is aimed at an honest exploration of these limitations, and can be viewed as part of a process that might ultimately point the way to a more impressive multiculturalism.

THE MANY FACES OF DIVERSITY

But the diversity canvassed in this volume refers more explicitly to intellectual constructs than the generic attributes of its authors. Its literary source of inspiration is twofold: Hoffmann's monolithic depiction of IR as an American social science in his 1977 essay, and Kalevi J. Holsti's exploration of intellectual hegemony in his 1985 work *The Dividing Discipline*. It is arguable that both of these works have received less attention than they deserve, with the former essay simply cementing for many what they already knew, and the latter book mined largely for its insights on the state-of-the-art in IR. Perhaps the time for sustained attention to the problem of hegemony and diversity in international thought had not quite come by the mid-1980s. Even the most cursory glance at the theoretical literature today could not generate the same conclusion. The mood of disarray, division, and theoretical drift addressed by Holsti has given way to virtual intellectual chaos, and ushered in an era of unprecedented crisis, at least in those admittedly small circles that interest themselves in international theory.

Thanks in large measure to Holsti's earlier intervention, we are now at least better able to distinguish genuine normative shifts from approaches that merely finesse the core assumptions and concerns of what he calls the "classical tradition." While some measure of diversity is an unavoidable feature of our enterprise, there is little to be gained by automatically conferring the status of "new school" on every innovation. But in broaching the issue of intellectual hegemony, reminding us that "almost all of what we call international theory today has been developed by observers from . . . Great Britain and the United States" (Holsti, 1985, vii–ix), Holsti also reminds us that the existence of a single unifying tradition is no more automatic a virtue than the existence of diversity. Each is of value only to the extent that it generates usable insights about the substantive problems of international relations. What these are, however, is increasingly contested, and at least partly forged in the many fires of national experience. A genuinely international discipline, therefore, ought not to further national over global interests, or vice versa, unless it can be shown that the two are indistinguishable. Beyond a very high level of generality, however (e.g., a general, globalized aversion to nuclear annihilation) there is strong prima facie evidence to suggest that the theoretical enterprise in international relations is one of multiple worlds, and that the discipline of IR may be more like a galaxy than a globe.

But how far do we take diversity? Are we dealing with multiple galaxies as well as multiple worlds—the Western intellectual tradition versus its civilizational rivals for example? Clearly the alleged parochialism and ethnocentrism of the Western traditions of social and political inquiry are important issues, but we leave these largely to the explorations of others (one possible exception is the contribution to this volume by Pal Ahluwalia and Michael Sullivan). This volume marks a point of departure, not an end-point, and we are content to assume that the notion of a homogeneous Western tradition of international thought falsely masks an important diversity. It is better in our view that the possibility of national differences within the discipline as normally understood be explored first if judgments about its unitary conception of things are to have more than merely rhetorical appeal. In terms of situating the volume, then, we see it sitting somewhere between the explosion of theoretical/personal viewpoints, orientations, and epistemologies that have exaggerated diversity in world politics, and the notion of a classical tradition that has tended to overstate similarity. In providing an analysis of the aptitude for "hegemony" and "diversity" in the field, our volume takes the first step on the path to a more informed, inclusive assessment of IR's disciplinary parameters and credentials.

Because what constitutes a discipline of IR in the first instance is an issue unresolved (and often unacknowledged) in the literature per se, no attempt is made to address it is in this collection. Indeed, IR research has typically done without the sort of explorations offered in many of these essays, despite their obviously predisciplinary character. There is an element of arbitrariness in the attempt to organize any diverse collection of essays and a volume such as this poses special challenges. For the sake of convenience, however, it is divided into three parts, each of which corresponds to a particular aspect of the hegemony/diversity issue that individual authors have been asked to address. The first of these broad themes deals with the problem of hegemony and diversity at the disciplinary level. Each of these essays either takes the idea of IR as a universally valid science for granted, or seeks to demonstrate the feasibility of some sort of disciplinary project in defiance of seemingly insuperable fragmentary forces.

Part I ("Hegemony and Diversity in International Thought") is anchored by Hoffmann's essay, which, again, functions as an intellectual springboard for the volume as a whole, whether or not the essays that follow deal explicitly with this work. The original essays are led off by Molly Cochran whose eminently sensible point of departure is to ask what it means to be an American social science in the first place. Her main point is that the direction the discipline took in the post–World War II era was understandable in terms of Hoffmann's analysis of the particular constellation of ideological, material, and historical circumstances in which it was nurtured, but that its eventual turn toward an almost exclusively empirical, naturalistic bent was by no means inevitable. One of the different tributaries into which a uniquely American social science of IR might have flown, she argues, is that of American pragmatism, an orientation typified by John Dewey.

In the next essay, Kalevi J. Holsti undertakes a detailed symptomatology of the perceived crisis in international relations theory, and suggests that what now resembles intellectual chaos should be placed in the comparative context of a field well accustomed to acrimonious disputes, and might ultimately be an indication or harbinger of growing disciplinary self-consciousness, maturation, and philosophical depth. It may also, however, portend several mutually exclusive directions or "travelogues" for the discipline, some of which include its disappearance. The main concern raised by Holsti's essay then is that, however diverse the discipline should and must become, it should remain focused on the actual political dilemmas in the world it tries to comprehend.

In his essay, D. S. L. Jarvis focuses on exploring the new diversity implied by postmodern and radical feminist international relations scholarship, especially as this relates to their proposed methodologies, agendas, and empirical foci. Since the first wave of discipline-defining debate in the early 1980s, he argues, feminist scholarship has been among the most forceful and "subversive" of the new approaches, and is aimed ultimately at advancing new research agendas, and "reinscribing" the role, function, and purpose of IR as an academic discipline. This proposed restructuring goes beyond diversity in the usual methodological sense, and includes an agenda to broaden the social composition of the profession in the name of an "identity politics" that insists on representation for "voices," "peoples," and "issues" traditionally "silenced" or "marginalized" in the field. Jarvis argues that, while theory need not always be capable of being operationalized in the service of public and foreign policy, some of it at least should be, and that too much attention to the dilemmas of knowledge tends to come at the expense of sustained attention to the dilemmas of international politics, the lives of whose inhabitants—whatever their identify—are made perilous because of them. While feminist perspectives have made valuable contributions and enhanced our understanding of international politics, Jarvis concludes, such perspectives have yet to make a convincing case for the intellectual revolution and refocused research agendas they so earnestly propose.

Tony Porter closes out part I by suggesting that it is only minimally useful to speak about "national perspectives" on international relations. He suggests that investigative energy is better directed to understanding how the enterprise of intellectual reflection itself, especially in the context of the disciplinary concerns that comprise IR, serves to marginalize, or perhaps even suppress, the role of nationality, if not substantially transcend it. Drawing upon the experiences and reflections of Canadian

IR scholars, Porter argues that nationality and theorizing are only nominally related and that the Canadian experience, while not likely to be generalizable, probably parallels that of national research communities located at a similar social and spatial distance from the center of our contemporary world. If this locational effect can be called nationality, he concludes, it is a nationality that is ambiguous, open, and only moderately distinctive.

Part II brings together a set of essays united by their exploration of the sometimes subtle influences of national perspectives in IR scholarship, influences that—for some—make the very idea of IR as a genuinely international discipline problematic. The essays in this part ("National and Transnational Identities in International Theory") share the view that there is something inherently myopic and ethnocentric about IR theory, but disagree over the extent to which this is shaped by American perceptions, the way in which it is manifested, and the degree to which national difference matters in the face of other, perhaps more fundamental, points of divergence like gender and/or class.

A. J. R. Groom and Peter Mandaville start the discussion by suggesting that IR theory is "all a matter of perspective." Using the metaphor of the telescope, what one finds out in or about the field, they argue, depends on where they focus attention, whether or not the instrument is placed to the blind eye, which end of the instrument they look through, and so forth. The question of whether IR is still an American social science depends on the locale, and the vantage point, from which one views the discipline. Groom and Mandaville begin their survey (in the double sense of a questionnaire of the field's participants and a topographical evaluation of its contours) from the confines of the contemporary European Union rather than the more conventional American point of departure. They roam wide and far across the disciplinary landscape, frequently repositioning the lens, and refocusing and redirecting the telescope, to build an image of the multiple national influences that have historically gone into the composition of the discipline, and continue to define its various foci and theoretical tools. In stark contrast to the notion of IR as an American discipline, Groom and Mandaville claim to demonstrate that a robust, and increasingly influential, European set of influences have always been part of the field's topography.

In the essay that follows, Kim Richard Nossal shifts the emphasis away from IR theory as a self-conscious intellectual activity amongst a small cabal of mutually acknowledged experts, to the teaching of the subject through textbooks, which is, he argues, itself a more or less systematic and theoretical construction of the world. What happens, asks Nossal, if the same "American" characteristics that Stanley Hoffmann attributed to the discipline of IR as a whole are reflected in the textbooks that are used to introduce students to the field? After surveying fourteen books that were written as textbooks designed to be adopted in introductory IR courses, Nossal argues that these teaching implements operate in the same "zones of relative darkness" that Hoffmann suggests characterize the American approach to IR as a whole. Nossal concludes that this theoretical rendering of the world is thoroughly Americo-centric, self-replicating, and destined to persist until, or unless, the hermetic vacuum in which it is sealed is finally broken.

In their contribution, Martin Griffiths and Terry O'Callaghan argue that the popular, American-influenced, presupposition that IR is compatible with a self-standing discipline of inquiry based on consensus over how to define, apply, and understand the purpose of theory is simply incompatible with those features of the world that justify sustained examination, including its division between conflicting national visions. Their aim is to challenge the particular understanding of IR that developed in the United States after 1945, and fostered a monistic, rather than pluralistic, attitude to the pursuit and development of its theory. This attitude, they suggest, precludes any meaningful reflection on what is meant by "a discipline," and fails to demonstrate why IR should enjoy any more substantial a consensus than, say, history or political theory. For example, it is one of their contentions that the traditional conception of IR as a world divided among sovereign states has tended to assert and assume the centrality of the particular substantive phenomenon of war, rather than argue for such a core problematic through exhaustive and serious consideration of other possibilities. The result, they conclude, is a bland and narrow definition of IR that runs counter to the complexity and diversity of the materials that comprise its subject matter, and that students of IR would do well to abandon in favor of a more open, pluralistic, less American conception of the field.

Chris Brown follows in a similar vein, but makes the counterintuitive claim that the real problem with IR is that it's not American enough! What he means is that the sort of intellectual background out of which the modern discipline has emerged has been a form of liberal rationalism which is wedded to the universal, has found especially fertile soil in American IR, and—like American popular culture in general—sets the seemingly relevant standards for the world as a whole along the lines of prevailing American notions of what constitutes worth. This universalist, rather than genuinely parochial, orientation, argues Brown, has tended to entomb an earlier, essentially communitarian and continental (European) theoretical tradition that constitutes a genuine international diversity of thought, but one that cannot be fully appreciated without dismantling the American academic discipline which presently conceals it from view.

Robert M. A. Crawford also emphasizes the methodological, as opposed to directly, national, character of American intellectual hegemony in IR but suggests that the national uniformity of the field is exaggerated by its customary depiction as an American or Anglo-American enterprise. Even as it currently stands, he suggests, the field is marked by a diversity of national approaches, though these are limited to only two distinctive versions of the subject as an academic discipline: American IR and British IR. Though differences between American and British approaches to the subject are acknowledged in the literature, Crawford argues, they are treated as differences of degree within a single discipline—distinguished by different methodological orientations for example—rather than recognized for what they are: almost entirely separate disciplines of IR based on a deep epistemological divide that is obscured by an American propensity to deny any fundamental difference, and (prior to the onset of critical theory) a British proclivity to quietly accept, rather than assert, any difference. Crawford points to the flowering of discipline-defining debate in British IR, and its virtual absence in the official channels of the American discipline, as prima facie evidence for a distinctive set of presuppositions about theory and knowledge in international relations that are explored more fully via reexamination of the field's dominant origin story.

In the next essay, Mark Neufeld and Teresa Healy argue that IR theorists, no less than anyone else, are a product of their contexts, and that national and other identities (e.g., gender, race, and class) are an inherent aspect of understanding and evaluating their offerings. This position tends to support Nossal's claim that "national identity" and situational context are an important part of the construction of the American discipline, the world it purports to explain, and the textbooks that convey its imagery to students. It is the traditional view of social science as a "value-neutral" enterprise, argue Neufeld and Healy, that keeps acknowledgment and exploration of its richly contextual, value-laden nature, out of sight, and off the research agenda. In sharp contrast to the position taken by Tony Porter, Neufeld and Healy undertake an evaluation of thinking (and teaching) IR in Canada that purports to demonstrate the existence of a distinctly and uniquely Canadian "thinking space."

Jan Pettman closes out Part II by drawing attention to gender and class as underanalyzed aspects of the global political economy and international relations. In conventional accounts, suggests Pettman, conflicts between individual identity and nationality treat the world as an entity fragmented between more or less self-contained units. Gender and class, as explicitly transnational categories, can thus help to propel IR beyond its current propensity for narrowly male, white, English-speaking, and national narratives. She also argues that recognizing the experiences of women as globalized through gender and class can correct perceived biases and parochialisms in existing feminist IR scholarship, drawing attention, for example, to race, nationality, and location as other sources of difference and diversity. Contrary to Jarvis, Pettman concludes that paying attention to the ways in which IR is constructed around masculinist versions of public space and power does not "come at the expense of sustained attention to the dilemmas of international politics" so much as it tells the story of IR from previously underexamined perspectives, and previously unheard accounts of what constitutes a dilemma in the first place.

The third and final part of this collection is comprised of essays that offer a small sampling of the sorts of directions the study of international relations might be expected to take in the new millennium, both in terms of its substantive focus and its status as an academic field. A uniting theme in these otherwise disparate contributions is the notion that IR as a free-standing and self-sufficient science must be made to yield at least some of its theoretical ground to new or extant approaches, whether or not Griffiths and O'Callaghan, or Brown, are justified in advocating the dismantling of the discipline in its currently dominant form. While some of the approaches discussed in this part ("Toward Diversity in International Thought") might be viewed as new or underexamined paradigms *within* the discipline of IR, the temptation to regard them thus may be yet another symptom of the field's habitual need for consensus and uniformity. It seems increasingly clear that there may be no stable discipline of IR in which to house the burgeoning roster of perspectives now on offer, and this part is intended as no more than an admittedly meager sampling of research by scholars laboring outside the geographical and intellectual mainstream of the discipline.

This sampling of new approaches, in conjunction with the essays in the volume as a whole, is offered with the assumption that it is only through establishing the relevance and meaningfulness of IR (or IRs?) on a more convincingly global scale that we can hope to avoid the sort of intellectual oblivion that Holsti warns may presently lie in wait. We can begin, James Richardson suggests, by being receptive to new theoretical openings without being taken in by diversity for its own sake. The problem with the dominant conception of IR, he suggests, is that it is too wedded to the pallid abstractions of the economics discipline, which include an ahistorical idealization of the status quo, and an apolitical reduction of individual interests to universalized rational choices. If postmodernist influences have supplied a useful corrective to this narrowness, argues Richardson, these are drawn too far in the direction of an individualized agenda that deconstructs, rather than reconfigures, the discipline as a whole. His main concern is that diversity, in much of its current form, seems unable to distinguish fruitful lines of inquiry from theoretical blind alleys. One fruitful, well-established, but underacknowledged line of inquiry, he suggests, is historical sociology, an approach that promises to keep the core issue of international systemic change on the theoretical agenda without confining it to its presently static boundaries. His claim is that historical sociology is not just one more theory to be added to the intellectual melting pot of IR, but the most promising starting point for theorizing about a central issue (historical change) that the discipline has thus far been unable to address.

In the next essay Roger Epp calls for a "theoretical clearing" for indigenous peoples and practices in IR, suggesting that the discipline has not neglected "diplomacies" of this sort so much as it has turned them into forms of marginal presence. Indigenous diplomacies, he argues, are front and center in the early-modern jurists' accounts of the law of nations, and in the social contract theorists' crude state-of-nature anthropologies that continue to shape IR's basic assumptions. But these diplomacies, like the peoples from which they derive, are assumed to have been "domesticated" in the so-called expansion of international society, and continue to mark the outside limits of acceptable decolonization. Epp, therefore, sets himself two basic tasks: (1) to contribute to a rethinking of the stories the discipline tells as regards indigenous diplomacies, and; (2) to encourage attentiveness to the complex mediations embedded in these indigenous practices. The main objective, he concludes, is to take IR beyond the mere incorporation and silencing of indigenous voices to a situation of genuine attentiveness to alternate modes of speaking, and a real willingness to listen. Epp thus provides a glimpse of what a more genuinely inclusive IR might look like.

Like Epp, Roger Spegele points toward the existing corpus of international thought, rather than entirely new approaches, as the most promising source of theoretical rejuvenation. Spegele's particular concern is the problem of ethics in international relations, and his primary purpose to refute the widely shared assumption that political realism, in all its guises, is a form of moral skepticism. This view, argues Spegele, rests on a crude caricature that impedes recognition of a distinctly realist moral theory that he calls "soft moral realism." Ironically, he adds, the Neo-Kantian–inspired critique that has most contributed to the false impression that realism is an amoral apology for brute force is just as likely as realism to "wear" moral skepticism. There is, he concludes, no basis for the view that political realism maintains unequivocally that moral claims have no truth value, that their truth or validity are relative to moral frameworks, or that it is impossible to test moral claims for truth or validity. Because the supposed moral bankruptcy of political realism has been a major source of theoretical misgiving in IR (one increasingly expressed in terms of a crisis), Spegele's essay could well lead to a reevaluation of the problem of theory in the discipline as a whole.

In their closing essay, Pal Ahluwalia and Michael Sullivan do not concern themselves with debates and perspectives internal to IR, but argue that the production and policing of its "truths," since the Cold War at least, reflects the hegemony of the discipline as an "American social science." The primary evidence presented for this claim is the discipline's failure to draw on perspectives from outside the self-declared boundaries of mainstream American social science (and IR), no matter how insightful, rich, or persuasive the theoretical work of cognate fields might be. A particularly telling example, they suggest, is the work of Edward Said, whose pioneering efforts to draw attention to numerous issues of direct relevance to world politics, has been almost entirely ignored by mainstream IR theorists, despite his status as a preeminent public intellectual, and the ready availability of his works. Ahluwalia and Sullivan aim primarily to correct this oversight, as they undertake the task of critically assessing Said's contributions to understanding the world. The principal contribution of Said's postcolonial theory, they conclude, is its ability to disrupt traditional academic boundaries and their implied uniformity of identity, nationality, and IR in favor of a genuinely diverse conception of these experiences that promises nothing more extravagant, yet nothing less worthwhile, than a rejection of all universal conceptions of the world and its problems.

STILL AN AMERICAN SOCIAL SCIENCE?

One question often begets another. Once defined as an American discipline it is natural to ask if IR continues to hold that dubious distinction, but it is tempting to take things back a step and ask *was it ever an American social science*? There are many ways in which this claim can be disputed, including Brown's suggestion that the discipline has never been American enough, Crawford's contention that the existence of a distinctive British conception of IR predates its emergence in the United States and renders unacceptable its depiction in singular terms (e.g., *the* discipline), or Porter's assertion that national perspectives of every stripe are largely irrelevant.

The question of whether IR is still an American social science is also oddly contradictory, since we do not normally associate the generality that is the promise of science with the particularism that is the reality of a geographically bounded research community. Ideas of course do not need passports and, in principle, the particularities of a country's geography, culture, historical experience, place in the international pecking order, and so forth are compatible with knowledge gathering. But they are incompatible with a genuinely cosmopolitan learning, unless it can be assumed that the country in question epitomizes the larger intellectual, moral, and cultural unity of the world as a whole. This is surely too much to ask of any country, however liberal, pluralistic, or tolerant its academic marketplace. On the particular and most germane issue of intellectual multiculturalism, moreover, there is little in American political culture—and American political theory—to suggest that it places much stock or value in diversity, except when it serves the utilitarian objective of long-term progress, understood largely in material terms. There is a strong commitment to procedural equality that demands, among other things, laws that are blind to color, race, ethnicity, gender, sexual preference, and other possible modes of differentiation. This view has never gone unchallenged, but surely enjoys the status of a dominant idea, a background presumption that frames debate, and sits uneasily beside the presumption that culturally defined collectivities should be assumed, *a priori*, to have equal worth (Rawls, 1971; Taylor, 1994, 56 and 72). It is impossible to believe that American IR can stand apart from this broader context of American political theory, and we would be foolish to expect it to do so. The idea of IR as a distinctively American undertaking, therefore, is useful, but the notion that it is also a social science seems a bit of a stretch. In what sense, for example, is American IR analogous with other "sciences"—or even other "social" sciences? Is there an American biology? an Australian epidemiology? a Brazilian sociology? or a British economics? Perhaps there are such things but, if so, we are even more compelled to either drop all pretensions to science, or do a better job of exploring its various possible meanings. Until recently, there has been little to suggest that explorations of the latter sort are much welcome in the American discipline of IR, a field that has sometimes more resembled the foreign affairs and relations branch of American public policy than a social science. Perhaps this is more than a peculiarly American phenomenon and endemic to the enterprise of international relations theory per se. This would certainly account for its virtual absence as a sustained field of interest in countries poorly placed to do much about changing the world. Hence, what we today envision as a discipline (or set of disciplines) called IR might be better imagined as comparative international public/foreign policy.

The point is not that American scholarship has failed to make a positive and lasting contribution to IR. The question, rather, is whether room can be found for other constructions of the discipline and its thematic motifs, some of which might eschew its often unspoken commitments to positivism, methodological cosmopolitanism, and great power concerns. But there is clearly a danger of making the story too pat and yielding to the sorts of stereotypes and caricatures to which, ironically enough, a globalized conception of IR seems inevitably to lead. In a sense American scholarship has never been able to live up to its own positivistic and rationalistic ambitions, as witnessed by the discernible weakening of the stylized commitment to monoscience so forcefully articulated by Kenneth Waltz (1979). If some of the contributions to this volume appear to conflate the problem of American nationality and positivist epistemology, it is because, to a significant extent, these elements have been inextricably fused in mainstream thinking. It is precisely because intellectual hegemony in the field—rendered American by the sheer demographic preponderance of its research community—has taken on a strongly methodological character that it has become easy to overlook the important reality that American scholarship has never been universally positivist. This said, it is important to acknowledge the existence of a much ignored, non-positivistic, and very American literature on domestic influences on IR, as well as the field's recent, American-led "turn" toward "constructivism," a theoretical output whose emphasis on intersubjectivity, understandings, and experience departs strongly from the usual rationalist emphasis of American IR (Katzenstein, 1996; Frieden and Starr, 1997; Wendt, 1992, 1998). Constructivism has not merely emerged as a valuable guide to empirical research across a number of issue areas, but has attracted a sizable following outside its American site of origin, raising the prospect of a possible weakening of parochialism in the years to come (see Hobbs, forthcoming). That the mainstream may be weakening is also suggested by the increased prominence of critical IR scholars (many of whom are American) in leading American journals like *International Studies Quarterly*, *International Organization*, and *World Politics*. These literatures demonstrate that there is decidedly more texture to American IR than its once unquestioned commitment to consensus would lead us to expect, but it is far too early to anticipate the overall direction of what remains an American-dominated field. Does the appearance of critical orientations within the traditional publishing centers of the discipline herald a new diversity, or the "mainstreaming" of once heretical theoretical positions (Crawford, 2000)? Will constructivism pave the way toward an alternative conception of disciplinarity in IR or, like regime theory before it, fail ultimately to escape the long shadow of positivism (Kratochwil and Ruggie, 1986; Crawford, 1996, 2000; Dessler, 1999)? Since the tendency to date has been either to ignore theoretical innovations, or regard them as investigative techniques that can be made to fit within the infinitely malleable boundaries of positivist social science, a healthy dose of skepticism is in order.

Assuming for the sake of argument that Hoffmann was right in 1977 to call IR an American social science, are we in any position today to contradict him? Miles Kahler suggests that we are: "on the basis of institutional development and research infrastructure, international relations no longer is an American social science" (Kahler, 1993). While it is to Kahler's credit that he resists the obvious, unavoidable, and self-perpetuating tendency of mainstream American IR to ignore its own propensity for theoretical hegemony, he is unable to transcend its built-in proclivity for evaluative judgments that are self-referential. In what sense, for example, can the increasingly global diffusion of made-in-America research institutions and techniques be considered a barometer for anything other than the field's (and the world's) increased Americanization, unless—as seems wholly indefensible—the version of IR nurtured in the United States is perfectly suited to the interests and experiences of the world as a whole? However remote, the latter possibility cannot be ruled out, but neither can it be seriously entertained until it is actually acknowledged as an issue worthy of discussion. It is a dialogue of this sort that the present volume is designed to provoke. While there is no clear and absolute consensus on the issue of whether IR continues to be (or ever was) an American social science, the essays that follow collectively point toward the conclusion of an overwhelming preponderance of American theoretical influences. Again, the diversity canvassed below tends to refer more explicitly to intellectual constructs than the "national identity" or "location" of particular individuals, though influences of this sort will be as obvious in this collection as they are inside and outside the boundaries of the discipline it problematizes. One of the more telling and least contestable findings of recent inquiry, after all, is that national prefixes no longer delineate discrete lines of ethnicity in an age of hypermobility and mass migration. For many in this collection, however, and countless others for whom it cannot speak, the problem lies not in this observation but in the fact that most of those who "do IR" in the restrictive sense of the word, tend to have been acculturated to its ways, methods, and theories in one of the hegemonic (teaching) centers of global power (i.e., North America, Western Europe, and, to a lesser degree, Australia and New Zealand) each of which has demonstrated a marked dependency on, or propensity to follow, American constructs.

If the theoretical hegemony of American IR posed insuperable barriers to the exploration and cultivation of a genuine international or multicultural "diversity" volumes of this sort would be pointless. Obviously, we do not believe either of these things to be true, but neither is an argument for the existence, or desirability, of multiple "national pre-fixes" itself a good, or reliable, indicator of diversity. But it is a start, and springs from legitimate concern that things "American" still tend to predominate. It will not have escaped the notice of an attentive reader, for example, that this volume is : (1) published in the United States; (2) aimed primarily at an IR and, thus, largely American, read-ership; and (3) conforms to American spelling and academic referenc-ing styles. The latter requirement is fair enough, but mildly symp-tomatic of, and analogous to, the often unreflective, even unconsciously generated, pressures for conformity that exist in any context of an unequal distribution of power and influence, whether overtly political or academic. The question of a largely American readership is simply a function of academic demographics. While we suspect that this volume will attract a much wider readership, its focus on the American disci-pline is also a function of the reality that there is not much point in preaching to the converted.

Undoubtedly, the American forum for this volume is testimony to the great openness of American intellectual life and its capacity for critical self-examination. This openness, however, is less pronounced in the more specialized field of IR, where all assumptions tend to be filtered through an American lens. The messages and warnings explicit and implicit in Hoffmann's essay do not appear to have been heeded, and not a single major introductory IR textbook with which we are familiar, nor many of the texts that deal explicitly with the problem of IR theory, make even a passing reference to it. It is our conviction, however, that the time is right for questions of this sort to be raised again, and that the crisis-weary discipline of IR is ready for construc-tive alternatives to the current menu of destructive denial and decon-structive chaos that has settled in to the discipline as normally con-structed. There are, at least, reasons to suppose that IR may finally be undergoing some sort of geographical and intellectual diaspora. In the narrow geographic sense described by Kahler, the study of IR is clearly widening relative to only a few decades ago. Western Europe, in par-ticular, has seen tremendous growth in the number of research insti-tutes and university programs that now research and teach IR. What-ever its inspiration in these developments, it is difficult to imagine the "American discipline" permanently forestalling a more parochial, home-grown IR in these locales, evidence for which is already at hand below. More obviously, the phenomenal growth of interest in interna-tional issues in the last few decades, in part as a result of "globaliza-tion" (whatever its ultimate meaning and reality) is heightening the prominence of international relations globally as an academic subject. Impressionistic evidence suggests that demand for IR programs and courses throughout the world has never been higher and is continuing to grow. This will undoubtedly change the spatial dimensions of IR, if not its subjects and objects of inquiry and its epistemological frameworks. Needless to say, those of us who have been involved in this project welcome these developments in the conviction that they will lead the field of international relations forward, even while we cannot say yet with much conviction where it might be going.

NOTE

1. For a collection of essays more along these lines, see Kahler (1993).

REFERENCES

Buzan, Barry. (1993). "From International System to International Society: Structural Realism and Regime Theory Meet the English School." *International Organization* 47(3), 327–352.

Crawford, Robert M. A. (1996). *Regime Theory in the Post–Cold War World*. Aldershot, U.K.: Dartmouth.

Crawford, Robert M. A. (2000). *Idealism and Realism in International Relations: Beyond the Discipline* London: Routledge.

Dessler, David. (1999). "Constructivism within a Positivist Social Science." *Review of International Studies* 25.

Diebert, R. (1997). *Altered Worlds: Communication Technologies in the Transformation of Political Authority*. New York: Columbia University Press.

Friedman, Gil, and Harvey Starr. (1997). *Agency, Structure, and International Politics: From Ontology to Empirical Inquiry*. London: Routledge.

Hobbs, Heidi (ed.). (Forthcoming). *Pondering Postinternationalism*. Albany: State University of New York Press.

Hoffmann, Stanley. (1965). *The State of War*. New York: Praeger.

Hoffmann, Stanley. (1977). "An American Social Science: International Relations." *Daedalus* 106(3), 41–60.

Holsti, K. J. (1985). *The Dividing Discipline*. Boston: Allen and Unwin.

Kahler, Miles. (1993). "International Relations: Still an American Social Science?" In Linda B. Miller and Michael Joseph Smith (eds.), *Ideas and Ideals*. Boulder, Colo.: Westview Press.

Katzenstein, Peter (ed.). (1996). *The Culture of National Security: Norms and Identity in World Politics*. New York: Columbia.

Kratochwil, Friedrich and John Gerard Ruggie. (1986). "International Organization: A State of the Art on the Art of the State." *International Organization* 40(4).

Morgenthau, Hans. (1948). *Politics among Nations*. New York: McGraw-Hill.

Rawls, John. (1971). *A Theory of Justice*. Cambridge, Mass.: Belknap Press of Harvard University Press.

Taylor, Charles. (1994). *Multiculturalism: Examining the Politics of Recognition*. Princeton, N.J.: Princeton University Press.

Wendt, Alexander. (1992). "Anarchy Is What States Make of It." *International Organization 46.*

Wendt, Alexander. (1998). "On Constitution and Causation in International Relations." *Review of International Studies 24.*

PART I

Hegemony and Diversity in International Thought

CHAPTER 1

An American Social Science: International Relations

Stanley Hoffmann

In the past thirty years, international relations has developed as a largely autonomous part of political science. Even though it has shared many of political science's vicissitudes—battles among various orientations, theories, and methods—it also has a story of its own. What follows is an attempt at neither a complete balance sheet nor a capsule history— merely a set of reflections on the specific accomplishments and frustrations of a particular field of scholarship (see Hoffmann, 1960; 1965, chaps. 1 and 2).

ONLY IN AMERICA

Political science has a much longer history than international relations. The attempt at studying systematically the patterns of conflict and cooperation among mutually alien actors—a shorthand definition of the subject matter—is recent. To be sure, we can all trace our ancestry back to Thucydides, just as political scientists can trace theirs to Aristotle. But Thucydides was a historian. He was, to be sure, a historian of genius, rightly convinced that he was writing for all times because he was using one particular incident to describe a permanent logic of behavior. Yet he was careful to avoid explicit generalizations, "if . . . then" propositions, and analytic categories or classificatory terms. Modern sociology and political science emancipated themselves from political and social history, political philosophy, and public law in the nineteenth century. International relations did not, even though the kind of social (or asocial) action described by Thucydides never disappeared from a fragmented world, and flourished particularly in the period of the European balance of power. One can wonder why this was so. After all, here was a realm in which political philosophy had much less to offer than it did to those who wondered about the common good in the domestic order. Except for the vast body of Roman Catholic literature preoccupied with just war, and not very relevant to a world of sovereign states, there were only the recipes of Machiavelli; the marginal comments on the international state of nature in Hobbes', Locke's, and Rousseau's writings; some pages of Hume; two short and tantalizing essays of Kant; compressed considerations by Hegel; and oversimplified fragments by Marx. Even so, the little political philosophy that was available should have been sufficiently provocative to make students want to look into the realities. For the philosophers disagreed about the nature of the international milieu and the ways of making it more bearable; and they wrote about the difference between a domestic order stable enough to afford a search for the ideal state, and an international contest in which order has to be established first, and which often clashes with any aspiration to justice. Similarly, the contrast between the precepts of law and the realities of politics was sufficiently greater in the international realm than in the domestic realm, to make one want to shift from the normative to the empirical, if only in order to understand better the plight of the normative. Without a study of political relations, how could one understand the fumblings and failures of international law, or the tormented debates on the foundation of obligation among sovereigns unconstrained by common values or superior power? And the chaos of data provided by diplomatic history did not require any less ordering than the masses of facts turned up by the history of states and societies.

Why did a social science of international relations nevertheless fail to appear? The answer to the discrepancy may well be found in that sweeping phenomenon which Tocqueville identified as the distinctive feature of the modern age: democratization. As domestic societies moved from their Old Regimes to their modern conditions—parties and interests competing for the allegiance of large classes of citizens; the social mobilization of previously dispersed subjects; the politics of large agglomerations and unified markets; an increasingly universal suffrage; the rise of parliamentary institutions or plebiscitarian techniques; the fall of fixed barriers, whether geographic or social, within nations—the study of flux began in earnest, if only in order to provide concerned observers and insecure officials with some clues about regularities and predictions of somewhat less mythical, if also less sweeping nature than those grandiosely strewn around by philosophers of history. With democratization, as Comte had predicted, came the age of positivism (his only mistake was to confuse his own brand of metaphysics, or his grand speculations, with positive science). But international politics remained the sport of kings, or the preserve of cabinets—the last refuge of secrecy, the last domain of largely hereditary castes of diplomats.

Raymond Aron has characterized international relations as the specialized activity of diplomats and soldiers. However, soldiers, to paraphrase Clausewitz, have their own grammar but not their own logic. It is not an accident if armies, having been democratized by the ordeals of the French Revolution and Napoleonic era, found their empirical grammarian in Clausewitz, whereas the still restricted club of statesmen and ambassadors playing with the fate of nations found no logician to account for its activities. Indeed, the historians who dealt with these succeeded only in keeping them beyond the pale of the kind of modern science that was beginning to look at societies, by perpetuating the myth of foreign policy's "primacy," isolated from domestic politics. There was, to be sure, one country in which foreign policy was put under domestic checks and balances, knew no career caste, and paid little respect to the rules and rituals of the initiated European happy few: the United States of America. But this country happened to be remarkably uninvolved in the kinds of contests that were the daily fare of other actors. Either it remained aloof, eager merely for continental consolidation and economic growth; or else it expanded, not by conflicts and deals with equals, but by short spurts of solipsistic exuberance at the expense of much weaker neighbors. International relations is the science of the tests and trials of several intertwined actors. Where they were intertwined, no science grew. In the United States before the 1930s, there was no reason for it to grow.

It was only the twentieth century that brought democratization to foreign policy. Diplomatic issues moved from the calculations of the few to the passions of the many, both because more states joined in the game that had been the preserve of a small number of (mainly European) actors and (mainly extra-European) stakes, and above all because within many states parties and interests established links or pushed claims across national borders. And yet, a world war that saw the mobilization and slaughter of millions, marked the demise of the old diplomatic order, and ended as a kind of debate between Wilson and Lenin for the allegiance of mankind, brought forth little "scientific analysis" of international relations. Indeed, the rude intrusion of grand ideology into this realm gave a new lease of life to utopian thinking, and delayed the advent of social science. Not "how it is, and why," but "how things should be improved, reformed, overhauled," was the order of the day. Old liberal normative dreams were being licensed by the League of Nations covenant, while at the same time the young Soviet Union was calling for the abolition of diplomacy itself.

It is against this reassertion of utopia, and particularly against the kind of "as if" thinking that mistook the savage world of the 1930s for a community, the League for a modern Church, and collective security for a common duty, that E. H. Carr wrote the book which can be treated as the first "scientific" treatment of modern world politics: *Twenty Years Crisis* (Carr, 1939)—the work of a historian intent on deflating the pretenses of liberalism, and driven thereby to laying the foundations both of a discipline and of a normative approach, "realism," that was to have quite a future. Two paradoxes are worth noting. This historian who was founding a social science, did it in reaction against another historian, whose normative approach Carr deemed illusory—Toynbee, not the philosopher of the *Study of History*, but the idealistic commentator of the *Royal Yearbook of International Affairs*. And Carr, in his eagerness to knock out the illusions of the idealists, not only swallowed some of the "tough" arguments which the revisionist powers such as Mussolini's Italy, Hitler's Germany, and the militaristic Japan had been using against the order of Versailles—arguments aimed at showing that idealism served the interests of the status quo powers— but also "objectively," as Pravda would say, served the cause of appeasement. There was a triple lesson here: about the springs of empirical analysis (less a desire to understand for its own sweet sake, than an itch to refute); about the impossibility, even for opponents of a normative orientation, to separate the empirical and the normative in their own work; and about the pitfalls of any normative dogmatism in a realm which is both a field for objective investigation and a battlefield between predatory beasts and their prey.

But it was not in England that Carr's pioneering effort bore fruit. It was in the United States that international relations became a discipline. Both the circumstances and the causes deserve some scrutiny. The circumstances were, obviously, the rise of the United States to world power, a rise accompanied by two contradictory impulses: renewed utopianism, as exemplified by the plans for postwar international organization; and a mix of revulsion against, and guilt about, the peculiar prewar brew of impotent American idealism (as symbolized by the "nonrecognition" doctrine), escapist isolationism (the neutrality laws), and participation in appeasement. Two books brought to America the kind of realism Carr had developed in England. One was Nicholas Spykman's *America's Strategy in World Politics* (Spykman, 1942), which was more a treatise in the geopolitical tradition of Admiral Mahan or Mackinder than a book about the principal characteristics of interstate politics; but it told Americans that foreign policy is about power, not merely or even primarily about ideals, and it taught that the struggle for power was the real name for world politics. The other book was Hans Morgenthau's *Politics Among Nations* (Morgenthau, 1948). If our discipline has any founding father, it is Morgenthau. Unlike Carr, he was not a historian by training; he had been a teacher of international law. Like Carr, he was revolting against utopian thinking, past and present. But where Carr had been an ironic and polemical Englishman sparring with other Englishmen about the nature of diplomacy in the thirties—a discussion which assumed that readers knew enough diplomatic history to make pedantic allusions unnecessary—Morgenthau was a refugee from suicidal Europe, with a missionary impulse to teach the new world power all the lessons it had been able to ignore until then but could no longer afford to reject. He was but one participant in the "sea change," one of the many social scientists whom Hitler had driven to the New World, and who brought to a country whose social science suffered from "hyperfactualism" and conformity the leaven of critical perspectives and philosophical concerns (cf. Hughes, 1975). But he was, among his colleagues, the only one whose interests made him the founder of a discipline.

Eager to educate the heathen, not merely to joust with fellow literati, Morgenthau quite deliberately couched his work in the terms of general propositions and grounded them in history. Steeped in a scholarly tradition that stressed the difference between social sciences and natural sciences, he was determined both to erect an empirical science opposed to the utopias of the international lawyers and the political ideologues, and to affirm the unity of empirical research and of philosophical inquiry into the right kind of social order. He wanted to be normative, but to root his norms in the realities of politics, not in the aspirations of politicians or in the constructs of lawyers. The model of interstate relations which Morgenthau proposed, and the precepts of "realism" which he presented as the only valid recipes for foreign policy success as well as for international moderation, were derived from the views of nineteenth-century and early twentieth-century historians of statecraft (such as Treitschke, and also Weber). Hence the paradox of introducing to the America of the Cold War, and of making analytically and dogmatically explicit, notions and a "wisdom" about statecraft that had remained largely implicit in the age to which they best applied, and whose validity for the age of nuclear weapons, ideological confrontations, mass politics, and economic interdependence was at least open to question.

Be that as it may, Morgenthau's work played a doubly useful role—one that it may be hard to appreciate fully if one looks at the scene either from the outside (as does Aron), or thirty years later, as does the new generation of American scholars. On the one hand, his very determination to lay down the law made Morgenthau search for the laws, or regularities, of state behavior, the types of policies, the chief configurations of power; by tying his sweeping analyses to two masts, the concept of power and the notion of the national interest, he was boldly positing the existence of a field of scientific endeavor, separate from history or law. On the other hand, the very breadth of his brushstrokes, the ambiguities hidden by his peremptory pronouncements about power, the subjective uncertainties denied by his assertion of an objective national interest, and even more the sleights of hand entailed by his pretense that the best analytic scheme necessarily yields the only sound normative advice—all of this incited readers to react and, by reacting, criticizing, correcting, refuting, to build on Morgenthau's foundations. Those who rejected his blueprint were led to try other designs. He was both a goad and a foil. (Indeed, the more one agreed with his approach, the more one was irritated by his flaws, and eager to differentiate one's own product.) A less arrogantly dogmatic scholar, a writer more modest both in his empirical scope and in his normative assertions, would never have had such an impact on scholarship. Less sweeping, he would not have imposed the idea that here was a realm with properties of its own. Less trenchant, he would not have made scholars burn with the itch to bring him down a peg or two. One of the many reasons why Raymond Aron's monumental *Peace and War* (Aron, 1962, 1966)—a book far more ambitious in its scope and far more sophisticated in its analyses than *Politics Among Nations*—incited no comparable reaction from scholarly readers may well have been the greater judiciousness and modesty of Aron's normative conclusions. Humane skeptics invite nods and sighs, not sound and fury; and sound and fury, are good for creative scholarship. Moreover, Aron's own scholarship was overwhelming enough to be discouraging; Morgenthau's was just shaky enough to inspire improvements.

Still, *Politics Among Nations* would not have played such a seminal role, if the ground in which the seeds were planted had not been so receptive. The development of international relations as a discipline in the United States results from the convergence of three factors: intellectual predispositions, political circumstances, and institutional opportunities. The intellectual predispositions are those which account for the formidable explosion of the social sciences in general in this country, since the end of the Second World War. There is, first, the profound conviction, in a nation which Ralf Dahrendorf has called the Applied Enlightenment (Dahrendorf, 1963), that all problems can be resolved, that the way to resolve them is to apply the scientific method—assumed to be value free, and to combine empirical investigation, hypothesis formation, and testing—and that the resort to science will yield practical applications that will bring progress. What is specifically American is the scope of these beliefs, or the depth of this faith: they encompass the social world as well as the natural world, and they go beyond the concern for problem-solving (after all, there are trial-and-error, piecemeal ways of solving problems): they entail a conviction that there is, in each area, a kind of masterkey—not merely an intellectual, but an operational paradigm. Without this paradigm, there can be muddling through, but no continuous progress; once one has it, the practical recipes will follow. We are in the presence of a fascinating sort of national ideology: it magnifies and expands eighteenth-century postulates. What has ensured their triumph and their growth is the absence of any counterideology, on the right or the left, that challenges this faith either radically (as conservative thought did, in Europe) or by subordinating its validity to a change in the social system. Moreover, on the whole, the national experience of economic development, social integration, and external success has kept reinforcing this set of beliefs.

Second, and as a kind of practical consequence, the very prestige and sophistication of the "exact sciences" were bound to benefit the social ones as well. The voices of gloom or skepticism that lament the differences between the natural world and the social world have never been very potent in America. Precisely because the social world is one of conflict, precisely because national history had entailed civil and foreign wars, the quest for certainty, the desire to find a sure way of avoiding fiascoes and traumas, was even more burning in the realm of the social sciences. The very contrast between an ideology of progress through the deliberate application of reason to human concern—an ideology which fuses faith in instrumental reason and faith in moral reason—and a social reality in which the irrational often prevails both in the realm of values and in the choice of means, breeds a kind of inflation of social science establishments and pretensions. At the end of the war, a new dogma appeared. One of the social sciences, economics, was deemed to have met the expectations of the national ideology, and to have become a science on the model of the exact ones; it was celebrated for its contribution to the solution of the age-old problems of scarcity and inequality. This triumph goaded the other social sciences. Political science, the mother or stepmother of international relations, was particularly spurred. It was here that the temptation to emulate economics was greatest. Like economics, political science deals with a universal yet specialized realm of human activity. Its emphasis is not on the origins and effects of culture, nor on the structures of community or of voluntary association, but on the creative and coercive role of a certain kind of power, and on its interplay with social conflict. This also drew it closer to that other science of scarcity, competition, and power, economics, than to disciplines like anthropology or sociology, which deal with more diffuse phenomena and which are less obsessed by the solution of pressing problems by means of enlightened central action.

Nations in which this grandiose and activist ideology of science is less overwhelming have also known, after the Second World War, a considerable expansion of the social sciences. But the United States often served as model and as lever.[1] And political science abroad has usually been more reflective than reformist, more descriptive than therapeutic; although, here and in sociology, foreign social scientists reacted against the traditional intelligentsia of moralists, philosophers, and aesthetes by stressing that knowledge (not old-fashioned wisdom) *was* power (or at least influence), they were not driven by the dream of knowledge *for* power. Moreover, when (inevitably) disillusionment set in, it took often far more drastic forms—identity crises within the professions, violent indictments outside—than in the United States. An ideology on probation cannot afford a fall. An ideology serenely hegemonial reacts to failure in the manner of the work horse in Orwell's *Animal Farm*, or of Avis: "I will try harder."

A third predisposition was provided by a transplanted element: the scholars who had immigrated from abroad. They played a huge role in the development of American science in general. This role was particularly important in the social sciences. Here, they provided not merely an additional injection of talent, but talent of a different sort. No social science is more interesting than the questions it asks, and these were scholars whose philosophical training and personal experience moved them to ask far bigger questions than those much of American social science had asked so far, questions about ends, not just about means; about choices, not just about techniques; about social wholes, not just about small towns or units of government. So they often served as conceptualizers, and blended their analytic skills with the research talents of the "natives." Moreover, they brought with them a sense of history, an awareness of the diversity of social experiences, that could only stir comparative research and make something more universal of the frequently parochial American social science. In the field of international relations, in addition to Morgenthau, there was a galaxy of foreign-born scholars, all concerned with transcending empiricism: the wise and learned Arnold Wolfers, Klaus Knorr, Karl Deutsch, Ernst Haas, George Liska, and the young Kissinger and Brzezinski, to name only a few. They (and quite especially those among them who had crossed the Atlantic in their childhood or adolescence) wanted to find out the meaning and the causes of the catastrophe that had uprooted them, and perhaps the keys to a better world.

The last two names bring us to politics. And politics mattered. Hans Morgenthau has often written as if truth and power were bound to be enemies (Hannah Arendt has been even more categorical). And yet he shaped his truths so as to guide those in power. The growth of the discipline cannot be separated from the American role in world affairs after 1945. First, by definition (or tautology), political scientists are fascinated with power—either because they want it, at least vicariously, or because they fear it and want to understand the monster, as Judith Shklar has suggested with her usual devastating lucidity.[2] And in the postwar years, what part of power was more interesting than the imperial bit? America the sudden leader of a coalition, the sole economic superpower, the nuclear monopolist, later the nuclear superior, was far more interesting to many students than local politics, or the politics of Congress, or the politics of group pluralism. Almost inevitably, a concern for America's conduct in the world blended with a study of international relations, for the whole world seemed to be the stake of the American-Soviet confrontation. Here was a domain which was both a virgin field for study and the arena of a titanic contest. To study United States foreign policy was to study the international system. To study the international system could not fail to bring one back to the role of the United States. Moreover, the temptation to give advice, to offer courses of action, or to criticize the official ones was made even more irresistible by the spotty character and the gaffes of past American behavior in world affairs, by the thinness of the veneer of professionalism in American diplomacy, by the eagerness of officialdom for guidance—America was the one-eyed leading the cripples. Thus, two drives merged, for the benefit of the discipline and to its detriment also, in some ways: the desire to concentrate on what is the most relevant, and the tendency (implicit or explicit) to want to be useful, not only as a scientist, but as an expert citizen whose science can help promote intelligently the embattled values of his country (a motive that was not negligible, among newcomers to America especially). For it was all too easy to assume that the values that underlie scientific research—the respect for truth, freedom of investigation, of discussion, and of publication—were also those for which Washington stood in world affairs.

Second, as I have just said, what the scholars offered, the policymakers wanted. Indeed, there is a remarkable chronological convergence between their needs and the scholars' performances. Let us oversimplify greatly. What the leaders looked for, once the Cold War started, was some intellectual compass which would serve multiple functions: exorcise isolationism, and justify a permanent and global involvement in world affairs; rationalize the accumulation of power, the techniques of intervention, and the methods of containment apparently required by the Cold War; explain to a public of idealists why international politics does not leave much leeway for pure good will, and indeed besmirches purity; appease the frustrations of the bellicose by showing why unlimited force or extremism on behalf of liberty was no virtue; and reassure a nation eager for ultimate accommodation, about the possibility of both avoiding war and achieving its ideals. "Realism," however critical of specific policies, however (and thus self-contradictorily) diverse in its recommendations, precisely provided what was necessary. Indeed, there was always a sufficient margin of disagreement between its suggestions and actual policies, and also between its many champions, to prevent it from being nothing but a rationalization of Cold War policies. And yet the first wave of writings—those of Morgenthau, Wolfers, Kissinger, Kennan, Osgood, Walt Rostow, or McGeorge Bundy—gave both the new intellectual enterprise and the new diplomacy the general foundations they needed. The second wave—roughly, from 1957 to the mid-1960s—turned strategy in the nuclear age into a dominant field within the discipline. This coincided with the preoccupation of officialdom to replace the reassuring but implausible simplicities of massive retaliation with a doctrine that would be more sophisticated; but it also reflected the conviction that force, in a mixture of nuclear deterrence and conventional (or subconventional) limited uses, remained both the most important aspect of power and a major American asset. Here again, in the literature, the attempt at finding principles for any "strategy of conflict" in a nuclear world is inseparable from the tendency to devise a strategy for America, at a time when both sides had weapons of mass destruction, and when there were serious problems of alliance management, guerrilla wars, or "wars of national liberation." A third wave is quite recent: I refer to the growing literature on the politics of international economic relations. It coincides with what could be called the post–Viet Nam aversion for force, and with the surge of economic issues to the top of the diplomatic agenda, caused by a combination of factors: the degradation of the Bretton Woods system, the increasing importance of economic growth and social welfare in the domestic politics of advanced societies, the resurgence of aggressive or protectionist impulses in order to limit the bad effects or to maximize the gains from interdependence, the revolt of the Third World. Once more, the priorities of research and those of policy-making blend.

The political preeminence of the United States is the factor I would stress most in explaining why the discipline has fared so badly, by comparison, in the rest of the world (I leave aside countries like the Soviet Union and China, in which it would be hard to speak of free social science scholarship!). Insofar as it deals primarily with the contemporary world, it seems to require the convergence of a scholarly community capable of looking, so to speak, at global phenomena (i.e., of going beyond the study of the nation's foreign policy, or of the interstate politics of an area) and of a political establishment concerned with world affairs; each one then strengthens the other. When the political elites are obsessed only with what is happening to their country, because it lacks the power to shape what is happening elsewhere, or because this lack of power has bred habits of dependence on another state (such as the United States), or because (as in the case of Japan and West Germany) there are severe constraints on the global use of the nation's power, the chances are that the scholars will not have the motivation or receive the impulse necessary to turn individual efforts into a genuine scientific enterprise, and will either turn to other fields with more solid traditions and outlets (such as, say, electoral behavior in France and Britain) or merely reflect, more or less slavishly, and with some delays, American fashions; or else there will be often brilliant individual contributions, but unconnected and unsupported: a Hedley Bull in Australia (and England), a Pierre Hassner in France, to name just these two, do not make a discipline. Even in England and France, which have become nuclear powers, strategic studies have been to a very large extent the preserve of a few intellectual military men, concerned either with reconciling national policy with the predominant doctrines of deterrence, or with challenging these. But the predominant doctrines have remained American, as if even in the more abstract efforts at theorizing about a weapon that has transformed world politics, it mattered if one was the citizen or host of a country with a worldwide writ. Scholars do not like to think about their intellectual dependence on the status of their country, and on the ambitions of its political elite; it disturbs their sense of belonging to a cosmopolitan, free-floating community of science. Even the sociology of knowledge, which has often looked at the debts of scholars to their countries, has been singularly coy about this particular kind of bond. And yet, the link exists. And it is sometimes reinforced by institutional arrangements.

In the case of the United States, there have been three institutional factors that have acted as multipliers of political connection—factors which have not existed, and certainly not simultaneously, elsewhere. One is the most direct and visible tie between the scholarly world and the world of power: the "in-and-outer" system of government, which puts academics and researchers not merely in the corridors but also in the kitchens of power. Actually, it may be wise to distinguish two phases. In the late forties and fifties, those kitchens remained the preserves of the old establishment: a mix of career civil servants, businessmen, and lawyers. They had to cope with the whole world, with a persistent enemy, with the travails of economic reconstruction and the turmoil of nuclear deterrence. They needed both data and ideas, and they turned to the universities. This was the age of the academic as consultant (officially or not), and this was the period in which much research got funded by those departments that had the biggest resources

(Defense more than State). The year 1960 was a turning point. Academics became proconsuls and joined the old boys; often they tried to prove that they could cook spicier dishes and stir pots more vigorously than their colleagues. If one had some doubts about "policy scientists," these could only be doubled by the spectacle of scientific policy-makers. Be that as it may, the Washington connection turned an intellectual interchange into a professional one. In countries with a tight separation between the career of bureaucracy or politics and the academic *métier*, such exchanges are limited to occasional formal occasions—seminars or colloquia—and frequent *diners en ville*; but the former tend to be sterile, and the latter hover between witty debates on current affairs, and small talk.

A second institutional factor of great importance is the role of what I have elsewhere called the relays between the kitchens of power and the academic salons. The most important of these dumbwaiters is the network of foundations that fed international relations research after the war, and whose role is essential if one wants to understand exactly why the three waves of scholarship coincided so aptly with the consecutive concerns of the statesmen. A combination of intellectual encouragement to "frontiers of knowledge" and civic desire to be of service, the sociological peculiarities of boards of directors composed, to a large extent, of former academics and former officials, the happy accident of vast financial resources that kept growing until the end of the sixties, all this made of the foundations a golden half-way house between Washington and academia. Wasps served in the CIA—pardon, the institution—as well as State; ex-State officials served in the foundations; and even those professors who had some reservations about serving in the government, had no objection to applying to the foundations. It was a seamless pluralism. These precious relays exist virtually nowhere else.

The third institutional opportunity was provided by the universities themselves. They had two immense virtues. They were flexible; because of their own variety, which ensured both competition and specialization, and also because of the almost complete absence of the straitjackets of public regulations, quasifeudal traditions, financial dependence, and intellectual routine which have so often paralyzed the universities of postwar Europe. The latter got caught in the contradiction between their own past—a combination of vocational training and general education for the elites—and the sudden demands of mass higher education; they could vacillate from confusion to collapse, but the one thing they could rarely do was to innovate. The other virtue of American universities resulted in part from the fact that mass higher education was already a *fait accompli*: they had large departments of political science, which could serve as the matrices of the discipline of International Relations.

In France until the late sixties, in Britain until the spread of the new universities, international relations remained the handmaid of law, or the laughingstock of historians; and when political science departments began to mushroom, the other reasons for the development of the discipline in America were still missing. Only in America could a creative sociologist write about the university as the most characteristic institution of the postindustrial age, the laboratory of its discoveries (cf. Bell, 1973). In other countries, universities are rarely the arenas of research: and when they are, the research funded by public institutions concentrates on issues of public policy which are rarely international—partly for the political reason I have mentioned above, partly because the existence of a career foreign service with its own training programs perpetuates the tendency to look at international relations as if it were still traditional diplomacy. Civil servants obliged to deal with radically new tasks such as urbanization, the management of banks and industries, or housing sometimes think they can learn from the social sciences. Civil servants who deal with so "traditional" a task as national security and diplomacy do not always realize that the same old labels are stuck on bottles whose shapes as well as their content are new. And when diplomats discover that they too have to cope with the new, technical issues of technology, science, and economics, it is to "domestic" specialists of these subjects that they turn—if they turn at all.

EVEN IN AMERICA

If one looks at the field thirty years after the beginning of the "realist" revolution, can one point to any great breakthroughs? The remarks which follow are, of course, thoroughly subjective, and undoubtedly jaundiced. I am more struck by the dead ends than by the breakthroughs; by the particular, often brilliant, occasionally elegant, but generally nonadditive contributions to specific parts of the field, than by its overall development; by the contradictions that have rent its community of scholars, than by its harmony. The specific contributions have been well analyzed in a recent volume of the *Handbook of Political Science* (Greenstein and Polsby, 1975), and I shall not repeat what is said there. If I had to single out three significant "advances," I would list the concept of the international system, an attempt to do for international relations what the concept of a political regime does for "domestic" political science: it is a way of ordering data, a construct for describing both the way in which the parts relate, and the way in which patterns of interaction change. It emerged from the first period I have described above, and continues to be of importance. Next, I would mention the way in which the literature on deterrence has analyzed and codified "rules of the game" which have been accepted as such by American statesmen, and which have served as the intellectual foundation of the search for tacit as well as explicit interstate restraints: MAD ("Mutual Assured Destruction") and arms control are the two controversial but influential offsprings of the doomsday science. Third, there is the current attempt to study the political roots, the originality, and the effects of economic interdependence, particularly in order to establish whether it shatters the "realist" paradigm, which sees international relations as marked by the predominance of conflict among state actors. And yet, if I were asked to assign three books from the discipline to a recluse on a desert island, I would have to confess a double embarrassment: for I would select one that is more than two thousand years old—Thucydides' *Peloponnesian War*, and as for the two contemporary ones, Kenneth Waltz's *Man, the State and War* (Waltz, 1959), is a work in the tradition of political philosophy, and Aron's *Peace and War* is a work in the grand tradition of historical sociology, which dismisses many of the scientific pretenses of the postwar American scholars, and emanates from the genius of a French disciple of Montesquieu, Clausewitz, and Weber. All three works avoid jargon; the two contemporary ones carry their erudition lightly: the sweat of toil is missing. How more unscientific can you get?

Let us return to the ideology I alluded to earlier. There was the hope of turning a field of inquiry into a science, and the hope that this science would be useful. Both quests have turned out to be frustrating. The desire to proceed scientifically, which has been manifest in all the social sciences, has run into three particular snags here. First, there was (and there remains) the problem of theory. I have discussed elsewhere at some length the difficulties scholars have encountered when they tried to formulate laws accounting for the behavior of states, and theories that would explain those laws and allow for prediction. A more recent analysis, by Kenneth Waltz, comes to an interesting conclusion: if theory is to mean here what it does in physics, then the only "theory" of international relations is that of the balance of power, and it is unfortunately insufficient to help us understand the field! The other so-called general theories are not more than grand conceptualizations, using "confused, vague and fluctuating definitions of variables" (Greenstein and Polsby, 1975, 8). This may well be the case; Waltz seems to blame the theorists, rather than asking whether the fiasco does not result from the very nature of the field. Can there *be* a theory of undetermined behavior, which is what "diplomatic-strategic action," to use Aron's terms, amounts to?

Aron has, in my opinion, demonstrated why a theory of undetermined behavior cannot consist of a set of propositions explaining general laws that make prediction possible, and can do little more than define basic concepts, analyze basic configurations, sketch out the permanent features of a constant logic of behavior, in other words make the field intelligible (Hoffmann, 1965, chap. 2). It is therefore not surprising if many of the theories dissected, or vivisected, by Waltz, are, as he puts it, reductionist, such as the theories of imperialism, which are what he had called in his earlier book "second image" theories (they find the causes of interstate relations in what happens *within* the units); or else, the theories he dismisses were all produced during the first phase—the neophytish (or fetish) stage—of postwar research: the search for the scientific equivalent of the philosopher's stone has been far less ardent in the past twenty years. Waltz' own attempt at laying the groundwork for theory is conceptually so rigorous as to leave out much of the reality he wants to account for. I agree with him that a theory explaining reality must be removed from it and cannot be arrived at by mere induction; but if it is so removed that what it "explains" has little relation to what occurs, what is the use? One finds some of the same problems in all political science; but Waltz is right in stating that international relations suffers from a peculiar "absence of common sense clues": the key variables are far clearer in domestic political systems, whereas here "the subject is created, and recreated, by those who work on it" (Greenstein and Polsby, 1975, 8). Still, here as in the rest of political science, it is the fascination with economics that has led scholars to pursue the chimera of the masterkey. They have believed that the study of a purposive activity aimed at a bewildering variety of ends, political action, could be treated like the study of instrumental action, economic behavior. They have tried in vain to make the concept of power play the same role as money in economics. And they have acted as if the mere production of partial theories unrelated to a grand theory was tantamount to failure.

A "science" without a theory may still be a science with a paradigm; and, until recently, the paradigm has been that of permanent conflict among state actors—the realist paradigm. However, in the absence of a theory, a second question has been hard to answer: what is it that should be explained? The field has both suffered and benefited from a triple fragmentation—benefited, insofar as much ingenious research has been brought to each fragment, yet suffered because the pieces of the puzzle do not fit. First, there has been (and still is) the so-called level of analysis problem. Should we be primarily concerned with the international system, that is, the interactions among the units? Or should we concentrate our efforts on the units themselves? There are two conflicting hypotheses behind these strategies. One postulates that the system has, so to speak, some sort of life of its own, even if some of the actors obviously have a greater role than others in shaping and changing the rules of interaction. The other approach postulates that the actors themselves are the strategic level for understanding what goes on among them. One says, in effect: Grasp the patterns of interaction, and you will understand why the actors behave as they do; the other one says: Look at the actors' moves, and you will comprehend the outcomes. Students of the international system and students of foreign policy making have never really blended their research. My own conclusion is that of a writer who has worked both sides of the street: I am dissatisfied with each, but I admit that it is hard to be on both at once. The study of the international system provides one with a fine framework, but no more—precisely because the system may well put constraints on and provide opportunities for the actors, but does not "dictate" their behavior; and the study of the actors tells you, inevitably, more about the actors than about the interactions. But what used to be called linkage theory (before linkage became a Kissinger-inspired technique), that is, propositions about the bonds between foreign policy and international politics, has remained in the frozen stage of static taxonomies.

Second, there has also been fragmentation at each level of analysis. One could say, not so flippantly, that each student of international systems has hugged his own version of what that abstract scheme "is." Aron's is not Richard Rosecrance's, which is not Morton Kaplan's. Moreover, each one has tended to took at the postwar international system in a different way (once again, in the absence of a single theory, it is not easy to determine authoritatively the dynamics of a particular system that still unfolds under one's eyes). A dozen years ago, scholars acted as if they were competing for a prize to the best discourse on the subject: are we in a bipolar system? Waltz, Liska, Kissinger, and many others (including me) took part, but since there was no Academy, there was no prize. In recent years, the new contest is about "Persistence or Demise of the Realist Paradigm?": Is the state-centered concept of international politics, with its focus on the diplomatic-strategic chessboard and its obsession with the use of force, still relevant to the age of interdependence? Aron, Joseph Nye and Robert Keohane, Edward Morse, Bull, and many others (including myself) are busy evaluating this. As before, I suspect that the verdict will be history's, and that like the long-awaited Orator in Ionesco's *Chairs*, it will speak in incomprehensible gibberish. At the other level of analysis, we have accumulated masses of studies of concrete foreign policies, and moved from the period of Chinese boxes—the decision-making theories of the 1950s—to the age of the "bureaucratic politics" model. The former provided endless items for laundry lists; the other one draws attention to the kitchen where the meal is being cooked, but forgets to tell us that what matters is whether the chefs cook what they want or what they are ordered to prepare, and assumes all too readily that what they do is determined by their particular assignment in the kitchen, rather than by what they have learned outside, or their personal quirks.

Third, there has been functional fragmentation as well. If there is, or can be, no satisfactory general theory, if the "overarching concepts" are excessively loose-fitting clothes, why not try greater rigor on a smaller scale? At the systemic level, we have thus witnessed such clusters of research as work on regional integration (where, for once, the theoretical ingenuity of scholars has far outreached the practical, "real-life" accomplishments of statesmen), modern theories of imperialism, arms race models and measurements of wars, recent studies of transnational relations and international economics. At the foreign policy level (although it tries to straddle both) the main cluster has been that of strategic literature; and there is now a growing literature on decision-making in the United States. Unfortunately, each cluster has tended to foster its own jargon; and this kind of fragmentation has had other effects, which will be discussed below.

Finally, the quest for science has led to a heated and largely futile battle of methodologies, in answer to a third question: Whatever it is we want to study, how should we do it? Actually, it is a double battle. On the one hand, there is the debate between those "traditionalists" who, precisely because of the resistance the field itself opposes to rigorous theoretical formulations, extol the virtues of an approach that would remain as close to historical scholarship and to the concerns of political philosophy as possible (this is the position taken by Hedley Bull), and all those who, whatever their own brand of theorizing, believe that there can be a political science of international relations—if not in the form of a single theory, at least in that of systematic conceptualizations, classifications, hypotheses, and so on—a science which can be guided in its questions by the interrogations of past philosophers, yet finds reliance on philosophical discourse and diplomatic intuition both insufficient and somewhat alien to the enterprise of empirical analysis. There is little likelihood that this debate will ever come to a conclusion—especially because neither side is totally consistent, and each one tends to oversimplify what it actually does. On the other hand, here as in other branches of political science, there is the battle of the literates versus the numerates; or, if you prefer, the debate about the proper place and contributions of quantitative methods and mathematical models. The fact that the practitioners of the latter tend to hug the word science, and to put beyond the pale of science all those who, while equally concerned with moving "from the unique to the general" and with considering "classes of events and types of entities," believe that these cannot be reduced to numbers or that science does not consist in "accumulating coefficients of correlation" . . . "without asking which theories lead one to expect what kind of a connection among which variables" (Greenstein and Polsby, 1975, 12)—this fact has made for rather strained relations among scholars of different methodological persuasions. In domestic political science, behaviorists and old-fashioned scholars have found coexistence easier, because their respective approaches fit separate parts of the field—electoral behavior or the behavior of legislative bodies lends itself to mathematical treatment. In international affairs, such a functional division of labor is much harder to apply. As a result, the prophets of quantitative methodologies dismiss as mere hunches based on "insight" (a word they often use as if it were an insult) the elaborate ruminations of their opponents, and these in turn ridicule the costly calculations that tell one nothing about causes or lump together different types of the same phenomenon (say, wars), and the endless correlations among variables lifted from their context, that all too often conclude that . . . no conclusive evidence can be derived from them: endless nonanswers to trivial questions.

If there is little agreement as to what constitutes a science, and little enthusiasm for the state of the science of international relations, what about the other great expectation, that of usefulness? I am struck by one apparent contradiction. The champions of a science of international affairs have, on the whole, declared their independence from philosophy and their allegiance to objective empiricism. And yet, most of them have wanted to draw consequences for the real world from their research: the greater the drive to predict (or the tendency to equate science, not just with intelligibility but with control and prediction), the greater the inclination to play the role of the wise adviser or of the engineer. It is in the nature of human affairs, and of the social sciences.

But in this specific realm, there are some very peculiar problems. The first could be called: advice to whom? Many scholars, especially those whose level of analysis is systemic, implicitly write as if they were addressing themselves to a world government, or as if they aimed at reaching those who wish to transcend the traditional logic of national self-righteousness and state calculations (the same can be said, even more strongly, of theorists of regional or functional integration; they tend to distribute recipes for going beyond the nation-state). Unfortunately, the chair of world statecraft is empty, and change comes (if at all) through the operations of state agents. And so, scholars of this kind oscillate from condemnation of state practices that make for conflict, or retard integration, or promote injustice, to advice to state agents on how to transcend the limits of the game which it is however these agents' role and duty to perpetuate, or advice to international secretariats and subnational bureaux on the best strategy for undercutting and turning the resistance of national statecraft. These are all perfect guarantees of unhappy consciousness for the scholars.

Other scholars, especially among those whose level of analysis is national decision-making, see themselves as efficient Machiavellians—they are advising the Prince on how best to manage his power and on how best to promote the national interest. This is particularly the case of the strategists, the group which contains the highest proportion of researchers turned consultants and policy-makers. "Systemic" writers who are fully aware of the differences between an international system and a community of mankind, that is, the "realists," do their best to make advice to the only Prince who still matters—the national states-man, bound to enhance the interests of his state—coincide with their views of the interests of the whole. They advocate "enlightened" con-cepts of the national interest, or "world order" policies that would somewhat reconcile the needs of the part and of the whole. But this is a difficult exercise. The logical thrust of "realism" is the promotion of the national interest, that is, not unhappy global consciousness but happy national celebration. "Realists" who become aware of the perils of real-ism in a world of nuclear interconnection and economic interdepen-dence—writers like Morgenthau, or myself—suffer from the addition of two causes of unhappiness: that which afflicts all "systemic" writers in search of a radically new order, and that which comes from knowing only too well that utopianism does not work.

Thus, basically, in their relations with the real world, the scholars are torn between irrelevance and absorption. Many do not like irrele-vance, and want even the most esoteric or abstract research to be of use. The oscillation I have described above is what they want to escape from, and yet they do not want to be absorbed by that machine for self-righ-teousness, the service of the Prince. But their only excuse is the populist dream—the romantic hope that "the people" can be aroused and led to force the elites that control the levers of action, either out of power alto-gether or to change their ways. Much of peace research, once it got tired of advocating for the solution of world conflicts the discrete techniques used for accommodation in domestic affairs, has been traveling down that route. It is one on which scholarship risks finding both irrelevance and absorption, for the policies advocated here do inspire both those intelligentsias that want to displace certain elites in developing countries, and those established elites that are eager to boost national power against foreign dominance. Yet if the former come to power, and if the latter follow the advice of "dependencia" theorists, the result is not likely to be a world of peace and justice, but a world of revolutions, and new conflicts, and new inequities.

As for the scholars who want to avoid esoterica or romanticism and who set their sights on Washington, they, in turn, run into problems. There are two reasons why the Washingtonian temptation is so strong. There is the simple fact that international politics remains the politics of states: whether or not, in the abstract, the actor is the shaper of or is shaped by the system, in reality there is no doubt that the United States remains the most potent player. And there is the fact that a science of contemporary politics needs data, and that in this realm, whereas much is public—in the records of international organizations, speeches, published state documents—a great deal remains either classified or accessible only to insiders: the specific reasons for a decision, the way in which it was reached, the bargains that led to a common stand, the meanderings of a negotiation, the circumstances of a breakdown. Far more than domestic political science, international relations is an insider's game, even for scholars concerned with the systemic level.

But a first problem lies in the fact that gathering information from and about the most potent actor, creates an irresistible urge to nudge the player: the closer the Washingtonian connection, the greater the temptation of letting oneself be absorbed. Second, outsider advice always suffers from oversimplification. When it comes to tactical suggestions, the insiders, who control not only all the facts but also the links connecting separate realms of policy, have the advantage. This increases the scholar's urge to get in closer. Third, once one starts rolling down the slope from research-with-practical-effects, to practical-advocacy-derived-from-research, the tendency to slight the research and to slant the advocacy for reasons either of personal career or of political or bureaucratic opportunity, will become insidious. Which means that the author may still be highly useful as an intelligent and skilled decision-maker—but not as a scholar. Either his science will be of little use, or else, in his attempt to apply a particular pet theory or dogma, he may well become a public danger. This does not mean that the experience of policy-making is fateful to the scholar, that the greatest hope for the science would lie in blowing up the bridge that leads across the moat into the citadel of power. A scholar-turned-statesman can, if his science is wise and his tactics flexible, find ways of applying it soundly; and he can later draw on his experience for improving his scholarly analytical work. But it is a delicate exercise which few have performed well.

BECAUSE OF AMERICA

The problems I have examined have arisen mainly in America, because the profession of international relations specialists happens to be so preponderantly American. Insofar as it flourishes elsewhere, the same difficulties appear: they result from the nature of the field. But because of the American predominance, the discipline has also taken some additional traits which are essentially American, and less in evidence in those other countries where the field is now becoming an object of serious study.

The most striking is the quest for certainty (see Hirschman, 1970, 329–343). It explains the rage for premature theoretical formulation, the desire to calculate the incalculable (not merely power but status), the crusade to replace discussions of motives with such more objective data as word counts and vote counts, the crowding of strategic research (here, the ends are given, and it becomes a quest for the means). International relations should be the science of uncertainty, of the limits of action, of the ways in which states try to manage but never quite succeed in eliminating their own insecurity. There has, instead, been a drive to eliminate from the discipline all that exists in the field itself—hence a quest for precision that turns out false or misleading. Hence also two important and related gaps. One is the study of statecraft as an art. With very few exceptions (such as *A World Restored*) it has been left to historians. (One could say much of the same about domestic political science.) The other is the study of perceptions and misperceptions, the subjective yet essential side of international politics. Robert Jervis' work is beginning to fill that gap, but it is not certain that his example will be widely followed (see Jervis, 1976). Almost by essence, the study of diplomatic statecraft and of perceptions refuses to lend itself to mathematical formulations, or to a small number of significant generalizations (one may generalize, but the result is likely to be trivial). Taxonomies and case studies do not quench the thirst to predict and to advocate.

A second feature, intimately tied to the discipline's principal residence rather than to its nature, is the preponderance of studies dealing with the present. Historians continue to examine past diplomatic history in their way. Political scientists concerned with international affairs have concentrated on the politics of the postwar era; and when they have turned to the past, it has all too often been either in highly summary, I would say almost "college outline" fashion, or in the way long ago denounced by Barrington Moore Jr., which consists in feeding data detached from their context into computers. This is a very serious weakness. It leads not only to the neglect of a wealth of past experiences—those of earlier imperial systems, of systems of interstate relations outside Europe, of foreign policy-making in domestic policies far different from the contemporary ones—but also to a real deficiency in our understanding of the international system of the present. Because we have an inadequate basis for comparison, we are tempted to exaggerate either continuity with a past that we know badly, or the radical originality of the present, depending on whether we are more struck by the features we deem permanent, or with those we do not believe existed before. And yet a more rigorous examination of the past might reveal that what we sense as new really is not, and that some of the "traditional" features are far more complex than we think.

There are many reasons for this flaw. One is the fear of "falling back into history"—the fear that if we study the past in depth, we may indeed find generalizations difficult and categorization either endless or pointless; and we may lose the thread of "science." A related reason is the fact that American political scientists do not receive sufficient training either in history or in foreign languages, indispensable for work on past relations among states. A third reason is to be found in the very circumstances of the discipline's birth and development. In a way, the key question has not been, "What should we know?" It has been, "What should we do?"—about the Russians, the Chinese, the bomb, the oil producers. We have tried to know as much as we needed in order to know how to act—and rarely more: a motivation that we find in other parts of political science (the study of political development, for instance), where some disillusionment has set in. But we can say to ourselves that there are no shortcuts to political development, that the United States cannot build nations for others, and that we should go back to the foundations, that is, to an understanding of the others' past. We are unable to say to ourselves that we must stop having a diplomacy, and impose a moratorium on our advising drive until we have found out more about the past of diplomatic-strategic behavior. And the interest which, quite naturally, the government and, less wisely but understandably, the foundations have shown in supporting research that deals with the present (or extrapolates it into the future, or scrutinizes the near future so as to discern what would be sound action in the present) has kept the scholars' attention riveted on the contemporary scene.

The stress on the present and the heavily American orientation have combined to leave in the dark, at least relatively, several important issues—issues whose study is essential to a determination of the dynamics of international politics. One is the relation of domestic politics (and not merely bureaucratic politics) to international affairs—we need to examine in far greater detail the way in which the goals of states have originated, not (or not only) from the geopolitical position of the actors, but from the play of domestic political forces and economic interests; or the way in which statesmen, even when they seemed to act primarily for the world stage, nevertheless also wanted their moves abroad to reach certain objectives within; or the way in which external issues have shaped domestic alignments and affected internal battles. The desire to distinguish the discipline of international relations from the rest of political science is partly responsible for this gap; scholars who study a given political system do not usually pay all that much attention to foreign policy, and the specialists of international politics simply do not know enough about foreign political systems. The only country for which the bond between domestic and external behavior has been examined in some depth is, not so surprisingly, the United States. Here again, an assessment of the originality of the present—with its visible merging of domestic and foreign policy concerns, especially in the realm of international economic affairs—requires a much deeper understanding of the past relations between domestic politics and foreign policy. We may discover that the realist paradigm, which stresses the primacy of foreign policy, has to be seriously amended, not only for the present but for the past.

Another zone of relative darkness is the functioning of the international hierarchy, or, if you prefer, the nature of the relations between the weak and the strong. There has been (especially in the strategic literature) a glaring focus on bipolarity, accompanied by the presumption that moves to undermine it (such as nuclear proliferation) would be calamitous (it may not be a coincidence if the French have, on the whole, taken a very different line). Much of the study of power in international affairs has been remarkably Athenian, if one may refer to the famous Melian dialogue in Thucydides (the strong do what they can, the weak what they must). How the strong have often dealt with the weak in ways far more oblique, or less successful than the simple notion of a high correlation between might and achievements would suggest; how and under what conditions the weak have been able to offset their inferiority—these are issues which, until OPEC came along, had not been at the center of research and for which, again, far more historical work ought to be undertaken.

What was supposed to be a celebration of creativity seems to have degenerated into a series of complaints. We have found here an acute form of a general problem that afflicts social science—the tension between the need for so-called basic research, which asks the more general and penetrating questions that derive from the nature of the activity under study, and the desire of those who, in the real world, support, demand, or orient the research, for quick answers to pressing issues. And if the desire often seems more compelling than the need, it is because of the scholars' own tendency to succumb to the Comtian temptation of social engineering. This temptation is enhanced by the opportunities the United States provides to scholar-kings (or advisers to the Prince), or else by the anxiety which scholars, however "objective" they try to be, cannot help but feel about a world threatened with destruction and chaos by the very logic of traditional interstate behavior.

Born and raised in America, the discipline of international relations is, so to speak, too close to the fire. It needs triple distance: it should move away from the contemporary, toward the past; from the perspective of a superpower (and a highly conservative one), toward that of the weak and the revolutionary—away from the impossible quest for stability; from the glide into policy science, back to the steep ascent toward the peaks which the questions raised by traditional political philosophy represent. This would also be a way of putting the fragments into which the discipline explodes, if not together, at least in perspective. But where, in the social sciences, are the scientific priorities the decisive ones? Without the possibilities that exist in this country, the discipline might well have avoided being stunted, only by avoiding being born. The French say that if one does not have what one would like, one must be content with what one has got. Resigned, perhaps. But content? A state of dissatisfaction is a goad to research. Scholars in international relations have two good reasons to be dissatisfied: the state of the world, the state of their discipline. If only those two reasons always converged!

NOTES

This article is reprinted in its entirety from the original, which appeared in 1977 in *Daedalus: American Academy of Arts and Sciences 106* (3), 41–60. We gratefully acknowledge the publishers of *Daedalus* for their permission to include it in this volume.

1. See the forthcoming Ph.D. thesis (Harvard University, Department of History) of Diana Pinto, who deals with postwar sociology in Italy and France.

2. Judith Shklar, in an introduction to the field of political science written for Harvard freshmen.

REFERENCES

Aron, Raymond. (1962). *Peace and War*. Paris: Calmann-Levy. 1962.

Bell, D. (1973). *The Coming of Post-Industrial Society*. New York: Basic Books.

Carr, E. H. (1939). *Twenty Years Crisis*. London: Macmillan.

Dahrendorf, R. (1963). *Die angewandte Aufklarung*. Munich: Piper.

Greenstein, F. I., and N. W. Polsby (eds.). (1975). *Handbook of Political Science: International Politics*. Vol. 8. Reading, Mass.: Addison-Wesley.

Hirschman, Albert O. (1970). "The Search for Paradigms as a Hindrance to Understanding." *World Politics* (April): 329–343.

Hoffmann, Stanley. (1960). *Contemporary Theory in International Relations*. Englewood Cliffs, N.J.: Prentice Hall.

Hoffmann, Stanley. (1965). *The State of War*. New York: Praeger.

Hughes, H. S. (1975). *The Sea Change*. New York: Knopf.

Jervis, Robert. (1976). *Perception and Misperception in International Politics.* Princeton, N.J.: Princeton University Press.

Morgenthau, Hans. (1948). *Politics among Nations.* New York: Knopf.

Spykman, N. (1942). *America's Strategy in World Politics.* New York: Harcourt, Brace.

Waltz, Kenneth. (1959). *Man, the State and War.* New York: Columbia University Press.

CHAPTER 2

What Does It Mean to Be an American Social Science? A Pragmatist Case for Diversity in International Relations

Molly Cochran

INTRODUCTION

The central theme of this book is the question of whether or not International Relations (IR) remains an American social science, as Stanley Hoffmann so famously characterized it in his *Daedalus* article reprinted in this volume. I want to take this back a step, however, and examine what it might mean to be an American social science in the first place. This essay thus undertakes a close analysis of Hoffmann's position, leaving the issue of nationality broadly construed largely to the exploration of others in this volume; diversity is treated here in its methodological sense, and refers to competing traditions of social science within an explicitly American intellectual context. Nevertheless, the alternative, pragmatist conception of social science I introduce below is less parochial than the one described by Hoffmann, in that it connects to traditions and questions previously forestalled by IR's single-minded quest for scientific certainty.

    The point I wish to emphasize is that the trajectory the academic discipline of IR took after World War II does not reflect the only direction a uniquely American social science can take. Hoffmann's characterization of the American ideology which shaped IR as a social science merely taps into important and dominant intellectual currents of the time, and does not consider the different tributaries into which those currents might flow. Hoffmann cannot be blamed, of course, for describing the idea of social science that IR actually grew out of and adopted. But this essay is less about describing the American social science of IR as it is, than envisioning an alternative (though still American) conception of a discipline. This alternative conception exists presently "outside" the artificial boundaries of the discipline in the form of American pragmatism, the most illuminating exponent of which is John Dewey. I want to suggest that it might be interesting to consider what IR would yield if reoriented to this alternative notion of social science. The central point of this essay, then, is that the particular idea of a social science that IR followed in the post–World War II era is a contributing factor to the ills Hoffmann diagnoses, and that the contribution of pragmatism to IR would be to provide a different, more encompassing, understanding of the way of conducting social scientific research.

I will retrace the structure of the argument in Hoffmann's article. The first section will examine the particularly American ideology that proved to be fertile intellectual ground for the growth of IR as a social science. Here, I will outline Dewey's contribution to this ideology and how he deviates from the foundational certainty that was at the base of the variant of American social science that Hoffmann identifies as fundamental to IR. The second section will examine how uniformity in ideological convictions does not necessarily lead to uniformity in how to carry out those convictions. I will update Hoffmann's characterization of fragmentation within the discipline to argue that, now more than ever, IR requires an approach that can serve as a bridge between IR camps, however you want to characterize them: empirical versus normative, positivist versus post-positivist, or rationalist versus reflectivist (see for examples of each categorization Hoffmann, 1977 and this volume; Smith, 1996; and Keohane, 1989). Finally, in section three, I will consider Hoffmann's suggestions about the places where he sees room for improvement in the state of IR as an American social science. Pragmatism can serve as the bridge-building alternative between the empirical and normative approaches that are so important to Hoffmann. Therefore, I will argue that an American pragmatist orientation to social science might better fulfill Hoffmann's prescription for progress in IR.

ONLY IN AMERICA: NARROW AND UNIVERSAL CONCEPTIONS OF SOCIAL SCIENCE

Hoffmann's argument for the development of IR as an American social science begins on a striking note when he points out that, although the British historian E. H. Carr wrote the first "scientific" account of world politics, Carr's book was not sufficient to kick-start the development of

IR as a social science (Carr, 1964). The idea of a "scientific approach" required a certain kind of environment to take root and that environment was available only in America. More specifically, Hoffmann attributes the development of IR as an "American social science" to three factors at work in the United States after the Second World War: intellectual predispositions, political circumstances, and institutional opportunities (Hoffmann, 1977, 45). It is under the heading of intellectual predispositions that Hoffmann develops his idea of the particularly American ideology that, as he writes, accounted for "the formidable explosion" of social science in America (Hoffmann, 1977, 45). Thus, I will concentrate on this set of factors in order to elucidate Dewey's role in shaping this ideology and his alternative, more "universal" understanding of American social science. Moreover, I also suggest that the second and third factors discussed by Hoffmann may offer reasons why the American social science of IR did not develop along the lines of the pragmatist model.

Hoffmann, it seems, has an endearing, Hegelian penchant for trichotomies as he throws up another set of "three factors" that account for the nature of American intellectual predispositions: a faith in scientific method, a belief that science would be useful to society, and the influence of immigrant scholars. He describes the first element as:

> the profound conviction . . . that all problems can be resolved, that the way to resolve them is to apply scientific method—assumed to be value free, and to combine empirical observation, hypothesis formation, and testing—and that the resort to science will yield practical applications that will bring progress. (Hoffmann, 1977, 45)

What constitutes this conviction as a particularly American ideology for Hoffmann is the wide extent to which these beliefs are held and the depth of American faith in "scientific method" to solve social problems. As Hoffmann explains, the depth of this faith manifests itself in the belief that in all areas of social inquiry there is a "masterkey" or "operational paradigm" that yields practical recommendations (Hoffmann, 1977, 45). Hoffmann attributes the "triumph" of this national ideology to the fact that there was no counterideology to shake this faith. Ultimately, of course, Hoffmann is correct: there was no radically different alternative ideology from which a conception of "American social science" might have evolved. Pragmatism, however, represents such an alternative that would have held, and perhaps still might, radically different implications for IR as an American social science.

Pragmatism à la Dewey

Dewey's pragmatism was imbued with a strong faith in scientific method: he believed that natural science got many things right that his own discipline, philosophy, had got wrong. Across almost seventy years of academic writing, from the 1880s until the late 1940s, Dewey was persistent in his efforts to reconstruct philosophy and its understanding of its role as a purveyor of absolute knowledge or truth. He wanted to overturn philosophy's privileging of thought, for example about "Being" and other such universals and fixities, over the practical, material problems of human existence and coexistence. Dewey's project was to recast philosophy an intellectual activity oriented toward social action and critique guided by a particular form of inquiry: scientific method. For Dewey, philosophy should remake itself as a social science. It should be engaged with the social problems of the day and systematically study the general method of inquiry suggested by natural science and its application to "human processes."

Why was scientific method important to Dewey? What does it get right exactly? To answer these questions it is important to understand what Dewey identified as the intellectual crisis of his day. The crisis, as he defined it, was that of the incursion of science into everyday life, usurping the traditional forms of authority represented by religion and morality (Dewey, 1948, xxi–xxii, xxvii–xxviii). Radical change had taken place and shaken the metaphysical comfort and certainty represented by religion and morality. What natural science had over philosophy was that, by the force of its own developments, it abandoned what philosophy for centuries had not been able to let go: fixity. Absolutes had been put up for question by the great scientific revolutions of his day: Darwin's theory of evolution and Einstein's theory of relativity. For Dewey, it was scientific method that brought us these revolutions and their accompanying radical conclusion that knowledge is not fixed. And for those seeking authority in their insights and knowledge, such conclusions at first glance are highly discomforting. What Dewey aimed to demonstrate, however, and where he made his contribution to the development of the American ideology identified by Hoffmann, was that the effects of scientific method had generated beneficial consequences. While there were the technological advances to be mentioned, what was most important to Dewey was that natural science and scientific method had two added benefits. First, they made it painfully clear that philosophers should redirect their energies away from the futility of pursuing "universal knowledge" or "truth"; that is, being less epistemologically centered and becoming more human-centered, focused on "understanding and rectifying specific social ills" (Dewey, 1948, 211). Second, natural science provides us with a method of inquiry that can be used across disciplines to remedy those social ills. It is a generalizable method of inquiry that is self-correcting, and oriented to invention and discovery, such that it affords a "positive intellectual direction to man in developing the practical" (Dewey, 1948, xxxiii).

As noted above, Hoffmann argues that faith in scientific method is a particularly American ideology because of the scope and depth with which it is held. Dewey is not exempt from the kind of American parochialism that Hoffmann describes. Dewey found that scientific method provided a general formula for inquiry which had a wide scope for use in intellectual endeavors. Also, Dewey was firmly convinced by the critical and positive powers of this method. In fact, sympathetic critics accuse him of having perhaps too much faith in this general method of inquiry to cure social, political, and economic problems (West, 1989, 102). However, there is an important point of difference in Dewey's faith from the kind of faith that resulted in the development of IR as an American social science on Hoffmann's terms. This difference is important because it explains why Dewey offers an alternative understanding of social science for IR.

According to Hoffmann, IR as an American social science engages in scientific inquiry to produce results with explanatory power for the purposes of prediction and control. The expected outcome is knowledge that we can invest with authority. Dewey, on the other hand, finds that the outcomes which result from the application of scientific method can no longer be regarded as independent foundations of truth or authoritative knowledge. Therefore, when Hoffmann goes on to characterize this first element of American intellectual predispositions as having the conviction that there is a "masterkey" in all areas of inquiry that, once found, yields answers and solutions, pragmatism follows a different path. There is no "masterkey" to be found for pragmatists. There are only individual and temporary solutions to particular problematic situations. For Dewey, it is the recognition of problematic situations that gives occasion to employ the general method of inquiry borrowed from natural science. Hypotheses are suggested as to the possible consequences of plans offered as solutions to problematic situations. The success of an inquiry is judged by whether the plan of action suggested by a hypothesis, and the execution of that plan (the experiment) resolve the doubt raised by the indeterminate situation (Dewey, 1938, 105–110). However, the solution reached for that particular situation is not generalizable across other problematic situations, even of like kind, and most important, the solution reached is not regarded as truth, but as warranted assertibility. Warranted assertibility is the recognition of fallibilism, a central proposition of American pragmatism. Fallibilism holds that any solution, claim, or principle has an element of miscalculation and cannot be known with certainty to be true. Thus, the claim can only hold a provisional status, meaning that it is always open to revision. Consequently, Dewey's idea of a social science puts a question mark over the idea that there is an answer out there for any or each field of inquiry, universal and generalizable within it, which needs only to be discovered for progress to follow naturally. Rather, solutions are particular to their problems and serve only as temporary resting places until inquiry begins again. Therefore, Dewey's understanding of social science as fallible suggests that studying human relations "scientifically" does not necessarily provide authoritative and reliable solutions to social problems, a conclusion very different from the expectations inherent in Hoffmann's depiction of IR as an American social science.

Dewey and Hoffmann on Science and Society

Having mapped out the alternative terrain of Dewey's own ideological fervor, I will now turn to the second element Hoffmann attributes to American intellectual predispositions: the idea that "the very prestige and sophistication of the 'exact sciences' were bound to benefit social ones as well" (Hoffmann, 1977, 47–48). As demonstrated above, Dewey did not share the view that natural science is "exact" nor, as a matter of course, that its supposed exactness is its particular benefit. However, he did think that scientific method held particular promise for the study of social problems. Although it could not confirm solutions absolutely, it could, nonetheless, generate ways to help us cope better in our social worlds. Indeed, Dewey saw it as an ethical responsibility to pursue inquiry via this method with diligence and intelligence. His project is centrally concerned with elucidating the relationships between science, society, and morality. Dewey was attentive to the untold social effects of the progress of science, and was anxious that natural science and the study of human activity and human values should not be regarded as separate intellectual activities. They impact on each other too much and, thus, any separation is artificial. For Dewey, natural science is social activity. As discussed above, the problems which give rise to the use of scientific method are the product of doubt; that is, the recognition of an indeterminate situation. These situations, according to Dewey, are inherently social and he sees inquiry itself to be a socially shared, collaborative process within critical, scientific communities. From the perspective of studying human activity and values, Dewey is clear that in applying scientific method as a general method of inquiry, the procedures of evaluation in science do not differ in their application or usefulness from any range of moral, political, economic, or social decisions.

However, while Dewey's pragmatist understanding of social science shares this second element identified by Hoffmann, once again it stands apart precisely because it takes seriously the idea that scientific activity is social activity and that it is social activity which is evaluative. What is deemed important for study and what is regarded as fact is socially conditioned. Science is an evaluative process in which value cannot be separated from fact. Thus, the empirical and the normative are interlinked for Dewey, whereas IR as an American social science embraces the idea that science is value-free. As Hoffmann nostalgically notes, it did not always attempt to separate the empirical and the normative (Hoffmann, 1977, 44–45, 51). However, it has moved in a decidedly empirical direction since Morgenthau, a move that Dewey's idea of a social science would regard as a narrow and limited idea of social inquiry.

Toward a Richer Social Science

This brings us to the third element of Hoffmann's characterization of the intellectual predispositions evident in America: immigrant scholars whose "philosophical training and personal experience moved them to ask far bigger questions than those much of American social science had asked so far" (Hoffmann, 1977, 46). What Hoffmann appreciates most about these scholars is that they were infusing "frequently parochial" American social science with wider questions about ends, choices, and social wholes making American social science "something more universal" (Hoffmann, 1977, 46–47). The purpose which motivated their scientific inquiry was indisputably normative. As Hoffmann puts it, they "wanted to find out the meaning and the causes of the catastrophe that had uprooted them, and perhaps the keys to a better world" (Hoffmann, 1977, 47). While IR as an American social science has steadily built upon one aspect of inquiry introduced by these immigrants, a focus on social wholes, or the international system, it has turned its back on much they added that according to Hoffmann made American social science more rich: a focus on normative ends and historical experience. American IR, as it has developed since the contributions of these immigrant scholars, has by Hoffmann's own measure become an increasingly narrow field. In light of Hoffmann's analysis, what is most interesting about Dewey's pragmatist idea of a social science is that it would "universalize" American social science as the immigrants had. It would reconnect inquiry in IR with philosophical traditions and an understanding of history as lived experience that could draw contemporary IR out of its increasingly narrow compass of inquiry.

Why IR Did Not Follow Dewey

Before I bring this section to a close, it will be useful to offer some brief suggestions as to why IR did not develop along the alternative, pragmatist route to social science outlined here. This is particularly interesting since, as Cornel West writes, the "coming-of-age of American pragmatism occurs just as the United States emerges as a world power" (West, 1989, 85). He finds that the events are not mere coincidence and that Dewey's thought was influenced by the new role of the United States in the world. Dewey wrote numerous essays on war and peace, America's role in the world, the League of Nations, the World Court, and morality and the conduct of states (Dewey, 1929). Yet, IR as a discipline was not influenced by Dewey. Perhaps these writings were unknown. Dewey was more popularly known for his writings on education, liberalism, and democracy. Or perhaps, if IR scholars were aware of them, they nonetheless ignored them since these essays were written in the midst of what was commonly regarded as the fog of the interwar utopian vision and would lack social science credentials. Although, quite to the contrary, one cannot help but be reminded of Carr when Dewey writes in 1920 that:

> The peace settlement is loudly proclaimed in the name of ideals that stir man's deepest emotions, but with the most realistic attention to the details of economic advantage distributed in proportion to physical power to create future disturbances. (Dewey, 1948, 128)

There are other reasons why Dewey would not have been in the minds of budding IR social scientists. IR did not emerge as a social science until after the Second World War and it was then that pragmatism was being eclipsed by analytic philosophy. However, even if Dewey had been in the minds of those who shaped IR as a discipline, there are other factors which would have precluded IR from taking a pragmatist turn. Those, in large part, are the two other factors identified by Hoffmann as contributing to the development of IR as an American social science: political circumstances and institutional opportunities. As Hoffmann writes, the policy makers wanted what the scholars aimed to produce—an "intellectual compass which would serve multiple functions"—and Realism provided that "compass" or "masterkey" (Hoffmann, 1977, 48). Realism served as an operational paradigm that produced authoritative grounds for action, and in addition, institutional factors unique to the United States "acted as multipliers of political connection" (Hoffmann, 1977, 49). However, as the discussion above notes, Dewey was not in the business of providing what policy-makers wanted: authoritative and generalizable principles for action. Thus, IR became a tool for policy-makers, while pragmatism on the other hand is a tool for the social critic, engaged in her social world, hoping to find not only instrumental means for coping in that realm, but ways of making it more meaningful as well. It is the blend of the empirical and the normative desired by Hoffmann, but rejected by IR as it eventually emancipated itself from philosophy and history.

EVEN IN AMERICA: HARMONY FOR SOME

In 1977, Hoffmann asked what breakthroughs had taken place in thirty years of the development of IR as an American social science. On the whole, he found that there was more cause for frustration than celebration since IR's quest to become more like a science and its hope that, as a science, it would be useful, have met obstacles at every turn. I will examine the difficulties Hoffmann identifies on both fronts and discuss any changes that may have taken place since. Also, I will elaborate what a pragmatist understanding of IR as a social science might contribute in addressing the divisions and contradictions which concerned Hoffmann.

Hoffmann was particularly struck by the division of opinion as to how IR should be pursued as a social science. He identified three obstacles: problems of theory formation, questions as to what should be explained, and questions about how we should study it (Hoffmann, 1977, 51–54). Concerning theories, Hoffmann notes that IR has had a difficult time formulating laws that can account for the behavior of states. Where Kenneth Waltz wants to blame the theorists for these difficulties, Hoffmann suggests that there may be something inherent in the field which precludes theory formation, particularly a theory of undetermined behavior (Hoffmann, 1977, 52). What is interesting is that since the publication of Waltz's *Theory of International Politics*, two years after the publication of Hoffmann's *Daedalus* article, there has been a growing consensus within American IR that Waltz was right. It is not that there is something about IR as a field that makes it impenetrable for the purposes of theory formation. Waltz, by the accounts of many in the field, has produced a theory of international relations or at least demonstrated that one can be formulated. Any problems are the result of the fact that IR theorists have not been rigorous enough, they have not been good scientists. The repercussion of this lesson for the field has been to consolidate the idea that IR must work to be more exact, and so American IR finally has separated itself off from the diffuseness introduced via its association with the fields of history, philosophy, and law. As Hoffmann notes, IR maintained its connections with these fields long after Economics and Political Science moved on to a "science of scarcity, competition and power" (Hoffmann, 1977, 46). However, since Waltz's 1979 book, American IR also has followed suit. Yet, as Hoffmann notes, in the United Kingdom, Hedley Bull maintained those long held IR links to traditions of law, history, and philosophy.

Second, Hoffmann writes that there was a "triple fragmentation" as to what should be explained in IR. He points to differences over the level of analysis problem, fragmentation at each level of analysis, and functional fragmentation resulting in clusters of research in different areas

(Hoffmann, 1977, 52). Since 1977, unlike the consensus around the possibility of a theory of IR—that of Waltz—there remains much division over what should be the focus of explanation. A well-rehearsed disagreement is what is labeled the neorealist-neoliberal debate: neorealists focus on changes in the capabilities of state actors in an anarchic system and neoliberal institutionalists focus upon changes in the intentions of actors, generally states operating within international institutions (Baldwin, 1993, 3–25). A recent and powerful intervention in the American IR debate has been that of constructivists or sociological institutionalists who suggest that we should focus on processes of identity formation and how actors are socialized into particular behaviors within the international system (Wendt, 1992; Katzenstein, 1996). Ultimately, these are epistemological matters concerning what counts as knowledge. However, this is not to suggest that there are not aspects of convergence on epistemological issues among these three groups. First, there is a large measure of agreement that IR should conduct systems level analysis. There have been recent calls to develop links with studies of domestic policy (Baldwin, 1993, 23). Nonetheless, the difficulties of integrating both are undertheorized (Katzenstein, 1996, xii), suggesting that engagement in American IR with subsystem analysis amounts to not much more than putting a toe in to test how the water feels. Second, while there is divergence on what IR should focus upon, there appears to be more clarity about what does not count as knowledge within IR. Basically, it amounts to anything that cannot be demonstrated as having explanatory power and results in degrees of wooliness or introduces diffuse phenomena. For example, anecdotal stories of women and the ways in which international politics affects their lives and how their lives impact upon the practice of international politics, or more generally, questions about the nature of proper relationships between individuals, states, and institutions and the meaning of those relationships within international practice. Interestingly, these more "diffuse phenomena" have a more receptive audience in the British IR community, where links with other fields have been maintained.[1]

For Hoffmann, the final obstacle that IR as an American social science has encountered is divided opinion over methodologies. There are two camps he identifies: traditionalists, who view the field as requiring historical and philosophical scholarship rather than scientific study, and those who want a science of IR and are wedded to empirical analysis (Hoffmann, 1977, 54). As noted above, the lesson imparted by Waltz on the possibility of theory has marginalized members of the traditionalist camp within American IR due to the requirement of exactness. While neoliberal institutionalists may be sympathetic to the institutionalism of the traditionalist Bull, they do not take on board the same interest that

Bull had in exploring the normative implications of his work, particularly questions of order and justice—a partisan and messy business (Keohane, 1989). Since Hoffmann wrote this piece, one can say that concerning methodology as well, there has been a growing consensus in American IR around the scientific camp, that IR should pursue empirical analysis.

Bridging Normative and Empirical Approaches:
Pragmatism and Hoffmann's "Wish-List"

It is interesting that Hoffmann's underlying message in this section—that IR would benefit as a discipline if we worked towards greater harmony in its study—seems to be a reason for the efforts towards theoretical and epistemological consensus and behind methodological unity in American IR. As Baldwin and Katzenstein write in the introductions to their edited collections, one on the Neorealist-Neoliberal debate in IR, the other on the contributions of sociological institutionalism to national security studies, progress in the discipline is more likely when its players agree to meet on the same playing field (Baldwin, 1993, 3; Katzenstein, 1996, 11). For contemporary IR as an American social science, that playing field is now positivism: what counts as knowledge is that which can be proven to have explanatory power and we study it empirically. The irony is that the thrust of Hoffmann's underlying message had a different intent. It was not to find harmony in the discipline by narrowing the range of questions asked, since this only serves to make American IR more parochial. This is all the more evident when one thinks of how marginal to mainstream American IR are recent developments in the United Kingdom and isolated North American locales which have explored IR's connection to the insights of political theory, for example, normative, critical, feminist, and poststructuralist theories, or to the insights of history, for example, recent historical materialist approaches.[2] It is exactly this kind of engagement with broader questions that Hoffmann wants to see. What Hoffmann intends by "harmony" in the discipline is an idea of IR as a social science that bridges empirical and normative approaches so that they can work productively together. This is needed now more than ever if IR wants to be more than a narrowly defined field capable of studying only that which can be "explained" in international politics.

I now want to address the extent to which pragmatism could serve as that bridge by examining what it has to contribute to the above points on theory, epistemology, and methodology. I will not go into detail in elucidating how pragmatism might operationalize the priorities discussed here. However, I will try to offer some suggestions related to Hoffmann's own "wish-list" for progress in IR.

What Dewey has to say about theory formation is to be found in his writings on logic. Like Waltz, Dewey would agree that theories do not tap into reality as such, but are constructions that are judged by their usefulness. As Dewey writes, "verification is in consequences . . . the hypothesis that works is the true one" (Dewey, 1948, 156). Dewey also shares with Waltz the idea that theories are made creatively, and for Dewey, one of the particular benefits of scientific method is the creativity that it inspires. However, Dewey and Waltz part company when Dewey defines logic as a "clarified and systematized formulation of the procedures of thinking" that efficiently provides for the "reconstruction of experience" (Dewey, 1948, 135). Logic for Dewey is empirical and normative. Usefulness is not judged by explanatory and predictive powers alone, but also a product of whether or not the result is meaningful. Thus, it maintains that connection to the interpretative in philosophy from which Waltz separates his idea of theory (Waltz, 1979, 6).

Epistemologically, American IR as a social science wants to be able to isolate what counts as knowledge in the field; that is, what most requires explanation in IR. However, pragmatism, as discussed above, regards knowledge as illusive. It suggests that we focus on learning instead of knowledge; that is, the growth gained by learning from lived experience. Attempts to fix what counts as knowledge ultimately close off otherwise potentially imaginative solutions to problematic situations that happen to fall outside of that category of knowledge as it is historically and contingently defined. In American IR as a social science, what at present falls outside of that category is a wide range of experience that it labels as reflexive or normative. As a consequence, what gets lost, according to Dewey's pragmatist understanding of social science, is the idea that experience, from which problematic situations arise, has principles of "connection" and "organization" in it which are both practical and meaningful rather than epistemological (Dewey, 1948, 82–91). Inquiry into ways that help us cope better in our social world cannot be separated out from the normativeness of society and how its constitutive practices influence us in our organization of experience. Indeed, inquiry arises from that normativity.

However, when we talk about "how" we study international practice, this does not mean that from a pragmatist perspective we cannot inquire into empirical conditions. For Dewey, the individual's situatedness in society is an empirical fact. The act of describing a problematic situation is an empirical matter and the solution that emerges from experimentation is empirical. Thus, methodology for the pragmatist does not suggest a choice between empirical and normative analysis, but employs both.

This orientation toward both the empirical and the normative spares pragmatists the other dimension to IR's frustration as an American social science identified by Hoffmann: its goal of being useful. Hoffmann finds that IR's will to be useful contradicts its "allegiance to objective empiricism" because it wants an advisory role for itself (Hoffmann, 1977, 54–55). The contradiction here is represented in the fact that the inclination to be useful is ultimately normative. This recognition is at the heart of Dewey's pragmatism and its self-understanding, and thus, avoids the awkwardness of this contradiction within IR as an American social science. IR as a pragmatist social science would aim to be useful by pursuing inquiry into international practice wherever problematic situations arose. What is recognized as a problematic situation in IR would not privilege the objective over the subjective or be limited to the goal of enhancing the explanatory power of IR theory. Nor would it privilege one level of analysis over others. Instead, against the grain of the narrowing that has taken place in American IR, it would introduce a broader range of questions and diffuse phenomena at system, subsystem, or state and substate levels, since it would be open to inquiring into whatever situation in international social practice came to be publicly recognized as problematic. For Dewey, it is exactly the diffuse character of phenomena that makes inquiry imperative as we work to understand the indirect consequences that link us into wider publics. Our consciousness of these interconnecting but diffuse consequences and persistent inquiry into their empirical and normative aspects is at the base of pragmatism as an American social science and perhaps can serve as the base for the kind of bridge that Hoffmann deems important to IR.

BECAUSE OF AMERICA: WHAT IS TO BE DONE?

In the final part of his article, Hoffmann discusses further traits that he finds to be largely unrepresented outside of American IR and suggests that American IR would benefit from a "triple distance" from them. In this concluding section, I will discuss each of these in turn and what pragmatism would contribute to the distancing of these traits. Finally, I will suggest that IR as a pragmatist social science is a kind of bridge that has not been tried, but one that should be under construction if we share Hoffmann's prognosis of the state of the discipline.

The first and clearly the most vexing for Hoffmann is what he calls "the quest for certainty" in IR as an American social science. It is this quest that, according to Hoffmann, has led to an empiricism and quantification in the discipline that ignores whatever cannot be quantified. Thus, Hoffmann is concerned about what is lost in the discipline when it rules the nonquantifiable or unobjective out of what is understood to be legitimate for study in the field. For Hoffmann, this means that areas of study like statecraft as an art or work on perceptions and misperception in IR get marginalized due to their subjective nature (Hoffmann, 1977, 57). Today it is the recent work that has followed out of the connections that were left in place in the United Kingdom between IR and traditions of philosophy, history, and law that are suffering the consequences of the quest for certainty in the discipline. Oddly enough, Dewey wrote a book titled, *The Quest for Certainty* (Dewey, 1929) and it is a topic of concern in much of his other work as well. Dewey would disagree that this has been a particularly American quest, since he traces this as a phenomenon evident in the history of philosophy. However, it is important to note that this search has a different character for Dewey. For Dewey, "perfect certainty is what man wants" (Dewey, 1929, 21), but he believes that it is a certainty that has been cultivated in thought or philosophy rather than in practical matters, which are the subject matter of science. The world of the material is the realm of flux, change, and insecurity, whereas thought or knowledge can tap into the universal which is "fixed and immutable," untouched by the "perils of uncertainty" that are the practical affairs of human activity (Dewey, 1929, 6–7). As discussed in the first section above, the beauty of scientific method for Dewey was that it revealed this quest in philosophy to be a myth. Yet, despite his own contributions to, and investment in, the American faith in scientific method, Dewey would have been loath to renew the quest for certainty in a different guise. Indeed, this is what separates out his idea of a social science. His idea would not be able to sustain a quest for certainty, as his view of science is one that assumes fallibility. It is an understanding of social science that is more suitable to Hoffmann as it works against the grain of the new and unique quest for certainty Hoffmann identifies in IR as an American social science.

A second trait that concerns Hoffmann is the discipline's focus on the present, such that history is left unexamined. He finds that this feature of American IR results in a preoccupation with America's superpower status and leaves unexplored the relation of domestic politics to international politics and the hierarchical nature of relations between the weak and the strong (Hoffmann, 1977, 58). At first glance, it may not appear that pragmatism would represent an improvement in regard to examining history, since pragmatism is largely future oriented in its aim to improve our ways of coping with problematic situations and its concern with consequences. However, the idea of continuity is ever present in Dewey's work and that requires an orientation to the past as well. As H. S. Thayer writes, Dewey finds that "continuity is something seen and discovered as well as a way of seeing and discovering" (Thayer,

1981, 174). Also, where American IR is *a*historical, pragmatism is decidedly historical, since Dewey's idea of the situation is embedded in context and history. Situations are unique to time and place, as are their particular solutions. Yet it remains the case that we must be careful about the degree to which we defend pragmatism's credentials in regard to the examination of history. It is certainly not at the center of its focus. However, its focus on learning from lived experience requires an historical awareness, and it does manage to avoid the pitfalls that Hoffmann attributes to this second trait of American IR.

When Hoffmann writes that American IR "fears" history because it asks "what should we do?" instead of "what should we know," pragmatism is not altogether out of the line of fire. Pragmatists too ask "what should we do?" However, they do so not in the interest of knowledge, but of learning. Learning is meant to be a guide to action, but it is also a guide to finding meaning and one's own growth in connection with others. It is a basis for widening moral inclusion and responsibility through the public recognition of common problems that require common solutions. Such an orientation brings one back to the forgotten questions that concern Hoffmann, to the extent that there is recognition of the problems inherent in the relationships between domestic politics and international politics and relations between the weak and the strong in world politics. Dewey acknowledged problems in both of these areas. Dewey identified an indeterminacy in domestic and international relations because he recognized an elaborate and global network of indirect consequences that links us in an immense and impersonal great society lacking in political organization. He adds that existing political and legal forms are incapable of dealing with the kinds of transnational consequences made visible since the First World War. He writes that this doubt raises the need that "non-political forces organise themselves to transform existing structures: that divided and troubled publics integrate" (Dewey, 1927, 128–129). However, for Dewey, before this can happen, these publics have to become self-aware of their connection via indirect consequences. This requires inquiry into these consequences: that is, inquiry into the relation between domestic and international politics. Dewey's pragmatism also suggests that there is a problem that presents itself in the relations of the strong and the weak. Where Hoffmann, by referring to the strong and weak, means only to suggest power relations in the sense of military might, Dewey's work also has implications for the strong and weak in the economic sense of haves and have nots. Dewey's call for self-awareness about wide-reaching, indirect consequences, and the need to address the inadequacies of existing political structures to deal with them, arises out of a concern for democratic participatory parity, that persons affected by these consequences are represented when action is taken in regard to them. For Dewey, democratic participatory parity has a socioeconomic dimension, which means that actors must have the wherewithal to participate. This would require that one address the material inequalities related to both military and economic strength among actors in aiming to narrow gaps in participatory parity.

Therefore, a pragmatist understanding of IR as an American social science appears to be well equipped to assist in the triple distancing that Hoffmann requires when he writes about American IR that:

> it should move away from the contemporary, toward the past; from the perspective of a superpower (and a highly conservative one), toward that of the weak and revolutionary—away from the impossible quest for stability; from the glide into policy science, back to the steep ascent toward the peaks which the questions raised by traditional philosophy represent. (Hoffmann, 1977, 59)

IR by a pragmatist understanding is not without its American characteristics; that is, its deep faith in scientific method and its usefulness in helping us cope with international social practice. However, it is not limited by the narrowness that IR as an American social science has assumed. Pragmatist social science is more "universal" in the sense that Hoffmann uses the term, meaning that its links to traditions of philosophy and history open it up to broader, normative questions, and its refusal of quests for certainty in any guise means that it does not close off from inquiry aspects of human activity or levels of analysis that are not capable of generating certainty of the right kind. While it aims to be useful, its usefulness is not intended for the purposes of policy-making alone, but is geared to be of use to individuals too as a process of inquiry into inquiry which facilitates social criticism and helps them to improve the ways they cope and find meaning in their lives. This process of inquiry is inherently social for Dewey and he argues that the more those who conduct inquiries coordinate their efforts, the better the potential solutions that may result. Thus, a pragmatist approach to social science emphasizes harmony in diversity: that methodologically, normative and empirical analysis be integrated, and that epistemologically, we cling less desperately to the idea of certainty and founding knowledge, and instead pursue various, temporary solutions experimentally to find what there is to be learned from experience in regard to how it is lived.

Pragmatism is not the only alternative to those who share Hoffmann's concerns about IR as an American social science today. For example, recent forays into constructivism in the discipline aim to reestablish links between empirical and normative analysis. The important question though for any approach to international relations that wants to serve as a bridge between positivist and post-positivist, rationalist and reflectivist, or empirical and normative approaches is the extent to which it genuinely serves the purposes of each side. Steve Smith writes that constructivism has failed in this respect, because otherwise, "it would be the dominant theory in the discipline, since it could relate to all other approaches on their own terms" (Baylis and Smith, 1997, 183). I agree with Smith that constructivism, as Alexander Wendt has outlined it, favors the explanatory bent of rationalist IR. Ultimately, constructivism developed out of the line of thinking that Hoffmann calls "IR as an American social science" and is affected by American IR's quest for foundational certainty. However, I have my doubts about the degree to which any approach can serve this role, including pragmatism. I do not want to rule it out as a possibility at this stage, because there is much more to be said about what a pragmatist understanding of IR as a social science can contribute to these camps in the discipline as they have been set apart.

More modestly, and appropriate to what there has been space to suggest here, I think there is cause for thinking that there is the possibility of another bridge approach, as well as constructivism, within IR. Consistent with the doubts just expressed, I expect that pragmatism will be seen to favor the normative bent of reflectivist approaches. For now, I think this is fine, especially for purposes of balance, as we explore possibilities for collaboration and progress in the discipline. Where constructivism begins the construction of its bridge from the banks of mainstream American approaches described by Hoffmann, a pragmatist understanding of IR as a social science begins its construction from those reflectivist or normative approaches that have found their most comfortable home of late in British IR. Perhaps these two construction projects will meet somewhere over the Atlantic. Perhaps they will miss each other altogether. However, if one accepts Hoffmann's prescription for progress in IR, it recommends that pragmatism and its idea of social science is best suited to the task.

NOTES

1. As a small representative sample of a growing body of such literature, see Cynthia Enloe (1989), Jean Bethke Elshtain (1987), Mervyn Frost (1996), and Linklater (1990).

2. For examples of feminist and normative contributions, see note 1 above. For critical contributions, see Hoffman (1987) and Neufeld (1995). For poststructuralist work, see Campbell (1993), Der Derian (1992), and Walker (1993), Finally, for historical materialist approaches, see Rosenberg (1994).

REFERENCES

Baldwin, David. (1993). *Neorealism and Neoliberalism: The Contemporary Debate*. New York: Columbia University Press.

Campbell, David. (1993). *Politics without Principle: Sovereignty, Ethics and the Narratives of the Gulf War*. Boulder, Colo.: Lynne Rienner.

Carr, E. H. (1964). *The Twenty Years' Crisis: 1919–1939*. New York: Harper & Row.

Der Derian, James. (1992). *Antidiplomacy: Spies, Terror, Speed, and War*. Oxford: Blackwell.

Dewey, John. (1927). *The Public and Its Problems*. Athens, Ohio: Swallow Press.

Dewey, John. (1929). *Characters and Events: Popular Essays in Social and Political Philosophy*. Vol. 2. London: George Allen and Unwin.

Dewey, John. (1938). *Logic: The Theory of Inquiry*. New York: Henry Holt.

Dewey, John. (1948). *Reconstruction in Philosophy*. Boston: Beacon Press.

Jean, B. E. (1987). *Women and War*. Brighton, U.K.: Harvester Press.

Enloe, Cynthia. (1989). *Bananas, Beaches and Bases: Making Feminist Sense of International Politics*. London: Pandora Press.

Frost, Mervyn. (1996). *Ethics in International Relations: A Constitutive Theory*. Cambridge: Cambridge University Press.

Hoffman, Mark. (1987). "Critical Theory and the Inter-Paradigm Debate." *Millennium: Journal of International Studies* 16(2), 231–249.

Hoffmann, Stanley. (1977). "An American Social Science: International Relations." *Daedalus* 106(3), 41–60.

Katzenstein, Peter. (1996). "Preface" and "Introduction: Alternative Perspectives on National Security." In Peter Katzenstein (ed.), *The Culture of National Security: Norms and Identity in World Politics*. New York: Columbia University Press.

Keohane, Robert O. (1989). *International Institutions and State Power: Essays in International Relations Theory*. Boulder, Colo.: Westview Press.

Linklater, Andrew. (1990). *Men and Citizens in the Theory of International Relations*. London: Macmillan.

Neufeld, Mark. (1995). *The Restructuring of International Relations Theory*. Cambridge: Cambridge University Press.

Rosenberg, J. (1994). *The Empire of Civil Society*. London: Verso.

Smith, Steve. (1996). "Positivism and Beyond." In Steve Smith, Ken Booth, and M. Zalewski (eds.), *International Theory: Positivism and Beyond*. Cambridge: Cambridge University Press: 11–44.

Smith, Steve. (1997). "New Approaches to International Theory." In J. Baylis and Steve Smith (eds.), *The Globalization of World Politics: An Introduction to International Relations*. Oxford: Oxford University Press: 165–190.

Thayer, H. S. (1981). *Meaning and Action: A Critical History of Pragmatism*. Indianapolis, Ind.: Hackett.

Walker, R. B. J. (1993). *Inside/Outside: International Relations as Political Theory*. Cambridge: Cambridge University Press.

Waltz, Kenneth. (1979). *Theory of International Politics.* New York: McGraw-Hill.

Wendt, Alexander. (1992). "Anarchy Is What States Make of It: The Social Construction of Power Politics." *International Organization* 46(2), 391–426.

West, C. (1989). *The American Evasion of Philosophy: A Genealogy of Pragmatism.* Madison, Wisc.: University of Wisconsin Press.

CHAPTER 3

Along the Road of International Theory in the Next Millennium: Four Travelogues

Kalevi J. Holsti

Like most disciplines, the field or subject of International Relations undergoes change. In its narrative or policy-oriented guise, this is natural, as the problems punctuating the world's headlines change from day to day. As a theoretical enterprise, on the other hand, change should not be ubiquitous or fundamental since perennial issues of security, peace, equity, development, and quality of life transcend location, time, and personality. Today, we can read translated clay tablets dating from the third millennium B.C. or review accounts of relations between Sumerian cities (Watson, 1992) and find in them many characteristics and aspects of statecraft that are commonly observed still today. Problems of honor, power, commitment, reputation, and hegemony, also major themes in the Melian dialogues, suffuse international relationships as much today as they did 2,500 years ago. Nevertheless, our contemporary theoretical renderings of international relations also reflect public moods and great issues of the day that may find no historical counterparts. Theory is not divorced from the milieu in which it is developed (cf. Ferguson and Mansbach, 1988; Patomäki, 1992), and milieus change in a number of dimensions, though not as rapidly as the day's events.

While we can accept and even applaud scholarly innovation, new perspectives, and theoretical novelties if they help us make a complex world more intelligible, international theory may be entering into an era characterized less by normal scholarly debate and change than by crisis. An intellectual crisis includes some or all of the following characteristics:

1. The foundations of knowledge claims erode or are assaulted to such an extent that the intellectual community has no further confidence in the authority of theoretical work.

2. The discrepancies between theoretical renderings of a subject—designed to increase understanding and intelligibility—and the events, trends, and essential characteristics of international practice are so great that isomorphism and correspondence are no longer possible.

3. The field of study no longer has any core questions or problems to investigate. Scholars go their own way, intellectually, meaning that the "community" of scholars organized around a common set of problems disintegrates.

4. The social/ethical/moral problems around which the field originated and developed—war and peace in the case of international politics—is solved at the political level. That is, the problem no longer exists and thus scholars who try to understand it, possibly in order to manage, control, or solve it, are now out of business.

A CRISIS IN INTERNATIONAL THEORY?

We have heard frequently that the study of international relations is in a state of crisis because it lacks a normative, substantive, and epistemological consensus (cf. Lapid, 1989; Crawford, 1996). But the term crisis in the sense of disagreement may be used more for rhetorical effect than as a serious characterization of the theoretical enterprise. After all, since at least the late eighteenth century there has been a constant dialogue between various strands of thinking about international relations. Debate, disagreement, and difference do not by themselves indicate a crisis, as defined above. In fact, if there are heady disagreements, probably all is well. Fashion and faddism in the field are normal. But when a field threatens to disappear, become redundant, or fly apart into a maelstrom of intellectual individualism devoid of common purpose or interest, we can say that there is a crisis.

Is this the case today? It is the opinion of many. John Ruggie, for example, has argued that the predominant perspectives on international relations—in this case neorealism and neoliberalism—are characterized by an "impoverished mindset" (Ruggie, 1993, 143). James N. Rosenau charges that most IR theorists are stuck in "conceptual jails" (1990, chap. 2) that hinder the development of the field. Jim George (George, 1994) is convinced that neorealism, in whatever guise, is fundamentally flawed in its ontological and epistemological foundations. Rob Walker and Richard Ashley (Ashley and Walker, 1990, 375ff.) see the discipline of international studies (sic) as just one area of crisis in a more general "crisis of representation" that characterizes modernity. Roland Bleiker (1995, 1) judges approvingly that during the past decade the field has been in a state of "flux and turmoil. . . . Nothing has remained unchallenged. The railings and bridges of orthodox IR wisdom have fallen into the water and numerous attempts to replace them immediately met with the same fate. No consensus, no new and coherent paradigm is yet in sight." I recently observed (Holsti, 1993, 401) that contemporary international theorists "do not see the world in the same ways, nor do they agree on what is important to know, or how to know it." The testimonials of crisis go on at length. There are many in the field who are disappointed, dispirited, and dejected. Others, in contrast, are elated because the "orthodoxies" are under assault and intellectual "thinking space" grows when there is no canon. That there can be such different reactions to the state of affairs suggests a kind of disciplinary schizophrenia.

We can readily observe these four symptoms of crisis at work in current debates and discussions about international theory. The first symptom takes the form of the challenges—and opportunities—posed by critical theory and postmodernism in some of their many forms. The second derives from the uncertainties attending the end of the Cold War and the emerging speculation about the effects of "globalization" and technological innovation on political practice. The remaining two symptoms are also prominent. Let us review some of the evidence which suggests that we are in a condition far beyond the parameters of ordinary scholarly debates and disagreements within disciplines and fields of study.

Promises and Pitfalls of Postmodernism

Change in the field in the past usually went along several trajectories. First, there may be change in the sense that a new normative/ethical problem is identified. This problem requires theoretical attention and makes a claim for addition to the repertoire of international theory. Some analysts, in contrast, take a very different tack. The purpose of change and innovation, according to its adherents, is not just to shift the theoretical focus onto other ethical concerns—a new theoretical agenda, so to speak; nor is it to add actors, such as nongovernmental organizations, to the intellectual purview; nor is it to "soften" the rough edges of Realism by acknowledging the collaborative aspects of international relations; nor, finally, is it concerned about lack of isomorphism between the "real" world and theoretical characterizations of it.

What is at issue is the nature of knowledge and communication. This is not the place to engage in a dissection of postmodern thought, of which there are as many strands as there are authors, and for which no one individual can claim any foundational authority. What we are concerned with is a claim about crisis in a field of inquiry. Some critics of contemporary theories of international relations help to create a sense of crisis by arguing that the foundations of all previous knowledge claims in the field are wrong. Empiricism is a flawed epistemology. Knowledge is linguistically and socially constructed; and, despite some possibilities for intersubjective consensus, ultimately it can be held only *individually*. Intersubjective consensus is difficult to achieve because no two individuals occupy the same emotional, cultural, or historical space. Most knowledge is only a "text," which, like poetry, can be interpreted in numerous ways, none of which can lay claim to authority. There is no acknowledgment that text is a means of communication between author and reader (Nicholson, 1996, 112). And since the Aristotelian notion of a distinction between observer and observed is denied, ultimately there can be nothing but individual truth or a "text," the meaning of which is not established by the author's intent, but by the reader's response. No one can say which interpretation is correct, or even better, for that matter (cf. Spegele, 1995, 213). The purpose of critical thought, in the view of some postmodernists, is not to alter the field in the substantive sense of "adding" to knowledge or evaluating knowledge claims. It is, rather, to destroy "orthodoxies," to "open up thinking space," to avoid the contaminating effects of traditional concepts, and to play with language so that clear prose, representing a form of intellectual domination, cannot impose "closure." Poetry, imagination, irony, paradox, and games must replace the somber language-uses of ordinary scholarship. Some current exponents of poststructuralism adopt a form of extreme epistemological individualism that is hardly consistent with any standard ideas of theory, or of intellectual organizing devices such as a "subject," "field," or "discipline." Indeed, the whole purpose of a "discipline" is just another form of intellectual closure designed to marginalize, to silence, and to exclude. There is a disciplinary crisis precisely because in a "register of freedom," ethically conscious scholars will challenge all authority claims. According to Ashley and Walker (Ashley and Walker, 1990, 398):

> to read almost any dissident text is to find not only a formal refusal of paradigmatic conceit but also a series of textual moves that function to disrupt any attempt to conduct a memorializing reading and turn a text into a paradigm [sic] of any sort. . . . Amidst a global crisis of representation, paradigmatic conceits have become downright impracticable for any scholarly enterprise that would expect not only to speak to something called global politics but also to be taken seriously in anything approaching the global scope to which it speaks.

There cannot be an integrated theory in such circumstances, and so, if some proponents of epistemological individualism have their way, there is no longer a need to think about "the state of the field," since there is no—or should not be—any field to think about.

Some aspects of postmodernism, as well as critical theory, offer rich opportunities for theoretical innovation in the more positive sense of the term. In this reading, the development does not imply crisis so much as increased maturation. Reflexivity, methodological self-consciousness, a willingness to explore concepts and approaches that are, and have been, taken too long for granted, all offer avenues for progress. Sensitivity to nuances, suspicion of "totalizing" projects, and awareness of paradox and the inevitability of "rough edges" as part of the human condition, may all contribute to healthy disciplinary debate. We await in which directions the contributions of postmodernism and critical theory will lead the field.

Isomorphism

A second source of crisis is the lack of fit between our theories and approaches to the field and the appearance of new trends, phenomena, and social/ethical problems. This is the issue of isomorphism. It has become particularly acute since the end of the Cold War.

Consider some of the phenomena that are not consistent with any of the major theoretical approaches or "schools" of International Relations existing today:

1. The reemergence of private armed forces, reminiscent somewhat of privateers, pirates, religious armies, and armed gangs of the past (e.g., armed drug-running organizations, warlords, armed fundamentalist groups with no distinct homeland, and terrorists-for-hire). In many "weak" states, the concept of sovereignty as a state monopoly over the legitimate use of force is meaningless. In many contemporary wars, the distinction between combat and crime has broken down (e.g., Liberia and Sierra Leone).

2. The ideological demands of global capital, or "the market." A type of economic orthodoxy "demands" certain domestic policies—fiscal discipline—and impinges upon and frequently overrides government priorities, seriously compromising autonomy.[1]

3. The dramatic decline of interstate war, to the point where the fundamental raison d'être of security studies, international theory, and the United Nations is being undermined (K. J. Holsti, 1996).

4. The collapse of sovereign states to the point where international efforts have to be made to resuscitate them. Some call it "the com-

ing anarchy [sic]" (Kaplan, 1994). I join those who raise the ulti-mate question about the transferability of the Western state concept into societies and cultures whose political traditions are fundamen-tally different from those that developed in Europe during the past five centuries (Holsti, 1996; Choukri, 1994; Badie, 1992). Others have called it a "new paternalism," suggesting that the main task of international organizations, indeed of the entire international com-munity, is not to prevent wars between states—the problem of inter-national theory since the eighteenth century—but to sustain or resuscitate states that have not made a successful transition from colonialism. The immense movement and victimization of civilian populations in wars surrounding collapsing states create an entirely new set of humanitarian problems not factored into traditional approaches to the field.

These phenomena are on the verge of becoming more than anoma-lies. They are trends, and in some parts of the world, they have become almost defining characteristics. None of the major theoretical approaches to the field accounts for them. If we add to this list all the problems associated with the unprecedented growth of technological innovation, it seems evident that international theory is not keeping up. Whether it is because our concepts are dated (Ruggie, 1993; Rosenau, 1996), our perspectives are still Eurocentric (Holsti, 1992), or our epis-temologies are all wrong (George, 1994), is hard to say. But whatever the problem, it is clear that existing characterizations of international politics miss a good deal.

Lack of a Core Problem

While oversimplifying to a certain extent, we can argue that in each era there has been an overriding problem that has attracted and stimulated change in international theory.[2] In the 1920s, the great problem was to create and sustain forms of international governance that could help pre-vent the recurrence of the Great War. By the mid-1930s, the great prob-lem was the Nazi/Fascist and Hitlerian threats to liberalism and the fun-damental principles of the Westphalian system. Since 1947, the Cold War and all the threats to security, freedom, and independence it entailed, formed the political background in which the ideas of Realism flourished. Concerns of equity, reciprocity, and justice animated the development of international political economy and dependency theory in the 1970s, the era of détente. Today, is there a commanding problem or challenge that animates theory and debate? Looking at the lack of substance in most contemporary theoretical debates, one might be led to the conclusion that philosophy has replaced international politics and international relations: there is no core normative problem that drives systematic inquiry. Disciplinary disintegration is one consequence. Concern with "how to" questions—epistemology, ontology, the connection between theory and praxis—is another. In this milieu of epistemological soul-searching, questions of substance—e.g., "what to study"—take a back seat.

The Problem of International Politics Is Solved

Closely linked to the symptom of crisis above is the political solution of the problem(s) that gave rise to a field of study or discipline. War and peace were the problems that stimulated the minds of eighteenth-century philosophers such as Kant, Rousseau, and Bentham, as well as their nineteenth- and twentieth-century successors. International Relations as an academic discipline began before but flourished after the Great War, and was, indeed, a major response to that tragedy. There is now mounting evidence, however, that for whatever reasons, the probabilities of major war between a large number of states in the system has declined precipitously (Holsti, 1996, chap. 2). There are existing or emerging "pluralistic security communities" (Deutsch, 1954) in North America, Western Europe, South America, Southeast Asia, and a few other regions of the world. War within these regions is an extremely low probability. And what few interstate wars do break out are usually caused by internal armed conflict. Saddam Hussein's assault on Kuwait may be among the last classical interstate wars.

If these trends become characteristic, then we can speculate that at least one of the main sources of the field of International Relations is drying up. The intellectual turmoil in the field today may be a reflection of this fact. In the absence of a commanding *problématique*, scholars have to turn to other issues, of which there may be any number. But there may be another interpretation of this bit of evidence about a crisis in the field.

It is that the apostles of change—liberal triumphalism, globalization, "identity politics" and the idea that technology and modernity have obliterated space/time, class, and national distinctions—fail to acknowledge the persistence of more traditional problems of world politics. The search for novelty takes on a momentum of its own, and everything new is assumed to *replace* the old. Every analyst goes off into new recesses to discover novelty, but that does not mean that the world necessarily follows in the footsteps of academic theorists. More of this in the final section, below.

This is the evidence of a crisis at hand. It is not overpowering, but suggestive enough to warrant speculation or concern about the future.

The field of International Relations changed little in the quarter century after the beginning of the Cold War. The behavioral revolution introduced a new panorama of methodologies and attempted to cast the subject in the mold of science. But the core problems, the ethical and normative concerns, and the basic images of the world and its political actors, changed very little (Holsti, 1985). An analyst in 1953, let us say, could predict with some certainty that the essential contours of international theory would look strikingly similar two decades later. And she would have been correct. Today, in contrast, one cannot predict with any confidence that in 2017 international theory will resemble even slightly today's efforts.

CONSTRUCTING TRAVELOGUES

Most histories of the discipline of International Relations characterize it in terms of a linear development of succeeding intellectual hegemonies focused on a major problem in international politics. The crude characterization of the field, above, is typical of our self-understanding. This view is, of course, a vast oversimplification and is in some respects incorrect (Schmidt, 1994), not the least because while some approaches or schools may have commanded the era's research programs, the field has always been characterized by competing, multiple "voices" (to borrow a postmodernist term). Thus, in making predictions about the future, there is no reason to believe that any single "school" or approach will dominate to the *exclusion* of others. Among other reasons, this is the case because the normative agenda of international politics is growing and will probably continue to proliferate (Holsti, 1996a).

I have chosen four travelogues to explore the future of the field. I do not claim that these are the only possibilities. They are projections of *some* of the main currents and tendencies in the field today.

Why use the term "travelogue?" Because the alternative, *scenario*, tends to be static. It is a photo of a state of affairs at a given time. In contrast, the travelogue analogy suggests movement, development, the possibility of side-tracks, and no certain destination. The point is not to get from A (today's "state of the field,") to B (some imagined—preferable?—"state of the field"). The reader should develop her or his own preference or predictions. Rather, it is to point out some of the available routes, byways, and side-trips, as well as their main scenic characteristics. However, if large numbers of theorists choose particular routes certain destinations—disciplinary consequences—are likely to ensue.

The four travelogues can be termed (1) oblivion; (2) uncivil war; (3) new consensus; and (4) one thousand blooming flowers. While these alternatives may not exhaust the possibilities, they are mutually exclusive. Thus, there cannot be combinations of them, some grand synthesis or reconciliation. Let us proceed with each travelogue and explore various byways along the route.

Oblivion

In 1995, Roland Bleiker (1995) delivered a paper at the Second Pan-European Conference on International Relations entitled "Forget IR Theory." The paper is erudite and delves into some complex problems of language, the rise and domination of scholarly orthodoxies, and Nitzschean philosophy. The essay, among other virtues, makes some insightful observations about the use of language in scholarship. However, I am less concerned with its contents than with its symbolism. It is, in my view, symptomatic of a mood in the field today: boredom. The *substance* of international politics—the ideas, actions, and interactions of governments and other actors, and the problems they create—seems no longer to be of interest to a growing number of international theorists. Rather, epistemology, social linguistics, "emancipation," ontology, the ideas of fifteenth- and sixteenth-century commentators, and some forms of historical sociology take over. They literally remove the world of past and contemporary practice from cognizance and cogitation. Two hundred years of theory which sought to make diplomatic, military, and commercial life intelligible through description, analysis, and explanation, simply disappears. This byway leads to a dead end, or perhaps more accurately, to a new road with a destination that bears little or no relationship to international politics. Along this route we learn a great deal about the innumerably contested ways of *how to think* about a subject matter, but almost nothing about the subject itself. The scenery is decidedly scholastic rather than substantive. This observation brings to mind Hedley Bull's criticism of behavioral studies in international politics, those massive efforts that focused on methodology to the exclusion of history, context, change, and politics. These studies, he suggested, "are as remote from the substance of international politics as the inmates of a Victorian nunnery were from the study of sex" (Bull, 1969, 26).

A second oblivion byway branches into many paths, each with interesting individual characteristics and unique scenery. Collectively, the diverging roads lead to a kind of neighborhood. We might call it "Identityville." Travelers along these streets observe new epistemological identities; identity is the key word. Appearance, rather than substance, defines the inhabitants of "Identityville." There are postmodernists, poststructuralists, critical theorists, feminist standpointers of unlimited hues, hermeneuticians, empiricists, historical sociologists, symbolic interactionists, and post-Marxists, just to name some of the more prominent (cf. Smith, 1995, for a similar, but more restricted categorization). We are likely to have more candidates soon. Everything, in a sense, goes, and no one author or text warrants more than passing interest. A prime characteristic of "Identityville" is the inhabitants' narcissistic concern with who they are. It seems as if the purpose of scholarship in "Identityville" is not to come to greater understanding of a domain of practice and experience called international politics, but rather to define the self. Scholarship is about who one is, not what the subject is. This theme pervades some of the feminist scholarship. Christine Sylvester (1994, 59), for example, writes that:

> Whereas standpointers admonish us to theorize from the lives of those we have designated as "others," or "reinvent ourselves as others," . . . a postmodern feminist may wonder whether it is preferable within the feminist method to unlearn (deny) ourselves to hyphenate with others empathetically in ways that avoid "progressive" replications of past erasures and reborn nostalgia for unity. Hence the emphasis on multiple standpoints, on being (ontologically) several things at once in a prismatic postmodern world—a rural-black-mother-agriculturalist-socialist-cooperator—and therefore, being homeless as a single-identity knowing Self.

Later, she concludes that "all feminisms are percolating through our postmodern time, debating each other and all others, scripting and rescripting their own texts and identities as they confront a world that once fixed us and now is a bit unhinged" (Sylvester, 1994, 155). It is difficult to see where an academic subject fits into these "narcissistic" forays into identity and subjectivities.[3]

A third byway has the street name "Forgetting." It branches off from "Identityville," but is still part of the neighborhood because part of the path of subjectivism and identity is dependent upon forgetting our ancestors who *did* have an overriding interest in substance. Moreover, many of these figures made truth claims and commanded a certain amount of authority, both attributes rejected as conceit by many of the denizens of "Identityville." Many inhabitants along "Forgetting Street" see our ancestors as little more than egotists trying to perpetuate themselves and their orthodoxies through graduate student groupies. Indeed, to some, one important purpose of international theory is precisely to "emancipate" us from such authority (and for a few, "totalitarian") figures. To achieve such emancipation, we have to free ourselves from the shadow of the past. We learn only by moving ahead, not by regarding our predecessors. Why should we bother reading Quincy Wright, E. H. Carr, Raymond Aron, and any other number of antecedents tainted by empiricism and other Enlightenment philosophical fallacies?[4]

"Forgetting Street" may indeed lead to a liberation of sorts. Anything will go, identities will be established—however fleetingly—and for some, the political agenda will command full-time attention. The subject, in the meantime, will disappear either because of boredom or through a deliberate attempt to erase its history. According to some inhabitants of "Identityville," intellectual emancipation comes only when methodological and epistemological canons and foundational figures or concepts have been eliminated. Critical "thinking space," imagination, and play will replace evidence as the foundation for scholarship.

Finally, the field may disappear because the fundamental distinction between the domestic realm and the realm between states—the latter always imagined, according to some—breaks down. This route is populated by many who do not accept the distinction between inside and outside. Intellectual constructs, such as sovereignty, which sustain the distinction, are coming under increasing critical scrutiny from numerous directions. Moreover, in using terms such as "governance" or "international civil society" to describe the international management of global problems or the growth of a world community, the distinction between national and international also begins to wear thin. The domestic analogy has always informed the analysis of international politics, particularly in its reform guise. But if the domestic analogy becomes a reality, then aren't the problems of international relations the same as the problems of political philosophy? Terry O'Callaghan (1995, 14) writes:

> There may be no valid ontological distinction between the international and domestic spheres. . . . [I]t needs to be asked whether it still makes sense to speak of international politics at all. . . . Indeed, it is appropriate to ask whether the discipline now only has an arbitrary existence within the social sciences; an existence based on nothing more than intellectual convention?

If we answer O'Callaghan's question in the affirmative, we are either out of jobs or we must become political philosophers and sociologists. This is a bold question indeed and it needs serious consideration.

Uncivil War

It is possible, of course, that fundamental differences of identity, purpose, and epistemology can coexist with a continued fascination with the subject matter of the field. There are many virtues to intellectual pluralism. But coexistence must be based on certain attitudes and mentalities. These would include either benign neglect or tolerance based on mutual understanding and respect. The first attitude would not solve the problem of oblivion, for fundamentally incompatible epistemologies and methodologies would likely lead to extreme fragmentation that may be inconsistent with the idea of a "field," "subject," or "discipline." The second attitude is not likely to predominate for reasons enumerated below.

The road of uncivil war is in fact already being chosen by some. Why? Because the stance taken by advocates and activists of the various methodological and epistemological persuasions often do not invite expansion, compromise, synthesis, or reconciliation. Elsewhere (Holsti, 1996a), I have spoken of the "monopoly syndrome," the attitude that "my approach to the subject is right, and yours is wrong." This is a zero-sum situation that does not accommodate strategies of amendment, change, working at the edges, deepening, or broadening the field.[5] Rather, the attitude promotes strategies of replacement, deletion, or total nonacceptance. Zealots of science in the 1950s and 1960s adopted this attitude, and we can see it today among some who argue that traditions, areas of cumulation, or existing approaches to international theory are fundamentally flawed because of wrong-headed epistemologies/methodologies, or because the purposes of inquiry are deemed illegitimate or are not sufficiently emancipatory. Usually it is a combination of all. Likewise, some proponents of more traditional approaches to the field have dismissed virtually all attempts at epistemological inquiry or interrogation as "silly" and worse.

But there is more along the road of uncivil war than the monopoly syndrome. There is also deep suspicion and fear of conspiracy, hidden agendas, and unspoken political motivations. The assumption of some postmodernists, Marxists, and critical theorists that theory and praxis are inextricably combined necessarily leads them to look for nonbenign, and sometimes nefarious, purposes in scholarship. The claim that all scholarship is necessarily political is likely to infuriate those who believe otherwise. Those engaged in more conventional scholarship are equally convinced that emancipatory purposes, whatever those might be, are inconsistent with the canons of good science or the rigor demanded of high-quality analysis.

But why is this road "uncivil?" Principally because of the fundamental incompatibilities involved, but also because of the exclusionary devices developed to establish notoriety and distinctiveness. Schools of thought sometimes take on the characteristics of an exclusive club; at other times, they may resemble a gang. There are entry rituals, there is a pantheon of intellectual heroes, there is a distinct jargon, and yes, there are even distinct journals and publishers that cater only to specific groups. There are also distinct denunciatory vocabularies (Rengger, 1996, 226).

We saw these phenomena during the early days of the behavioral revolution in the 1950s and 1960s. Today, we see similar symptoms of irreconcilability. The objects of attack from the newer methodologies/epistemologies are not likely to concede gracefully that 2,500 years of the study of politics based on observation, classification, and comparison—the Aristotelian legacy—should be thrown out because Nietzsche and other continental philosophers—but not experts on international relations—have declared that rationalism and empiricism are the sources of much that ails the world today. There is, in other words, a great deal at stake. Much of postmodernism and certain aspects of "standpoint" epistemologies are also inviting targets for robust denunciations, critiques that are not likely to heal wounds or undo deep cleavages. Along this road we are likely to see threats, denunciations, exposures, and occasional name-calling.

There is some evidence that this road is attracting travelers, perhaps in increasing numbers. Jim George's (1994) major study of Realism and neorealism has a great deal to recommend it as a primer on alternative epistemologies and as a critique of conventional approaches to international politics. Yet its tone is often denunciatory rather than scholarly. The objects of his attacks are labeled either in his text or, citing approvingly others' criticisms, as "totalitarian" (p. 173), "of little substance" (p. 119), and "shallow" and "sterile" (p. 133). Works of some repute in many quarters "reek" of empiricism or of "primitivism" (pp. 132, 124, 127, 133).

There is not much of Realism that can be salvaged from George's demolition derby. One would certainly be convinced that reading Rousseau, E. H. Carr, Hans Morgenthau, and Kenneth Waltz (in particular) would be a major waste of time at minimum, but more likely it would be complicit with American imperialism, the arms race, innumerable wars (including Bosnia and Kosovo), and the Holocaust.[6] Realism and neorealism are not just abstract explanatory theories of a world "out there," according to George. They are major reasons why the world is as bad off as it is and thus anyone who "subscribes" to it by, for example, teaching it or using it as an analytical framework, adds to the complicity.

Publications require a certain decorum. Denunciations must at least use a vocabulary that has some intersubjective meaning and meets minimum (quite!) standards of etiquette. Such restrictions are not similarly in play at seminars, conferences, and other formal and informal gatherings. At the 1996 International Studies Association meetings, I heard second-hand of one denunciatory outburst that was, to put it mildly, unprofessional. I personally witnessed another where a scholar characterized a group of colleagues with an expletive commonly featured in bar-room brawls. And in the milieu of campus political correctness, professors who do not teach every conceivable trendy topic in their introductory and advanced courses are denounced as racists and sexists. Anecdotes such as these do not of course establish a trend. But they are a new and disturbing phenomenon, not seen even in the heydays of behavioralist-traditionalist warfare.

The scenery along the road of uncivil war is not very pretty. There are many victims—or at least scholars feel victimized—the vocabulary is often excessive, and suspicion lurks everywhere. And uncivil wars among scholars, like those within states, tend to be long, nasty, and brutish. The conflicts tend to become personalized after enough uncivil behavior appears. The struggle over ideas may become a fig leaf for more personal vendettas. The profession as a whole suffers, and outsiders in particular will marvel at the ways that academics sometimes conduct their debates. They will note that today theorists of international politics appear to quarrel over metaphysical rather than substantive issues, and they will see little of relevance to their own lives. In a decade or so we might look back—some with nostalgia, others with relief—on the "Great Epistemological Pause" of the 1990s. Or, just possibly, a new wave, fashion, theory, or problem will conquer everyone's imagination, fascination, dedication, and research funds.

A New Consensus

This would mean a new consensus. There would be a main highway that sustains and guides traffic in one direction. Side-roads exist, but they are less densely populated. Debates between the followers of this route refer primarily to technical aspects of the way rather than to ultimate destinations. A new *problématique*, accompanied by an epistemological consensus, would command moral, political, social, and therefore, scholarly attention.

During the past few decades many problems have commanded theoretical attention. These include issues of reciprocity and equity (international political economy and dependency theory), social power relations (gender studies), and issues of quality of life and aesthetics (environmental problems), and international ethics. This proliferation of moral/political concerns has led to the diversification of the field and to the development of many competing and often incompatible theoretical designs. All of them, nevertheless, go under the term "international theory." I have argued elsewhere that while all these endeavors have value, interest, and a proper place in an expanded field, their theoretical renderings are essentially incommensurable (Holsti, 1970, 1985, 1996). Is it possible that, in contrast, any single socially constructed problem will once again gain predominance, as the problem of peace and war held for more than two centuries?

We might briefly list some candidates:

1. *Equity, Reciprocity, and Affluence*: Dependency theory had great appeal precisely because it addressed a glaring problem that remained outside the purview of Realism and various forms of liberalism: the inequitable distribution of welfare throughout the world. But there are many reasons why this problem is not likely to unify the field of international theory. The United Nations annual *Human Development* reports chronicle an amazing growth of human welfare in the past decades, even though this record is marred by continued severe deprivations and even worsening conditions in some countries since the 1960s. In comparative historical terms, however, there has been a marked and progressive transformation in the human condition, and there appears to be massive public optimism (or is it indifference?) that this progress will continue. Moreover, financial shortages, high unemployment rates, donor "fatigue," environmental concerns within and among the richer countries, and the seeming victory of orthodox economics also militate against the world equity *problématique*. The persistence of massive corruption, human rights abuses, and autocratic politics in poor countries do not help the cause either.

2. *Global governance*: This second candidate, linked at least in part to the first, has numerous possibilities in both diagnostic and prescriptive dimensions. A variety of questions come to mind: (a) under what circumstances is there likely to be the rise or development of international means of regulation, management, or reform? (b) how can these work effectively alongside national governments? (c) what does the growth of international governance mean for the concept and practices of sovereignty? and of political, social, and cultural diversity? (d) what are the possibilities for and limitations of domestic analogies? (e) and from a prescriptive point of view, how can we reconcile more global governance with freedom and liberty? (cf. Waever, 1996.)

The study of global governance reemerged under the title of "liberal institutionalism" in the 1980s and 1990s. This subfield has become among the most fully articulated theoretical and comparative ventures available today. But the idea of global governance may not be sufficiently attractive to form a new core of international theory. Those concerned with environmental issues will continue to point to the need for state-coordinated, or centralized world management. But others hold deep reservations about using domestic analogies, particularly those emanating from Western liberal experience, as a template for global management and institutions. Governance suggests control, influence, power, and even dictation. It goes without saying that system-wide governance of any form will largely reflect the values, interests, and policy priorities of the rich. Global governance also clashes with some peoples' desiderata of localism, spontaneity, and ideas about a growing international civil society. There may be a contradiction between the ostensible *need* for global and regional governance, and the ideological preference for local action and, above all, for "emancipation." Another problem is that in these domains partisanship may clash with high quality diagnosis and theory construction.

3. *System transformation*: There is already a vibrant literature that seeks to uncover the essential characteristics of, and the main trends in, the contemporary international system. Since the end of the Cold War we have seen theses that there will no longer be any fundamental ideological conflicts with the victory of liberal capitalism (Fukuyama), or of a much more pessimistic bent, that conflicts will become even more intractable because they will reflect deep cultural cleavages (Huntington, 1993) rather than mere state interests. Prognostications for the Third World, or what remains of it, are even more pessimistic (Kaplan, 1994). Several have suggested that we are now entering an era of two different types of international politics: the first will become an expanding pluralistic security community where war will become an exceptional event, and where common values will help mute commercial rivalries (Goldgeier and McFaul, 1992; Singer and Wildavsky, 1993). The second will see continuing and even accelerating conflicts, mostly surrounding the collapse of Third World states, and ethnic and religious wars (Holsti, 1992; 1996). We will need, then, to employ different conceptual apparatuses to understand the dynamics and sources of change in the "two worlds" (for other examples, see Scott 1982; Paul Elkins, 1991; Rosenau, 1990; Zacher, 1992; Spruyt, 1994; David Elkins, 1995; Linklater, 1996; Rosenau, 1996; and Deibert, 1997).

Can the themes of systemic change reunify the field? At first glance, one would think that many of the fissiparous tendencies of international theory over the past decade could be reduced or slowed down by a *problématique* as interesting and significant as system transformation.

But most analysts of systemic change have focused so far on all those elements that seem to be bringing the world closer together and/or subverting the concept and practices of sovereignty. We appear to be myopic on this score, for parallel to the manifold processes of "globalization" are the continuing processes of fragmentation. Political fragmentation, often manifested by the quest for sovereignty, has been a trend with surely as much significance as integration or "globalism." I wrote (Holsti, 1980) some time ago that the most significant political trend is not the "withering" of the state so much as the growing number of new states. Any international system that grows from fifty-two sovereign members to almost two hundred states in one-half century is undergoing a fundamental transformation in the sense that, as Lenin argued, at some point quantitative change produces qualitative change. I also suggested that the blossoming of statehood may be a *response* to the homogenizing forces of globalization. Rosenau (1996) has similarly acknowledged that globalization is not the only game in town, and that what he calls "localism" may be in part a response to those processes and forces that apparently "shrink" the world. We thus have a paradox that could set an agenda for significant theoretical work in the future: if sovereignty as an institution, concept, and set of practices is being undermined, or is waning, why is it that today we have almost four times as many sovereignties as we did a mere half-century ago? And why is it that, given present trends, we may have another dozen new sovereignties within another decade?[7] There are rich possibilities for significant theoretical work focused on the *problématique* of system transformation. But for many who believe that the most significant issues revolve around "identity," this is not the way to go. The problem of system change, they might suggest, is too imbued with respect for the status quo and not sufficiently "emancipatory."

There is a further problem. To what extent are the changes so notably theorized about in the contemporary literature strongly biased by geography and culture? Analysts of "globalization," "planet earth," the destruction of space/time distinctions, the "erosion of sovereignty," the growth of a universal "civil society," and the like, notably overlook some persisting characteristics that are more than local artifacts or anomalies. For one, a large portion of the world's 6 billion inhabitants are not hooked cognitively, commercially, or emotionally into any sort of community beyond their village or valley. Hundreds of millions remain illiterate, have no conception of societies other than their own, scratch out a subsistence living, and have absolutely no prospect of being "tuned in" or "wired" during their lifetimes. The approximately 80 million mostly white, male, high-income, North American and European Internet users are hardly representative of the global population. Other trends are equally problematic. Despite the availability of global news media, the overwhelming proportion of "news" remains local and national. There is little evidence that most people are today, compared to the past, better informed, more knowledgeable, or more interested in events, trends, and practices outside of the communities with which they identify.[8] If universal system change is going to be a primary focus for future theoretical effort, there must be a major attempt to rid the subject of its cultural and geographic biases and limitations.

4. "*Emancipation*": This term has been used both in the epistemological and political sense, with an explicit connection between the realm of ideas and action. This theme reflects the continuation of a long intel-

lectual tradition, going back to Marx and beyond. The claim here is that scholars have an *obligation* to promote certain types of change. Theory and practice, à la Marx, are inseparable, although frequently in this type of analysis the demands for change take precedence over scholarly rigor. Nevertheless, many recent statements by international theorists are making the case for emancipation as the predominant function of the field (cf. Hazel Smith, 1996). But, as in the case of terrorism, one person's emancipation could well be regarded by others as a means of guaranteed serfdom. A great discussion about the *ends* of political action is not likely to promote values of scholarly discourse or the definition of a field. In the absence of a fundamentally new conception of the nature and purposes of scholarship, the emancipatory agenda is not likely to form the core of future theories of international relations.

5. *An entirely new perspective on international relations or international politics:* From somewhere in the world's political peripheries, an entirely new conceptualization of international studies could emerge. It could have great appeal because it will carry no Cold War baggage, or the conceptual apparatus of classical European diplomatic/military institutions and behavior. It will reflect fundamental processes that are at work in large areas of the world and which have significant impacts on political-commercial-military life. There are no candidates on the horizon, but we must leave open the possibility that someone will conceptualize the world, its trends, and processes in ways that are at once intellectually attractive, politically relevant, and nonparochial.

6. *A candidate already?* One can make the case that the theoretical aspects of international politics are no longer predominantly an American enterprise. Despite the threats of oblivion, irrelevance, and scholasticism, there is much evidence that vibrant theoretical work is being undertaken, primarily in the United Kingdom and, increasingly, in Europe, including Scandinavia. Where is the theoretical action today? It is in the pages of periodicals such as *Millennium*, the *Review of International Studies*, and the *European Journal of International Relations*. Where do the authors reside? In the United Kingdom, predominantly, but also in Australia, Canada, Sweden, Finland, Germany, and Italy. Not an inconsiderable number of American scholars are now also publishing in these new theoretically oriented journals. But while these patterns represent a major shift from post-1945 practices, they do not necessarily resolve the problems represented by the scenic routes of oblivion and uncivil war. There is nothing in the publications, moreover, to suggest any new harmony, consensus, or theoretical hegemony. Extreme epistemological and theoretical individualism reign, analytical problems proliferate, and the multiplication of theoretical purposes continues apace. The lack of interest in substance is perhaps the most worrying

element or theme underlying much of the new work. The problem is not that the world lacks serious problems that should command theoretical attention—one of the signs of a crisis in the field—but that theorists have *chosen* to focus on epistemological and scholastic problems rather than substance.[9] "How to" questions have largely replaced "what to study" issues. Outsiders might be excused from laying accusations of the ivory tower syndrome against contemporary international theorists. Academics are speaking to each other, or even more narrowly, to their own "converted," not to students and the broader public who might benefit from analyses that go beyond what passes for international news on television.

THE FOURTH TRAVELOGUE:
ONE THOUSAND BLOOMING FLOWERS

The assumption that the field can be unified around a single normative problem, as it was for most of its history, should not be uncritically accepted today. The past of the field, constructed around the antinomies of international conflict and cooperation, is no necessary template for future developments. Indeed, if we can avoid the oblivion and uncivil war travelogues, we might continue along a trajectory that is already established: the vibrant proliferation of problems, epistemologies, levels of theoretical reflexivity, and issue areas. The pluralism of international theory, expressed already in the age of Rousseau and Bentham, is blossoming today to include all sorts of new developments. The increased number of journals and other publications in the field reflects the luxuriant growth of perspectives, debates, and approaches. There is much to be said for this view, and anyone who compares the present state of discourse with what was available in the 1950s or 1960s would have to acknowledge that the field is more intellectually vibrant today than it has been for a long time. Indeed, one could argue that International Relations in its theoretical guise is following the trend of other social science disciplines: increased specialization and fragmentation, but also increased theoretical self-awareness.

A development of thousands of blooming intellectual flowers would be consistent with the *zeitgeist* of some postmodernists and most poststructuralists. Theories, or disciplines, in their view, are constraining, authoritarian devices, quite in opposition to the emancipatory spirit of the times. All boundaries, all logocentric practices, all conceptual exercises are open to "interrogation." In this spirit, there can be no theory of international relations, or, indeed, international theory. Any attempts to codify, to construct categories, to adhere to methodological canons, to build explanatory systems, to diagnose the sources of problems, or to build disciplinary walls around a subject so that it can become amenable to systematic analysis, is suspect. Intellectual achievement becomes "conceit," definitional exercises "exclude" and "marginalize," and cumulation in a "crisis of representation" becomes an oxymoron (see Ashley and Walker, 1990, 378). We may have international thought, but that is not international theory. The field would be characterized by hyperfragmentation, with no possible standards to choose between what is "sense" and what is "nonsense."

The thousands of flowers travelogue, featuring streets, paths, highways, tracks, and culs-de-sac that go in no particular direction nor toward any destination, might bring a good deal of discomfort for those who use frameworks, concepts, lenses, and other devices that help make sense of complexity. Those who are comfortable with all the "voices" of international theory who have presented antinomies, argument, debate, and powerful insights—ranging from Heeren to Hertz, Rousseau to Russett, Bentham to Bull, Wilson to Waltz, Kant to Keohane, and Hobson to Hoffmann, to mention just a few—will miss the rich tapestry of high-level intellectual debate. In a more populist, poststructural mode, however, we would listen to the voices of all of those who have been marginalized and excluded in those debates. Microperspectives would replace macroperspectives. The denizens of fish markets, peasant rebellions, the members of the Talibans of the world, and other marginalized and "silenced" voices would provide the substance of a discourse taking place in an environment of flux, paradox, fragmentation, and no known certainties.

Can there be synthesis in this fourth travelogue? Can the best of the many blooming flowers serve as some beginning point (as opposed to "foundation") for analysis? I think not. In previous debates in the field, there was a corpus of intersubjective consensus on the means to knowledge and an agreement on what are the crucial problems to explore and to explain. Disagreements arose out of questions of *how best to describe and characterize* the main features of a limited domain populated by diplomats, governments, warriors, and commercial agents, *how best to explain patterns and anomalies*, and *how best to solve the problems* that these figures create for humanity. In the fourth travelogue, there is no agreement on substance, but more important, there is not even agreement on the question of "how do we know?" Indeed, as I have argued, most of the so-called Third Debate in International Relations is a debate about thought, not about substance. The problem is that the numerous positions that have developed on "how to think" are mostly incommensurable and incomparable. Consider table 3.1, which outlines some of the main tenets of two epistemological extremes: a rigorous "scientific" approach compared to a poststructuralist approach.

TABLE 3.1
Characteristics of Theoretical Inquiry: Two Extremes

Main Characteristics	"Science"	Poststructuralism(s)
Functions of theory	1. causal analysis/correlations 2. make complexity more intelligible 3. knowledge 4. provide authoritative foundations for problem-solving/prescription	1. emancipation 2. create identities 3. empathy with marginalized "voices" 4. interrogate all previous knowledge claims
Main units of analysis	1. macro (elitist) (governments, systems, leaders, institutions)	1. micro ("popular") (exiled, dissident, marginal "voices") 2. identities of ordinary people 3. identities of scholars
Role of historical/social/cultural context	1. variable, depending upon theoretical framework, but generally held constant to enable cross-temporal and cross-spatial comparisons	1. all-important
Bases of truth claims	1. disciplined observation 2. replication 3. consensus of peers 4. confidence in data 5. isomorphism 6. previous achievement	1. extent to which knowledge advances emancipation 2. truth claims are social constructs and texts, open to innumerable interpretations and meanings 3. epistemological individualism
Substance of the field	1. practices/ideas/purpose of major actors 2. sources, nature, and changes in international institutions 3. dynamics/change of international system	1. "interrogation" of truth claims, critical examination of concepts approaches, paradigms, etc. 2. listen to "marginalized"/excluded "voices" 3. locate identities
Results	1. cumulation 2. confidence 3. consensus—discipline 4. theory	1. situated knowledge 2. celebrate paradox, flux, change 3. freedom

The table demonstrates the vast distances that separate the two extremes in terms of the functions of theory (the most important question), actors, the role of context, and the like. There is nothing here to synthesize. One can become more sensitive to the role of context in political analysis, which necessarily moves the diagnosis from the pure science format to something that incorporates more judgment and individual interpretation. But one cannot combine at once the desideratum of generalization, which is the hallmark of theory, to a wholesale commitment to the study of individual "voices" and "identities," which are by definition highly contingent, unique, and nonrecurrent. And can one combine a commitment to rigorous method, consensual knowledge, and replicability with a more overriding commitment to emancipation? One can try, of course, as Marxists did for more than one century. Political necessity—emancipation—ruled "truth," or put in another way, truth served the interests of emancipation and millions perished as a result. The reader can judge to what extent there is room for synthesis in the remaining categories of the table.

The fourth travelogue, then, is an exploration of the benefits and costs (excuse the logocentrism here) of hyperfragmentation. However much some may decry the notion of a "field," "discipline," or "subject," and the ways that they *may* constrict and constrain, without some guiding notions of substance, there can be only the conclusion of "anything goes." This, of course, is a recipe for self-destruction and since I have been one of the beneficiaries of the agonies and delights for several decades of theorizing about international politics, I will not endorse this as a productive road to the future. At some point, choices will have to be made. Some will no doubt feel marginalized and victimized, but there is always the alternative of migrating to intellectual homesteads that are more congenial to questions of identity, ethnography, and anthropology.

The solution to the problem of hyperfragmentation, as Chris Brown has suggested (1994, 236), is neither to decry the loss of a central guiding problem, nor to celebrate uncritically any noise that rings with the "register of freedom." It may be, rather, "a time for making distinctions, for (gently) weeding out seedlings that do not seem likely to grow, while giving sustenance to others which seem to be taking root." The motto might be "growth with discipline."

CONCLUSION

I have outlined several possibilities that might develop to bring a new coherence to the field. All remain possibilities, some of them remote, others with a higher probability. The reader no doubt can make his or her own judgments about the future. My comments are designed to think about theory. As a subject for debate, discussion, and policy prescription commentators on "international affairs" will go on no matter what theorists do. But, I would argue, international theory has a lengthy tradition and a valuable scholarly and public role to play: it can make more intelligible a world often characterized by observable patterns, repetitions, and structural regularities. Theory creates *understanding* of the larger picture, the background, the basic trends, the links between what on first sight may appear noncomparable, and the commonalties and differences that transcend time, place, and personality. Theory also helps identify true anomalies, and shows us how practices, institutions, and ideas combine to produce that which often endures as well as that which is genuinely changing. There are just too many people who are interested in more than the opinion on the latest events of the day. If we cannot conceive of political science, sociology, or psychology without theory, it is equally hard to envision the vast realm of international politics as one that fails to generate systematic speculation, characterization, and explanation.

At this stage debate, uncertainty, epistemology, and political programs predominate. Some will applaud this theoretical "self-consciousness"; but its other side is the loss of concern with substance. This is exactly why international political economy can make a claim that *it* represents the future of the field, and that its normative repertoire of reciprocity and equity concerns are more important than the traditional ones of war, peace, and security. In the English-speaking world, at least, there are strong signs that political economy is replacing international theory the concerns of which focus on the security *problématique*.

If I am pressed to make a prognostication, it would be reasonably optimistic despite the evidence that the roads to oblivion, uncivil war, and hyperfragmentation are already densely populated. I have faith that those who practice erasing, exclusionary, or denunciatory strategies will ultimately tone down their rhetoric and come to realize that there is much of value in the tradition of the field. And those who resist new approaches, once they come to appreciate their contributions, may well begin incorporating their perspectives. Rather than resist at all costs, they can mine new epistemologies and methodologies for insights, analytical frameworks, and other tools for a broadened scholarship. While international theory will never again be a unified field because its normative sources differ (Holsti, 1996), in more optimistic moments we might envisage a field that matures in philosophical depth and self-consciousness, but which is also aware of actual political dilemmas in the world.

NOTES

1. An analogy can be made between the current ideological hegemony of global capitalism and the religious hegemony of the Church in Europe during the mediaeval era (Deibert, 1996).

2. Change does not imply innovation. The major themes of international theory over the past three centuries have remained notably similar, even if the vocabularies and styles differ. For an essay that examines the underlying similarities in the field over an extended period of time, see Gabriel (1994).

3. In some cases, questions of identity may affect politics, although I suspect they have been largely overemphasized. In much of the contemporary theoretical literature, in contrast, the sources, nature, and consequences of identity are becoming more important than *interests* and *ideas* in the framing of foreign policy and its analysis. But if we think that the concept of "national interest" was vague and subjective, problems of identity are infinitely more complex, and raising it into a central concern of the field will probably condemn the field to oblivion.

4. Commonly acknowledged as one of the greatest scholars of international relations of the twentieth century, Quincy Wright's works are rarely cited today. Robert Beck (1996, 120, n. 13) reports that in a "job talk" he attended given by an applicant from a major graduate program in the United States, the candidate, whose theoretical focus was the problem of war, acknowledged that he had not read *any* of Wright's works. Forgetting is not confined to some postmodernists, though they may be the only ones to adopt a *deliberate* strategy of erasure.

5. There is an inconsistency in some critiques of "orthodoxy." On the one hand, they promote the value of "inclusiveness" and open-minded dialogue. On the other, they deny any legitimacy to "orthodox" representations and explanations of international politics. The purpose of the critiques is not to amend, but to destroy, particularly all versions of Realism. For example, see George (1994) and Bleiker (1995).

6. One wonders how many critics of Realism have actually read Morgenthau's works. Many ritual denunciations reveal a serious lack of familiarity with his *oeuvre*. That Morgenthau was a telling critic of American foreign policy and that his highly articulated views on the social context of science were quite similar to many postmodernists is overlooked by almost all critics of his work. Mark Neufeld's (1995) analysis of the field is one prime example of the omissions, distortions, and lack of familiarity typical of critiques of Morgenthau's thought.

7. Candidates include Quebec, the formal partition of Somalia (already de facto), Myanmar, Northern Ireland, Sri Lanka, Bougainville, Taiwan, and Bosnia, and Cyprus.

8. Some anecdotal evidence supports the claim. *Figaro*, a major national daily in France, in its edition of May 19, 1995, contained less than one-half page of foreign news in a total of thirty-nine pages for the issue. CNN's "Prime News" on May 29, 1997 contained only ten seconds of news that did not directly involve the United States. CNN's *World News* of the same date, a one-

hour review of the day's events, contained not a single item of news about events outside of the United States. At the time, elections were going on in France and Canada, the new president was sworn into office in the Congo, and many other foreign items in the *New York Times* of that date were not even mentioned.

9. The periodical *International Organization* is the premier theoretically oriented publication in the United States. Most of its theoretical contributions sustain a debate between Realists and liberals. In recent issues, constructivist approaches have become more prominent. The theoretical purview of British journals is substantially broader. I am grateful to Darryl Jarvis for the point about choice.

REFERENCES

Ashley, Richard, and R. B. J. Walker. (1990). "Reading Dissidence/Writing the Discipline: Crisis and the Question of Sovereignty in International Studies." *International Studies Quarterly 34*(3), 367–416.

Badie, B. (1992). *L'État importé: Essai sur l'occidentalisation de l'ordre politique*. Paris: Fayard.

Beck, R. J. (1996). "*A Study of War* and *An Agenda for Peace*: Reflections on the Contemporary Relevance of Quincy Wright's plan for a 'New International Order.'" *Review of International Studies 22*(2), 119–147.

Bleiker, R. (1995). "Forget 'IR' Theory." Paper presented at the Second Pan-European Conference on International Relations, Paris, September 13–16.

Brown, Chris. (1994). "Turtles all the Way Down: Anti-Foundationalism, Critical Theory and International Relations." *Millennium 23*(2), 213–235.

Bull, Hedley. (1969). "International Theory: The Case for a Classical Approach." *World Politics 18*(3), 363–377.

Choucri, E. (1994). "La genèse de l'État péripherique." *Globe: Revue de recherche et d'études universitaires en science politique 3*(4) (Spring/Autumn), 5–25.

Commission on Global Governance. (1995). *Our Global Neighborhood: The Report of the Commission on Global Governance*. New York: Oxford University Press.

Crawford, Robert M. A. (1996). *Regime Theory in the Post–Cold War World: Rethinking Neoliberal Approaches to International Relations*. Aldershot, U.K.: Dartmouth Press.

Deibert, R. (1996). "*Exorcismus Theoriae*: Constructivisim, Metaphors, and Global Change." Department of Political Science, University of British Columbia, Vancouver, Canada (mimeo).

Diebert, R. (1997). *Altered Worlds: Communication Technologies in the Transformation of Political Authority*. New York: Columbia University Press.

Deutsch, Karl. (1954). *Political Community at the International Level: Problems of Definition and Measurement*. Garden City, N.Y.: Doubleday.

Elkins, David. (1995). *Beyond Sovereignty: Territory and Political Economy in the Twenty-First Century*. Toronto: University of Toronto Press.

Elkins, P. (1991). *A New World Order: Grassroots Movements for Global Change*. London: Routledge.

Ferguson, Yale, and Richard Mansbach. (1988). *The Elusive Quest: Theory and International Politics*. Columbia: University of South Carolina Press.

Fukuyama, F. (1991). "Liberal Democracy as a Global Phenomenon." *PS: Political Science and Politics* 24(4), 659–663.

Gabriel, J. M. (1994). *Worldviews and Theories of International Relations*. London: Macmillan.

George, Jim. (1994). *Discourses of Global Politics: A Critical (Re)Introduction to International Relations*. Boulder, Colo.: Lynne Rienner.

Goldgeier, J. M., and M. McFaul (1992). "A Tale of Two Worlds: Core and Periphery in the Post–Cold War Era." *International Organization* 46(2), 465–491.

Holsti, K. J. (1971). "Retreat from Utopia: International Relations Theory, 1945–1970." *Canadian Journal of Political Science* 4, 165–177.

Holsti, K. J. (1980). "Change in the International System: Integration and Fragmentation." In Ole R. Holsti, R. Siverson, and A. George (eds.), *Change in the International System*. Boulder, Colo.: Westview Press: 23–53.

Holsti, K. J. (1985). *The Dividing Discipline: Hegemony and Diversity in International Theory*. London: Allen and Unwin.

Holsti, K. J. (1992). "International Theory and War in the Third World." In B. Job, (ed.), *The Insecurity Dilemma: National Security of Third World States*. Boulder Colo.: Lynn Rienner: 37–62.

Holsti, K. J. (1996a). *The State, War, and the State of War*. Cambridge: Cambridge University Press.

Holsti, K. J. (1996b). "Hindrances to Understanding in International Politics." Paper presented at the Annual Meetings, International Studies Association, San Diego, April 19.

Huntington, Samuel. (1993). "The Clash of Civilizations"? *Foreign Affairs* 72, 22–49.

Kaplan, R. (1994). "The Coming Anarchy." *The Atlantic Monthly* 273, 44–65.

Lapid, Y. (1989). "The Third Debate: On the Prospects of International Theory in a Post-Positivist Era." *International Studies Quarterly* 33(3), 235–254.

Linklater, A. (1996). "Citizenship and Sovereignty in the Post-Westphalian State." *European Journal of International Relations* 2(1), 77–103.

Mueller, J. (1988). *Retreat from Doomsday: The Obsolescence of Major War*. New York: Basic Books.

Neufeld, Mark. (1995). *The Restructuring of International Relations Theory*. Cambridge: Cambridge University Press.

Nicholson, M. (1996). *Causes and Consequences in International Relations*. London: Frances Pinter.

O'Callaghan, Terry. (1996). "The Real World of Normative Theory in International Relations." Department of Politics, University of Adelaide, South Australia (mimeo).

Onuf, N. (1989). *World of Our Making: Rules and Rule in Social Theory and International Relations*. Columbus: University of South Carolina Press.

Rengger, Nicholas J. (1996). "Clio's Cave: Historical Materialism and the Claims of 'Substantive Social Theory' in World Politics." *Review of International Studies* 22(2), 13–31.

Rittberger, Volker. (1993). *Regime Theory and International Relations*. London and New York: Oxford University Press.

Rosenau, James. (1996). "The Dynamics of Globalization: Toward an Operational Formulation." Paper presented at the Annual Meetings of the International Studies Association, San Diego, California, April 18.

Rosenau, James. (1992). "Governance, Order, and Change in World Politics." In James Rosenau and E. Czempiel (eds.), *Governance without Government: Order and Change in World Politics*. Cambridge: Cambridge University Press: 1–29.

Rosenau, James. (1990). *Turbulence in International Politics: A Theory of Change and Continuity*. Princeton, N.J.: Princeton University Press.

Ruggie, John. (1993). "Territoriality and Beyond: Problematizing Modernity in International Relations." *International Organization* 47(2), 139–174.

Schmidt, B. C. (1994). "The Historiography of Academic International Relations." *Review of International Studies* 20(4), 349–367.

Scott, Andrew M. (1982). *The Dynamics of Interdependence*. Chapel Hill: University of North Carolina Press.

Singer, M., and A. Wildavsky (1993). *The Real World Order: Zones of Peace/Zones of Turmoil*. Chatham, N.J.: Chatham House Publishers.

Smith, H. (1996). "The Silence of the Academics: International Social Theory, Historical Materialism and Political Values." *Review of International Studies* 22(2), 191–212.

Smith, Steve. (1995). "The Self-Images of a Discipline: A Genealogy of International Relations Theory." In Ken Booth and Steve Smith (eds.), *International Relations Theory Today*. University Park: The Pennsylvania State University Press: 1–37.

Spegele, Roger. (1995). "Political Realism and the Remembrance of Relativism." *Review of International Studies* 21(2), 211–236.

Spruyt, H. (1994). *The State and its Competitors: An Analysis of Systems Change*. Princeton, N.J.: Princeton University Press.

Sylvester, C. (1996). "The Contributions of Feminist Theory to International Relations." In Steve Smith, Ken Booth, and M. Zalewski (eds.), *International Theory: Positivism and Beyond*. Cambridge: Cambridge University Press: 254–278.

Sylvester, C. (1994). *Feminist Theory and International Relations in a Postmodern Era*. Cambridge: Cambridge University Press.

Waever, O. (1996). "Emancipation and Governance: Who's on First, What's on Second?" Paper presented at the Annual Meetings, International Studies Association, San Diego, April 19.

Watson, A. (1992). *The Evolution of International Society: A Comparative Historical Analysis*. London and New York: Routledge.

Zacher, M. W. (1991). "The Decaying Pillars of the Westphalian Temple: Implications for International Order and Governance." In James Rosenau and E. Czempiel (eds.), *Governance without Government: Order and Change in World Politics*. Cambridge: Cambridge University Press: 58–101.

CHAPTER 4

Identity Politics, Postmodern Feminisms, and International Theory: Questioning the "New" Diversity in International Relations

D. S. L. Jarvis

INTRODUCTION

Few in the social sciences and humanities will have missed the rise of what Christina Sommers described recently as "militant gynocentrism and misandrism" (Sommers, 1994, 275). Since the advent of critical and subversive postmodern and deconstructive theory in International Relations (IR) in the early 1980s, feminist scholarship has been one of the most forceful of such perspectives, exploring a panoply of issues, ontologies and epistemologies, all aimed broadly at advancing new research agendas and "reinscribing" the role, function, and purpose of IR (see Enloe, 1989; 1993; Peterson and Runyan, 1993; Pettman, 1996, Sylvester, 1994; 1996; Tickner, 1997). Diversity, especially in terms of epistemological and ontological perspectives, but also in terms of the social composition of the profession, has become the new catch-phrase of the 1990s, invoking the precepts of "identity politics" with its insistence on representation for "voices," "peoples," and "issues" otherwise "silenced" or "marginalized" in the traditional canons of the discipline.

This essay seeks to explore some of the implications of this new diversity, focusing on the contributions of postmodern and radical feminist scholars to IR and their suggested methodologies, agendas, and empirical foci. I begin by outlining the objections postmodern feminists raise about IR and then turn to a critical analysis of their theoretical contributions, especially as these relate to the issue of identity politics, and their empirical observations.

FEMINIST OBJECTIONS TO
INTERNATIONAL RELATIONS

"Professionalized IR discourse," notes Jean Bethke Elshtain, "is one of the most dubious of many dubious sciences that present truth claims that mask the power plays embedded in the discourse and in the practices it legitimates." For Elshtain, as for others (Sylvester, 1994; Tickner, 1997; Steans, 1998), IR is a site pervaded by "masculinized" images, theories, approaches, and biases, excluding women and other "marginal" peoples and perspectives, but in ways not apparent from the "normal" viewing positions associated with elite, privileged, male theory (see Pettman, this volume). Simply "adding women" and assuming gender parity will reorient the discipline in ways more sensitive and inclusive of gender issues, while a celebrated beginning for postmodern feminists is, nonetheless, viewed as less than adequate; a development that in and of itself will not "un-write" the discipline's hegemonic "discourses" or refocus its substantive concerns. On the contrary, for Elshtain, the increasing participation of women in IR only confirms that many have been "prepared to take their place among the ranks of the purveyors of the hegemonic discourse—whatever it may be at any given moment in the academy and its journals" (Elshtain, 1987, 90–91). "Adding women" to the Realist/positivist/security equation is co-optation, not emancipation, which, for postmodern feminists, suggests the means to "true" understanding reside in formulating "new" equations and drawing upon the experiences of those whose histories and stories have otherwise been expunged from mainstream (or what Mary O'Brien calls "malestream") discourse (as quoted in Zalewski, 1993, 17). The task thus proscribed is to "rewrite" the discipline's theory, methods, and concerns, demonstrating how "women" and feminist perspectives have been "ghettoised" and how the discipline and world politics have been "encoded" as "masculine territory" to exclude and repress women (Sylvester, 1993, 77; Zalewski, 1994, 225). In the process, such perspectives aspire to "reread" the canonical texts of IR and reveal the gendered narratives hidden beneath the facade of "gender-neutrality"; how, for example, Realism and security politics derive from masculinist inscriptions that hide their epistemological essence by cloaking them in a realm of "necessity" and "anarchy" deemed to be beyond governance (Wight, 1996, 293). Postmodern feminist scholarship has therefore been promoted as a necessary activity if the emperor is to be disrobed, "his" hidden practices of oppression and expulsion exposed, and IR remade in a way that is sensitive to different ontological beginnings, questions, perspectives, and peoples.

For Elshtain, feminist analyses have thus emerged in the wake of those women who have managed to "escape the snare of these modes of professionalization and emerge from their training still able to grapple with the complexities of history, the vagaries of events, and the unpredictability of human passions" (Elshtain, 1987, 91). This is where contemporary feminist scholarship cuts into the "Third Debate," chastising not only orthodox theory for "androcentric metatheoretical assumptions" evident "in the traditional definitions of the legitimate and substantive concerns of the discipline; that is, with 'high politics' or military security," but also "[m]ale scholars concerned with reflexivity" who have ignored the "relevance of philosophical debates within contemporary feminisms" (Ship, 1994, 131–133). Christine Sylvester, for example, accuses the early phase of the "Third Debate" of excluding feminism, indeed for not even making Yosef Lapid's categorical list as one of its constituting "isms." "Women," she notes, "are beyond studied dissidence," and enjoy only "passing nods in the alternative international relations literature." This, too, is "androcentric," "masculine," and displays "shared understandings biased to one side" so that "even dissidence is more credible when it is represented to us mostly by men."[1] For Sylvester, it is not just the case that IR has ignored feminist scholarship, but that the discipline is diseased by "rampant sexism and misogyny," where it is all "too commonplace for self-defined critical social theorists to pay homage to the Critical Theorists, postmodernists and post-structuralists and to relegate the 'words of women to the after hours of academic work, to a hobby one never gets around to'" (as discussed in Zalewski, 1994, 417, 421). In fact, she suggests, there is "yet another sovereign voice singing IR, this time with dissident-sensitive lyrics that hint at but do not belt out a feminist message." Feminist writings and "women" have been equally "marginalized or preempted by those who plead for a more inclusive IR," do not "appear in the citation list of third debaters," or count "among the categories of contestation that Lapid notes" (Sylvester, 1994, 8–9). Those "males" who otherwise claimed "victimization" because of their own intellectual "dissent" (Ashley, 1989; Ashley and Walker, 1990), are now themselves accused of perpetrating crimes of exclusion, of ignoring the other "other" and operating in a "masculine territory" that belittles the contributions of feminist theory and "women." Even the likes of Richard Ashley and Robert Walker, the very emissaries of "dissidence," Sylvester condemns, when, as editors of the *International Studies Quarterly* special edition titled "Speaking the Language of Exile: Dissidence in International Studies," they address "women" but in a manner so "cursory" that the "dilemmas of gender are not considered important enough to warrant article-length treatment" (Sylvester, 1993, 87). Likewise, when Andrew Linklater poses "The Question of the Next Stage in International Relations Theory" (Linklater, 1992), ostensibly to probe the possibilities of critical-theoretic, postmodern and feminist perspectives, in Sylvester's eyes he merely perpetrates "silence" by making "women" invisible. "He says that women are among the excluded groups whose individual perspectives must be taken into account in developing critical theory. Nonetheless, feminists, and the 'women' they talk about, must be the illegitimate daughters of the really diverse ones because there is not one citation in Linklater's article to a feminist 'woman.' The postmodernists are cited. The critical theorists are cited. Feminist 'women,' however, have no names" (Sylvester, 1994, 210–211). This, for Sylvester, demands a new level of subversion beyond that proposed by "male" dissidents: dissidence from the (male) "dissidents" (Wight, 1996, 293). Under this new dissident "dissidence," the "real victims" are "women" and feminist writings, who now stand up to profess their "victimization" not just from the intellectual practices of orthodox theorists, but from those self-declared heretics like Ashley and Walker who now stand accused of being part of the tyranny of exclusion.

The "Third Debate" has thus evolved a new addendum, one where "gender" and "identity politics" questions even "dissident thought," labeling it an equally suspect discourse propagated largely by white middle-class heterosexual males. This represents a new, deeper, subversive tendency in "dissident" scholarship. This time the charge is not just that we have been "thinking wrong," or "not thinking at all," but when "not thinking" we have been actively constructing gender gulags, excluding "women" by "segregating" and denying" them access to "International Relations." In its most overt form practitioners are charged with being "misogynist," sexist, "racist," and "homophobic." In less provocative language, V. Spike Peterson laments the failure of feminist literature "to be taken seriously in International Relations" (Peterson, 1992, 191). For feminists, such a predilection represents an "androcentric system of thought inherited from early western state making[,] . . . revitalized in the Enlightenment," and now cemented in IR as a form of "masculinism" but one that is "rendered so invisible as to be absent in even critical and postmodern accounts" (Peterson, 1997, 186–187). IR thus represents a form of professionalized "bigotry," evolved through the natural outgrowth of unreflective "men" theorists who are wedded implicitly "to an unacknowledged and seemingly commonplace principle that international relations is the proper homestead or place for people called men." Men of all political stripes have, according to Sylvester, been "winking" at feminists as they walk by, failing to read them, appoint them, take them seriously, or acknowledge them (Sylvester, 1994, 4, 211). In such a "chilly climate," women have been systematically "evacuated" from "IR," forced into "their assigned places at home," and even when they have managed to break free of such "places" "[t]heir words have been lost, or covered-up and stored in the basement, . . . ignored because they are the views of people called women and 'women' have no place in the political places of 'men'" (Sylvester, 1994, 9). Of "all the institutionalized forms of contemporary social and political analysis," concludes R. B. J. Walker, IR is "the most gender-blind, indeed crudely patriarchal" (Walker, 1992, 179).[2]

Indictments such as these circumscribe the "need" for feminist perspectives/critiques of the discipline and its theoretical approaches. Patriarchy, gender, and "masculinism," for feminists, become as pertinent to understanding international relations as do strategic studies, nation-states, and military force. "[A] gender-sensitive lens," notes V. Spike Peterson, "illuminates mounting tensions and even contradictions between the 'deeper historical structures' of masculinism (bequeathed to us by the success of western civilization) and multiple transformations in 'events-time' (the dimensions of today's structural crisis)" (Peterson, 1997). For feminists, gender is a "central facet of human identity," and identities are "constructed by others who have a stake in making up certain social categories and in trying to make people conform to them." In fact, for Jill Krause, gender is the ontological essence of "self," being, and identity: "our view of ourselves, how we relate to others and how we understand our world and our place in it are all coloured by our perception of ourselves and others as gendered individuals" (Krause, 1996, 106–107). Gender, in other words, is an indispensable ingredient in the study of international politics, a means of understanding not just the systemic basis of the international system, but of the power structures embedded in these relations. Without feminist perspectives, IR is adduced as being "illegitimate," "dominated mostly by white, English-speaking background intellectuals, located mainly within the Anglo-North America academic establishment," and this "dominated by men, asking questions and pursuing interests that" affect them (Pettman, this volume). Gender, in other words, is both the problem in international relations (and International Relations) because of its untheorized, unconscious, unrecognized importance to the play of global politics and their analysis, and also the solution to these problems that, once "out of the closet," will yet elucidate the systemic basis of aggression, war, identity, discrimination, power, and territoriality. The need for gendered perspectives and "gender sensitive lenses" is thus self-evident for feminists, representing "a more powerful variable than anarchy or power for understanding international relations" (Henry Nau as quoted in Tickner, 1996, 147). "Gender," it seems, "makes the world go round" (Enloe, 1989).

Despite these self-congratulatory adulations, Adam Jones concluded recently that, while innovative in terms of the research they have brought to the discipline, feminist "critiques are far from constituting an adequate account [or even an inclusive framing] of gender and IR. The wider task—theorizing and narrating the international politics of gender—remains" (Jones, 1996, 429). For feminists who suggest they have found "better" ontological viewing points from which to theorize the realities, causes, and issues of international politics, this is stinging criticism. Indeed, it renders problematic the "gender variable" as the principal ontological starting point for investigating international politics and makes apparent how premature are adages announcing "gender makes the world go round." That feminist epistemologies, especially postmodern feminisms, are not above being problematic, underscores how important is the need for further investigation before we all don postmodern "gender lenses" and view the world through this singular and unifocal lens.

QUESTIONING "IDENTITY POLITICS"

Critical research agendas of this type, however, are not found easily in IR. Critics of feminist perspectives run the risk of denouncement as either a "misogynist" malcontent or an androcentric keeper of the gate. At work in much of this discourse is an unstated "political correctness," where the historical marginalization of women bestows intellectual autonomy, excluding those "outside" the identity group from "legitimate" participation in its discourse. Only feminist women can do "real," "legitimate," feminist theory, since, in the mantra of "identity politics," discourse must emanate from a positional (personal) ontology. Those sensitive or sympathetic to the identity politics of particular groups are, of course, welcome to lend support and encouragement, but only on terms delineated by the groups themselves. In this way, they enjoy an uncontested sovereign hegemony over their own self-identification, insuring the group discourse is self-constituted and its parameters, operative methodology, and standards of argument, appraisal, and evidentiary provisions, self-defined. Thus, for example, when Sylvester calls for a "homesteading" of IR she does so "by [a] repetitive feminist insistence that *we be included on our terms* (my emphasis)." Rather than an invitation to engage in dialogue this is an ultimatum that a sovereign intellectual "space" be provided and insulated from critics who question the merits of identity-based political discourse. Instead, Sylvester calls upon IR to "share space, respect, and trust in a re-formed endeavor," but one otherwise proscribed as committed to demonstrating not only "that the secure homes constructed by IR's many debaters are chimerical," but, as a consequence, to ending IR and remaking it along lines grounded in "feminist postmodernism" (Sylvester, 1994, 211, 226). Such stipulative provisions might be likened to a form of negotiated sovereign territoriality, where, as part of the settlement for the historically aggrieved, border incursions are to be allowed but may not be met with resistance or reciprocity. Demands for "entry" to the discipline are thus predicated on conditions that insure two sets of rules, cocooning postmodern feminist "spaces" from systematic analyses while "respecting" this discourse as it hastens about the project of deconstructing IR as a "male space." Sylvester's impassioned plea for tolerance and "emphatic cooperation" is thus confined to like-minded individuals, those who do not challenge feminist epistemologies but accept them as a necessary means of reinventing the discipline as a discourse between postmodern identities(the most important of which is gender (True, 1996, 218). "Intolerance" or "misogyny" thus become the ironic epithets attached to those who question the wisdom of this "reinvention" or the merits of the "return of identity" in international theory (see, for example, the recent edited collection by Lapid, 1996). Most strategic of all, however, demands for "entry" to the discipline and calls for intellectual "spaces" betray a self-imposed, politically motivated "marginality." After all where are such calls issued from other than "the discipline" and the intellectual—and well established—"spaces" of "feminist IR"?

Postmodern feminists thus deflect as "illegitimate" criticism that derives from skeptics "whose vantage" points are labeled "privileged." And "privilege" is variously interpreted historically, especially along lines of race, color, and sex, where the denotations "white" and "male," to name but two, serve as intergenerational mediums to assess the injustices of past histories. "White males," for example, become generic signifiers for historical oppression, indicating an ontologically "privileged" group by which the historical experiences of the "other" can then be reclaimed in the context of their related "oppression," "exploitation," and "exclusion." "Legitimacy," in this context, can then be claimed in terms of one's group "identity" and the extent to which the history of that particular group has been "silenced." In this same way, self-identification or "self-situation" establishes one's credentials, allowing admittance to the group and legitimating the "authoritative" vantage point from which one speaks and writes. Thus, for example, Jan Jindy Pettman includes among the introductory pages to her most recent book, *Worlding Women*, a section titled "A (personal) politics of location," in which her "identity" as a woman, a feminist, and an academic, makes apparent her particular ("marginal") "identities" and "group" loyalties (Pettman, 1996, xi). Similarly, Christine Sylvester, in the introduction to her book, insists that "[i]t is important to provide a context for one's work in the often-denied politics of the personal." Accordingly, self-declaration reveals to the reader that she is a feminist, went to a Catholic "girls" school where she was schooled to "develop your brains and confess something called 'sins' to always male forever priests," and that these provide "some pieces" to her "dynamic objectivity" (Sylvester, 1994, 17–19). Like territorial markers, self-identification permits entry to intellectual spaces whose "sovereign authority" is "policed" as much by "marginal" subjectivities as they allege of the "oppressors" who "police" the discourse of Realism, or who are said to walk the corridors of the discipline insuring the replication of patriarchy, "hierarchical agendas," and "malestream" theory. If Sylvester's version of "feminist postmodernism" is projected as tolerant, perspectivist, and encompassing of a multiplicity of approaches, in reality it is as selective, exclusionary and dismissive of alternative perspectives as mainstream approaches are accused of being.

Skillful moves of this nature underscore the adroitness of postmodern feminist theory at emasculating many of its logical inconsistencies. In arguing for a "feminist postmodernism," for example, Sylvester employs a double theoretical move that, on the one hand, invokes a kind of epistemological-deconstructive-anarchy-cum-relativism in an attempt to "decenter" or make insecure "fixed" research gazes, identities, and concepts ("men," "women," "security," and "nation-state"), while, on the other hand, turning to the "lived experiences" of "women" as if ontologically given and assuming their experiences to be authentic, "real," substantive, and authoritative interpretations of the "realities" of international relations. "Women" at the peace camps of Greenham Common or in the cooperatives of Harare, for example, represent, for Sylvester, the *real* coal face of international politics, their experiences and strategies the *real* politics of what she terms "relations international." But why should we take the experiences of these "women" to be ontologically superior or more insightful than the experiences of other "women" or other "men?" As Sylvester admits elsewhere, "[e]xperience . . . is at once always already an interpretation *and* in need of interpretation." Why, then, are experience-based modes of knowledge more insightful than knowledges derived through other modes of inquiry? (Joan Scott quoted in Sylvester, 1996, 262). Such epistemologies are surely crudely positivistic in their singular reliance on osmotic perception of the "facts" as they impact upon the personal. If, as Sylvester writes, "sceptical inlining draws on substantive everydayness as a time and site of knowledge, much as does everyday feminist theorising," and if, as she further notes, "it understands experience . . . as mobile, indeterminate, hyphenated, [and] homeless," why should this

knowledge be valued as anything other than fleeting subjective perceptions of multiple environmental stimuli whose meaning is beyond explanation other than as a personal narrative? (Sylvester, 1996, 271). Is this
what Sylvester means when she calls for a "revisioning" and a repaint-
ing of the "canvases of IR," that we dissipate knowledge into an
infinitesimal number of disparate sites, all equally valid, and let loose
with a *mélange* of visceral perceptions; stories of how each of us *perceive*
we experience international politics? If this is the case then "feminist
postmodernism" does not advance our understanding of international
politics, but leaves untheorized and unexplained the *causes* of international relations. Personal narratives do not constitute theoretical discourse, nor indeed an *explanation* of the systemic factors that procure
international events, processes, or the actions of certain actors.

"Feminist postmodernism," especially as propounded by Christine
Sylvester, also proves disappointing if only for its proclivity for double
standards and tendency to self-contradiction. Sylvester, for example, is
adamant that we can not really know who "women" are, since to do so
would be to invoke an "essentialist concept," concealing the diversity
inherent in this category. "Women" don't really exist in Sylvester's estimation, since there are black women, white women, Hispanic, disabled,
lesbian, poor, rich, middle-class, and illiterate women, to name but a
few. The point, for Sylvester, is that to speak of "women" is to do violence to the diversity encapsulated in this category and, in its own way,
to "silence" those "women" who remain unnamed. Well and good. Yet
this same analytical respect for diversity seems lost with "men." Politics
and international relations become the "places of men." But which
"men?" All men? Or just white men, or rich, educated, elite, upper-class,
heterosexual men? To speak of "political places" as the places of "men"
ignores the fact that most men, in fact the overwhelming majority of
men, are not in these "political places" at all, are not decision-makers,
elite, affluent, or powerful. Much as with Sylvester's categories, there are
poor, lower-class, illiterate, gay, black, and white men, many of whom
suffer the vestiges of hunger, poverty, despair and disenfranchisement,
just as much as women. So why invoke the category "men" in such
essentialist and ubiquitous ways while cognizant only of the diversity in
the category "women"? These are double standards, not erudite theoretical formulations, betraying, dare one say, sexism toward "men" by
invoking male gender generalizations and crude caricatures.

Problems of this nature, however, are really manifestations of a
deeper, underlying ailment endemic to discourses derived from "identity
politics." At base, the most elemental question for identity discourse, as
Zalewski and Enloe note, is "Who am I?" (Zalewski and Enloe, 1995,
282). The personal becomes the political, evolving a discourse where

self-identification, but also one's identification by others, presupposes multiple identities that are fleeting, overlapping, and changing at any particular moment in time or place. "We have multiple identities," argues V. Spike Peterson, "e.g., Canadian, homemaker, Jewish, Hispanic, socialist" (Peterson, 1993, 4). And these identities are variously depicted as transient, polymorphic, interactive, discursive, and never fixed. As Richard Brown notes, "Identity is given neither institutionally nor biologically. It evolves as one orders continuities on one's conception of oneself" (Richard Brown quoted in Peterson, 1993, 3). Yet, if we accept this, the analytical utility of "identity politics" seems problematic at best. Which "identity," for example, do we choose from the many that any one subject might display affinity for? Are we to assume all "identities" of equal importance or some more important than others? How do we know which of these identities might be transient and less consequential to one's sense of "self" and, in turn, politically significant to understanding international politics? Why, for example, should we place gender identity ontologically prior to class, sexual orientation, ethnic origin, ideological perspective, or national identity?[3] As Zalewski and Enloe ask, "Why do we consider states to be a major referent? Why not men? Or women?" (Zalewski and Enloe, 1995, 283). But by the same token, why not dogs, shipping magnates, movie stars, or trade regimes? Why is "gender" more constitutive of global politics than, say, class, or an identity as a cancer survivor, laborer, or social worker? Most of all, why is gender essentialized in feminist discourse, reified into the most preeminent of all "identities" as the *primary* lens through which international relations *must* be viewed? Perhaps, for example, people understand "difference" in the context of "identities" outside of gender. As Jane Martin notes, "How do we know that difference . . . does not turn on being fat or religious or in an abusive relationship?" (Martin, 1994, 647).[4] The point, perhaps flippantly made, is that "identity" is such a nebulous concept, its meaning so obtuse and so inherently subjective, that it is near meaningless as a conduit for understanding global politics if only because it can mean anything to anybody.

For others like Ann Tickner, however, "identity" challenges the assumption of state sovereignty. "Becoming curious about identity formation below the state and surrendering the simplistic assumption that the state is sovereign will," Tickner suggests, "make us much more realistic describers and explainers of the current international system" (Zalewski and Enloe, 1995, 284; see also Tickner, 1992). The multiple subjects and their identities that constitute the nation-state are, for Tickner, what are important. In a way, of course, she is correct. States are constitutive entities drawn from the amalgam of their citizens. But such observations are somewhat trite and banal, and lead IR into a devolving

and perpetually dividing discourse based upon ever emergent and trans-
forming identities. Surely the more important observation, however,
concerns the bounds of this enterprise. Where do we stop? Are there limits to this exercise or is it a boundless project? And how do we theorize
the notion of multiple levels of identities harbored in each subject person? If each of us is fractured into "multiple identities," must we then
lunge into commentaries specific to each group? We might well imagine,
for example, a discourse in IR between white feminist heterosexual
women, white middle-class heterosexual physically challenged men,
working-class gay Latinos, transgendered persons, ethnic Italian New
York female garment workers, and Asian lesbian ecofeminists. Each
would represent a self-constituted "knowledge" and nomenclature; a
discourse reflective of specific identitygroup concerns. Knowledge and
understanding would suffer from a diaspora, becoming unattainable in
any perspicacious sense except in localities so specific that its general
understanding, or inter-group applicability, would be obviated. Identity
groups would become so splintered and disparate that IR would
approach a form of identity tribalism, with each group forming a kind
of intellectual territory, jealously "policing" its knowledge borders from
intrusions by other groups otherwise seen as "illegitimate," nonrepre-
sentative or opposed to the interests of the group. Nor is it improbable
to suppose that "identity politics" in IR would evolve a *realpolitik*
between groups; a realist power-struggle for intergroup legitimacy or
hegemonic control over particular knowledges or, in the broader polity,
situations of intergroup conflict. With what "legitimacy," for example,
do middle-class, by and large "white," "affluent," "feminist," "women"
IR scholars speak and write for "black," "poor," "illiterate," "gay,"
"working-class," "others" who might object, resist, or denounce such
empathetic musings? The "legitimacy" with which Sylvester or Enloe
write, for example, might be questioned on grounds of their "identities"
as elite, educated, privileged women, unrepresentative of the experiences
and realities of those at the "coal face" of international politics.

Celebrating and reifying "difference" as a political end in itself thus
runs the risk of creating increasingly divisive and incommensurate discourses, where each group claims a "knowledge"- or experience-based
legitimacy but, in doing so, precluding the possibility of common understanding or intergroup political discourse. Instead, "difference" produces antithetical discord and political tribalism: only "working class
Hispanics living in South Central Los Angeles," for instance, can speak
of, for, and about "their" community, its concerns, interests and needs;
only female Afro-Americans living in "the Projects" of Chicago can
speak "legitimately" of the housing and social problems endemic to
inner-city living. "Discourse" becomes confined not to conversations

between identity groups (since this is impossible), but storytelling of personal/group experiences where the "other" listens intently until their turn comes to tell their own stories and experiences. Appropriating the "voice" or "pain" of "others" by speaking, writing, or theorizing on issues, perspectives, or events not indicative of one's "group-identity," becomes not only "illegitimate" but a medium of "oppression" and a means to "silence others." The very activity of theory and political discourse as it has been understood traditionally in IR, and the social sciences more generally, is thus rendered inappropriate in the new milieu of "identity politics."

Politically, progressives obviously see a danger in this type of discourse and, from a social scientific perspective, understand it to be less than rigorous. Generalizing, as with theorizing, for example, has fallen victim to postmodern feminist reactions against "methodological essentialism" and the adoption of what Jane Martin calls the instillation of "false difference" into identity discourse. By reacting against the assumption that "all individuals in the world called 'women' were exactly like us" (i.e., white, middle-class, educated, etc.), feminists now tend "a priori to give privileged status to a predetermined set of analytic categories and to affirm the existence of nothing but difference." In avoiding the "pitfall of false unity," feminists have thus "walked straight into the trap of false difference" (Martin, 1994, 631). "Club words" now dominate the discourse. "Essentialism," "*a*historicism," "universalism" and "androcentrism," for example, have become the "prime idiom[s] of intellectual terrorism and the privileged instrument[s] of political orthodoxy" (Martin, 1994, 650). While sympathetic to the cause, even feminists like Jane Martin are critical of the methods that have arisen to circumvent the evils of "essentialism," characterizing contemporary feminist scholarship as imposing its own "chilly climate" on those who question the methodological proclivity for "difference" and "historicism." Postmodern feminists, she argues, have fallen victim to "compulsory historicism," and by "rejecting one kind of essence talk but adopting another," have followed a course "whose logical conclusion all but precludes the use of language" (Martin, 1994, 631). For Martin, this approaches a "dogmatism on the methodological level that we do not countenance in other contexts. It rules out theories, categories, and research projects in advance; prejudges the extent of difference and the nonexistence of similarity" (Martin, 1994, 654). In all, it speaks to a methodological trap that produces many of the same problems as before, but this time in a language otherwise viewed as "progressive," "sensitive" to the particularities of "identity" and "gender," and destructive of conventional "boundaries" in disciplinary knowledge and theoretical endeavor.

Lurking behind such positions, of course, is the highly problematic assumption that a fundamental shift in the political, social, and economic worlds has occurred; that "people, machinery and money, images and ideas now follow increasingly nonisomorphic paths," and that because of this there is a "deterritorializing mobility of peoples, ideas, and images," one overcoming the "laborious moves of statism to project an image of the world divided along territorially discontinuous (separated) sovereign spaces, each supposedly with homogeneous cultures and impervious essences" (Soguk, 1996, 285). In this "new" world where global space-as-territory has been "obliterated," where discrete national cultures no longer exist but are "dissolved" by cosmopolitanism and ubiquitous images peddled by "hypermodern communications," all that remains as tangible referents for "knowledge" and "understanding," we are told, are our own "fractured identities" (Stienstra, 1994, 3). While, for feminists, this is profoundly liberating, allowing them to recognize a "multiplicity of identities," each engaged in a "differing politics," it also betrays how narrow is the intent of "feminist postmodernism," that stands "not toward any other ends" except "the eradication of essentialism" (Stienstra, 1994, 3). Much like Richard Ashley (1986) saw in "positivism" tyrannical structures of oppression, so in "essentialism" postmodern feminists see the subjugation of "diversity" amid "universal" narratives. Yet the reification of "difference" as the penultimate ontological beginning and end-point seems disingenuous in the extreme. The question is not whether there are "differences," of course there are, but whether these are significant for IR, and if so in what capacity? Historically, the brief of IR has been to go out in search of those things that unite us, not divide us. Division, disunity, and "difference," have been the unmistakable *problems* endemic to global politics, and overcoming them the objective that has provided scholars with both their motivating purpose and moral compass. In venerating "difference," identity politics unwittingly reproduces this problematique: exacerbating "differences" beyond their significance, fabricating disunity, and contributing to social and political cleavage. Yes, we are not all the same. But the things that unite us are surely more important, more numerous, and more fundamental to the human condition than those that divide us. We all share a conviction that war is bad, for example, that violence is objectionable, global poverty unconscionable, and that peaceful interstate relations are desirable. Likewise, we all inhabit one earth and have similar environmental concerns, have the same basic needs in terms of developmental requirements, nutrition, personal security, education and shelter. To suppose that these "modernist" concerns are divisible on the basis of gender, color, sexuality, or religious inclination, seems specious, promoting contrariety where none really exists from the perspective of IR. How, for example, amid the reification of ever divisible "difference," do we foster political community and solidarity, hope to foster greater global collectivity, or unite antithetically inclined religious, segregationist, or racial groups on the basis of their professed "difference"? How this is meant to secure "new visions" of international politics, solve the divisions of previous disputations, or avert violent factionalisms in the future, remains curiously absent from the discourse of "identity politics."[5]

Methodologically, the implications of reifying "false difference" are also far from benign for IR, but betray a devolution of disciplinary knowledge and theory amid sundry "narratives" captive to personal "travelogues," attempts to "re-create histories" or enumerate a catalogue of previous "silences" simply on the basis that such has not been done before. The result is a type of agenda inflation; sprawling research topics that, from a more traditionalist perspective, would seem unrelated to IR. Consider, for example, Birigit Weiss, who, when attempting to extol the virtues of an identity-based research agenda for IR, suggests that we think of "symbols such as phone boxes, mail boxes, or the little green man flashing electronically above pedestrian crossings. [These] are national (identity) symbols which we seldom notice as such," she writes. "Only: [sic] once we are away from home do we perceive them as different. First deduction. Being abroad we learn to know what home means" (Weiss, 1997, 8). Travel, and the "distance" associated with it, for Weiss "helps us to define who we are (and where we come from)— which is a necessary condition for developing an international perspective." The old adage that "travel does round the individual" is now reiterated in postmodern form, and IR exalted to become "interNETional" or "intercultural" studies where, for example, Weiss notes that with the Internet "one can travel from ocean to ocean, from continent to continent, from country to country and around the globe in one night— through cyberspace." One can only suppose that play on the Internet assists in the formation of our personal "identities," makes us better scholars, and that reflections on this can constitute discourse in "InterNETional" studies. As a final reflection on what "Intercultural" as opposed to "International Relations" might look like, Weiss recalls the *Container 96—Art Across Oceans* exhibition held in Copenhagen, where "artists coming from 96 seaport cities . . . created art works inside the containers. The visitors were able to 'circumnavigate the globe in just a few hours' and could 'take a walk from continent to continent, from climazone to climazone and from seaport to seaport and enter into visions and realities, as perceived by artists from near and far'" (Weiss, 1997, 13). "In my view," Weiss writes, "this exhibition is an example for an alternative vision of international relations, and might help us look beyond the scope of the discipline" (Weiss, 1997, 13).

Similarly, Marysia Zalewski in a recent paper titled "Posthuman Bodies? Invasion, Erasure, Alienation" (Zalewski, 1997), concerns herself "with the intersection between the international political economy and pregnant women's bodies," and addresses concerns such as the "ethics of 'quality-controlled babies'," the relationship between "eugenics" and "economic ideologies," and how the "ubiquitous use of ultrasound is incrementally erasing the presence of the mother" while "the fetus is imagined as a sort of extra-terrestrial floating in 'space'." Her discussion is counterpoised against questions that reflect on popular cultural images like the movies *Three Men & A Baby*, *Junior*, and *Tootsie*. Ultimately, she is concerned with "what might happen when men can have babies? Or when the boundary between women and machine collapses? What might this do to our notions of subjectivity? Have reproductive technologies heralded the arrival of the posthuman body—the cyborg—at the end of the twentieth century?" (Zalewski, 1997, 20). Likewise, Cynthia Enloe sees the purview of IR extending to such topics as the "dating practices of American soldiers" and the rumors surrounding "'barracks girls', young British girls who leave home and in time become resident sexual partners of American male soldiers" (Enloe, 1989, 65). Issues and topics germane to IR Enloe extends to inter-racial liaisons and romances between Afro-American GI's and British women, the sexual proclivities of U.S. soldiers, and observations that "women can seem as much a threat as a comfort to the modern warrior. A women is to be destroyed just as the enemy is to be destroyed." Or, that some soldiers are "far more ambivalent about women as a direct result of their militarized sexuality" (Enloe, 1989, 68–71, 74).

While interesting, one wonders if the disciplinary parameters of IR are now so porous as to be meaningless. If, as Martin Griffiths and Terry O'Callaghan suggest, "anyone can 'join' IR, regardless of their formal training," is there any longer an intrinsic meaning or purpose to what we do other than engage in academic musings for their own sake? (Griffiths and O'Callaghan, this collection). Does this mean, for example, that no formal training or grounding in world politics will suffice as preparation for studying them, that there is no "core" to our subject, no central concerns or recurring themes that warrant at least rudimentary attention if one is to have an elementary grasp of things international? The obliteration of "intellectual boundaries," the suggestion that there is "no valid distinction between the international and domestic spheres" (O'Callaghan, 1996, 14), and that *all* issues are germane to IR, supposes that we can not only "forget IR theory," as Roland Bleiker urges (as cited in Molsti, this collection), but read, write, and research anything of nominal interest to us and call this international politics. Birigit Weiss' "vision" of "container art exhibitions" or Cynthia Enloe's reflections on the "posthuman body—the cyborg," threatens not just to expand the vistas of our discipline but, in doing so, make us little more than a compendium of the visual arts, science fiction, "identities," personal stories, and research whims whose intellectual agendas are so disparate as to be meaningless. Indeed, how, precisely, this makes for better knowledge and a better understanding of global politics, or how such "agendas" or "concerns" are related to global events and processes, we are never told. The only objective evident in the new "identity politics" seems to be the "transgression of boundaries," where everything no matter how disparate is assumed to be related to IR, and where the purview of our disciplinary lenses are counseled to have no focus but be encompassing of *all* things social, political, and economic.

FEMINIST (RE)VISIONS OF THE "FACTS"

Apart from the problematic nature of identity discourse as a theoretical avenue germane to IR, there is much else in postmodern feminist writings that is questionable. Adam Jones, for example, is concerned at the exclusivity with which "women" are made the ontological essence of "gendered" analyses, creating skewed commentaries that, rather than frame the important question of "gender" in more *inclusive* ways, tend to imprison it amid a radical matriarchal discourse (Jones, 1996, 405–429). Unfortunately, this all too often leads to narratives and modes of analysis whose treatment of the "facts" in international relations is, at best, suspect. One of the recurrent themes in feminist analyses of international politics, for example, is that women everywhere suffer more violence, intimidation, torture, mutilation, and abuse, than do men who otherwise perpetrate these crimes. When Ann Tickner attempts to draw attention to the "particular vulnerabilities of women within states," for instance, "the phrase 'particular vulnerabilities' suggests not just an analytically separable category, but a disproportionate degree of vulnerability" (Jones, 1996, 423). Yet, if we look at the facts the contrary is true: men direct the overwhelming majority of their violence toward other men. In terms of random violence, it is "young men," notes Lorraine Radford, "who are most at risk from 'stranger-danger,'" not women. According to British Home Office figures for 1992, "men are more than twice as likely than are women to be killed by strangers" through acts of random street violence (as quoted in Radford, 1996, 235). This figure is even greater in the United States where men accounted for 76.3 percent of the 18,954 homicide victims in 1989 (Schmittroth, 1991). Likewise, rape statistics released by the United

States Department of Justice in 1990, show that 130,000 women were the victims of rape, while male-to-male prison rape claimed a reported 290,000 victims.[6]

Yet, according to V. Spike Peterson, "male violence constitutes a 'global war against women'," perpetrated with "state complicity" because of patriarchal relations that invariably see women suffer far more than men (Lori Heise quoted in Peterson, 1992, 46). In Peterson's estimation, women suffer a heavier burden than do men, suffer more emotional stress and bear the burden of patriarchal state expenditures that benefit men at the expense of women. "Systematic violence," things like "sexual harassment, battery, rape and torture," Peterson and Ann Runyan argue, "is the persistent price that women pay for the maintenance of large militaries" (Peterson and Runyan, 1993, 158). The implication, of course, is that men pay no price and enjoy freedom from violence when, in fact, we know that "hazing rituals," physical and verbal abuse, torture and mental torment, are daily occurrences throughout the armies of the world and these staffed almost exclusively by men. "Human rights, too," suggest Peterson and Runyan, are "compromised" by militarization. "Amnesty International vividly documents examples of military and police forces around the world terrorizing, imprisoning, and even torturing women who seek information about family members who have 'disappeared' at the hands of government-sponsored death squads." What Peterson and Runyan forget to add, however, is that by Amnesty International's own estimation, the overwhelming number of political prisoners in the world who suffer cruel and inhumane treatment happen to be men; that those who "disappeared" under Argentina's military junta and Nicaragua's and El Salvador's U.S.-sponsored death squads in the 1980s, were disproportionately male, and that torture of political prisoners by sheer weight of numbers therefore concerns, disproportionately, the torture of male political prisoners.[7]

Even the traditional concerns of IR, war and conflict studies, are not spared from the biased framing of the gender variable. Cynthia Enloe, for instance, tells of the plight of women during the Bosnian war, and how Bosnian, Serbian and Croatian men used rape as an instrument of terror. By implication, however, we are left to assume that men in the Bosnian conflict endured no terror, brutality, or deprivations, but were simply the perpetrators of atrocities (Enloe, 1993, 238–244). Similarly, in discussing the Gulf War, Enloe is highly exclusive in dealing with gender, adequately narrating the plight of female migrant workers in Kuwait who suffered atrocities like rape and torture at the hands of Iraqi troops, but neglecting the "wider Iraqi process of detention, torture, execution, and forced removal . . . of tens of thousands of Kuwaitis" that, "judging from the human-rights and media reports [were] virtually all male" (Jones, 1996, 423–424).

Narratives of this type reveal how exclusive has been the framing of the "gender" variable in IR, where "men" are characterized as a "hegemonic gender-class" whose interests, concerns, actions, and writings are "opposed" to the interests and well being of women (Jones, 1996, 423). As Sylvester writes: "states and their regimes connect with people called women only to ensure . . . that the benefits of regime participation will flow from 'women' to 'men' and *not ever* the other way round" (as quoted in Jones, 1996, 423). With such a mind-set, facts become superfluous to the argument(s), leading to a fallacy of composition where assertive prose is itself offered as evidence of the "disproportionate" level of burden or "victimization" that women suffer. Thus, for example, Jones is plainly bemused at Ann Tickner's assertion that women have been forced to enter "the military primarily in the lower ranks." But, asks Jones, "how *else* does one enter the military, except at the lower levels?" (Jones, 1996, 422). Likewise, Peterson and Runyan assert that "the plight of both Third World and Western women has been exacerbated by the debt crisis" (Peterson and Runyan, 1993, 101). Third World and Western men, apparently, were untouched by this same debt crisis. And when commenting on the migration south of the border of "the jobs of many working-class women in the United States," Peterson and Runyan announce with horror how, between "1979 and 1983, 35 percent of the workers who lost jobs because of plant closings in the United States were women." What they fail to point out, of course, is that this means that fully 65 percent of those who lost their jobs because of these same plant closings were men (Peterson and Runyan, 1993, 101; Jones, 1996, 426–427). Moreover, if we look at the available evidence for issues like murder, suicide, homelessness, life expectancy and mortality rates, we find that rather than a "hegemonic gender-class," statistically men kill each other at a far greater rate than they do women, commit suicide at a rate almost three times that of women, constitute about 80 percent of the homeless in the United States, throughout virtually every community in the world live shorter lives than do women, and in the developed world suffer a mortality rate due to disease twice that for women.[8]

Crude characterizations of a "hegemonic gender class" thus display an anomalous capacity to ignore completely those facts that do not accord with ideological belief. And postmodern feminists have been most adroit at this, substituting the evidentiary requirements of systematic observation and reasoned argument, for identity discourses that rely on "perceptions" and "feelings." In a recent survey conducted for the International Studies Association (ISA) by the "Committee for Study on the Status of Women in IR," for example, Marie Henehan and Meredith Reid Sarkees frame their survey in such a way as to measure the subjective *perceptions* of respondents. "The respondents were asked whether they had perceived gender bias in the course of their career" (International Studies Newsletter, 1997, 8). In an alternate survey conducted for the same ISA committee, Christine Sylvester notes that "many respondents report feeling isolated within their departments and from major networks in the field" (International Studies Newsletter, 1996, 12). Aside from the obvious fact that "perceptions" of bias or "feelings" of isolation are not exclusive to women, questions of the methodological appropriateness of anecdotal evidence need also to be explored. That the reality of any situation can be gauged from personal narratives based exclusively upon "perception" makes for bad social science and leads, ultimately, to destructive debates that hurl about subjective accusations.[9] Witness, for example, the claims of matriarchal superiority when standpoint feminists insist that "women have a distinctive, superior view of the world, distinctive because shaped by those features of their experiences that distinguish them from men, superior on the . . . basis that the oppressed are capable of a higher form of awareness than the oppressor" (Brown, 1997, 241). This is simply inverted patriarchy, premised on little more than fanciful whims about the innate characteristics of women vis-à-vis men. It replicates the privileging of one gender over another, and discharges all hope of equality between genders on the basis of merit alone. Moreover, it invokes a crude and unsubstantiated argument derived through intuition, that women "feel" more deeply, are better "knowers" and thus have better understandings of international politics. But how is this different from patriarchal-chauvinist claims that men are more "rational," "logical, "strategic" and women more "emotional," less reasoned and captive to their biological cycles? Both arguments are equally preposterous and need to be abandoned, not invoked as a means "forward" for understanding international relations. More obviously, such silly "methods" tend toward a perverse hierarchical index of who suffers the most, who bears the most burden, feels the most hurt. When Judy True notes that "states demand sacrifices of gendered citizens: mother's, for example, who are forced to devote "their lives to socializing these dutiful [male] citizens for the sovereign state as masculine deity," lest we should forget that male citizens have typically been the cannon fodder who have sacrificed their lives and limbs for the state (True, 1996, 234–235). If we wish to construct hierarchies of pain and suffering, none can be higher than the "ultimate sacrifice," a sacrifice made throughout history overwhelmingly by male combatants.

The point of all of this, however, should not be to countenance against one type of suffering and in favor of others. Rather, the point is to take issue with those who view suffering, or at least "disproportion-ate" suffering, the preserve of one gender, women, and inflicted by another gender, men. More importantly, the point for IR must be to affirm as illegitimate *all* suffering and work actively to develop ways of understanding and prescriptions that might help in its eradication. The "gender variable" is not inappropriate in this regard, but only when used in *inclusive* ways.

TOWARD SOME CONCLUSIONS:
POSTMODERN FEMINISMS, "GENDER BIAS,"
AND INTERNATIONAL RELATIONS

"One variable," notes Tom Kando, "does not make a theory." Gen-der, while important, on its own is only one element among many in international politics. Its contribution to IR might thus be assessed as only partial: part of a multitude of perspectives that attempt to con-tribute to our understanding of domination, exploitation, and inequal-ity in the context of global politics (Kando, 1996, 26–27). Yet this is not the way postmodern feminists position themselves in the disci-pline, admonishing all who stand opposed to making the "gender vari-able" the principal ontological vantage point from which to explain and understand international politics. Among radical feminists there is a deep-seated suspicion of IR, especially toward the discipline's tradi-tional subjects of inquiry and modes of analysis. Not that this is unique to IR. The social sciences and humanities generally, and West-ern culture and Enlightenment thought in particular, are now viewed ominously. As Patricia Lança observes, for radical feminists the mod-ernist-rational intellectual edifice is now "seen as a shelter from which malign entities (embodied in the bourgeoisie) especially since the Enlightenment, have sought to exercise power," while "the house of western culture" is depicted not as a "place of welcome where all mankind may find a place but of exclusion." Contributions to this "edifice" in whatever form are thus rendered "complicitious" in the "project of oppression," and the spread of "western culture" as coter-minous with "imperialist exploitation" and "cultural genocide." Like-wise, "meaning attributed to language by ordinary mortals" becomes "a delusion," and "true" meaning the preserve of those who disas-semble language itself. "Nothing is as it seems and the realists who believe otherwise are victims of logocentrism, or more radically, phal-lologocentrism where those who exercise control over the power sys-tem are essentially males who impose 'compulsory heterosexuality' on the unwilling masses of man and womankind" (Lança, 1996, 41).

While Lança's comments are harsh, they probably explain the spate of nefarious and ideologically opinionated "isms" that masquerade as theoretical formulations but which incite "revolt," "disturbance," and "repudiation" in favor of "relativism and tribalism" (Walsh, 1996, 36). The irony in all of this, of course, is that such repudiationist formulations display a near panegyric celebration of the writings of white European men, Foucault, Derrida, and Nietzsche, for example, who never once wrote about the plight of women but are now lionized as the emissaries of their emancipation. This makes "male deconstructionists and their female epigones . . . the product of the narrowest Eurocentrism," while uniquely adept at rejecting all that is "western," "European," "modernist," "rational" and "scientific" (Lança, 1996, 42). Indeed, the outright rejectionism of Enlightenment and Western values seems all the more peculiar considering how instrumental they have been in extending to women rights and freedoms that, elsewhere in the world, are only dreamt about. As Lança again observes, "if it were not tragic it would be hilarious that western female intellectuals, a privileged class indeed by global or even purely American standards, should demonize white, European, upper-class males and blame the power structures of western society for women's ills. For where has women's emancipation progressed further than in these very societies and, what is more, with the help, support and open initiative of many such males?" (Lança, 1996, 43).

Similar sentiments might be extrapolated into IR where the discipline, its practitioners and theories, are castigated by postmodern and radical feminists for crimes of "elitism," "sexism," "racism," and for "marginalizing" not just "women" but their ideas, perspectives, and approaches. The ISA "Committee for the Study of the Status of Women in IR," for example, complained that "research by women is poorly integrated into the corpus of scholarship in this field" and that, overall, there is an "underrepresentation of women in . . . ISA journals." (Tetreault, 1997, 2–3). Again, however, the facts would seem to make anomalous these accusations. As William Thompson and Brian Pollins, the editors of the ISA's *International Studies Quarterly* (ISQ) noted in responding to these allegations, while "women submitted fewer papers than one might expect," the "probability of success" was nonetheless "what one would expect given the submission numbers."[10] In all, they added, the available data indicates "that the problem may lie more with what is submitted, where it is submitted, and how well it is crafted than it does with alleged bias on the part of specific journals."[11]

Cries of "victimization" and professional "marginalization" nonetheless persist, albeit issued from rather prestigious corners of the academy. Christine Sylvester, for example, issues hers via Cambridge

University Press and the distinguished series "Cambridge Studies in IR," Cynthia Enloe via the University of California Press, Berkeley, and V. Spike Peterson via Westview Press (Sylvester, 1994; Enloe, 1989; Peterson and Runyan, 1993).[12] "Marginalization" of this nature, not unnaturally, is the career goal of most junior faculty! Nor is there evidence of systemic discrimination in the academy in terms of hiring practices. As most junior faculty will be only to familiar with, affirmative action policies and an acute awareness of equity issues, regales throughout advertisements for faculty vacancies: the "University is an Equal Opportunity/Affirmative Action employer; applications from women and minority candidates are specifically invited."[13] A "commitment to diversity," an enhanced sensitivity to correcting historical disciplinary gender disparities, and an awareness of sexism, have all made for a more even playing field in terms of academic recruitment practices. Sheilah Mann of the American Political Science Association (APSA), for example, reports that for graduating candidates in 1995–1996, the "placement success rates differ overall by gender and ethnicity," and that "more of the women graduates seeking jobs were successful (70%) than the men (62%)." Mann further notes that "among U.S. citizens, a higher percentage of each group of minority doctoral students got jobs than did all men and, to a lesser degree of difference, all women. Placement success rates were 77 percent for Latin Americans, 74 percent for Latinos, and 83 percent for Asian Americans."[14] Systemic discrimination, "racism," "bigotry" and "gender bias," are thus far from endemic, or even evident, across all the subfields of political science. This probably explains why allegations of such "bias" are typically only asserted and never substantiated with reference to fact or professional actualities.

But putting aside the ambit claims of postmodern feminists, the more important question for IR concerns the relevance of the strategies and theoretical approaches they recommend for the discipline. What might IR look like, do, research, and produce under the "theoretical" formula suggested by postmodern feminists? Are we to assume that observations derived through the experiences of "Ruby the elephant" a sufficient ontological starting point for the research agendas of the discipline as Sylvester suggests in the introduction to her book? (Sylvester, 1994). Will accusatory gender finger pointing help in eradicating injustice, global poverty, and war? How do highbrow postmodern discourses or feminist ontologies help the truly needy, destitute, and impoverished? Can such insights be operationalized, used as tools to inform public policy, or utilized as formula to help negotiate peaceful resolutions to ethnic conflict or territorial wars? Can we settle for a series of ongoing questions concerning "what it means to know, who may know, where knowers are located, and what the difference among them mean for the knowledges that result?" (Sylvester, 1996, 256–257). Can the histiography of the Cold War really be understood by reference to the "T-shirts" worn by U.S servicemen and the "sex industry in the Philippines"? (Zalewski, 1996, 349). Should we prioritize the study of "marriage" and "venereal disease," as Enloe suggests, as equal to that of "studying military weaponry?" (Enloe, 1989, 195). Is theoretical endeavor really an attribute of "journal" entries from the travels of a "U.S. academic living on a kibbutz" in Israel, or the recollections of those who gather at ISA meetings and exchange narratives? (see, for example, the contribution by Ferguson, 1996, 435–454). Does theoretical endeavor really extend to "how to make cups of tea, about washing clothes, about using the word processor, about driving a car, about collecting water, about joking," as Marysia Zalewski contends? (Zalewski, 1996, 346).

Not all theory, of course, has to conform to the strictures of utilitarian principles, able to be operationalized and used in an instrumental way to inform public and foreign policy. But some of it probably should, save the relevance of what we do might be lost on those at the "coal face" of international politics if not also many of its professional practitioners and academicians. Stimulating our theoretical imaginations, "pushing the envelope," and exploring discursively the epistemological grounding of our collective knowledge is all good and well. But to suppose that this is all we should do, or the most important of our activities, would seem to marginalize the continuing dilemmas of international politics and those whose lives are made perilous because of them. Doubtlessly, feminist perspectives have made valuable contributions and enhanced our understanding of international politics, but such perspectives have yet to make a convincing case for the intellectual revolution and refocused research agendas they so earnestly propose.

NOTES

1. Sylvester's sense of "exclusion" is related to us when she notes: exclusion "is especially evident in the special issue of *International Studies Quarterly* 34 (3) (1990) titled 'Speaking the Language of Exile: Dissidence in International Studies,' where women are mentioned but our dilemmas of gender are not considered important enough to warrant article-length treatment" (Sylvester, 1993, 87).

2. Despite Walker's assertion, Jane Marcus insists that, in the humanities at least, it is philosophy and musicology, and in the sciences, mathematics that have "been the fields most zealously guarded" and gender blind disciplines. In comparison to these, the case could be made that IR is a little more progressive than Walker's glib remark would otherwise suggest (see Marcus, 1982, 218).

3. Feminists, of course, insist that they do not privilege "gender" ontologically but use it as a variable for understanding the configuration of power

relations. As Griselda Pollock puts it: "It is a common misunderstanding that feminism is a perspective or approach which prioritizes gender over all other structures of oppression. I would argue that by focusing on issues not only of sex and gender but of sexual difference, feminism explores the complex con-figurations of power and difference which do indeed specify the question of sexual difference, but not exclusively." My objection stands, however. This position seems somewhat nonsensical, suggesting that while gender is not "essentialized," it is "essential" to understanding such relationships! To make the point further, Pollock employs the standard variety of postmodern speak, suggesting "feminism signifies a set of positions, not an essence; a critical prac-tice, not a doxa; a dynamic and self-critical response and intervention, not a platform." I remain unconvinced that this clarifies anything, accept perhaps that Pollock's position is even more opaque than it first appears. See Pollock (1993, 98, 100).

4. We might also ask why amid the discourse of ever emergent "identi-ties" the issue of nationalism and "national identity" is so absent from feminist postmodern discourses? Indeed, why is nationalism and "national identity" rejected as unimportant when, for example, John Hutchinson and Anthony Smith note that in nationalism there is "power, of national loyalties and identi-ties over those of even class, gender, and race" (see Hutchison and Smith, 1994).

5. On the reification of "difference," Patricia Lança makes the poignant, if stinging, observation that, "The worst sin of both types of cultivators of these particular poisoned fruits of postmodernism is that they are attacking the essen-tial unity of the human race. It is, after all, our capacity for rationality which goes hand in hand with the development of language, that brings people together." For Lança, all said and done, all of us are united by our basic capac-ity to reason, to think, and communicate. "Difference" is thus really only a sub-structural set of variances on our essential commonalties whose impotence is secondary, and not constitutive, of our human natures. See the discussion in Lança (Lança, 1996).

6. This figure is somewhat higher than the FBI "Uniform Crime Report" for 1990, which indicated that 102,560 women had been the victims of rape or attempted rape. See the discussion in Sommers (Sommers, 1995, 209, 225; Don-aldson, 1993, 29).

7. See, for example, Forrest and the report by Amnesty International (Forrest, 1996; Amnesty International, 1993). The findings by Adam Jones are also instructive, who, using a diverse collection of empirical evidence, notes that during the era of the "dirty war" in Argentina, 70% of the victims who disap-peared were male. Or, in the case of Nicaragua after the 1979 revolution, 93.4" of those killed in the insurrection were male. See Jones (1996, 426–427).

8. The mortality rate for men per 1000 of the population in developed countries is 3.37 compared to 1.50 for women; a female to male ration of 0.45. See *The Worlds Women 1995: Trend and Transformation* (New York: United Nations), 72. See also Jones (1996, 423).

9. I am reminded at this juncture of a speech delivered to the Melbourne Writer's Festival by Germaine Greer, who, as Catharine Lumby reports, made associations between the "revival of punk fashion featuring models with dark

eye shadow and lipstick" as "evidence that girls magazines encourage male violence" (Lumby, 1997, 21).

10. The editors of the *International Studies Quarterly* (ISQ) further note that "this information was communicated to the Committee, and it is unfortunate that it evidently was not taken into consideration" (Thompson and Pollins, 1997, 4).

11. To these comments the editors of ISQ further noted that "it is the current policy of ISQ to employ reviewers who share or, at least, do not reject out of hand the epistemological assumptions of submitted manuscripts. If submitted manuscripts are rejected at ISQ, it is usually because reviewers with similar orientations encountered serious problems with the manuscript and recommended against publication—and not because of glass ceiling gender bias or epistemological hostility" (Thompson and Pollins, 1997, 4).

12. Similarly, Marysia Zalewski, Cynthia Enloe, and Christine Sylvester have also been published in an edited volume for Cambridge University Press (see Smith, Booth, and Zalewski, 1996).

13. This example is taken from the *American Political Science Association Personnel Service Newsletter* 4(5) (January 1997), 9, for a faculty position at Colgate University in "International Relations." Examples of such wording are, of course, numerous.

14. "This overall positive placement record for 1995–1996 American minority doctoral students is consistent with the placement experience of their cohorts in the last several years" (Mann, 1997, 604–605).

REFERENCES

"Gender Discrimination in the Academy? Yes, Survey Indicates." (1997). *International Studies Newsletter* (February), 5–6.

"Oral Histories Reveal That Junior Female Scholars Expect More from the Academy Than Their Senior Counterparts." (1996–97). *International Studies Newsletter* (December/January), 5–8.

Amnesty International. (1993). *Getting Away with Murder: Political Killings and "Disappearances" in the 1990s.* London: Amnesty International Publications.

Ashley, Richard K. (1986). "The Poverty of Neorealism." In Robert O. Keohane (ed.), *Neorealism and Its Critics.* New York: Columbia University Press: 225–286.

Ashley, Richard K. (1989). "Living on Border Lines: Man, Poststructuralism, and War." In James Der Derian and Michael J. Shapiro (eds.), *International/Intertextual Relations: Postmodern Readings of World Politics.* New York: Lexington Books: 259–321.

Ashley, Richard K. (1996). The Achievements of Poststructuralism." In Steve Smith, Ken Booth, and M. Zalewski (eds.), *International Theory: Positivism & Beyond.* Cambridge: Cambridge University Press: 240–254.

Ashley, Richard K., and R. B. J. Walker. (1990). "Reading Dissidence/Writing the Discipline: Crisis and the Question of Sovereignty in International Studies." *International Studies Quarterly* 34(3), 367–416.

Ashley, Richard K., and R. B. J. Walker. (1990). "Speaking the Language of Exile: Dissident Thought in International Studies." *International Studies Quarterly* 34(3), 259–268.

Brown, Chris. (1997). *Understanding International Relations*. London: Macmillan.

Donaldson, S. (1993). "The Rape Crisis Behind Bars." *New York Times*, December 29.

Elshtain, J. B. (1987). *Women and War*. New York: Basic Books.

Enloe, Cynthia. (1989). *Bananas, Beaches and Bases: Making Feminist Sense of International Politics*. Berkeley: University of California Press.

Enloe, Cynthia. (1993). *The Morning After: Sexual Politics at the End of the Cold War*. Berkeley: University of California Press.

Ferguson, K. (1996). "From a Kibbutz Journal: Reflections on Gender, Race, and Militarism in Israel." In Michael J. Shapiro and Hayward Alker (eds.), *Challenging Boundaries: Global Flows, Territorial Identities* (Borderlines, Volume 2). Minneapolis: University of Minnesota Press: 435–454.

Forrest, D. (1996). *A Glimpse of Hell: Reports on Torture Worldwide*. London: Cassell: Amnesty International.

Hutchison, J., and A. D. Smith (eds.). (1994). *Nationalism*. Oxford: Oxford University Press.

Jones, Adam. (1996). "Does Gender Make the World Go Round?" *Review of International Studies* 22, 405–429.

Kando, T. (1996). "Postmodernism: Old Wine in New Bottles?" *International Journal on World Peace* 13(3).

Krause, Jill. (1996). "Gendered Identities in International Relations." In Jill Krause and N. Renwick (eds.), *Identities in International Relations*. New York: St. Martin's Press: 99–117.

Lança, P. (1996). "Comment on Postmodernism: Old Wine in New Bottles?" *International Journal on World Peace* 13(3), 41–44

Lapid, Yosef, and Friedrich Kratochwil. (1996). *The Return of Culture and Identity in IR Theory*. Boulder, Colo.: Lynne Rienner.

Linklater, A. (1992). "The Question of the Next Stage in International Relations Theory: A Critical-Theoretical Point of View." *Millennium: Journal of International Studies* 21(1), 77–100.

Lumby, Catharine. (1997). "For Her Peers, No Milk of Kindness." *Sydney Morning Herald* (Friday, October 24), 21.

Mann, S. (1997). "Placement of Political Science Doctoral Students in 1996: Degrees Matter." *Political Science and Politics* 30(3), 602–610.

Marcus, J. (1982). "Storming the Toolshed." In N. O. Keohane, M. Z. Rosaldo, and B. C. Gelpi (eds.), *Feminist Theory: A Critique of Ideology*. Chicago: University of Chicago Press: 217–235.

Martin, J. R. (1994). "Methodological Essentialism, False Difference, and Other Dangerous Traps." *Signs: Journal of Women and Culture in Society* 19(3), 630–657.

O'Callaghan, Terry. (1996). "The Real World of Normative Theory in International Relations." Mimeograph, Department of Politics, University of Adelaide, South Australia.

Peterson, V. Spike. (1992). "Security and Sovereign States: What Is at Stake in Taking Feminism Seriously?" In V. Spike Peterson (ed.), *Gendered States: Feminist (Re)Visions of International Relations Theory*. Boulder, Colo.: Lynne Rienner: 31–64.

Peterson, V. Spike. (1997). "Whose Crisis? Early and Postmodern Masculinism." In Stephen Gill and H. Mittleman (eds.), *Innovation and Transformation in International Relations Theory*. Cambridge: Cambridge University Press: 185–206.

Peterson, V. Spike. (1992). "Transgressing Boundaries: Theories of Knowledge, Gender and International Relations." *Millennium: Journal of International Studies 21*(2), 186–206.

Peterson, V. Spike. (1993). "The Politics of Identity in International Relations." *The Fletcher Forum* (Summer), 1–12.

Peterson, V. Spike, and A. S. Runyan. (1993). *Global Gender Issues*. Boulder, Colo.: Westview Press.

Pettman, Jan Jindy. (1996). *Worlding Women: A Feminist International Politics*. London: Routledge.

Pollock, G. (1993). "The Politics of Theory: Generations and Geographies, Feminist Theory and the Histories of Arts Histories." *Genders 17*, 97–120.

Radford, L. (1996). "Women, Crime and Violence." In B. Madoc-Jones, and J. Coates (eds.), *An Introduction to Women's Studies*. Oxford: Basil Blackwell: 228–249.

Schmittroth, L. (1991). *Statistical Record of Women Worldwide*. Gale Research, Inc. Detroit.

Ship, S. J. (1994). "And What about Gender? Feminism and International Relations Third Debate." In Claire T. Sjolander and W. S. Cox (eds.), *Beyond Positivism: Critical Reflections on International Relations*. Boulder, Colo.: Lynne Rienner: 131–133.

Smith, Steve, Ken Booth, and M. Zalewski (eds.). (1996). *International Theory: Positivism and Beyond*. Cambridge: Cambridge University Press.

Soguk, N. (1996). "Transnational/Transborder Bodies: Reexistence, Accommodation, and Exile in Refugee and Migration Movements on the U.S.-Mexican Border." In Michael J. Shapiro and Hayward Alker (eds.), *Challenging Boundaries: Global Flows, Territorial Identities*. Minneapolis: University of Minnesota Press: 285–325.

Sommers, C. H. (1994). *Who Stole Feminism: How Women Have Betrayed Women*. New York: Simon & Schuster.

Steans, J. (1998). *Gender and International Relations: An Introduction*. New Brunswick, N.J.: Rutgers University Press.

Stienstra, D. (1994). *Womens's Movements and International Organizations*. New York: St. Martin's Press.

Sylvester, Christine. (1993). "Homeless in International Relations? 'Women's' Place in Canonical Texts and Feminist Reimaginings." In M. Ringrose and A. J. Lerner (eds.), *Reimagining the Nation*. Buckingham, U.K.: Open University Press: 77–97.

Sylvester, Christine. (1994). *Feminist Theory and International Relations in a Postmodern Era*. Cambridge: Cambridge University Press.

Sylvester, Christine. (1996). "The Contributions of Feminist Theory to International Relations." In Steve Smith, Ken Booth, and M. Zalewski (eds.), *International Theory: Positivism and Beyond*. Cambridge: Cambridge University Press: 254–278.

Tetreault, M. A. (1997). "Study Finds Underrepresentation of Women in an ISA Journals." *International Studies Newsletter* 24(4), 1–3.

Thompson, W. R., and B. Pollins. (1997). "ISQ Editors Respond to Recent Critiques of the Journal." *International Studies Newsletter* 24(6), 3–4.

Tickner, J. Anne. (1992). *Gender in International Relations: Feminist Perspectives on Achieving Global Security*. New York: Columbia University Press.

Tickner, J. Anne. (1997). "You Just Don't Understand: Troubled Engagements Between Feminists and IR Theorists." *International Studies Quarterly* 41(4), 611–632.

Tickner, J. Anne. (1996). "Identity in International Relations Theory: Feminist Perspectives." In Yosef Lapid and Friedrich Kratochwil (eds.), *The Return of Culture and Identity in IR Theory*. Boulder, Colo.: Lynne Rienner: 132–147.

True, J. (1996). "Feminism." in S. Burchill and A. Linklater (eds.), *Theories of International Relations*. New York: St. Martin's Press: 210–251.

United Nations. *The World's Women 1995: Trend and Transformation*. New York.

Walker, R. B. J. (1992). "Gender and Critique in the Theory of International Relations." In V. Spike Peterson (ed.), *Gendered States: Feminist (re)Visions of International Relations Theory*. Boulder, Colo.: Lynne Rienner: 179–202.

Walsh, T. G. (1996). "Reflections on the Antecedents of Postmodernism." *International Journal on World Peace* 13(3), 35–40.

Weiss, B. (1997). "Reconstructing International/Intercultural Relations: Beyond Feminist Disturbances and Postmodern Deconstruction." Mimeograph. Paper presented at the panel "Feminist Transformations of International Theory," Thirty-eighth Annual Convention of the International Studies Association, Toronto, March 18–22.

Wight, C. (1996). "Incommensurability and Cross-Paradigm Communication in International relations Theory: 'What's the Frequency Kenneth?'" in *Millennium: Journal of International Studies* 25(2), 291–319.

Zalewski, M. (1993). "Feminist Standpoint Theory Meets International Relations Theory: A Feminist Version of David and Goliath?" *The Fletcher Forum of World Affairs* 17(2), 13–32.

Zalewski, M. (1994). "The Women/Women Question in International Relations." *Millennium: Journal of International Studies* 23(2), 407–423.

Zalewski, M. (1994a). "What's New? Feminist Observations on the New Europe." In W. Carlsnaes and Steve Smith (eds.), *European Foreign Policy: The EC and the Changing Perspectives in Europe*. London: Sage: 223–237.

Zalewski, M. (1996). "All These Theories Yet the Bodies Keep Piling Up: Theory, Theorists, Theorising." In Steve Smith, Ken Booth, and M. Zalewski (eds.), *International Theory: Positivism and Beyond*. Cambridge: Cambridge University Press: 340–353.

Zalewski, M. (1997). "Posthuman Bodies? Invasion, Erasure, Alienation." Mimeograph. Paper presented Thirty-eighth Annual Convention of the International Studies Association, Toronto, March 18–22.

Zalewski, M., and Cynthia Enloe. (1995). "Questions about Identity in International Relations." In Ken Booth and Steve Smith (eds.), *International Relations Theory Today*. University Park: Pennsylvania State University Press: 279–305.

CHAPTER 5

Can There Be National Perspectives on Inter(national) Relations?

Tony Porter

INTRODUCTION

What do Kenneth Waltz, Richard Ashley, Cynthia Enloe, and Craig Murphy have in common? All are well-known international relations scholars and all have played an important part in initiating new international relations theorizing and research. And all happen to teach at American universities. It is difficult, however, to see that they share much else in common. Enloe, for example, is a "standpoint" feminist, Waltz has pioneered neorealist theory, Ashley has developed insights derived from postmodern and poststructural theory, and Murphy is a proponent of Gramscian historicism. These scholars differ markedly in theoretical outlook, and the often ferocious debates between them would even seem to preclude the possibility of "commonality." Nationality, therefore, seems an insignificant determinant of the intellectual development of ideas, theory, and approaches to the study of international politics.

In this essay I take this anecdotal example as a starting point for arguing that it is only minimally useful to speak about "national perspectives" on international relations. Rather, I argue, it might be of greater worth attempting to understand how the enterprise of intellectual reflection itself, especially in the context of those disciplinary concerns that comprise International Relations (IR), serves to marginalize or perhaps even suppress the role of nationality, if not substantially transcend it. This paper is divided into two sections. The first begins with a general discussion of the suggested lack of relationship between nationality and theoretical perspective, revisiting traditional debates on this topic as they have been addressed in IR over the past number of decades.

131

The second section of the paper then draws upon the example of Canada as a case study to assess and test the hypothesis that nationality and theorizing are only nominally related.

NATIONALITY AND PARADIGMS:
THE AMBIVALENT SCIENCE OF POLITICAL REALISM

In the aftermath of World War II the discipline of IR developed two well-recognized features with quite contradictory implications for the perceived relevance of nationality on theorizing and research. On the one hand, there was a strong desire to develop scientific generalizations that were applicable across time and space, and, therefore, free of the influence of nationality. On the other hand, Realism, the dominant approach, stressed the centrality of the nation-state in international affairs, suggesting, at least implicitly, that nationality would invariably shape all ideas, including scholarly approaches to international relations.

In the immediate post–World War II period, however, the impulse for scientific generalization, especially in the context of America's new-found need for policy-relevant theory and prescription, marginalized investigations into the implications of political Realism for the discipline's philosophy of science. Hans Morgenthau's scientific ambitions, for example, evident in the second chapter of his much celebrated book *Politics Among Nations* (Morgenthau, 1967), made explicit what he described as "The Science of International Politics." Ideology, to the extent that it is studied "scientifically," is analyzed only in terms of its role in the enhancement of national power—similar to E. H. Carr's discussion of the "adjustment of thought to purpose" (Carr, 1939, 68). Not unlike his contemporaries, Morgenthau did not consider the possibility that his own ideas could be treated as "ideology," and thus be connected to the power and interests of the American nation-state from within which he wrote. On the contrary, it was Morgenthau's idealist rivals that he labeled "ideological," with his stated goal of attempting to "see through these ideological disguises and grasp behind them the actual political forces and phenomena." As confirmation of this, Morgenthau counterposed his own positive portrayal of the balance of power as "a universal principle for all pluralist societies" while he dismissed the "universally valid abstract principles" upon which idealist approaches were based (Morgenthau, 1967, 94, 4, 3). Morgenthau's "universal principles," he assumed, were based on "historical precedent" and were therefore "scientific" rather than "ideological." Indeed, he could subsume American ideological biases beneath the mantle of power politics: "A policy of the status quo," he wrote, "can often afford to reveal its true nature and dispense with ideological disguises because the status quo has already, by virtue of its very existence, acquired a certain moral legitimacy" (Morgenthau, 1967, 86). Moreover, this tendency to suppress the contradictory implications of political Realism with, on the one hand, its aspiration to universalistic science and, on the other, its emphasis on the subservience of ideas to power became even more pronounced as enthusiasm for behavioralism and quantification swept through the discipline.

By contrast, Stanley Hoffmann's article (Hoffmann, 1977; and this volume; see also Cochran in this volume) drew out these implications and proclaimed explicitly that international relations *was* "An American Social Science." Hoffmann insightfully analyzed the way in which Realist-dominated IR had been influenced by "power" and the "national interest" of the American state, and by the peculiarities of American national culture. Although there are echoes of Realism's scientific aspirations in Hoffmann's emphasis on "distance" as a corrective to U.S.-centrism, these themes are subordinate to his analysis of the subservience of ideas to national power—the order is reversed from that of Morgenthau and earlier Realists.

Hoffmann's highlighting of the relationship between nationality and IR perspectives was further reinforced by the increased attention paid to the existence of a lively alternative literature in the form of British IR (Smith, 1985; see also Crawford this volume), more sensitive to philosophy, law, and history—apparently another case where nationality had contributed to a distinctive approach—and by periodic studies (Holsti, 1985) charting the continued preeminence of U.S. scholars in the discipline.

THE THIRD DEBATE, PARADIGMS, AND NATIONALITY

In the past two decades increasing degrees of skepticism have been expressed about the discipline of IR's scientific aspirations. Yosef Lapid, for instance, identified a "Third Debate" between positivists and post-positivists and applauded the latter's gains. Notions of "paradigms" were imported into the discipline from Thomas Kuhn's analysis of scientific discovery in the history of physics: testable theories were treated as embedded in large-scale, untestable, and often incommensurable paradigms that, in turn, were embedded in the shared norms and values of particular scientific communities. Aspirations to test empirically universal generalizations were thereby downgraded substantially (Lapid, 1989, 235–279).

One might assume that this change in the discipline would lead to greatly increased acknowledgment of the role of nationality in international relations theorizing: skepticism toward "value-free" universal social scientific theorizing, for example, had weakened substantially the ability of scientistic claims to forestall examination of the potential impact of national norms and values on the norms and values of the IR scholarly community.

Yet this was not to be the case. Instead, the prevailing tendency was to discern three major IR paradigms, none of which was explicitly linked to nationality (see, for example, Groom and Mandaville in this volume). Although a wide variety of labels have been used the trichotomy usually referred to some variant of Realist, liberal (e.g., neofunctionalism, transnationalism, globalism, interdependence, neoliberal institutionalism) and critical approaches (e.g., world systems, dependency theories, Gramscian approaches) (see, for instance, Banks, 1985, 7–26; Maghroori and Ramberg, 1982; Viotti and Kauppi, 1987; McGrew and Lewis, 1992; Doyle, 1997). Even where these approaches were identified, either by their proponents or their opponents, as having political consequences (as, for instance, with dependency theorists' advocacy of enhanced power for the Third World), it was groups of states or social locations (the "core" and "periphery") that were highlighted and *not* the interests of particular nation-states.

During the 1990s, however, the use of a threefold typology of paradigms to classify IR theories became increasingly problematic, principally for three reasons. First, relatively new approaches that did not "fit" into the trichotomy became more prominent, most notably feminism and postmodernism. Postmodernism, for instance, shares an emphasis on the ceaseless and anarchic clashes of power politics with Realism, an emphasis on the importance of language and the individual subject with some variants of liberalism, and, at the same time, an emphasis on challenging the status quo with critical approaches, but differs sharply with each in other respects. Second and relatedly, there was a shift away from the more directly political or substantive theoretical differences (e.g., are states, nonstate actors, or social classes most important in international relations? should IR be concerned primarily with war and peace, with economic growth, or with economic inequality?) that characterized the trichotomy to more metatheoretical differences about epistemology, ontology, and methodology, such as distinctions between "rationalistic" and "reflective" approaches (Keohane, 1988, 379–396), or positivist versus post-positivist approaches (Kratochwil and Ruggie, 1986, 753–776). These metatheoretical differences cut across the three major paradigms.[1] Finally, theoretical innovation in the form of neoliberal institutionalism and regime theory rendered the trichotomous paradigm approach problematic, especially since these research perspectives so obviously overlapped the spaces that had been assumed previously to divide the three paradigms. Regime analysis, for example, sought explicitly to bridge the gap between the liberal tradition, with its emphasis on cooperative norms, and the Realist tradition, with its insistence on the preeminence of the state (Krasner, 1983).

Once again one might expect this heightened sensitivity to the often politicized process by which knowledge is produced, combined with growing skepticism about universalistic claims, and recognition of the ubiquity of persistent cultural differences within the community of IR scholars, would lead increasingly to widespread recognition of national differences in IR theorizing.

There are, however, a number of reasons why this has not occurred and is not likely to do so in the future. These form the analytical core of my argument and highlight why there cannot be national perspectives on international relations. I will discuss each of these in turn.

First, the weakening of scientific claims to universality does not only make space for the idea of national IR perspectives—it simultaneously weakens claims that national identities are anything more than one variant among countless other possible contemporary "identities." This is not simply the collateral effect of a fashionable rejection of "fixed identities" in influential social theories such as poststructuralism or structuration theory, for example, from which many IR theorists are now drawing. And while it is likely a reflection of actual social practices which these social theories seek to analyze, it is also more than this: the metatheoretical disposition that highlights the arbitrariness of scientific claims inevitably highlights the arbitrary and constructed nature of *national* identities.

Second, and relatedly, the increased reflexivity of contemporary life and social theorizing directs our attention not just to what exists, but also to what *should* exist.[2] This is a central feature of the Marxist tradition of critical theory (Cox, 1986) but is even more pronounced in those reflexive approaches that reject the constraining effects of the Marxist emphasis on a degree of centrality for economic factors and social class (Laclau and Mouffee, 1985). When counterposed to the ethical correlates of nationality as a foundation for thought, the alternative ethical imperative of cross-boundary communication appears to have a decisive advantage. This, in part, was the appeal of the aspiration to scientific generalization and, although the negative tendency of scientific generalization to portray the "particular" as "universal" and thereby suppress diversity has been effectively exposed, the more positive desire to transcend discursively one's particular location remains an influential feature of the positivist tradition. At the other end of the epistemological spectrum, postmodern approaches, in the very act of making metaclaims about the nature of difference, reveal a similar inclination. Moreover, contemporary work on postmodern ethics in IR as elsewhere, indicates that an emphasis on the recognition of difference can be seen as part of a larger effort to enhance understanding and respect across these differences. In short, even if nationality was now recognized as influential in IR theorizing, prevailing ethical inclinations, supported by the discipline's increased reflexivity, would lead the discipline to seek to transcend it.

Third, the very nature of a discipline requires at minimum a common set of shared understandings that would be contradicted almost by definition by the notion of national IRs. Many years ago, Martin Wight argued that, among other reasons, there could be no international theory because of the persistence of national outlooks on politics that saw international activities as a mere extension of the national polity (Wight, 1966, 17–34). The abundance of IR theory today suggests that Wight overall was wrong—but his identification of the incompatibility of national perspectives and IR theory remains logically convincing.

Fourth, despite the importance of sociology of knowledge approaches such as Hoffmann's it is a mistake to overstate the degree to which the power and financial resources of the state or the cultural predispositions of a country's citizens are able to determine the content of a scholarly community's ideas. States have always paid for foreign policy ideas, ranging from simple propaganda to sophisticated advice for policy-makers. These ideas are not, however, the type of ideas we refer to when we talk about international theories produced by scholars working in the discipline of IR. Disciplines have developed powerful institutional mechanisms to protect against nonacademic influences in the production of ideas, including peer review and the extended socialization of graduate training. While academic autonomy is always threatened by the influence of states and markets, to a very considerable degree these disciplinary institutional mechanisms reduce the likelihood that states can foster coherent national IR perspectives. States and markets merely become one among many influences that impact upon the course of theoretical development and debate. Moreover, the often dissimilar outlooks on the part of policy-makers and citizens in the countries in which scholarly disciplines are tolerated tends to augment academic autonomy rather than confine it. In part, this accounts for the enduring influence of theories that seek to promote international cooperation and peace in the United States, while other "American" theorists gravitate toward Realist, structural-Realist, Gramscian, or political-economy perspectives.

Fifth, technological advances erode the controlling effect of territorial cultures and states on scholarly ideas—even more so than in other areas of contemporary life. Universities have played a decisive role in the creation of the Internet. With the Internet scholarly collaboration can be almost as easy with colleagues abroad as with those in nearby cities. A glance at the small number of countries represented in the programs of the International Studies Association meetings will confirm that constraints imposed by distance persist. Nevertheless, the overall secular effect of technological innovation appears in the discipline of IR, as elsewhere, to undermine the potential influence of nationality and territoriality.

Sixth, Hoffmann's insightful article notwithstanding, it can be argued that there never have been national IRs and, therefore, there is no historical foundation upon which national approaches could now be built. Despite the importance of Hoffmann's focus on the links between the U.S. state, U.S. culture and IR theories, it would be a mistake to conclude that it is therefore best to treat IR theory as characterized significantly by the effects of nationality. It is not clear why we should attribute the degree of centralized impact these theorists and theories have as correlated most significantly with nationality. Those less Realist than Hoffmann might see them as located alternatively at the core of the world economy; or in the West; or at the imperial center; or at the center of the "free world"; or near the helm of the NATO alliance; or as tied to a Atlantic ruling class. This point is reinforced by the absence of any alternative center of "national" theories except, perhaps, the British, itself just as easily categorized with these alternative designations. Second, as Hoffmann himself acknowledged, key figures in the creation of "American" IR were European émigrés, including Morgenthau and Karl Deutsch, among others. The analytical utility of nationality, in this context, becomes blurred: which "nationality" in the case of Morgenthau or Deutsch, for example, does one attribute to the formation of their intellectual ideas?

In sum, there are good theoretical reasons to suppose that we will *not* see the emergence of significant national perspectives on international relations. This does not mean that there will not be variation across countries in the character of IR theorizing—but it does suggest that such variation is not likely to be correlated primarily with nationality. Middle power theorizing may differ from great power theorizing; or peripheral theorizing from core theorizing; or a distinctive IR may emerge from the former Second World—but these are not *national* distinctions. Moreover, there is no reason to suppose that differences in perspectives *between* countries will outweigh differences in perspectives *within* countries, or that similarities among IR communities *within* particular countries will outweigh similarities among particular IR communities *across* countries. Realists, liberals, feminists, Gramscian theorists and scholars working in other well-defined theoretical perspectives are likely to have more in common with their ideological/intellectual counterparts in other countries than with their compatriots working out of alternative perspectives. The failure of the interparadigm debate to focus on national differences despite its expected compatibility with an investigation of the effects of nationality on theorizing, is likely, then, to be due more to the greater hold of the ideological differences represented by the paradigms over theorists' loyalties than simple oversight.

Nor does this argument against the relevance of nationality imply that the type of sociology of knowledge questions asked by Hoffmann are irrelevant—on the contrary, the influence of post-positivism in IR suggests that such self-critical exploration of the knowledge producing process is likely to continue and be fruitful, but more sophisticated analyses of transnational epistemic communities or subnational policy networks are more likely to yield meaningful results than analyses that seek coherent and unified national knowledge-producing processes.

CANADIAN IR AS A CASE STUDY

Because I am discussing the development of ideas, the types of interpretive problems identified by post-positivists in the decisive empirical testing of hypotheses apply even more to my arguments rehearsed above than might be the case with some other types of assertions about the practice of international relations. Nevertheless, it is useful to provide some evidence, albeit cautiously, to confirm or refute the theoretical logic of the previous section.

An analysis of the Canadian case offers both disadvantages and advantages in exploring the effect of nationality on IR. On the one hand, the geographic, linguistic, cultural, political, economic, and strategic closeness of Canada to the United States makes it hard to generalize vis-à-vis other countries from a finding that Canadian nationality has little influence. On the other hand, there has historically been a vigorous nationalist sentiment in Canada, evident not only in acrimonious debates over free trade agreements with the United States, but also the way in which universities have been "Canadianized" through heavy government expenditures in the postwar period on new construction, research funding and hiring, and through the creation of legal restrictions on the hiring of "foreign scholars." In addition to their contribution to "Canadianization," these expenditures also set in place the necessary institutional structures that would have otherwise allowed the development of a specifically "Canadian IR" and thus Canadian IR theory.

With these hypotheses in mind, I start with an analysis of the responses to a questionnaire sent to academics teaching IR across Canada and assess the significance of these responses for the arguments made in the previous section.

The questionnaire, which was entitled "Is there a distinctively Canadian approach to IR?" was sent to full-time permanent teaching staff of international relations throughout Canada. It aimed to explore Canadian IR scholars' own perceptions of the influence of Canadian nationality. One might argue that the individuals surveyed may not themselves be aware of the influence of nationality over their own scholarship. This type of "false consciousness" argument, problematic at the best of times, is doubly dubious here because the people in question are by profession expected to be familiar with, and be able to explain, variations in international relations perspectives and the etiological development of intellectual ideas. Put differently, it is hard to see how a distinctively Canadian IR perspective could be produced if there was nothing that could be pointed to as holding together or distinguishing a community of Canadian IR scholars.

Before reporting on the responses to the questionnaire it is important to acknowledge its limitations. The 188 full-time permanent faculty members teaching IR at Canadian universities to which the questionnaire was directed are not the only set of people relevant in the production of Canadian IR perspectives. One might argue that graduate students, part-time instructors, or Canadians teaching abroad should be included, or that foreign nationals teaching IR in Canada should be excluded. Additionally, only fifty-eight responses (31%) were received. It must be emphasized, therefore, that this is not a comprehensive survey, nor can it be used to produce statistically rigorous measurements. It does, however, provide a better picture than would be possible based simply on intuition and personal impressions. Responses were received from all regions of Canada, from thirty of the forty-one universities to which letters were sent and from both senior and junior scholars.[3]

The first two questions asked respectively "Do you think that there is a distinctively Canadian approach to the study of international relations?" and "Have your ties to Canada influenced your own approach to IR?" Respondents were asked to check off one of three options. The results are summarized in table 5.1. The responses to question 1 indicate that a Canadian approach to IR, if it exists, is not well defined. Interestingly, the second question picks up a much stronger indication of the influence of nationality on IR in Canada.

Question 1 also followed up with an opportunity to provide a qualitative response to "If distinctive, how would you describe it?" and several themes emerge that help clarify the significance of the figures in

TABLE 5.1
Summary of Responses to Questions 1 and 2

		Yes, Definitely	Moderately	No	Total
Is there a distinctively Canadian approach to IR?	Count	5	37	16	58
	Percent	9%	64%	28%	100%
Have your ties to Canada influenced your own Approach to IR?	Count	25	22	12	59
	Percent	44%	37%	20%	100%

table 5.1 and the difference in the responses to the two questions. First, a number of respondents indicated that the distinctiveness was based, as Michael Tucker put it, "chiefly in terms of issue areas and focus rather than theoretical constructs." Similarly, Akira Ichikawa stated that "my belief that there is no distinctively Canadian approach to the study of IR hinges on the meaning of 'approach' (i.e., a general analytical strategy)but doesn't deny certain emphases—low policy, 'middlepowermanship', 'multilateralism,' for example—detectable in studies of IR by Canadians or in Canada." Or, as Fen Hampson noted, "if there is a 'Canadian' approach (and I'm not sure about it) it is one characterized by a concern for multilateral institutions (UN, regional organizations) and multilateral approaches to the management of global problems, conflict and trade." Others cited peacekeeping. Maureen Appel Molot comments, "clearly Canadians are less preoccupied with issues of hegemony."

Second, a set of respondents felt, paradoxically, that "if there is a Canadian approach it is defined by its eclecticism . . . there is no orthodoxy" (Paul Evans), a sentiment echoed in David Welch's view that there is "less grand theory or metatheory" but also that Canadian IR is "more heterodox metatheoretically than US or UK IR." George MacLean comments "short of describing it as fence-sitting, I would suggest that a balance of sorts is sought, drawing orthodoxy together with non-traditional approaches"—Blema Steinberg finds herself "somewhat more critical and less defensive in teaching U.S. foreign policy than her U.S. counterparts." Perhaps (at least at some "second-tier" universities) "more space exists to pose critical questions of mainstream thinking"

(Mark Neufeld). Rob Walker suggests that "the broader Canadian political economy tradition has reduced the influence of the U.S. IPE tradition in some places."

Third, and relatedly, Canadian distinctiveness was defined by a "greater sensitivity to interests/actions of countries other than the US" (Kal Holsti)—or put differently, there is "un regard moins ethnocentrique que la pensée politique américaine," Michel Duquette suggested. The British influence, in part because of Britain's former imperial role in Canada, is notable but Continental Europe, Latin America, Asia, Africa, and indeed the Arctic Innu and native influences were also cited.

Canada's distinctiveness is "perhaps a reflection of Canada's non–great power status rather than anything uniquely Canadian" (Tom Keating). Claire Cutler points to the importance of "Canada's position as a 'smaller' or 'weaker' partner to a hegemon" and suggests that "many Canadians have a close understanding of the impact of asymmetrical power relations and that this finds its way into their scholarship."

None of the above four elements of Canadian IR's distinctiveness make for a coherent, easily identifiable presence. As Alistair Edgar puts it, "the distinction is more in terms of what a Canadian approach is '*not*' rather than what it '*is*'—which puts IR study in line with much of the rest of Canadian life."[4] The image is one of openness and diversity, "une sensibilité multiculturelle" (Michel Duquette).

On the other hand, a number of respondents also pointed to more defined theoretical traditions as part of Canadian IR's distinctiveness. A number noted that Canadians are less quantitative and would concur with Helene Pellerin's view that Canadians are "more historical, if not historicist." Others suggested that Canadian IR was functionalist, more case-study oriented, more attentive to domestic sources of foreign policy, Grotian, or undergirded by "a reformist liberalist orientation" (W. Andy Knight).

In part, the distinctiveness derives from the Canadian state: concern with multilateralism reflects the orientation of the policy-making community (Fen Hampson, W. Andy Knight). In James F. Keeley's words,

> interactions with Canadians have been important to me, primarily through work I have done for the Department of Foreign Affairs in the area of controlling weapons of mass destruction. This has put me into contact with other Canadians similarly doing research for DFAIT, and much of my output of papers has been related to workshops, etc., arising in conjunction with these projects.[5]

The Canadian state is not the only one influencing the Canadian IR community however: for instance, another respondent noted his interactions with the U.S. state that resulted from his scholarship on terrorism.

Taken as a whole, then, the responses to questions 1 and 2 indicate that Canadian IR may be distinguished by openness to a variety of influences, domestic and international, a concern with particular issues such as multilateralism, less enthusiasm for Realism and more for liberal internationalism and less quantitative and more historical methodologies. Nevertheless, the prevailing view is that there is no coherent and sharply distinctive Canadian approach.

This does not mean, however, that one's location in Canada is irrelevant—on the contrary, most respondents felt that their ties to Canada were important. We have, then, an interesting paradox evident in the differing responses to questions 1 and 2: Canadian IR's distinctiveness is its nondistinctiveness. Scholars value being *in Canada* in part because they can more easily appreciate a diversity of *foreign influences* than might be the case in the United States. Can we call this an effect of nationality on IR theorizing? I return to this question below after considering the responses to the rest of the survey.

The survey also attempted via three other questions to gauge the cohesiveness and autonomy of the Canadian IR community. The first of these asked "Regarding the relative importance for you of the Canadian and foreign/international audiences that you seek to influence with your scholarly publications, roughly what proportion of your effort is expended on each (e.g., 60/40, 30/70, etc.)?" There was great variation in the response, but the average level of importance attributed to the Canadian and international audiences were 33 percent and 67 percent respectively.

The second of these questions asked "roughly what proportion of the material on your IR course outlines was chosen in part because of Canadian content?" The most frequent response was zero (13) but here too there was large variation and the average response was 19 percent.

The third of these questions was "what proportion of your collaborative interactions (conference participation, joint authorships, participation in edited volumes, collaborative research) are with Canadians as opposed to foreigners?" The average response here was 48 percent.

Despite the impossibility for respondents of estimating precisely the answers to any of the above three questions the figures are an indication of the perceived importance of Canadian connections in the production and dissemination of IR. They suggest a set of scholars who are, collectively, substantially "internationalized" in their networks of interaction. National allegiance plays a relatively small role in the selection of material used to educate Canadian IR students. Can we even speak of a "Canadian IR community" when foreign connections are more important than domestic ones, as would be suggested by the answers to these three questions? We return to this issue below.

The final question sought to assess the importance of nationality to respondents' scholarly identity by comparing it to other possible ways of identifying oneself. The question stated "please rank on a scale of 1–5 [from unimportant to very important] the following ways to differentiate approaches to indicate their relative importance to your scholarly identity, recognizing that there are overlaps and ambiguities in any such differentiating schemata." This was followed by a list of seven categories: nationality (Canadian, Quebecois . . .); IR subfield (international political economy, international law, international organization . . .); issue area (trade, arms control, environment . . .); major IR "paradigm" (Realist, liberal, world systems, feminist . . .); concept or research program (regimes, long cycles, hegemony . . .); regional focus (Europe, Asia-Pacific . . .); and epistemology or methodology (behavioralist, institutionalist, interpretive, rational choice, historicist . . .). Spaces were provided for the respondents to insert and rank other categories as well. Several respondents indicated that they either did not like or were not entirely clear on the significance of this question. Rob Walker, for instance, added two other categories, "theoretically interesting questions" and "politically interesting questions" and ranked them well above the other categories, adding that "it is not all that difficult to identify worthwhile scholarship whatever the 'approach.' Far too much energy is spent classifying such approaches, usually in a very crude way, and far too much boring research and writing is produced as a consequence." Similarly, David Long commented, "I guess I regard the only genuine scholarly identity as 'maverick.' Accepting any of the above is an admission that you have stopped thinking."

Nevertheless, fifty-seven respondents answered the question and the average scores appear in table 5.2.

TABLE 5.2
Scholarly Identities

Category	Average Score
IR subfield (PIE, IO . . .)	3.63
Issue area (trade, arms control . . .)	3.60
Region (Europe, Asia-Pacific . . .)	3.16
Epistemology or methodology	3.14
Major IR "paradigm" (realist, liberal . . .)	3.03
Concept or research program (regimes . . .)	2.71
Nationality (Canadian, Quebecois . . .)	2.13

These figures suggest that respondents are less likely to identify themselves as "Canadian IR scholars" than with some other designation, such as IPE scholars, arms control specialists, or Europeanists. However, these averages conceal much variation and a subset of respondents felt strongly about their Canadian scholarly identity: nine assigned nationality a value of 4 (none assigned a 5). This, then, corresponds with the other answers: nationality has *some* influence, but it is a modest one.

CONCLUSION

What lessons can we draw then from these Canadian scholars' impressions of the relevance of nationality, and do they lend support or not to the theoretical arguments made in the first part of this essay? I will make three analytical points in turn.

First, it is clear that there is no widely recognized Canadian approach to IR. While many individuals do perceive certain distinctive attributes of the Canadian study of IR this distinctiveness is felt by most to be only moderate. Moreover, the distinctiveness for many is a set of things that Canadian IR is not, or a particular mix of influences from outside Canada rather than an "approach" in the sense of a system of positive and coherent beliefs about the world. It would be difficult to argue that the overall impressions of the fifty-eight scholars surveyed are wrong: these are people whose job it is to be aware of contemporary thinking about IR. Moreover, echoing Benedict Anderson's well-known notion of the national as "imagined community," one could say that a national IR cannot only exist as a hidden essence or a vague and variegated sentiment, but can only be brought into being and be sustained by a shared imagining of what it is. It would be difficult to argue that this is present among Canadian IR scholars.

Second, it also seems clear, however, that location matters—in particular, it makes a difference whether one is "in Canada" or the United States. In part, this appears to be due to the types of state and cultural influences highlighted by Hoffmann in his analysis of the United States. The Canadian government, through its own policy-making inclinations, has some impact on Canadian IR scholars. Similarly, as one respondent put it, "l'approche canadienne reflète le nationalism canadien et ses ambiguités." Such influences provide support for the view that nationality does matter.

If nationality in this sense does matter, it seems clear that it is a paradoxical nationality: state influence is perceived as fostering a commitment not to the Canadian state itself but to multilateralism, and nationalism is seen not as a set of indigenous and self-contained shared beliefs positively defining the meaning of "Canadian," but rather, an awareness of a set of relationships and differences with citizens of other countries. This corresponds with the insights of theorists of globalization such as Roland Robertson and A. Appadurai who argue that contemporary nationalism is "relational" and that people define the nation increasingly in relationship to other nations or identities rather than as evolving from an imagined common past (Robertson, 1992, 293–311). This is both positive, in the sense of an awareness of new possibilities for collective self-expression stimulated by globalization, and negative, as a perceived need to construct a haven from the hazards associated with globalization. As such, contemporary nationalism is, paradoxically, an expression of the social presence of the global. Further, as suggested by the responses to the survey, this set of relationships is not free-floating, but is structured and historical: for Canada it is a set of relationships with the United States and the desire to draw on other relationships to offset the overwhelming power and influence that the U.S. represents.

To what degree is the Canadian experience likely to be comparable to that in other countries? This is a question, of course, that can only begin to be answered with larger efforts such as the project of which this book is an expression. It seems very possible, however, that Canadian scholars' experience parallels that of others similarly located at a social and spatial distance from the center of our contemporary world. One could interpret this locational effect as one of nationality, but if so, it is a nationality that is ambiguous, open, and only moderately distinctive.

NOTES

The author wishes to warmly thank the respondents to the survey. Research assistance on this project has been provided by Bill Hogg, Manisha Thomas, and Priscilla Parmar.

1. With respect to Realism, compare for instance Alexander Wendt's social constructivist but state-centric approach (Wendt, 1992), to the positivist Realist work analyzed by John Vasquez (Vasquez, 1983).

2. On reflexivity see the work of Ulrich Beck, Anthony Giddens, and Scott Lash (Beck, Giddens, and Lash, 1994). Reflexivity is, for Beck, not just reflection but "self-confrontation" (p. 5). For an application of the concept of reflexivity to IR, see Mark Neufeld (Neufeld, 1994, 11–35). Neufeld states that "theoretical reflexivity can be defined as reflection on the process of theorizing" (p. 13).

3. The eleven universities from which no responses were received included twenty IR scholars in total.

4. One senior Canadian scholar noted "Canadian IR scholars exhibit the same kind of attraction/repulsion vis-à-vis the U.S. that we see in the English-Canadian population as a whole: hate those Yanks, but love 'em and their good

works at the same time. Look at our referents of 'excellence' in scholarship: we bend over backwards to publish in U.S. journals. We rush to cite the latest 'discoveries' by US academics. We adopt their IR textbooks even while we grumble about their tendency to be written in the first person plural."

5. Rex Brynen similarly noted the effect of his involvement in the Canadian foreign policy process. Keeley distinguishes his work on nuclear proliferation from his work on international regimes. In the latter area "questions of Canadian identity scarcely arise."

REFERENCES

Appadurai, A. (1991). "Global Ethnoscapes: Notes and Queries for a Transnational Anthropology." In R. G. Fox (ed.), *Recapturing Anthropology: Working in the Present.* Santa Fe, N.M.: School of American Research Press, and Seattle University of Washington Press: 293–311.

Banks, Michael. (1985). "The Inter-Paradigm Debate." In M. Light and A. J. R. Groom (eds.), *International Relations: A Handbook of Current Theory.* London: Pinter: 7–26.

Beck, U., Anthony Giddens, and S. Lash. (1994). *Reflexive Modernization: Politics, Tradition and Aesthetics in the Modern Social Order.* Stanford: Stanford University Press.

Carr, E. H. (1939). *The Twenty Years' Crisis.* London: Macmillan.

Cox, Robert W. (1986). "Social Forces, States and World Order: Beyond International Relations Theory." in Robert O. Keohane (ed.), *Neorealism and Its Critics.* New York: Columbia University Press: 204–254.

Doyle, M. (1997). *Ways of War and Peace.* New York and London: W. W. Norton.

Hoffmann, Stanley. (1977). "An American Social Science: International Relations." *Daedalus* 106(3), 41–60.

Holsti, K. J. (1985). *The Dividing Discipline: Hegemony and Diversity in International Theory.* Boston: Allen & Unwin.

Kahler, M. (1993). "International Relations: Still an American Social Science?" In L. B. Miller and M. J. Smith (eds.), *Ideas and Ideals: Essays in Honor of Stanley Hoffmann.* Boulder, Colo.: Westview: 395–414.

Keohane, Robert O. (1988). "International Institutions: Two Approaches." *International Studies Quarterly* 32(4), 379–396.

Krasner, Stephen D. (ed.). (1983). *International Regimes.* Ithaca and London: Cornell University Press.

Kratochwil, F., and J. G. Ruggie. (1986). "International Organization: A State of the Art on the Art of the State." *International Organization* 40(4) (Autumn), 753–776.

Lapid, Yosef. (1989). "The Third Debate: On the Prospects of International Theory in a Post-Positivist Era." *International Studies Quarterly* 33(3) (September), 235–279.

Maghroori, R., and B. Ramberg (eds.). (1982). *Globalism versus Realism: International Relations' Third Debate.* Boulder, Colo.: Westview.

McGrew, A. G., and P. G. Lewis et al. (eds.). (1992). *Global Politics: Globalization and the Nation-State*. Cambridge: Polity.

Morgenthau, Hans. (1967). *Politics among Nations: The Struggle for Power and Peace*. 4th ed. New York: Alfred A. Knopf.

Neufeld, Mark. (1994). "Reflexivity and International Relations Theory." In C. T. Sjolander and W. S. Cox (eds.), *Beyond Positivism: Critical Reflections on International Relations*. Boulder, Colo.: Lynne Reiner: 11–35.

Robertson, R. (1992). *Globalization: Social Theory and Global Culture*. London: Sage.

Smith, Steve (ed.). (1985). *International Relations: British and American Perspectives*. Oxford: Basil Blackwell and the British International Studies Association.

Vasquez, J. A. (1983). *The Power of Power Politics: A Critique*. New Brunswick, N.J.: Rutgers University Press.

Viotti, Paul, and Mark Kauppi (eds.). (1987). *International Relations Theory: Realism, Pluralism, Globalism*. New York: Macmillan.

Wendt, Alexander. (1992). "Anarchy Is What States Make of It." *International Organization* 46(2), 391–426.

Wight, Martin. (1966). "Why Is There No International Theory." In H. Butterfield and M. Wight (eds.), *Diplomatic Investigations*. London: George Allen and Unwin: 17–34.

PART II

National and Transnational Identities in International Theory

CHAPTER 6

Hegemony and Autonomy in International Relations: The Continental Experience

A. J. R. Groom
and
Peter Mandaville

INTRODUCTION

The question of whether International Relations (IR) is still an American social science, as Stanley Hoffmann once so famously asserted (Hoffmann, 1977), invariably evokes different perspectives depending on the locale and the vantage point from which one views the discipline. Much like looking through a telescope, one's perspective and view of the disciplinary landscape can be as much a function of how one positions the instrument, which end they look through, and whether or not the instrument is placed to the blind eye, as it can a function of the disciplinary landscape itself. Perspective in IR is everything, no less so when dealing with the esoteric nuances of intellectual traditions whose borders are often porous and prone to movement and repositioning. This essay takes its cue from the metaphor of the telescope and searches wide and far, frequently repositioning the lens, its focus, and the direction in which it is pointed, to build an image of the multitude of national influences that historically went to make up the discipline of IR and which now define its various foci and theoretical tools. Contra the notion of "American hegemony" our survey shows a robust and increasingly influential European set of influences that have historically, and more recently, informed the disciplinary concerns and character of IR.

A GLOBAL HISTORIOGRAPHY
OF INTERNATIONAL RELATIONS

From the heartland of American neorealism, IR may seem to be an "American social science," particularly if the eye to the telescope can see no further than the boundaries of North America. Seen, however, from the confines of the contemporary European Union (EU), nothing fundamental would be lost if North American IR were simply to shut up shop and vanish from the purview of intellectual life. Everything that is of merit in North American IR, and there is much of very great merit in quality and impressive quantity, can be found too in EU IR—and more besides. Moreover, there is little difference in quality, although the quantity may be significantly less. Dross can be found everywhere. What's more, if the boundaries of the EU are to be extended eastward, to embrace all of Central and Eastern Europe, we move into the historic heartland of another intellectual tradition in IR—the fructuous intellectual breeding ground of the Marxist-Leninist approach. This tradition, together with the legal approach in France and Mediterranean Europe and a long tradition of administrative science, combined with a venerable background in area studies begotten by empire, however dubiously, are added strengths in diversity. To be provocative, if forced in a Darwinian selection to choose, it might be better to preserve European IR rather than its North American counterpart on grounds of comparable quality but much greater diversity. Such a question, however, denies the complex interdependencies of an intellectual world that is, in many ways, one, albeit that this world too has had in the past both its centers and peripheries. Today, however, what is remarkable is the degree of its homogeneity. But was this always the case?

Contemporary postmodern approaches aside, it is not difficult to conceive of the intellectual history of IR in terms of three traditions. Among the great names of European political thought, we can cite Hobbes, Grotius, and Kant as symbolizing these three general approaches (Bull, 1977). After the Second World War, Martin Wight characterized them as Realists, rationalists and revolutionists (Wight, 1991). More recently, a similar categorization has been invoked; Realist, pluralist or world society approaches, and structuralists (Banks, 1985), acknowledging thereby *inter alia* the Marxist tradition. This overall conceptual framework has proven useful as a guide to conceiving of the three generative traditions that have guided intellectual development in IR, and all of them owe little to North American IR.

Indeed, the disciplinary background of IR emanates from numerous corners, with most of them outside of North America and nearly all of them from traditions and approaches whose genealogy is distinctly

European. For the founding professors of IR this background was drawn, for example, in North America from international law and in the United Kingdom (UK) from diplomatic history. On the European Continent both these traditions prevailed, but with a predilection for law. So too, the founding professors inherited from the nineteenth century the three intellectual traditions with the balance of power, as institutionalized in the Congress and Concert System illustrating the Realist approach. The growth of liberal internationalism, and, particularly, the activities of intergovernmental and nongovernmental organizations and other nonstate actors as well as the attempts at creating systems of arbitration and arms control in the second part of the nineteenth century, exemplified the pluralist approach. And the structuralist approach could be found in the newly founded traditions of Marxism and geopolitics. The influence of North America in these developments, while important, was certainly not hegemonic or even primary.

In the nineteenth century the United States government kept clear, ostensibly, of the machinations of the European Great Powers, although it acted in a Realist manner in the Americas and Pacific. As the bourgeois liberal reformists began to exert their influence there was a strong American participation in the meetings of concerned individuals and private societies. Yet there was, in the Americas, little on the scale of the founding of the International Committee of the Red Cross or of the Anti-Slavery Movement as personified in Europe. There was, however, a major American contribution in the area of arbitration and the growth of mediation as a means of managing disputes. The Alabama Case between Britain and the United States was a case in point. Moreover, there was a growing willingness to accept legal obligations to submit to arbitration in the Americas, which was also a tribute to this pluralist liberal internationalist approach. On the other hand, in the structuralist revolutionary framework there is little to be found. Nevertheless, the writings of Admiral Mahan on the use of sea power by the British and earlier the Romans had great influence on the continent, especially in Germany, and gave credence to a different form of structuralism—geopolitics (Mahan, 1965). The great influence of the United States was not to come until later, principally in the philosophy and political drive to establish the League of Nations on the foundation of collective security, and, also, in the major role played by the United States in its thrust for arms control as exemplified by the Washington Naval Treaty. Here indeed the United States had a leading role and, it is worth noting, many reluctant European followers.

Such ambitions were naturally important for a country which had built itself from a group of often disparate and not always cooperating colonies to be the dominating power on the North American continent, and, on the basis of that experience, now proposed to create a new world order. The apogee of this approach of social engineering and institution building, based on the tenets of liberal internationalism, gave rise to the founding of IR as a discipline, both in the United States and the UK. This, it should be noted, was the foundation of the first consensus in the field.

For the British, and especially the Welsh, it has long been a matter of pride that the first Chair in IR in a modern university system was that funded by Lord David Davies at Aberystwyth in the University of Wales as the Woodrow Wilson Chair of International Politics.[1] In the aftermath of the First World War a number of chairs were founded in Britain, not only at Aberystwyth but also at Oxford, the London School of Economics, and at Chatham House (later to become the Royal Institute of International Affairs), which was established as a link between the academic world and that of government in pursuit of the "scientific study" of what was, and still remains, part of the agenda of the day, namely, the understanding of the *causes of war* and the *conditions for peace*. In the United States, chairs were also founded along with the sister institute of Chatham House, the Council on Foreign Relations.

Although much of the energy that led to the founding of these chairs and to the idea of progressive rationalism and social engineering had been shared widely throughout the continent, particularly in France, in the Low Countries, and in Switzerland, Germany and Italy, IR as a formal discipline did not flourish, except in Geneva where the Graduate Institute of International Studies was founded in 1927. The institute, which received a considerable sum of foundation money from the United States, although its directors were from France and Switzerland, quickly became a haven for refugees from fascism in all branches of international studies including history, politics, economics, and law. But despite its intellectual antecedents, the rise of fascism as a dominant political doctrine in Europe put liberal internationalism very much on the defensive, save for France, Britain, the Low Countries, Switzerland, and parts of Scandinavia where it was resisted. Elsewhere, all branches of political science, and not least IR, were stifled except where they were used as a prop for expansionist and racist theories, as in the use of geopolitics by the Munich School led by Haushofer to support Hitler's policies of *Drang Nach Osten* and racism. The political machinations of Europe and the War, it needs hardly be said, circumvented academic pursuits such that Britain and the United States benefited immensely from the intellectual plight and physical flight of scholars such as Georg Schwarzenberger and Hans Morgenthau (Schwarzenberger, 1964; Morgenthau, 1985), who, together with E. H. Carr (1939), were the intellectual pivots of the second consensus in IR on Realism (see the discussion in Brown, this volume).

A constellation of factors like the rise of fascism, social Darwinist theorists, the depression, the Second World War, along with the Cold War, conspired by the mid-1940s and 1950s for a climate in which liberal internationalism was found wanting. The dark tenets of a Hobbesian world of anarchy, self-help in a security dilemma and the drive to dominate came to blinker intellectual life. It was not that such phenomena did not exist—they did, and in plenitude—but that other phenomena were ignored. The pendulum, as perhaps in the 1920s, had once again swung too far. What cannot be gainsaid, however, is that Realist IR was now overwhelmingly dominant and, more importantly, dominant in the United States where the "subject" had essentially become based both in terms of the sheer numbers of the practitioners who theorized, studied, and taught international relations and, also, very often in terms of the quality of the work produced. Moreover, as the subject spread, it spread very much as the "American science of IR," whether in Africa, India, or elsewhere in the English-speaking world. On the European continent the Germans were learning their political science and IR from the Americans, while in many other countries IR had retreated into the rather arid framework of faculties of law. Some notable figures joined the "American debate" such as Raymond Aron (1967), and while there were some in Britain, such as Martin Wight who had a wider view imbued with Christianity, or who were diplomatic historians of an old school (Butterfield and Wight, 1966), their influence was nevertheless slight and the debate dominated by "American" theorists and practitioners—but not for long.

There were, of course, a number of challenges to Realism as the hegemonic discourse of the "American debate." Importantly, these mostly originated from outside the United States and by their very success in establishing alternative theoretical vistas were not insignificant factors in undermining the hegemony of the "American discipline of IR." John Burton, David Mitrany, Karl Deutsch, and James Rosenau, to name but a few (Burton, 1968, 1972; Mitrany, 1966, 1975; Deutsch, 1963, 1966; Rosenau, 1967, 1969), developed transnationalist ideas in different but related ways. Pluralist approaches were again in favor, albeit more popular outside the United States than within its national confines. Rosenau, for example, provided an eloquent and powerful indigenous American voice to these perspectives, although he was often a lone voice inside an American academic establishment still embellished with a hard-nose Realist ethos. And while neither Burton or Mitrany were British, both propagated their ideas from within the British IR establishment while Deutsch moved between the old and new worlds. The Realist approach also engendered a practical and theoretical response in the form of "nonalignment" under the intellectual authority of writers such as Leo Mates and A. P. Rana in India (Mates, 1972; Rana, 1979). Structural theories also reemerged as fashionable, emanating, initially, from Latin America but gradually spreading throughout the Third World then to Europe and eventually to North America where a number of prominent scholars embraced the dependency/structuralist approach, but only after currency had been given to these ideas elsewhere.[2] Ironically, rather as Marx and Lenin had predicted, the road to the citadels of capitalism, or rather its intellectual fortresses, was through the Third World.

A further challenge to Realism and thus the "American discipline" came from historical sociology. Leading figures in this area operated on both sides of the Atlantic, such as the British writer Michael Mann (Mann, 1986, 1993). Curiously, one area in which the challenge to Realism was strongest was in fact dominated, at times almost exclusively, by scholars from the United States; namely in the development of integration theory. Although the phenomenon was European, it posed a major anomaly for Realist theory. The intellectual lead in broaching this new phenomenon was essentially American, as the impact of the likes of Ernst Haas and Leon Lindberg attests (Haas, 1964; Lindberg, 1963). Nevertheless, on the whole what we can discern is that the cutting edge of IR in the 1960s and later was not only in the United States but elsewhere and, notably, beyond the confines of the developed world. If there had been an "American social science of IR," it was a short-lived phenomenon.

But what of the present situation? A quick perusal of the intellectual efforts of current-day theorists reveals a vibrant, perhaps dominant, non-American intellectual community. The high priests of both post-modernism and critical theory, such as Foucault and Habermas (Foucault, 1968; Habermas, 1972), for example, are not American, but those who have developed their ideas in the context of IR are mainly Anglo-Americans (Brown, 1994). Postmodernism, however, is likely to be a passing phase if only because it has nowhere to lead or practical future to offer. Postmodern theorists are thus not the best candidates by which to measure the pulse of those whom predominate in the discipline of IR and who provide it with intellectual nourishment. The postmodernist "turn" is itself on the wane and seems unlikely to gain currency in IR beyond the philosophical predilections of some, usually Finnish, Nordic scholars.

Critical theory, however, is an entirely different matter, since its manifest aim is liberation set within an historical context. It abjures us to be aware of and take seriously history and the intersubjective construction of meaning, norms, and identities, but without denying foundations and thus the postmodern tendency to deconstruct everything into dusty rubble. Its intellectual contributions thus hold out great promise. Yet its practitioners and principal theorists hail as much, if not more so, from outside the United States as they do from the critical voices that are now vocal within the United States.[3]

If we consider some of the principal subfields of IR at the present time we can see that there is a healthy mix of leading figures from the United States and elsewhere. In normative theory the thrust is as much in Britain as in the United States, but somewhat strangely, there appears not to be a strong interest on the continent. Much of the critical and postmodern literatures in IR are today more likely to come from Britain, or the anglophone peripheries, as they are from the United States. In international organization there is a clear division between the Anglo-Americans and the continental legal tradition, with scholars such as Marie-Claude Smouts (1995) bridging the divide. Conflict research, on the other hand, has had a very strong impulse from Europe, notably in Scandinavia where Johan Galtung[4] was one of the founding fathers, in the Netherlands from the Groningen School, in Germany with a long-standing and important contribution of the Hessen Institute, in France with Gaston Bouthoul (1962), and, not least, in Britain with a group lead by John Burton and others (Burton, 1969). International political economy (IPE) also has a long history in Britain, which has produced its "Mother Superior," Susan Strange (Strange, 1988), while the fundamental contribution of the Latin Americans has already been mentioned. Strategic studies was, for a long time, an American preserve with important contributions, but of a like ilk, from Britain and Australia. A different voice was heard from France, where one can conjure up names such as Gallois, Beaufre and, in a different context, Regis Debray (Gallois, 1961; Beaufre, 1965; Debray, 1967). While political geography has been kept alive by the French as much as anyone, foreign policy analysis, on the other hand, is very clearly a North American phenomenon. Feminist approaches to IR constitute an integral part of whatever hegemony the United States has in the field of IR generally (Light and Halliday, 1994). Harold and Margaret Sprout deserve our thanks for keeping the ecological aspects of human affairs on the agenda (Sprout, 1965), but environmental politics is well established in universities in Europe, as well as in practice through Green political parties.

If there has been a recent resurgence of uniquely American centered research this, obviously, has been in terms of the incessant debates surrounding neorealism, which has generated a veritable cottage industry over the last two decades and dominated by the work of Kenneth Waltz, Robert Keohane, and Stephen Krasner (Waltz, 1979; Keohane, 1991; Krasner, 1983). Yet this has been a largely North American phenomenon that has not been transplanted to Europe, or indeed, elsewhere. Outside of the United States, Waltz and Keohane are much more respected for the works of their youth (Waltz, 1959; Keohane and Nye, 1971).

The often nationally or regionally confined nature of much debate in IR, however, cannot be attributed solely to epistemological proclivities or cultural traditions alone. Language, too, has played, and continues to play, an important role. A great deal of the work of continental scholars is only known in Britain and the United States, for example, if it is translated into English. Thereby hangs a structural difficulty since it is likely that the work of continental scholars will be translated *only* if it concerns the central debates of the English-speaking world, either conceptually, methodologically, or in terms of substantive issue. It is thus, by extension, part of the American social science of IR, and to a lesser extent the British adjunct to it. We pick up, and in this instance, translate, that which we know, and we know that which we understand, or which is taken back to Europe from North America by graduate students and visiting lecturers. What we miss all too often is that which is hard to find because we do not know what we are looking for.

But is there something out there beyond that contained in the repositories of the English-speaking world? We know that there is a legal tradition in the study of IR in much of continental Europe, and indeed, Latin America. We know that there is a tradition of public administration studies and we also know that there is a rich tradition of area studies in the research institutes of the old imperial Powers of Britain, France, Italy, and the Netherlands. Where, then, are we in continental Europe now?

IR is strong in France, Germany, the Netherlands, Scandinavia, Austria, and Switzerland, and it is gaining strength in Italy, Spain, Greece, and Turkey. In Eastern Europe IR is weak, as is political science generally in that part of the continent. In the past, part of the general problem was a lack of institutionalization, in the sense that IR was part of a broad political science faculty or a law faculty. Those who taught it were distributed in penny packets around the faculties, research institutes, and the like. In many instances, there was not a critical mass, albeit cumulatively the number of individuals involved was significant. This situation is now changing with a growing professionalization of the discipline in Europe. Two pan-European conferences have been held of IR specialists, each of which attracted some five hundred participants from all parts of Europe and from different generations and genders. The European Standing Group for IR of ECPR circulates a newsletter of some three thousand copies, a *European Journal of International Relations* has been established and there are a number of English-language journals, especially in Scandinavia. Moreover, there is a growth in new professional IR journals in different languages in Europe that go beyond policy analysis. In Scandinavia, France, and Germany, for example, new professional IR associations have sprung up, or coherent IR sections in the broader political science associations have been established. A similar association in East Central Europe is in the process of formation. The North American International Studies Association (ISA), then, now has some *interlocuteurs valables*.

SURVEYING THE TRENDS

In part, as a means of attempting to map recent and present trends in the study of international relations, the authors of this paper have undertaken a quick, and, admittedly, dirty and very unprofessional survey of continental IR. A questionnaire was devised and sent to some 250 scholars on the continent, of whom 50 replied. Although the scholars were drawn from every country on the continent, the target methodology was less than scientific, with prospective respondents drawn from personal address books and business cards acquired at conferences. They do not represent a fair sample, and therefore the actual figures of responses to our questions will not be given because they would be misleading. What follows, therefore, as with what went before, is an intensely personal and subjective interpretation, the prime justification of which is that it may give rise to some testable hypotheses that could then be followed by a methodologically respectable survey and analysis.

The point has already been made that continental writing published in English may not be fully representative, because in order to be published in English it must, to some extent, reflect an Anglo-American discourse or the interests of those who are attracted to that discourse. The tip of an iceberg is no reliable indicator of the shape of its massive bulk below the surface. While the United States has its personalities and barons, such as Francis Fukuyama and Keohane, Britain has its eccentrics, such as Wight, and the continent has intellectuals such as Raymond Aron. The French contribution to IR theory, apart from Aron who was very much in the Realist tradition of American strategic studies, has been particularly apparent in the writings of Merle, Smouts, and Badie (Merle, 1988; Smouts and Badie, 1992). In the area of strategic studies and war, the names of Gallois, Beaufre, Debray, and Bouthoul, have already been mentioned, to which should be added those of Klein and Hassner (Klein, 1987; Hassner, 1995), but there are contributors in other domains too, notably in political geography and in political economy, such as the work of François Perroux (Perroux, 1984). It is particularly noteworthy that in area studies French scholars have the happy ability to fuse together conceptual thinking and detailed empirical work. This is a facility that also marks the quality press in France, such as *Le Monde*, and in the German-language press, such as the *Neue Zürcher Zeitung* and *Süddeutsche Zeitung* in a manner that cannot be matched by English-language broadsheets.

In Germany political science was decimated by the Nazis, and as the subject was reestablished in universities it came under heavy American influence. This has now passed and there are many names to conjure with, such as Czempiel, Rittberger, Albrecht, and Senghaas (Czempiel, 1981; Rittberger, 1993; Albrecht, 1986; Senghaas, 1988). The eminence of the Dutch in the early stages of peace research has been noted earlier, as has the immense contribution of the Scandinavians. In Southern Europe the writings of classic political scientists such as Gramsci, Pareto, and Mosca wield a contemporary influence beyond the Italian peninsula, and contemporary Italian IR has broken the legalistic cage as the writings of Bonanate and Attina will attest (Bonanate, 1992; Attina, 1989). Young scholars of great talent are manifesting themselves in Southern Europe, not least at the European University Institute in Florence, but also elsewhere in Italy, Spain, Greece, and in Turkey. Nascent programs are now also underway in Cyprus and Malta, and centers of excellence are emerging in some of the former socialist countries, such as in the Central European University and in Slovenia. But what did the fifty respondents to our questionnaire themselves wish to bring to our attention?

During the past decade there has been a change in the location of training of young scholars in IR on the continent. Whereas the traditional pattern of studying abroad in the United States, France, Britain and Russia continues, it does so to a lesser extent if only because the development of the subject on the continent, albeit unevenly, has now furnished the possibility for high-level training in local universities and research institutes. To this extent, there is no particular pattern, since it is now no longer necessary to go abroad to study to make a "successful" career in IR, although this may still be helpful in Greece and Turkey. This is one of the manifestations of the weakening or decline of North American hegemony in the field. A North American, French, British or Russian period of postgraduate training is no longer a *rite de passage*. While it is true that many continental scholars now write in English, they do it, not so much to break into the Anglo-American debate, although this is a factor, but because English has become the lingua franca of social science. Indeed, much postgraduate teaching and training, as well as research, takes place in English in continental universities and research institutes. In a sense too, money talks, in that the large American foundations are far more likely to give funding to a research project in English than one in another language. One of our respondents suggested that the real problem is not American or British hegemony, but rather, the overwhelming predominance of the English language in a discipline that lays claims to a global vision. Several of our respondents also noted that in some senses the use of English destroys the nuance of their thought and often leads to a loss of subtlety and insight. Because it imposes upon them the structures and thought patterns of a different culture, many feel that they cannot give the best of themselves. "There is a connection between language and thought," notes one respondent, "and IR would be impoverished as a worldwide undertaking if all important ideas were thought out in English." The point was also made that it is a matter of professional responsibility for scholars in a discipline such as IR to be aware of contributions from colleagues in other parts of the world.

There is no particular concentration of issue areas or subfields of IR in particular parts of the continent, although there are obvious regional strengths such as peace and conflict research in Scandinavia and Germany. The spread is, however, evening out in this field with centers in Spain, France, the Low Countries, Switzerland, Austria, and beyond.

Quite a lot of work in IR, particularly teaching, is hidden because it is not given an independent format in the shape of a degree program. There are, therefore, relatively few degree courses in IR at the undergraduate or postgraduate level designated as such, although there are exceptions in Greece, Turkey, and Russia. The separation of IR was itself an Anglo-Saxon development, reflecting a belief that the discipline was intellectually healthy, rich, and different enough to stand on its own (this, of course, is a highly contestable proposition. See, for example, the discussion in Griffiths and O'Callaghan in this volume). This attitude does not tend to obtain elsewhere and, on the whole, such courses are taught under the rubric of political science or law, but they are taught as IR courses. The texts used in such courses had in the past a strong influence from the United States and Britain, with some clear exceptions in France and Germany. This situation is now changing because even indigenous texts, which may have been in the past clones of the Anglo-American literature, are no longer so. New indigenous nonimported textbooks are arising, most notably, for example, in France and Russia, which reflect a very different experience compared to that of a world seen exclusively through the lens of a superpower.

One counterintuitive indicator gleaned through our survey, was the substantial number of female academic staff and postgraduate students in Spain, Greece, and the former Yugoslavia when contrasted with a low percentage in Norway, Switzerland, Netherlands, and Denmark. It may well be that in more traditional countries the university world provides upwardly mobile females with an easier career track than other professions or activities in their own societies, but such a comment could be more a desire to explain a counterintuition, and thus to reject it, than a valid argument.

The predominance of English as a medium of expression is reflected in the indication that when scholars do publish abroad they publish in journals in Britain, the United States, and Scandinavia, which are English-medium journals. This is probably an indicator of the decline of French and Russian as major languages for IR. Some respondents also felt that the provenance of many major journals gave North American colleagues a certain advantage in determining the agendas and debates of the discipline. Likewise, continental scholars visit conferences or colloquia in Britain and the United States, at least annually, although Greeks, Turks, and Eastern Europeans indicated a significantly higher rate of participation in such conferences and colloquia, demonstrating, perhaps, a type of center-periphery intellectual relationship in terms of IR conferences at least. In the case of East Europeans this may be partly explained by their previously exotic allure and the present travails of their countries, as well as their lack of access to information technology facilities. On the whole Germans, Scandinavians, and Dutch have good access to IT facilities, although one French respondent did note a lag on the arrival of e-mail facilities.

On the question of an Anglo-American hegemony in IR many of our respondents accepted some degree of initial influence, except, perhaps, in France, but the time of this has long since passed. Nevertheless, several also pointed to Britain and the United States as the primary sources of conceptual and theoretical approaches to IR. Interestingly, it was acknowledged that this influence had enabled scholars in the field to assert their identity as IR scholars in their home countries, sometimes in an institutional form. There was also some acknowledgment of French influence in this regard. Now, however, whatever hegemony that existed, and it was North American not British hegemony, has lessened to an exchange between equals, at least in quality if not in quantity. When asked whether any North American hegemony was welcomed, respondents split almost equally, with a clear rejection by the French and Germans. Interestingly, our continental respondents saw Britain primarily in European terms and as a major challenger to North American hegemony. This raises the interesting point that while it might have made sense to think of IR as an "Anglo-American" subject in the interwar period, and as one in which the United States dominated in the immediate postwar decades with Britain and Australia playing a minor role, this was certainly not the case from the mid-60s onward when Britain joined the continent in a process of intellectual emancipation from North American hegemony. What, perhaps, we experience today, then, is a position of "complex interdependence" between Western European and North American IR. Within this new multiplural intellectual world, the British have a distinctive voice, but so do the French, and increasingly the Germans.

Our respondents also looked to the future, and suggested that this will be characterized by increasing interdisciplinarity, with greater emphasis on the role of transnational nonstate actors such as social movements and humanitarian NGOs. Others spoke of a new focus on area studies centered upon emerging regional regime systems such as the EU and the OSCE. Some national distinctive voices are certainly valued, but set amid a nascent notion of a European approach to IR. Indeed, a number of respondents felt that IR has a key role to play in "converting Europeanization into everyday academic life."

We thus return to our starting point. What hegemony? There were certainly traditions of a positivistic approach in the pragmatic Anglo-American manner compared to the legal-administrative approach on the European continent. There were also differences in patterns of institutionalization of the discipline that tended to mask what was going on in some continental countries. There was also in some countries the devastating effects on intellectual life of the rise of fascism. Perhaps, however, what is very striking has been the isolation of three distinctive traditions, that of the Anglo-Americans, that of the French, and that of the Russians. What is exciting is that this polarization and isolation has broken down. There is now a nascent "European IR community" that is alive and well and living, for the most part, in the EU. It has the advantage of easy access to the glories of North American academia, but at the same time it can dig deeply into its national intellectual traditions conceived within a broader European framework. The Europeanization of IR is a notion whose time has come, and it interacts on a somewhat separate but largely equal basis with North American IR. There are, then, no hegemonies, something that may also be true beyond the confines of the EU and North America. May this continue.

NOTES

1. We should note that an important precursor was Emily Greene Balch who taught courses in international politics and economics at Wellesley College in the United States from 1896 to 1918. Dismissed from her post at Wellesley on account of her pacifism, Balch went on to win the Nobel Peace Prize in 1946 for her work with the Women's International League for Peace and Freedom. We are indebted to Craig Murphy for bringing this to our attention.

2. An initial impulse came from the work of the United Nations Economic Commission for Latin America under the direction of Raoul Prebisch.

3. See, for example, the discussion in Neufeld in this volume, who makes the observation of how central Canada has been as a national confine for producing some of the leading critical and feminist theorists of IR.

4. Galtung, a highly prolific writer, was also instrumental in forming the influential *Journal of Peace Research*.

REFERENCES

Albrecht, U. (1986). *Internationale Politik*. Munich: Oldenburg Verlag.

Attinà, F. (1989). *La politica internazionale contemporanea*. Milan: Angeli.

Aron, Raymond. (1967). *Peace and War*. London: Weidenfeld and Nicholson.

Badie, B., and M. C. Smouts. (1992). *Le retournement du monde*. Paris: Dalloz.

Banks, Michael. (1985). "The Inter-Paradigm Debate." In A. J. R. Groom and Margot Light (eds.), *International Relations: A Handbook of Current Theory*. London: Pinter: 7–26.

Beaufre, A. (1965). *Deterrence and Strategy*. London: Faber.

Bonanate, L. (1992). *Etica e politica internazionale*. Turin: Einaudi.

Bouthoul, G. (1962). *Le phénomène-guerre*. Paris: Payot.

Brown, Chris. (1994). "Critical Theory and postmodernism in International Relations." In Margot Light and A. J. R. Groom (eds.), *Contemporary International Relations: A Guide to Theory*. London: Pinter: 56–68.

Bull, Hedley. (1977). *The Anarchical Society*. London: Macmillan.

Burton, John. (1969). *Conflict and Communication*. London: Macmillan.

Burton, John. (1968). *Systems, States, Diplomacy and Rules*. London: Cambridge University Press.

Burton, John. (1972). *World Society*. London: Cambridge University Press.

Butterfield, Herbert, and Martin Wight (eds.). (1966). *Diplomatic Investigations*. London: George Allen and Unwin.

Carr, E. H. (1939). *The Twenty Years' Crisis*. London: Macmillan.

Czempiel, E. O. (1981). *Internationale Politik*. Paderborn: Ferdinand Schöningh.

Debray, R. (1967). *Revolution in the Revolution?* Hammondsworth, U.K.: Penguin.

Deutsch, Karl. (1966). *Nationalism and Social Communication*. Cambridge, Mass.: MIT Press.

Deutsch, Karl. (1963). *The Nerves of Government*. New York: Free Press.

Foucault, Michel. (1969). *L'archéologie du savoir*. Paris: Gallimard.

Gallois, P. (1961). *The Balance of Terror*. Boston: Houghton-Mifflin.

Haas, Ernst. (1964). *Beyond the Nation State*. Stanford: Stanford University Press.

Habermas, Jürgen. (1972). *Knowledge and Human Interests*. London: Heinemann.

Hassner, P. (1995). *La violence et la paix: De la bombe atomique au nettoyage ethnique*. Paris: Esprit.

Hoffmann, Stanley. (1977). "An American Social Science: International Relations." *Daedalus* 106(3), 41–59

Keohane, Robert O. (ed.). *Neorealism and Its Critics*. New York: Columbia University Press.

Keohane, Robert O., and Joseph S. Nye (eds.). (1972). *Transnational Relations and World Politics*. Cambridge, Mass.: Harvard University Press.

Klein, J. (1987). *Sécurité et désarmament en Europe*. Paris: IFRI-Economica.

Krasner, Stephen (ed.). (1983). *International Regimes*. Ithaca: Cornell University Press.

Light, Margot, and Fred Halliday. (1994). "Gender and International Relations." In A. J. R. Groom and Margot Light (eds.), *Contemporary International Relations: A Guide to Theory*. London: Pinter: 45–55.

Lindberg, L. (1963). *The Political Dynamics of European Economic Integration*. Stanford: Stanford University Press.

Mahan, A. T. (1965). *The Influence of Sea Power upon History*. London: Methuen.

Mann, M. (1986). *The Sources of Social Power*. Vol. I. Cambridge: Cambridge University Press.

Mann, M. (1993). *The Sources of Social Power*. Vol. II. Cambridge: Cambridge University Press.

Mates, L. (1972). *Nonalignment Theory and Current Policy*. Dobbs Ferry, N.Y.: Oceana.

Merle, M. (1988). *Sociologie des relations internationales*. Paris: Dalloz.

Mitrany, David. (1966). *A Working Peace System*. Chicago: Quadrangle.

Mitrany, David. (1975). *The Functional Theory of Politics*. London: Martin Robertson.

Morgenthau, Hans J. (1985). *Politics among Nations*. New York: Alfred Knopf.

Perroux, F. (1984). *A New Concept of Development*. New York: UNESCO.

Rana A. P. (1979). *The Imperatives of Non-Alignment*. New Delhi: Macmillan.

Rittberger, Volker (ed.). (1993). *Regime Theory and International Relations*. Oxford: Clarendon Press.

Rosenau, James N. (ed.). (1967). *The Domestic Sources of Foreign Policy*. New York: Free Press.

Rosenau, James N. (1969). *Linkage Politics*. New York: Free Press.

Schwarzenberger, G. (1964). *Power Politics*. London: Stevens.

Senghaas, D. (1988). *Konfliktformationen im internationalen System*. Frankfurt: Suhrkamp Verlag.

Smouts, M. C. (1995). "France and the UN System." In F. A. Chadwick, G. M. Lyons, and J. E. Trent (eds.), *The United Nations System: The Policies of Member States*. Tokyo: United Nations University Press.

Sprout, H., and M. Sprout. (1965). *The Ecological Perspective on Human Affairs*. Princeton: Princeton University Press.

Strange, Susan. (1988). *States and Markets*. London: Pinter.

Waltz, Kenneth N. (1979). *Theory of International Politics*. Reading, Mass.: Addison-Wesley.

Wight, Martin. (1991). *International Theory: The Three Traditions*. Edited by Gabriele Wight and Brian Porter. Leicester, U.K.: Leicester University Press.

CHAPTER 7

Tales That Textbooks Tell: Ethnocentricity and Diversity in American Introductions to International Relations

Kim Richard Nossal

INTRODUCTION

Although quarrels over theory in International Relations (IR) loom large in academic debates, it is worth remembering that these quarrels actively involve only a tiny percentage of the professoriate. There are thousands of postsecondary instructors of IR all over the world; but few of them actively contribute to the theoretical debates that are the focus of the contributions to this volume. The reality is that international theory is "produced" by an exceedingly small number of scholars, mostly English-speaking, and mostly based in American universities. The rest tend either to "consume" that theory, implicitly or explicitly, in their writing, or simply ignore the theoretical "produce" altogether.

Yet while most members of the IR professoriate do not take an active role in the debate over IR theorizing, there can be little doubt that the thousands of instructors who walk into classrooms, seminar rooms, and lecture halls all over the world each August, September, October, or February to teach courses that seek to introduce students to international relations are all engaged in IR "theorizing"—that is, constructing the world of international relations for their students in ways that are more or less systematic. However, we tend to overlook the fact that the way in which instructors introduce their students to the world of world politics—reflected in their course outlines, syllabi, and lecture schedules—is by its very nature "theoretical," even if the instructor remains totally (blissfully?) unaware of the theoretical machinations that mark the IR field. Likewise, what instructors ask (or demand) that their students read is of necessity "theoretical," even if not a single item on the reading list is explicitly about IR theory.

This is particularly true when an instructor assigns his or her students an IR textbook (as opposed to a book which might not have been written as a textbook but which is assigned as "required reading" to a course). We do not usually think of IR textbooks as works of theory, or as contributions to the broader debates that so persistently engage scholars in the discipline. But it can be argued that an IR textbook, whether an authored text or a book of readings, is a *highly* theoretical "product." By its very nature, an IR textbook is designed to organize the diverse phenomena of world politics into a more or less comprehensible whole and structured so that it can be "taught" (or, from the students' perspective, "studied" and "learned") within the relatively unforgiving time frames of a term, semester, quarter, or academic year. But in so doing, a textbook constructs IR for both the student who must read and study it, and also, it should be added, for the instructor who must work with, or from (or around, or against), it. It can thus be argued that an assigned textbook can be as important in defining the discipline of IR for students as other components of the course, such as lectures, seminars, tutorials, or the other readings assigned by the professor. In that sense, to the extent that its contents will be absorbed by the undergraduates who read and study it, and to the extent that a textbook helps shape the course for which it is assigned, a textbook has the capacity to shape theoretical understandings of world politics.

Given this, it can be asked whether the same "American" characteristics that Stanley Hoffmann attributed to the discipline of IR as a whole are reflected in the IR textbooks that are used to introduce students to the field. To what extent do American IR textbooks, like the American approach to the discipline as a whole, operate in what Hoffmann called "zones of relative darkness" (Hoffmann, 1977, 58)? To test this, I surveyed fourteen books that were written as textbooks designed to be adopted in introductory IR courses. All are "American": they were all written by Americans or scholars who are faculty at American universities or colleges; all were published in the United States by American publishing houses (even if in the changing firmament of the global publishing industry those publishers were owned by non-American firms or interests).[1] The texts included in this study are listed in box 7.1.

One of the most obvious defining characteristics of these textbooks is that they are written in the first person plural, figuratively if not literally. To be sure, only one of the texts surveyed—*The New World of International Relations* by Roskin and Berry—is quite literally written

---

Introductory IR Texts Surveyed

Joshua S. Goldstein. (1996). *International Relations*. 2nd ed. New York: HarperCollins.

Barry B. Hughes. (1997). *Continuity and Change in World Politics: Competing Perspectives*. 3rd ed. Upper Saddle River, N.J.: Prentice Hall.

Walter S. Jones. (1997). *The Logic of International Relations*. 8th ed. New York: Longman.

Charles W. Kegley Jr. and Eugene R. Wittkopf. (1997). *World Politics: Trend and Transformation*. 6th ed. New York: St. Martin's.

Howard H. Lentner. (1997). *International Politics: Theory and Practice*. Minneapolis: West Publishing.

Richard W. Mansbach. (1997). *The Global Puzzle: Issues and Actors in World Politics*. 2nd ed. New York: Houghton-Mifflin.

Dean A. Minix and Sandra M. Hawley. (1998). *Global Politics*. Belmont, Calif.: West/Wadsworth.

Daniel S. Papp. (1997). *Contemporary International Relations: Frameworks for Understanding*. 5th ed. Boston: Allyn and Bacon.

Frederic S. Pearson and J. Martin Rochester. (1992). *International Relations: The Global Condition in the Late Twentieth Century*. New York: McGraw-Hill.

Michael G. Roskin and Nicholas O. Berry. (1997). *The New World on International Relations*. 3rd ed. Upper Saddle River, N.J.: Prentice Hall.

John T. Rourke. (1997). *International Politics on the World Stage*. 6th ed. Guilford, Conn.: Dushkin/McGraw-Hill.

Bruce Russett and Harvey Starr. (1996). *World Politics: The Menu for Choice*. 5th ed. New York: W. H. Freeman.

Donald M. Snow and Eugene Brown. (1996). *The Contours of Power: An Introduction to Contemporary International Relations*. New York: St. Martin's.

Paul R. Viotti and Mark V. Kauppi. (1997). *International Relations and World Politics: Security, Economy, Identity*. Upper Saddle River, N.J.: Prentice Hall.

BOX 7.1

Fourteen Introductory IR Texts

in the first person plural: the authors of this text openly frame their discussion in terms of "we Americans," "our" foreign policy, and what foreigners do to "us." Other texts are more subtle in their rendition, phrasing the discussion of international relations in the third person. But the voice remains *figuratively* in the first person plural: the world of world politics represented in these texts revolves around the United States. These texts leave in no doubt that the readers being addressed are American students. The scholarly sources cited are invariably the writings of other Americans or scholars at American universities, or the output of publishing houses in the United States. The referents are overwhelmingly American; the examples chosen to illustrate points are American or have to do with the United States. And most of the texts surveyed have extensive sections on United States foreign policy. Indeed, it is likely that not one of the texts surveyed would pass a blind taste test: one could strip the names from any of the fourteen books but no reader would be left in any doubt as to the nationality of the authors.

Now the essential "Americanness" of these texts is neither surprising nor particularly noteworthy. After all, all of these textbooks are primarily aimed at the huge market of American undergraduates. Indeed, it would be surprising if these books did not use American examples or American referents. What is noteworthy, however, is that these texts tend to represent world politics in an essentially *Americocentric* way— in other words, as a phenomenon that has an essentially *American* core. This is reflected in at least three ways. First, it is revealed in the degree to which the scholarly discipline of IR is represented as something to which only Americans contribute. Second, it is revealed in the way in which the discipline of IR is portrayed as revolving around the United States. Third, it is revealed in the way that the "world out there"— beyond the water's edge—is constructed by these texts.

AN AMERICAN (CENTERED) SOCIAL SCIENCE

One of the purposes of a textbook is to acquaint students with some of the scholarly literature in the field, usually through the technique of citing works in footnotes or endnotes or in "For Further Reading" sections at the end of chapters, or in select bibliographies. Which scholars a textbook author chooses to cite, which journals students are implicitly (or explicitly) pointed to, whose books are identified as "must-reads"— these are all a useful reflection of the way in which the discipline is being represented for students who are coming to the study of world politics for the first time. On this measure, it is not difficult to conclude that American IR textbooks are deeply parochial.

One common observation, made more widely about the American academy and deeply reflected in the discipline of IR, is that American scholarship tends to be robustly unilingual; American IR textbook writers, like American IR scholars more generally, tend to read and reference only what is published in English. This, in turn, both reflects and reinforces the essential unilingualism of the American undergraduate audience who are the primary "consumers" of these texts. It must immediately be noted that this linguistic parochialism is by no means particular to Americans. The linguistic imperialism (if not linguistic laziness) that comes naturally to native speakers of a universal language is evident throughout the English-speaking world, and well reflected in the IR discipline. The fact is that students of IR in Australia, Britain, English-speaking Canada, and New Zealand tend to be as robustly unilingual as Americans; they also tend not to be exposed to any IR scholarship that is not either written in English in the original, or translated from another language into English. By contrast, consider how many undergraduate students in places like Germany, Hong Kong, Japan, Mexico, the Netherlands, Norway, Québec, or Taiwan might receive their instruction in their native language, but are nonetheless expected to be able to read English works in IR that are assigned by their invariably bilingual or multilingual instructors.

But even leaving the issue of language aside, we see clear evidence of a deep parochialism in American IR texts. Nearly all of the textbooks surveyed for this essay leave their readers with the unmistakable impression that there is no one writing in English outside the United States on world politics. With but few exceptions, overwhelmingly the references, the suggestions for further reading, and the selected bibliographies are the works of American scholars, writing in American journals, or for American publishing houses.

The exceptions are few. Goldstein's footnotes, which are designed to serve as a kind of IR bibliography for students, contain a few references to non-American authors. Kauppi and Viotti contains more than an occasional reference to the work of British scholars or works put out by British publishing houses. Of the texts surveyed, Lentner is unusual in the degree to which he regularly cites the works of non-American authors and the products of non-American publishing houses; perhaps, not coincidentally, Lentner spent several years in the early 1970s as chair of a political science department at McMaster University in Canada before returning to the United States.

For the rest, however, the scholarly world seems to stop at the water's edge. To be sure, non-American scholars are occasionally cited in these textbooks, but it tends to be when these scholars have published in American sources. Likewise, works of non-American scholars are often cited when they have been published in the United States via the U.S.-based subsidiaries of publishing houses that are organized on a global basis, such as Oxford University Press or Cambridge University Press, or who have "global alliances" (such as Macmillan and St. Martin's). In this regard, special mention should be made of two Boulder, Colorado publishing houses: both Westview Press and Lynne Rienner have worked hard to bring the IR scholarship of non-Americans to an

American audience. But generally speaking, if a book does not have an American imprint, it is likely to be invisible to American scholars more generally, and, therefore, to those who author textbooks and who take their referential cues from the writings of others. As a consequence, the incidence of citations to non-Americans who have been published in non-American journals or whose books have been published by non-American publishers is extremely low.

This invisibility is particularly true of the journal literature. Despite the existence of a large number of scholarly journals on world politics published in English outside the United States, one would never know of their existence from American textbooks, where the journal references are dominated by articles in *International Organization, Foreign Affairs, Foreign Policy, International Studies Quarterly, American Political Science Review, Journal of Conflict Resolution,* and other journals published in the United States. The only non-American journals to appear in the citations with any regularity (but even then with no great frequency) are the *Journal of Peace Research,* published in English in Oslo, and the *Jerusalem Journal of International Relations.* An occasional reference to such journals as *Review of International Studies* or *Millennium* may be found, particularly when an American academic has published an article there. Kegley and Wittkopf's *World Politics: Trend and Transformation* is nicely illustrative of this phenomenon: with approximately one thousand references spanning twenty pages of small-point text, Kegley and Wittkopf's bibliography provides readers with numerous references to articles in American journals, but there are only fourteen references to articles in non-American journals. Fully nine of those were to the *Journal of Peace Research* (one of which was to an article co-authored by Kegley himself, another to American scholar Carl Sagan). Of the remainder, two were references to *Review of International Studies,* the journal of the British International Studies Association (one of which was an article by American scholar Inis Claude); and two to the *Jerusalem Journal of International Relations.* There was but one reference to *Millennium,* the IR journal published by the students at the London School of Economics and Political Science—and that is to an article by the American scholar Robert O. Keohane.

AMERICA AT THE CENTER:
THE CASE OF HEGEMONIC STABILITY THEORY

A second commonality is that these texts tend to construct international politics as something that cannot be understood unless the United States is at the core. And nothing is more indicative of the Americocentric focus of American IR texts than how they tend to treat the notion of American leadership in world politics. Much of the story of the post-1945 period is told with the United States at the center of the action. And prominent in that story is the "theory" that has been invented by American scholars to "account" for American leadership—hegemonic stability theory. Most of the texts surveyed acquaint their student-readers with hegemonic stability theory (see Viotti and Kauppi, 1997, 189; Goldstein, 1996, 103–104; Minix and Hawley, 1998, 231–232; Kegley and Wittkopf, 1997, 210–211; Lentner, 1997, 147; Hughes, 1997, 129ff.). As importantly, they also tend to avoid acquainting their readers with critiques of this theory, such as that of Isabelle Grunberg (Grunberg, 1990), who gets only an occasional footnote citation (as, for example, in Goldstein, who merely observes that hegemonic stability theory "is not . . . accepted by all IR scholars" [Goldstein, 1996, 103]).

More or less the story gets told like this: at different times in world history, there will be a country that, because of its superordinate power and its desire for order, will selflessly apply its energies, its resources, and its power to the creation and maintenance of a stable world order. In the recent past, there have only been two such hegemonic powers creating such "hegemonic stability": Britain in the nineteenth century, and the United States in the twentieth. Considerable attention is usually devoted to an account of how after 1941 a succession of American administrations devoted the energies of the government in Washington—and the treasure of the American people—to creating, and then maintaining, a stable international economic and security order so that the world did not drift back into the economic disaster of another Great Depression—and the risk of another global war. In this version of the tale, Americans created the international institutions that shaped the post-1945 order; Americans created the many alliances that ringed a putatively expansionist Soviet Union; Americans devoted billions of dollars to providing security for friends and allies; hundreds of thousands of American lives were lost in the cause of freedom against German Nazis, Japanese imperialists, North Korean and Chinese expansionists, Vietnamese Communists, and Iraqi annexationists. To maintain and encourage a more vibrant and open global economy, Americans created the post-1945 recovery of both Europe and Japan, by donating billions of dollars in aid and opening its markets to their products.

Normally, all of this activity is described using the discourse of "public goods." In this rendition, the United States, through foreign policy decisions that result in the creation of alliances, or rules-based trading regimes, or stable exchange markets, "produces" "public goods," either for the international system as a whole, or for particular countries (e.g., Russett and Starr, 1996, 426–434). Moreover, these "public goods," by their very nature, are deemed to be "good" for whomever is out there consuming them. Consider, for example, Goldstein's globalized update of the old saw that "What's good for General Motors is good for the USA": a hegemon, Goldstein tells his students, "basically has the same interests as the common good of all states" (Goldstein, 1996, 103). In other words, "What's good for the USA is good for the whole world." Americans spend money and energy creating something positive for the world that can be enjoyed by all, even those who do not contribute to those "goods," and indeed even those who might not want to enjoy those goods.

Of course, the moment one slips into the discourse of "public goods," one cannot avoid the corollary: if these benefits can be enjoyed by all, then some folks must be enjoying the benefits created by Americans *without contributing*. Thus are American undergraduates introduced to the idea that other countries in the world are essentially "free riders," enjoying the security created by the United States, enjoying the economic benefits of an open and liberal global economy sustained by American leadership, but without having to pay the attendant costs. This leads inexorably into discussions of what is openly called the "free rider problem"—how to deal with those who enjoy the benefits provided by Americans but who do not pay their "fair share" of the costs (e.g., Russett and Starr, 1996, 399–400; Goldstein, 1996, 300; Kegley and Wittkopf, 1997, 212; Hughes, 1997, 130–131). And this, in turn, leads to telling undergraduates about "burden-sharing" in American-led alliances, and how the allies of the United States tend to be able to devote more of their social wage to social welfare (health care, education or, as the case may be, "research and development") because the American treasury is burdened with the costs of paying for the alliance. It also provides an opportunity to acquaint American students with "fair trade," a uniquely American term invented to describe the process by which trading partners of the United States, having been assisted by American largesse in the immediate post-1945 period, in essence kick their benefactors in the teeth by engaging in trade practices that hurt American interests. It also confirms for American students what they have already been told by President Bill Clinton in his second inaugural address: that their country is indeed the "indispensable country." Roskin and Berry put baldly what is implicit in most other texts: "The alternative to US leadership is chaos. Only the United States can have the breadth of vision to work toward a new world order" (Roskin and Berry, 1997, 67).

Although it is never painted this way by the American texts which so dutifully outline the theory, hegemonic stability theory is in fact a deeply nationalistic way of telling the tale of the post-1945 period. The theory portrays Americans as global "good guys," selflessly ensuring that the world didn't slip back into the blackness of the Great Depression of the 1930s, and working hard to keep other folks safe from the predations of the new expansionists in Moscow and Beijing—but always having to struggle against foreigners who are, if not enemies, then untrustworthy "free riders" or ungrateful "unfair traders." It is a tale in which Americans feature prominently, and the rest of the world characterized as merely responding to farsighted American leadership and extraordinary American generosity, or cast in the role of cheap/ungrateful/unfair (choose your adjective) "free riders" bludging off an always put-upon United States. As a nationalist tale, hegemonic stability theory no doubt achieves its purpose: it probably makes American undergraduates feel good about their country's generosity and annoyed at foreigners—in particular those allies and trading partners who have done so well by the United States.

But this is very much the story as it would be told by an American. Few others in the international system tell the story this way, not even those who would willingly grant that many elements of post-1945 American statesmanship, such as the Marshall Plan, represented statecraft of considerable vision and generosity on the part of those in the administration and Congress, and, indeed, on the part of Americans who sustained the postwar internationalists in power. But unfortunately for aficionados of hegemonic stability theory, foreigners find it hard to take the essential hubris of the theory and the fanciful conflation of the "common good of all states" with the "international public goods" being produced by Americans. Above all, non-Americans find it difficult to accept the theory's construction of the world as a simple we/they duality in which the United States is the "Important Self" and the rest of the world is, in essence, the "Unimportant Other." It is thus no coincidence that hegemonic stability theory is a tale that tends to be told only in the United States, or by those who are in thrall to Americocentric IR theorizing.

THE "IMPORTANT SELF" AND THE "UNIMPORTANT OTHER"

The essential ethnocentricity of these texts is also reflected in how non-Americans are portrayed. First, the obvious and necessary concomitant of an ethnocentric focus on the "Important Self" is that others are, by definition, unimportant. This is a not uncommon attitude among the leading members of the discipline in the United States. It is best exemplified by the comment of a senior American scholar, Stephen Krasner, to a panel on hegemonic stability theory at the 1990 meetings of the American Political

Science Association. Krasner is reported to have put the idea that those who did not enjoy a hegemonic position were essentially irrelevant this way: "Sure people in Luxembourg have good ideas. But who gives a damn? Luxembourg ain't hegemonic" (Higgott, 1991, 99). No less indicative was Kenneth Waltz' dismissive comment that "Denmark doesn't matter" in his discussion of the new world order (Waltz, 1996, 1993).

Given such views, it is perhaps not surprising that IR textbooks would also mirror these attitudes. Consider how one author, for example, characterizes the Solomon Islands for his readers:

> Admittedly, the Solomon Islands is a political entity significant to few others than its 385,000 residents. It has no oil and no industry, has not been the scene of major domestic or international strife since World War II, and is largely forgotten. . . . For the most part, most microstates, including the Solomon Islands, are important only in that they are voting members of the General Assembly . . . [where] their votes are as significant as those of the United States, Russia, China, Japan, and the European states. . . . Little more can be said about the Solomon Islands. . . . Most [states like the Solomons] are indeed in the backwaters of international life .(Papp, 1997, 350–351)

Little more can be said about such views, except to reiterate the obvious observation that how important one is deemed to be, or whether the water at the edge is "backwater," depends heavily on one's standpoint.[2]

On occasion, simple oversights or mistakes can result in a distortion of importance. For example, consider how the IR texts surveyed treat the creation of the Asia Pacific Economic Cooperation (APEC) forum, which for many people around the Pacific Rim is one of the most important international groupings in the post–Cold War era. Despite APEC's prominence, a number of texts (Lentner, 1997; Pearson and Rochester, 1992; Jones, 1997) get the name wrong. And some texts—Goldstein, Russett and Starr, Hughes, and Viotti and Kauppi—ignore APEC altogether: either the authors remain unaware of the forum's existence or they deem it to be not important enough to bring to the attention of their student-readers. Most of the texts that do mention APEC simply note its existence without exploring its origins (Kegley and Wittkopf, 1997; Lentner, 1997; Minix and Hawley, 1998; Roskin and Berry, 1997). Some imply that APEC started in 1993 (not coincidentally the year that President Bill Clinton hosted the first heads of government summit in Seattle), or in Bogor, Indonesia the following year (see Rourke, 1997, 521–522; Papp, 1997, 392). Four texts mention APEC's origin, and three get it wrong. Jones (Jones, 1997, 81) intimates that APEC evolved from ASEAN (Association of Southeast Asian Nations); Mansbach (Mansbach, 1997, 485) credits the United States with initiating APEC; Pearson and Rochester claim that Japan launched it (Pearson and Rochester,

1992, 455). In fact, APEC evolved from an initiative taken in 1989 by Bob Hawke, the Australian Prime Minister. Hawke proposed the idea in a speech in Seoul, South Korea in January 1989, and hosted a meeting in Canberra in November of that year (Evans and Grant, 1991, 121; Cooper, Higgott, and Nossal, 1993, 92–94). But only Snow and Brown (Snow and Brown, 1996, 361) attribute APEC's creation to Hawke.

The treatment of APEC underscores a more general problem evident in many of the IR texts surveyed: these texts are also noteworthy for what they do *not* tell their student-readers about international politics, those things deemed to be too unimportant to bother knowing about, or telling students about. A good example is the Commonwealth of Nations or the grouping of states known colloquially as *la francophonie* (including the *Agence de Coopération culturelle et technique* and the *Conférence des chefs d'État ayant en commun l'usage de français*). No doubt because the United States is not a member of either of these associations of states, they are generally not even mentioned in IR texts. Of the fifteen texts surveyed, the Commonwealth gets a passing mention in only three texts (Goldstein,1996; Papp, 1997; and Roskin and Berry, 1997); *la francophonie* is mentioned in two (Goldstein, 1996; Papp, 1997)—albeit not by name, official or colloquial.

It can be argued that such omissions are not trivial. Knowing nothing about the Commonwealth, for example, means that one cannot fully analyze the global struggle against apartheid in the 1980s, for a great deal of the international campaign occurred in the context of the Commonwealth. Likewise, knowing nothing about the Commonwealth distorts one's analysis of the origins of international development assistance in the 1950s. For example, not a single text of the fifteen surveyed mentioned the Colombo Plan of 1950, which was the first attempt to apply the lessons of the Marshall Plan to the development problems of the South. But because the United States was not at the meeting of the Commonwealth in Colombo in January 1950—and only joined the plan later—this germinal event in international development assistance is totally overlooked. Instead, the origins of development assistance are invariably represented to American undergraduates as having exclusively American roots: Hughes' discussion of "foreign aid" in the 1950s (Hughes, 1997, 97–98) provides a quintessential example of this.

"CAVE! HIC DRAGONES" REVISITED: GETTING THE WORLD WRONG

In her critique of regime theory, the late Susan Strange used the warning often found on medieval maps of the world beyond Europe to identify five "dragons," or pitfalls, that lie in wait for students of international regimes (Strange, 1982, 479). However, the phrase is no less useful to describe a common phenomenon in American IR texts: the representation of an assertion as authoritative fact based on little, no, or erroneous knowledge. It should be remembered that medieval map-makers drew pictures of dragons and inscribed *Cave!* on their maps not because of *lack* of knowledge; rather, they were trying to convey to readers of the map their *certainty* that the waters beyond Europe were populated by sea monsters, even though in reality they did not actually know much about the waters they were drawing. There is something of the medieval map-maker in American IR texts: the world beyond the United States is sketched out, dragons and all, but it is not always based on a great deal of *correct* knowledge. On the contrary, the authors of these textbooks often appear to know very little about the world beyond the water's edge, even though they represent the world "out there" to their readers with seeming authority and assurance.

A good example of an authoritative assertion is this description of contemporary Hong Kong in Goldstein:

> Hong Kong is a small territory with great internal disparities of wealth. Its rich neighborhoods are jammed with high-rise office buildings and expensive apartments; nearby are huge refugee camps providing cheap labour. (Goldstein, 1997, 512)

This appears following a photo of Hong Kong entitled "Hong Kong business district, 1987." But it is clear that neither Goldstein nor the production staff at HarperCollins who wrote the caption for the photo have ever been to Hong Kong. For the photo is in fact a picture shot from street level of a jetliner making "the turn"—the precarious right-hand turn at rooftop level that planes had to make seconds before touching down at the old Kai Tak airport. But "the turn" used to occur over Kowloon Tong—a district that is across the harbor and many kilometers from the business district in Central. Likewise, the written commentary will have those who know Hong Kong asking: What Hong Kong is Goldstein describing? After all, the only "refugee camps" in the last generation were those created to house several thousand Vietnamese refugees, most of whom were not allowed to provide labor, cheap or otherwise, to the local market. To be sure, squatters continue to be a feature of the urban landscape—their population was estimated in 1996 to be 32,000—but their numbers are reduced each year as they are relocated to public housing estates. Moreover, while there are disparities in wealth, Goldstein's intimation that Hong Kong is teeming with an impoverished laboring class does not square with either anecdotal observation or with the aggregate data. Hong Kong's per capita GDP income of US$21,800—a level higher than that enjoyed in Australia, Britain, or Canada—may not be distributed perfectly equally, but it is distributed in a way that allows fully 43.9 percent of households in Hong Kong either to own their flats or to participate in a government-sponsored home-ownership scheme.

Certainly no one would want to criticize Goldstein for not having been to Hong Kong. But students reading Goldstein will come away with entirely the wrong information about Hong Kong. (Moreover, this is not the only error in his text: for example, it has the Communists seizing power in China in 1949, and then has India achieving independence "around the same time" [475]; it has Vietnam invading Cambodia in 1979 rather than in 1978; it has Iraq attacking Iran in 1979 rather than in 1980 [55]; it has Israel attacking the Osiraq reactor in 1982 instead of 1981 [212]; it claims that the visit to Beijing of Mikhail S. Gorbachev in May 1989 touched off the pro-democracy movement in China [43]—rather than the death of Hua Guofeng in April.)

While it is perhaps unusual to see so many factual errors in a single text, the other textbooks surveyed are not free of erroneous representations of the world. Consider the fleeting mentions of the Commonwealth of Nations noted in the previous section. Only three texts mention the Commonwealth, but those texts all got it wrong. Both Roskin and Berry (Roskin and Berry, 1997, 314) and Goldstein (Goldstein, 1996, 91) call it the "British Commonwealth"—even though the adjective "British" has not been used by the Commonwealth itself for decades. Moreover, Roskin and Berry clearly are unacquainted with the role of the Crown in contemporary governance, or of the relationship of the Crown to the Commonwealth: they describe the Commonwealth as "a loose grouping of Britain and its former colonies, which call the queen their nominal sovereign" (Roskin and Berry, 1997, 314). They appear to be unaware that not a single member of the Commonwealth regards Elizabeth II as its "nominal" sovereign; that she is the actual head of state of sixteen Commonwealth members; or that she is acknowledged by all members to be the head of the Commonwealth (this being a necessary condition of membership in the association).

For his part, Papp (Papp, 1997, 287) has this to tell his student-readers about the Commonwealth: "Great Britain's global Commonwealth of Nations meets regularly, and the countries of the Commonwealth share the equivalent of the US concept of most favored nation trading status." No single sentence could more closely approximate the very essence of American ethnocentricity. First, the suggestion that the Commonwealth is somehow "Great Britain's" reflects essentially imperial assumptions about power as it is assumed to operate in any association of sovereign nation-states. After all, if one constructs Britain as a "former hegemon," it follows that Britain *must* remain hegemonic over members of its former empire. Such an assumption would, of course, draw a rueful snort from the British tabloid press, which regularly expresses the view that Britain should withdraw from the Commonwealth precisely because other members have so often proved willing to cross the British government. And the idea that the Commonwealth members share special nondiscriminatory trading arrangements is simply mistaken. Papp perhaps was thinking of the old Imperial Preference, but this has been dead and buried for decades. The idea that "most-favored-nation" treatment is a "United States concept" is equally erroneous. This practice had made its appearance in various European trade treaties for at least two hundred years before 1860, when the phrase that now describes it was legally entrenched in the Anglo-French treaty negotiated by Richard Cobden and Michel Chevalier.

Comparable errors can be found in discussions of the civilizational argument most commonly associated with Samuel P. Huntington (Huntington, 1993, 1996). Most texts refer to Huntington's contention that in the future the fault lines of global conflict will be on civilizational lines. Many reproduce the thesis without comment or criticism, leaving readers with the view that the civilizational argument is not at all contested (e.g., Hughes, 1997, 63; Goldstein, 1996, 207; Viotti and Kauppi, 1997, 279); two authors do draw attention to criticisms (Snow and Brown, 1996, 556–557; Rourke, 1997, 194–195; see also Ahluwalia and Sullivan, this volume). At least one textbook reproduces for students a map showing how Huntington divides the world into major civilizations (Minix and Hawley, 1998, 553). This map faithfully reproduces Huntington's often bewildering divisions, including the inclusion of Papua New Guinea (PNG) as a country of the "West," the mapping of Israel as an Islamic country, the characterization of Madagascar as "African," and the characterization of the Philippines as partly a Sinic country, partly an Islamic country.

But not one of the texts remarks on the degree to which these are odd ways to represent these countries. No one notices that Huntington and the cartographers at Simon and Schuster appear to believe that PNG is, like Tasmania, part of Australia and not a country of the South. Or, that Huntington is seemingly unaware of Madagascar's unique blend of cultural origins—still reflected today—that are as much Indonesian as they are African. Or, that perhaps he did not know that the population of the country he characterized as part Sinic, part Muslim is in fact 94 percent Christian and only 4 percent Muslim. No one comments on the strangeness of his exclusion of Israel from his definition of the West (an exclusion that is, however, no error: at different points in his book, Huntington makes quite clear that he does not think Israel is a Western country). Instead, Minix and Hawley simply reproduce Huntington's idiosyncratic characterizations and errors without comment or criticism (Minix and Hawley, 1998, 552–554).

Kegley and Wittkopf also discuss the civilizational thesis, though they do not use Huntington's civilizational phraseology. Instead, they divide the world into nine "cultural domains," declaring that these "world or transnational cultures recognize no international borders" (Kegley and Wittkopf, 1997, 177). They then produce a nine-color map of the world showing nine "cultures": European, Chinese, Russian, Islamic, Black African, Hindu, Latin American, South African, and "other" (which appears to be a category in which to dump Madagascar and Papua New Guinea).

It is alarming that thousands of American undergraduates are assigned this book each year—and thus might actually believe this map to be an accurate representation of world politics. There are, however, a series of errors that render the accuracy of this depiction of the world problematic. First, it is strange that the boundaries of these cultures that supposedly recognize "no international borders" all happen to correspond precisely and neatly to the existing borders of contemporary sovereign states. And the cultural divisions themselves are fanciful, to say the least. Among the more egregious errors include the representation of all the countries of South and Southeast Asia as part of a putatively "Hindu" domain—including the three states of Indochina, Indonesia, Thailand, Malaysia, Brunei, Singapore, Myanmar, and Bangladesh. The populations of these countries is in fact overwhelmingly Buddhist, Muslim, Christian, Taoist, and animist, and Bangladesh and Malaysia have only tiny Hindu minorities. And just like Huntington, Kegley and Wittkopf seem misinformed about the cultural makeup of the Philippines: they paint some islands of the Philippines as "European" and some as "Hindu"—even though 84 percent of the population is Roman Catholic, 10 percent are Protestants, 4 percent are Muslims, and Hindus are such a minuscule proportion of the population that they do not register on most data sets.

Unlike Huntington, however, Kegley and Wittkopf acknowledge that PNG is not part of Australia, and do not mistakenly paint the eastern half of the island of New Guinea as "Hindu" as they do with Irian Jaya. But they do not appear familiar with what kind of "culture" exists there, for it is marked merely "other."

Kegley and Wittkopf's knowledge of Africa is equally problematic. As noted above, South Africa is accorded its own unique cultural domain—"South Africa (mixed)"—but for some reason Madagascar is not accorded the same privilege. Instead of a separate category—"Malagasy (mixed)"?—the island of Madagascar is classified merely as "other," offering readers little clue of the rich and ethnically diverse history of the origins of the peoples of the island before and after the arrival of Europeans. For reasons not made clear, a number of African countries—Niger, Chad, Mali, and Ethiopia—are classified as Black African rather than Islamic.

Other parts of the world are equally misconstrued in this exercise. All of the countries and territories of the Caribbean and the Guiana coast are uniformly depicted as part of the "Latin American" cultural domain, which obliterates the many English, French, and Dutch-speaking peoples of the Caribbean basin. The Baltic republics—Estonia, Latvia, and Lithuania—and Ukraine are all considered by Kegley and Wittkopf to be part of the Russian cultural domain despite the presence of several strident nationalist groups. Likewise, Japan, the Koreas, and Mongolia are all painted "Chinese" (ditto).

How can one explain the many outright errors and erroneous characterizations outlined above? It could be a function of the stay-at-home parochialism of the American professoriate, which manifests itself in many ways, from a lack of world travel[3] to the incestuousness bred by reading only what other Americans have to say about the world. It could also be a function of a reviewing process that is relentlessly parochial and Americocentric. Consider how many people read these erroneous characterizations of the world beyond American borders before they appeared in print. It is sobering when one considers that all of these textbooks were reviewed in manuscript form by colleagues at other universities—and many of them have gone through at least one edition (and thus multiple reviews)—but not one of these errors was picked up by reviewers or readers of previous editions. But given the ethnocentric nature of the reviewing process, it is not particularly surprising. For publishers of American IR texts appear not to bother to send manuscripts to "foreigners" for review. For example, Goldstein (Goldstein, 1996, xxiii) lists thirty-one scholars who acted as reviewers; fully thirty came from universities all over the United States and only one non-American is listed as a reviewer—Akira Ichikawa of the University of Lethbridge in Canada. Other texts are even more Americocentric. For example, all seven of Kegley and Wittkopf's sixth edition reviewers came from American universities; all twenty-eight reviewers of Minix and Hawley are at American institutions; and all nineteen reviewers engaged for Snow and Brown, and all eighteen for Hughes.[4] Needless to say, relying to such a degree on Americans to review commentary on foreigners not only runs the risk that one will get it wrong, but the Americocentric nature of the reviewing process merely perpetuates the Americocentricity of the text.

But mostly, it can be argued, these errors stem from the lack of general knowledge of the authors—and their reviewers—about that which is deemed unimportant. In other words, it is okay to get things wrong if they are unimportant; it is not necessary to work to get *everything* right as long as one has the important stuff right.[5] What does it matter, after all, if American undergraduates are left with the impression that Hong Kong is a teeming slum, or that APEC was started by Bill Clinton in 1993, or that Indonesia is Hindu, or that Papua New Guinea is part of Australia? Who cares if they know who Queen Elizabeth II is, or how governance in a Westminster system actually works? Is it really important to know about the Commonwealth? Who cares if they think that the Iran-Iraq war started in 1979 rather than 1980, or that Vietnam invaded Cambodia in 1978 rather than 1979? After all, is this not all "the backwaters of international life"? Are these things not, when all is said and done, fundamentally unimportant?

CONCLUSION: IN THE "ZONE OF RELATIVE DARKNESS"

This essay has focused on an admittedly very partial reading of fourteen texts, many of which run to hundreds of pages and hundreds of thousands of words. It might therefore be asked whether it is fair to fix on a few errors or omissions or erroneous characterizations. After all, one can easily pick nits with any book, and few authors (or publishing houses) are immune from the errors in fact or interpretation that all too easily creep into any book. However, I focus on these characteristics of American texts because they reveal so well a critical element of the construction of IR in the United States: that is, the degree to which American IR textbooks contribute in important ways to how the tale of world politics is told, how a certain image of world politics is constructed and thus world politics understood, and how this is reproduced from one generation to the next in a hermetically sealed Americocentric vacuum. While they are not normally seen as contributions to IR theorizing, in fact they *are* theoretical contributions, for they organize and define world politics for hundreds of the professors who adopt them for their courses and thousands of students who are required to read them for examination purposes. And even a very partial reading of these texts reveals the degree to which IR, as they construct it, remains a deeply "American" enterprise, having changed little since Hoffmann was writing in the late 1970s. In other words, these texts portray the world to their readers from a uniquely *American* point of view: they are reviewed by Americans; the sources they cite are American; the examples are American; the theory is American; the experience is American; the focus is American; and in one case, the voice is also explicitly American. And, as the errors and omissions surveyed suggest, the "zones of relative darkness" that Hoffmann wrote about two decades ago are all too evident in these texts. Moreover, this "American" view of the world is being communicated to successive cohorts of American undergraduates, some of whom will themselves go on to get Ph.D.s and teach international politics in American universities to a future cohort of undergraduates—thus perpetuating and reproducing these zones of darkness.

NOTES

Readers should be aware that since joining this project, I myself have written an introductory IR text (Nossal, 1998)—partly in reaction to the findings outlined in this chapter and partly out of a belief that the existing IR texts on the Canadian market were so unabashedly Americocentric that it would be inappropriate to assign them to my students at McMaster University. However, the appearance of *The Patterns of World Politics* means that I am no longer as disinterested as I was when I joined the project; skeptics may be forgiven if they read the critique in this chapter as hopelessly self-serving.

1. Thus, at least one widely used text written by a scholar at a Canadian university and published in the United States has not been included in this survey: K. J. Holsti (1995), *International Politics: A Framework for Analysis*, 7th ed., Englewood Cliffs, N.J.: Prentice Hall.

2. Papp might have chosen the Solomons as an exemplar of the "Unimportant Other" rather more carefully: his characterization of the country as uninvolved in "strife" is simply wrong, as the former Papua New Guinea (PNG) Prime Minister Sir Julius Chan, Solomons Prime Minister Solomon Mamaloni, Francis Ona and the other rebels on Bougainville, not to mention the board members of CRA, the soldiers of the transnational security corporation Executive Outcomes, and the Australian government of John Howard would attest.

3. Consider, for example, the startling admission by one of the most productive American scholars in the field that between his wartime service and 1993 he had never actually been abroad (Rosenau, 1996, 24).

4. Rourke lists eighty-nine colleagues who "contributed" feedback; clearly not all were reviewers engaged by Dushkin, his publisher. Of the eighty-nine, only three were members of faculty of a non-American university—all in Canada.

5. If one were *really* churlish, one might be tempted to cite the observation by Roskin and Berry to their student-readers about the putative causes of "backwardness" in the world. Apparently, one of them obtained a pocket calendar in Yugoslavia, but discovered that it was one day off—because its maker had made an error, and forgotten to add an extra day in February for leap year. That, according to Roskin and Berry (Roskin and Berry, 1997, 183), was when they "discovered what backwardness was all about. It's not a shortage of tractors and telephones; it's a shortage of meticulous thinking, of doing things right the first time. Backwardness is slovenly attitudes." Indeed.

REFERENCES

Cooper, A. F., Richard A. Higgott, and Kim Richard Nossal. (1993). *Relocating Middle Powers: Australia and the Changing World Order.* Vancouver: University of British Columbia Press.

Evans, G., and B. Grant. (1991). *Australia's Foreign Relations in the World of the 1990s.* Carlton, Victoria: Melbourne University Press.

Goldstein, Joshua S. (1996). *International Relations.* 2nd ed. New York: Harper Collins.

Grunberg, I. (1990). "Exploring the 'Myth' of Hegemonic Stability Theory." *International Organization 44,* 431–478.

Higgott, R. A. (1991). "Towards a Non-Hegemonic IPE: An Antipodean Perspective." In C. N. Murphy and Roger Tooze (eds.), *The New International Political Economy.* Boulder, Colo.: Lynne Rienner.

Hoffmann, Stanley. (1977). "An American Social Science: International Relations." *Daedalus 101*(3), 41–59.

Hughes, Barry B. (1997). *Continuity and Change in World Politics: Competing Perspectives.* 3rd ed. Upper Saddle River, N.J.: Prentice Hall.

Huntington, Samuel P. (1996). *The Clash of Civilizations and the Remaking of World Order.* New York: Simon & Schuster.

Jones, Walter S. (1997). *The Logic of International Relations.* 8th ed. New York: Longman.

Kegley, Charles W. Jr., and Eugene R. Wittkopf. (1997). *World Politics: Trend and Transformation.* 6th ed. New York: St. Martin's.

Lentner, Howard H. (1997). *International Politics: Theory and Practice.* Minneapolis: West Publishing.

Mansbach, Richard W. (1997). *The Global Puzzle: Issues and Actors in World Politics.* 2nd ed. New York: Houghton Mifflin.

Minix, Dean A., and Sandra M. Hawley. (1998). *Global Politics.* Belmont, Calif.: West/Wadsworth.

Nossal, Kim Richard. (1998). *The Patterns of World Politics.* Scarborough, Ontario: Prentice Hall/Allyn and Bacon Canada.

Papp, Daniel S. (1997). *Contemporary International Relations: Frameworks for Understanding.* 5th ed. Boston: Allyn and Bacon.

Pearson, Frederic S., and J. Martin Rochester. (1992). *International Relations: The Global Condition in the Late Twentieth Century.* New York: McGraw-Hill.

Rosenau, James N. (1996). "Powerful Tendencies, Startling Discrepancies, and Elusive Dynamics: The Challenge of Studying World Politics in a Turbulent Era." *Australian Journal of International Affairs 50* (April), 23–30.

Roskin, Michael G., and Nicholas O. Berry. (1997). *The New World on International Relations.* 3rd ed. Upper Saddle River, N.J.: Prentice Hall.

Rourke, John T. (1997). *International Politics on the World Stage.* 6th ed. Guilford, Conn.: Dushkin/McGraw-Hill.

Russett, Bruce, and Harvey Starr. (1996). *World Politics: The Menu for Choice.* 5th ed. New York: W. H. Freeman.

Snow, Donald M., and Eugene Brown. (1996). *The Contours of Power: An Introduction to Contemporary International Relations.* New York: St. Martin's.

Strange, S. (1982). "*Cave! Hic dragones*: A Critique of Regime Analysis." *International Organization* 36(2), 479–496.

Viotti, Paul R., and Mark V. Kauppi. (1997). *International Relations and World Politics: Security, Economy, Identity*. Upper Saddle River, N.J.: Prentice Hall.

Waltz, Kenneth N. (1993). "The New World Order," *Millennium: Journal of International Studies* 22(2), 187–196.

CHAPTER 8

The End of International Relations?

Martin Griffiths
and
Terry O'Callaghan

The map appears to us more real than the land.
—D. H. Lawrence

INTRODUCTION

Unlike many contributors to so-called "great debates" in the discipline of international relations (hereafter referred to as IR to distinguish the discipline from its contested subject matter), we are less concerned with legislative proposals for its future health than with the presupposition that makes such legislation possible, namely, that the state of affairs that gives rise to IR is compatible with a self-standing discipline of inquiry in the social sciences. IR is not, to use Michael Oakeshott's (Oakeshott, 1975) famous phrase, an "enterprise association" in which there is a consensus over what is meant by international theory, the methods appropriate to its pursuit and evaluation, and its purpose. The absence of such a consensus has become a source of concern for many scholars in recent years, but we think that such concern may be exaggerated. Indeed, we argue in this essay that the desire for consensus and "discipline" in IR is incompatible with those features of the world that justify sustained examination in the academy. For a variety of well-known reasons that require no rehearsal here, IR has been a site of contestation and "great debate" in the past, but the spirit of such well-known fissures between Realists and idealists, behavioralists and historians, and, more recently, among defenders of various "paradigms," has rarely been one of dialogue and accommodation. On the contrary, the degree of anxiety they tend to provoke among so many self-anointed cartographers of dissent is possibly unparalleled in the social sciences. What is missing in much of the recent literature is any meaningful reflection on what is meant by "a discipline," and why IR should enjoy any more substantial a consensus than, say, history or political theory. For our part, we do not believe that IR constitutes a discipline in anything other than a weak sense; that is, the academic study of the consequences of, and possibilities for modifying, a world divided among sovereign states. This definition is weak in that it refuses to privilege a particular phenomenon such as war, and it neither presupposes nor promotes a hierarchical distinction between empirical and normative concerns. Most importantly, it does not smuggle in a substantive characterization of "relations" among states that needs to be argued for rather than asserted or assumed from the outset. Our aim, then, is to challenge that particular understanding of IR which developed in the United States after 1945. This understanding fostered a monistic, rather than a pluralistic, attitude to the pursuit and development of international theory.

IR is largely a North American creation. As Stanley Hoffmann (Hoffmann, 1987, 27) noted, it was "born and raised in America." This is not to discount the contribution of other countries to the early development and growth of the field, but simply to acknowledge that it was scholars in the United States who first established IR as a distinct and formal social science. As a result, the influence of American scholarship and research on the study of international relations has been enormous. Even today, the American conception of IR remains a powerful force in the study of international relations, although the advent of continental philosophy, as well as a more vigorous profile from scholars outside of the American core, indicate that this influence may be waning (see, for example, Groom and Mandaville, this volume).

It is not our intention, however, to disparage the efforts of American scholarship. It has been a fountain of great insight over the years. Yet there is something quite strange about a field that claims an *international* focus, but relies almost totally on research emanating from a hegemonic core. We need only consider the extent to which concepts, ideas, and themes developed in the United States remain the organizational center around which IR (and international political economy for that matter) is studied in Canada, Europe, and the Antipodes, or, for example, how negative mainstream American scholars are toward non-American–generated theories and ideas on international relations, to see that the universalism inherent in the idea of a discipline of IR is little more than a thinly disguised parochialism masquerading as a global field of study (see Nossal; Brown; and Crawford this volume). When we are told by Barry Buzan (Buzan, 1993) that "English School" Realism should be more like regime theory, or by Robert Keohane (Keohane, 1988) that critical theorists should develop research agenda that reflect the concerns of positivists at Harvard, it is clear that the meaning we attribute to the notion of a "discipline" is heavily skewed in one direction. The result, in our view, is a bland and narrow definition of IR that runs counter to the complexity and diversity of the materials that comprise its subject matter. The aim of our paper, then, is to counsel students of IR to abandon the American conception of "the discipline" in favor of a more open and pluralistic one.

The inherently interdisciplinary nature of IR—and all the social sciences for that matter—cannot be contained in a way that justifies a rigid academic division of labor between itself and other areas of study within political science. For that very reason, anyone can "join" IR, regardless of their formal training as economists, anthropologists, or historians. This ought not to be (mis)interpreted, however, as a belittlement of the field, or as an attempt to relegate it to the margins of political science. Nothing could be further from the truth. On the contrary, it is precisely our strong belief in the pertinence of international relations that makes us so suspicious of legislative proposals that seek to cordon off the discipline from "outsiders." Such proposals merely mirror the efforts of the sovereign state to guarantee its monopoly over the use of force within a given territory. Indeed, in light of the fact that the sovereignty of the state is itself now contested, it seems specious to insist on the sovereignty of the discipline whose borders should be no more impervious than those of its subject matter.

Despite this, defenders of "the discipline" of IR tend to advance two main arguments to defend its autonomy. First, IR has a distinct identity because of its concern with war, conflict, and endemic global violence; a concern that receives, and has always received, "inadequate" attention elsewhere in political science. Second, the autonomy of IR, and the possibility of consensus within it, is justified by the particular qualities of the domain in which relations between sovereign states take place. These are separate claims, neither of which we find very compelling. Let us examine each in turn.

IT'S WAR, STUPID

As a twentieth-century invention, IR began on the margins of political science. As David Armstrong (Armstrong, 1995, 362) observes, it

> developed as a distinct discipline both as a response to events like the
> two world wars and the cold war and because there were certain phe-

nomena—war, diplomacy, strategy, international law, the balance of power, the numerous ramifications of sovereignty—that were inadequately, or not at all, treated elsewhere in the social sciences.

In what sense were war and related issues "inadequately . . . treated elsewhere?" Armstrong is ambiguous. Were the other social sciences inadequate per se because they did not consider the phenomena that have become the staple diet of IR scholars? Or were they inadequate for those who believed that such phenomena were eminently suitable for academic study, and needed a "home" within the academy if they were to receive "adequate" attention? Unfortunately, the first question is never asked. As IR monopolized the phenomenon of war, other social sciences were never challenged to explore the implicit boundaries of their own legitimacy. Ironically, war, whose implications for the future of the human race are obvious, became the preserve of a "discipline" that defined itself in terms of what it was not.

Had students of international relations challenged the legitimacy of the boundaries of other social sciences at the time, rather than crediting themselves with the creation of a "new discipline," the dubiousness of establishing it around a single problem (war) might well have been seen more clearly. To employ the problem of war as the main criterion for justifying the autonomy of IR is no different than seeking to develop a "discipline" that takes democracy, freedom, or capitalism, for example, as its central concern. Yet all of us would recognize how bizarre and inappropriate would be any for these concepts as the delineating essence of a separate and autonomous discipline.

Not only was IR handicapped from the start by its peripheral status in political science, it was also (and in large part continues to be) burdened with the enduring problems of presentism, or what Robert Cox (Cox, 1986, 208) calls the ethos of "problem-solving." This manifests itself in a number of ways, but the combination of marginalization and problem-solving helps to explain the enduring state-centrism that has characterized IR this century. By this we do not mean that IR scholars should not take the state seriously as a unit of analysis. They should. But this does not mean taking the state for granted or ignoring important challenges to its power and legitimacy. The territorial boundaries of the state need not cohere with disciplinary boundaries, nor is there any reason why a concern with the problem of war between states should preclude attention to war within them. Arguably, intrastate war is replacing war between states as a source of global disorder (Holsti, 1996). Since this trend is inextricably linked with the collapse of state authority in many parts of the global periphery, even those who remain resolutely deaf to calls for a "new agenda" cannot fail to note that the traditional agenda has been seriously weakened in recent years. To claim that this question can be pursued adequately under the aegis of a self-standing discipline, then, is to fail to read the "sign of the times": a rather serious charge against a discipline that has always prided itself on its practical relevance to current political affairs. Moreover, as Fred Halliday (Halliday, 1985, 408) has pointed out, in terms of theory IR has always been "an absorber and importer, not a producer in its own right." Continuing to defend the traditional agenda, then, is not only to risk irrelevance, but also to perpetuate one of the most dubious myths to ever have cast its spell over the field. For neither in theory, nor in practice, does IR have the degree of autonomy its defenders claim or seek to bring about.

Even those "traditionally" trained scholars who find themselves in a position of acknowledging the extent to which intrastate war is replacing war between states, seem unwilling to confront the theoretical contradiction between this state of affairs and their earlier defense of the autonomy of international relations. Our argument is aimed as much at them, as it is against those who continue to live in the theoretical darkness.

Although war is undoubtedly of legitimate concern and deserves to remain a high priority, it is not a form of behavior that can be defined with sufficient precision to warrant the status of a "dependent variable." Not only is it quite problematic to speak of "International Relations" in these terms, but the concept of "aggression" is notoriously difficult to pin down in discourses of "just war" and "collective security," while the search for the cause(s) of war remains hampered by the elusiveness of precisely what it is that we are trying to explain. As Hidemi Suganami (Suganami, 1990) points out, in seeking the causes of war we must distinguish between three separate issues: the conditions in the absence of which war would not be possible, patterns of war and peace over space and time, and, finally, explanations of particular wars. Kenneth Waltz (Waltz, 1959), in his magisterial survey of the literature, observed (almost tautologically) that although the absence of world government made war possible no examination of the other issues could be pursued without acknowledging factors at levels of analysis other than the international. Moreover, if the empirical study of war is justified by the desire to achieve peace, the latter cannot be a privileged goal unless its achievement is accompanied by a reduction of all the factors that contribute to the onset of violence between states. Students of war must, therefore, be concerned with all forms and sources of global conflict. This challenge does not justify a "discipline," nor does it facilitate the identification of a specific and insoluble subject matter.

THE AUTONOMY OF "THE INTERNATIONAL?"

If war per se does not help in justifying IR as an autonomous discipline, what about the related claim that (international) theory is necessary because international relations are conducted in a discrete (non)place? According to this argument, it is not war or any other phenomenon that justifies IR. Rather, as Stanley Hoffmann (Hoffmann, 1959, 346) explains, "international relations take place in a milieu which has its own 'coherence and uniqueness,' its rules of the game which differ sharply from the rules of domestic politics, its own perspective." The uniqueness of this domain is the fact that it lacks a central government or power capable of exercising absolute legitimate control over the entire system. As Raymond Aron (Aron, 1973, 4) puts it, there is a multiplicity of power centers, "each of which claims the right to take justice into its own hands and to be the sole arbiter of the decision to fight or not to fight." In other words, international relations are conducted in an anarchical environment. On this view, the crucial difference between this realm and domestic politics is the existence of a legitimate authority with the capacity to rule over the citizenry. Domestic politics is hierarchically ordered. Within the state, individuals develop their talents and skills, and amass wealth in a realm of legal rights and duties that constitute (actually or potentially), a *res publica*.

It is worth exploring this claim further before noting its implications for international theory. The world is divided among sovereign states. War is an ever-present background possibility among states that coexist in a condition of anarchy. There is no world government, although elements of "international governance" in the form of international organizations and sustained patterns of cooperation no doubt moderate the extreme image of international relations as a "jungle." In this environment, political authority is dispersed along territorial lines. It is therefore difficult to coordinate global action to deal with global problems that do not respect territorial borders. As human beings, we may be upset by the images of starvation, cruelty, and injustice, for example, that bombard us daily on our television screens. It may strike us as arbitrary that we enjoy the privileges of peace and prosperity while other human beings suffer simply because they happen to have been born in Somalia rather than Australia, Canada, or the United States. Modernity, among other things, is an ethos of reason and belief in the growth of reason to control our environment so that it fulfils human purposes and contributes to the sum of our collective well-being. Suffering, of course, does not correlate with territorial boundaries, but the political capacity to respond to it does. Our cosmopolitan moral sentiments are constantly frustrated by our particularistic political identities as citizens. This is puzzling, frustrating, and apt to make us curious. How did this schism come about? What sustains it? How may it be overcome, if indeed it should? Such questions may explain the need for theory but they are questions of an ethical nature, rather than, or perhaps in addition to, the scientific urge to explain patterns of state behavior.

As students, of course, our duty or vocation is to understand. However, as Michael Banks (Banks, 1984, 4) points out, understanding in this area "is not a matter of hunting down immutable laws. It is an exploration of the manner in which some political ideas have become political facts, whereas others have not. . . . To seek understanding, therefore, is to take part in a debate between competing sets of ideas." One of the most interesting trends in IR over the last decade or so is an acknowledgment of the fact that the "the world" is not independent of the perceptual and conceptual horizons that allow us to organize, simplify, and select from "it" the data that constitute the "raw material" of empirical theory. Try as we might to occupy some Archimedean point from which to understand international relations "objectively," it is by no means clear how to achieve this goal. If this is the case, it implies that the pursuit of "consensus" at a disciplinary level is not only chimerical, but positively dangerous, involving the concealment or subordination of ideas and values incompatible with the hegemonic core. In this context, theoretical pluralism is a sign of health, not disarray.

"Consensus" and "discipline," in this context, are related terms. A "disciplinary consensus" implies some obedience to regulations, the acceptance of a preordained code, technique, or practice, or a system of rules to guide behavior. Yet, as Michel Foucault (Foucault, 1984, 181) reminds us, it is also a general formula of domination. Regimentation, conformity, and order are implicit in the notion of "consensus" in IR.

Of course, the appeal for consensus has never been limited to the realm of the subject matter, nor has IR ever been autonomous in the way its spokespersons have studied that subject matter. If "relations among states" is the ontological site of IR, the latter has also been dominated by an implicit consensus that its subject matter is amenable to the development of "theory" that obeys the alleged requirements of epistemological rigor regardless of ontological domain. In 1959, Hoffmann described many of the pitfalls that lay in store on what he called "the long road to theory," but the metaphor itself aptly expressed the confidence that even if the car had to be built from scratch, the road was already there. During IR's "long boom" years in the United States after 1945, the founding and expansion of the "discipline" not only required an initial agreement that international relations could be isolated analytically, but also that the domain was amenable to the systematic elaboration of empirical theory in a positivist mode. This enabled scholars to speak and understand each other through the use of a common vocabulary, prioritize research, set disciplinary goals, and provide a "neutral" epistemological framework so that research findings could be verified and tested against existing disciplinary knowledge.

The epistemology that accompanied the development of IR as a discipline (particularly after 1945) derived from the Enlightenment and the philosophies of the natural sciences. In large measure, the articulation of this historical relationship preordained the parameters for generating consensus on theoretical matters, for what it is for a subject to qualify as a science, and for the discovery of truth and knowledge. Although there have, of course, always been dissenters, and some, like Morgenthau, were never quite sure which side of the fence they sat on, generally speaking the discipline has accepted this epistemological bill on face value. Indeed, the very idea of consensus and agreement is an outgrowth of a scientific culture; a culture that believes that its achievement is the first and necessary step on "the royal road to truth and knowledge."

IR, then, comprises an autonomous discipline only insofar as it is possible to maintain a consensus on its epistemological as well as the ontological dimensions. This is continually reaffirmed by the use of such "consensus" generating phrases as "our discipline," "we scholars," and so on. This continual reaffirmation is one of the mechanisms by which the pulse of the "discipline" is taken, and its health assured. The former has roots deep in the psyche of modernity. The term "enlightenment," for example, is a metaphor used generally to denote the passage of human thought from darkness to illumination, mythology to knowledge, and conveys the movement of human consciousness from the irrational to the rational. To be "enlightened" is to see the world in the clear light of day; to escape from the shadows of the Platonic cave and see things as they really are. In the eighteenth century the term gained currency as a social and political movement which embraced the idea of progress, on the epistemological, social, and political fronts. The opposite of enlightenment is concealment. To conceal is to hide from view, to keep secret. For the thinkers of the eighteenth century, the church and the clergy conspired to conceal the liberative power of reason from the masses, to keep them in the dark and make them subservient to an ideology of tradition, authority, prejudice, and arbitrary power. Breaking the hold of this ideology was one of the things that made the thinkers of the eighteenth century revolutionaries and "enlighteners." Kant's (Kant, 1970, 54) famous statement about the need for individuals to escape from their self-imposed immaturity is the quintessential expression of this side of the Enlightenment's political agenda.

Neorealism, the target of voluminous criticism in recent years, stands squarely within this broad intellectual movement because of its commitment to the epistemological rationality of scientific progress as (re)presented by positivism. But that commitment is wedded to a set of ontological assumptions consistent with a "discipline" of IR that restricts progress to the instrumental reason of the great powers in providing what little order exists among states. The overall aim of neorealists, like all thinkers of a modernist hue, is enlightenment. They seek, through the application of reason, to determine the "true" nature of international relations. We can see this in their promise to cut through the rhetoric of state behavior, ideology, and moralism, and to discover the perennial laws of interstate behavior rooted in the structural necessities of the international system. In adopting this stance, neorealists believe that they are adding to the storehouse of knowledge, making the opaque clear, the dark light, and the complex world of international relations more transparent. To be "enlightened" on neorealist terms is to describe and explain the inner workings of the international system, to understand that it resists the forces of change and reform, and face a political world that is violent, hostile, and conflict-ridden in a "realistic" and cautious manner. Neorealists are epistemologically progressivist, even though they are highly skeptical of progress as a political goal.

Much (possibly too much) has been written about the hegemony of neorealism in IR. Much less has been written about the difficulties of drawing the emperor's attention to his lack of clothing without thereby destroying the empire itself. Richard Ashley (Ashley, 1991, 38) is one of the few to have pointed out the irony of a seemingly permanent critique whose reluctance to confront the implications of its success undermines the revolutionary enterprise:

> [If] challenging [neo]realism is itself a normal activity, already accommodated within the discipline's official self-representations, then how serious can the challenges be? Perennially challenged, [it] also seems to be perennially affirmed as the central paradigm to be challenged.

Is there any way out of the circle of repudiation/affirmation? If neorealism is the paradigm most committed to sustaining the unity of both dimensions of the "discipline," it would seem somewhat naive to ignore the implications of its repudiation for the "discipline" as a whole.

Our own response is to refuse to be seduced by ritualistic appeals for "disciplinary integrity" that generate legislative demands for "consensus" and concern for "division." These appeals are obviously necessary to sustain the myth that academic specialization is a prerequisite for knowledge, which, in turn, is a prerequisite for enlightened intervention. However, it is becoming increasingly difficult to sustain that myth in light of the dramatic failure of the "discipline" to predict the end of the Cold War on the basis of its existing stock of empirical theory. This is not to say that the ontological condition that gives rise to IR no longer exists. The world continues to be divided among states. Despite the ubiquity of references to globalizing forces of one kind or another, there is precious little evidence to suggest that this foreshadows the imminent transcendence of sovereignty as a constitutive principle of constitutional pluralism in international society. It is to say, however, that the academic study of international relations should not take this condition for granted, nor should it exclude "relations" and processes that are not usefully understood within a state-centric representation. Ideological, environmental, gender, and especially market capitalist "relations," to mention but four, are not adequately explored within a "discipline" that continues to operate on assumptions that informed its inception at the close of the First World War. Indeed, one major constraint to the systematic academic study of these questions is the persistence of an academic division of labor between students of "international," "domestic," and "comparative" politics. This division has sustained striking instances of mutual neglect between bodies of literature whose substantive concerns have obvious areas of overlap.

Perhaps the most glaring example of this is the problematic nature of "International Relations" in an era when nations and states are entities whose congruence in the form of the "nation-state" is an achievement that is both rare and extraordinarily difficult to replicate across the globe. Those who welcomed the end of the Cold War in the belief that the society of states was no longer confronted by powerful revisionist challengers to the traditional international legal order, failed to note the tensions within that order, between, on the one hand, the maintenance of state (territorial) sovereignty and, on the other hand, the political ideal of self-determination. Although the latter was subordinated to the former in the context of decolonization, it can no longer be contained within the constraints of the existing distribution of territorial boundaries unless the ideal of the nation-state as a unitary political agent is abandoned. If such tensions are to be resolved by peaceful means, then we also have to abandon the belief that we can examine the nature of international order independently of its domestic counterpart (see Griffiths, 1997, 44–68). In the 1990s, the relationship between territorial borders, political communities, and the rights and obligations of the "international community" should be at the core of any "research program" that seeks to be relevant in contemporary global politics. In exploring the complexities of that relationship, we need to draw on the insights of political theory, political science, comparative political analysis, and, of course, the voluminous literature on the history of nationalism.

REALISM: FOR AND AGAINST

If we entertain the possibility that the American "discipline" of IR is obsolescent, and that attempts to restore its unity and coherence by importing metatheoretical gurus from the increasingly fractured philosophy of science are unlikely to succeed, this does not imply that international relations no longer exist, nor that the elements of what Kalevi Holsti (Holsti, 1986, 7) calls "the classical tradition" no longer warrant our attention. There are, however, far more fruitful ways to engage in "international theory" than clinging to the idea that the latter must conform to epistemological criteria that may not be consistent with the phenomena—the ontological subject-matter—of international relations, even if they bear the promise of fulfilling "scientific" criteria for theoretical progress.

Instead of accepting the idea that international theory should explain patterns of state behavior by grounding them in the alleged imperatives of anarchy, a move that begs crucial questions about the source and nature of those imperatives, we need to be far more critical of the practices that sustain the autonomy of IR and that perpetuate the paradox of a seemingly endless critique of Realism. It is possible, in our view, to escape Ashley's (Ashley, 1991) paradox of constant repudiation/affirmation by not repudiating what is valid in Realism when it is understood solely as a codification of constraints on the use of reason to reform international relations. Whatever else international society may be, Hoffmann is quite right to insist that it is not an integrated system or a global community. It is hostile to any reforms that may undermine the principle of state sovereignty as a basis for the legitimate exercise of political power on a global scale. Indeed, it may well be the case that the principle of sovereignty still offers the most cogent explanation for what takes place in international relations on a day-to-day basis.

If Realism is understood in minimal terms as a constant reminder of the enduring tragedies of power politics that stem from the irrational association of sovereignty, territory, and statehood in differentiating humanity politically, then we should all be quite happy to be called Realists. At the same time, it would be quite wrong to argue that "Realism" has dominated the study of international relations. Political Realism is precisely what has been absent from the Anglo-American study of international relations. Instead, what Alan James (James, 1989, 215) calls "large-R-Realism" has been constructed—by both "its" champions and critics—as the guardian ghost of the autonomous "discipline" of IR. The ghostly metaphor is appropriate in light of the abject failure to identify "Realism" in a way that allows it to be defended or attacked.

What is Realism? Everyone is assumed to know, but none can agree, and even those who call themselves "Realists" are divided on what "it" is. It is not possible, for example, to defend a view of international politics couched in terms of "might is right," while, at the same time, appealing to the morality of states. To defend one set of arguments is to reject, or at least marginalize, the insights of many of the others. The absence of agreement is indicative of a deeper failure to establish IR as an autonomous "discipline" with its own theoretical approaches in which the terms of debate are widely shared. This has simply never been the case in IR, and it is clearly impossible today. Indeed, the degree of diversity in the 1990s is so great that it is not even possible to undertake the ambitious cartographic exercises that were so popular in the 1970s and 1980s. A decade ago, one could still get away with constructing trilogies of "schools of thought" employed by writers such as Holsti, Wight, and Bull (see, for example, the discussion in Porter this volume). Who would dare to continue in such a vein today? The fragmentation of IR is such that it includes fissures at many levels of analysis that cut across each other. In addition to the well-worn debates of yesterday, one must now acknowledge "isms" that simply do not fit criteria of selection and evaluation that are themselves at issue in these "post-positivist" days.

CONCLUSION

In attacking the idea that the study of international relations should be pursued within an autonomous "discipline," we should make clear that this does not entail a facile celebration of "diversity" for its own sake. We can avoid the false dichotomy between, on the one hand, Robert Keohane's (Keohane, 1988, 392) dogmatic appeal to "discipline" (show us your research program or we'll show you the door!), and, on the other, a relativistic clash of "global voices" (to use the misleading title of Rosenau's [Rosenau, 1995] edited collection). These are not the only alternatives. A third is to acknowledge the value of pluralism and debate in performing our role as students of international relations and as participants in their reform. It may be time to cease casting around for yet another "self-image" of the "discipline" as a whole within which to generate typologies of "schools of thought" as well as criteria for their evaluation. This has always been a popular activity for aspiring cartographers of IR, and one could fill many pages with the various "debates" said to constitute the "discipline" at various stages in its history. These exercises in disciplining disorder are increasingly problematic, although they are extremely valuable when presented for pedagogical purposes in arranging and organizing the ways in which particular substantive questions have been answered. For example, if one thinks that the question "what is international society?" is a good one to ask, then Martin Wight's (Wight, 1994) taxonomy of Realists, rationalists, and revolutionists may be useful to consider the range of responses to it. Similarly, if one's question is "what is international justice, and on what philosophical basis should one attempt to develop normative criteria for evaluating the use of force and the distribution of wealth in the world?" then Chris Brown's (Brown, 1992) book, based around a distinction between cosmopolitanism and communitarianism, is a good introduction. Alternatively, the question "what was the Cold War, and how did it begin?" may yield a completely different typology between orthodox, revisionist, and post-revisionist accounts. Typologies such as these, based on substantive questions generated independently of their answers, are extremely useful. Alternatively, the question "what are the main paradigms in IR?" is not an interesting question. Nor are a whole list of similar questions such as: What does postmodernism have to offer students of international relations? What is the relationship between neoliberalism and neorealism? How does feminism challenge the hegemonic discourse of Realism in contemporary international theory? What is a "great debate" in IR and how many of them have there been? What is the "next stage" in international relations theory? These, and a host of other questions that have obsessed academics and students in recent times, are second-order questions, not first-order questions about the world. While the raising of second-order questions is necessary, especially if we are to judge the viability of theoretical contributions from individual scholars, there is a need for discrimination. Second-order questions which amount to little more than disciplinary navel-gazing should be given up. For they perpetuate the myth so neatly expressed by Dougherty and Pfaltzgraff (Dougherty and Pfaltzgraff, 1971, 15) that "before we can develop theory, we must have at least a consensus within the community of scholars as to what the field of international relations entails." Only an academic in IR (and the social sciences) could make such a fatuous claim. There is no easier way to bore students of international relations to death than by taking them on a tedious journey through the "great debates" of IR. Unless one's interest is grounded in, and stays grounded in, substantive questions about the world, the fate of a marginal "discipline" will be of no interest to anyone but those who have some professional stake in its outcome.

NOTE

The authors would like to thank Roger Spegele, Darryl Jarvis, and Robert Crawford for their thoughtful comments on this paper.

REFERENCES

Armstrong, D. (1995). "Why Is There Too Much International Theory." *Australian Journal of Political Science 30*(4), 356–363.

Aron, Raymond. (1973). *Peace and War: A Theory of International Relations.* Abridged version. New York: Anchor Press.

Ashley, Richard K. (1991). "The State of the Discipline: Realism under Challenge." In Richard L. Higgott and James L. Richardson (eds.), *International Relations: Global and Australian Perspectives on an Evolving Discipline.* Canberra: The Australian University Press: 37–69.

Banks, Michael. (1984). "The Evolution of International Relations Theory." In Michael Banks (ed.), *Conflict in World Society: A New Perspective on International Relations.* Brighton, U.K.: Harvester Wheatsheaf: 3–21.

Brown, Chris. (1992). *International Relations Theory: New Normative Approaches.* London: Harvester Wheatsheaf.

Buzan, Barry. (1993). "From International System to International Society: Structural Realism and Regime Theory Meet the English School." *International Organization 47*(3), 327–352

Cox, Robert W. (1986). "Social Forces, States and World Orders: Beyond International Relations Theory." In Robert O. Keohane (ed.), *Neorealism and Its Critics.* New York: Columbia University Press: 204–254.

Dougherty, J. E., and R. L. Pfaltzgraff. (1971). *Contending Theories of International Relations.* New York: J. B. Lippincott Co.

Foucault, Michel. (1984). "The Docile Bodies." In P. Rabinow (ed.), *The Foucault Reader.* New York: Pantheon Books: 179–187.

Griffiths, Martin. (1997). "Multilateralism, Nationalism and the Problem of Agency in International Theory." In Richard Leaver and D. Cox (eds.), *Middling, Meddling, Muddling: Issues in Australian Foreign Policy.* Sydney, Aust.: St. Leonards: Allen & Unwin: 44–68.

Halliday, Fred. (1986). "A 'Crisis' in International Relations." *International Relations 8*(4), 407–412.

Hoffmann, Stanley. (1959). "International Relations: The Long Road to Theory." *World Politics 11*(3). 346–377.

Hoffmann, Stanley. (1987). "An American Social Science: International Relations." In Stanley Hoffmann, *Janus and Minerva: Essays in the Theory and Practice of International Politics.* Boulder, Colo.: The Westview Press.

Holsti, K. J. (1996). *The State, War, and the State of War.* Cambridge: Cambridge University Press.

Holsti, K. J. (1985). *The Dividing Discipline: Hegemony and Diversity in International Theory.* London: George Allen & Unwin.

James, A. (1989). "The Realism of Realism: The State and the Study of International Relations." *Review of International Studies 15*, 215–229.

Kant, Immanuel. (1970). "What Is Enlightenment?" *Kant's Political Writings*. Cambridge: Cambridge University Press: 54–60.

Keohane, Robert O. (1988). "International Institutions: Two Approaches." *International Studies Quarterly 32*(4), 379–396.

Oakeshott, Michael. (1975). *On Human Conduct*. Oxford: Clarendon Press.

Rosenau, James N. (1995). *Global Voices*. New York: State University of New York Press.

Suganami, H. (1990). "Bringing Order to the Causes of War Debate." *Millennium: Journal of International Politics 19*(1), 19–35.

Waltz, Kenneth N. (1979). *Man, The State and War*. New York: Columbia University Press.

Wight, Martin. (1994). *International Theory: The Three Traditions*. London: Leicester University Press.

CHAPTER 9

Fog in the Channel:
Continental International
Relations Theory Isolated
(Or an essay on the Paradoxes of
Diversity and Parochialism in IR Theory)

Chris Brown

INTRODUCTION

If the numbers of scholars engaged in the discourse is any kind of indicator, then it is difficult to deny that International Relations (IR) is an "American discipline," *pace* the evidence presented elsewhere in this volume by A. J. R. Groom. However, the "American" nature of the discipline is not simply a matter of numbers. IR is an American discipline in the sense in which Coca-Cola is an American drink and Macdonald's hamburgers are American beef patties; although lots of people in the rest of the world "do" IR, it is American IR that, for the most part, they are doing, just as Macdonald's are American burgers, even when ingredients, cooks, and consumers are all drawn from another continent. As with a Macdonald's franchise, the relevant standards are set in the United States in accordance with prevailing American notions of what constitutes scholarly work in the field. Put more precisely, the field itself is largely delimited by the American understanding of IR—one is only "doing" IR, as opposed to some other intellectual activity, if one is addressing problems recognized as such by the American discipline, and/or employing modes of reasoning recognized as appropriate in the United States—which is not to say that the American profession speaks with one voice; it is orthodox IR to which I refer here, and there are many minority voices in the United States who can be found in opposition to orthodoxy.

In this essay, I want to address three aspects of this situation. First, I want to suggest that while IR has always been a discipline dominated by English speakers, throughout its formative period in the interwar years, the English speakers in question were as likely to be British as they were to be American, and thus the fact that continental European influences were marginalized in those days was as much, if not rather more, the fault of English parochialism than of nascent American hegemonism. Second, I ask whether the dominance of English speakers matters in any substantive sense and argue that it does, because the English-speaking intellectual community that created the discipline had quite distinctive views on politics, views that were markedly different from those predominant on the Continent. To this day the discipline of IR is shaped by this difference, because, contrary to first impressions, this difference was reinforced rather than shaken by the rise of "Realism" and the substantial input made to the discourse by émigré scholars in Britain and, especially, the United States in the 1940s and 1950s.

The third aspect I wish to discuss concerns the paradoxes of parochialism, and is less easy to pose in short form. Perhaps the simplest way of making the point is to ask in what sense, if at all, is American IR "parochial"? It is parochial because the practical concerns of U.S. foreign policy continue implicitly or explicitly to dominate the thinking of a great many American scholars and this, though understandable enough, without doubt reflects a certain narrowness of view. However, there is another sense in which it can be argued that both American IR and the Anglo-American political tradition upon which it is based are not parochial enough, that is to say, do not pay sufficient attention to the parochial, the local, the sources of difference between states and communities. Paradoxically, to achieve diversity in international thought it may be necessary to make mainstream American IR more open to the parochial, less wedded to the universal—perhaps even more explicitly "American"—than it has been in the past. Even this may understate the task—it may be that the nature of the discipline of IR as such is at the heart of the matter, and that current American "ownership" of "the discipline" is incidental to a wider problem.

This essay addresses these problems, drawing on past work on international political theory and more recent work on the history of the discipline (Brown, 1992, 1997). However, it should be noted that the argument here is drawn with a very broad brush—the scope and range of the paper requires a great many generalizations that, in a different context, I would wish to qualify. Apologies to those, then, who might feel, with some justice, that their work has been cavalierly treated.

FOUNDATION

A number of statements about the twentieth-century origins of IR as a discipline would be very widely accepted, in particular; that it was largely the product of the experiences of the Great War of 1914–1918, that in its early years (the "first foundation") it was dominated by liberal internationalist thinking ("idealism" or "utopianism") and that in reaction to the rise of the dictators, and the stresses and strains of events in the 1930s and 1940s, it was reshaped on different lines ("Realism") by writers such as Carr, Niebuhr, Kennan, and Morgenthau (the "second foundation"), lines that have remained salient, albeit frequently amended, up to the present day. Less frequently made explicit, although present implicitly, is the assumption made by defenders of the conventional discourse that while the first foundation was certainly Anglo-American and liberal in inspiration, the second foundation provided the diversity the first foundation lacked—Marxists such as E. H. Carr, theologians such as Reinhold Niebuhr (and, more informally, Herbert Butterfield and Martin Wight), German-Jewish émigrés such as Hans Morgenthau, and Georg Schwarzenberger, even professional diplomats such as George Kennan, each in their different ways could claim to be not just a critic of the post-1918 consensus, but distanced from the mindset that produced that consensus. In the rest of this and the next section I will examine these assumptions, supporting most of them, but, also, in most cases, putting a slightly different spin on conventional wisdom.

In his 1923 inaugural lecture as the (second) Woodrow Wilson Professor of International Politics at the University College of Wales, Aberystwyth, C. K. Webster commented:

> This is the first Chair of International Politics founded in this country, and though in other countries there are professors whose duties are akin to mine, there is no general acceptance of the principles of the study. Indeed, even if such principles had existed before the Great War, that event has so sapped the foundations of international order, and *changed so remorselessly our conceptions of IR*, that a recasting of our ideas would be necessary. But, of course, no ordered and scientific body of knowledge did exist in 1914. Perhaps, if it had, the catastrophe might have been averted. (cited from Olson, 1972, 10, emphasis added)

This is revealing, especially as it comes from a writer who was a hard-nosed diplomatic historian, and not one of those thinkers of the twenty years' crisis who would later be castigated by the fourth holder of the Wilson Chair, E. H. Carr. Part of what Webster has to say is routine but the throwaway line that the Great War "changed so remorselessly our conceptions of IR" repays further study.

Many features of the Great War were, more or less, original to that conflict—in particular, of course, the impact of the technological and organizational capacities of industrial society to warfare and the very high human cost this impact produced. What is less obvious is that the Great War brought about changes in the conceptual apparatus by which we understand international relations. On the contrary, it could well be argued that the Great War actually vindicated the conceptions of international relations that had dominated thinking about the subject for the previous one hundred—if not three hundred—years. At a general level, the war was fought by states exercising their sovereign right to resort to violence in accordance with principles of international law that had been in operation since at least the early eighteenth century. More specifically, it was fought (and won) by a coalition of states united only by their determination to prevent one state from achieving military dominance over the continent, again, a motivation that would have been understood at any time in the previous three centuries. Even more specifically, it was a war that was initiated by the conflict-generating propensities of nationalism, as had been virtually every major war of the previous century. Paul Schroeder's comment is apposite

> . . . not Why World War? but Why Not? War was still the *ultima ratio regum*. World War I was a normal development in international relations; events had been building toward it for a long time. (Schroeder, 1984, 104)

In terms of outcomes, the war brought about the overthrow of three imperial regimes, changed radically the distribution of world power, and provoked social revolution in a number of countries—but much the same could be said of previous European-wide wars. So, then, what was the conception of international relations that had been, apparently, "changed so remorselessly"?

The answer is clear; what was changed by the war was the view that modern industrial society had outgrown such violent and irrational patterns of behavior. What the events of 1914–1918 allegedly demonstrated was that the approach to international relations characteristic of *bien-pensant* British liberals in the early years of the twentieth century—a belief in the atavistic nature of military force as a problem-solving mechanism, a belief in the peace-generating qualities of international economic relations—had been based on a fundamental misunderstanding. Moreover, this misunderstanding may actually have contributed to the outbreak of war, which is, perhaps, the unintentional implication of the final sentence of Webster's cited above. Thus is it that the need to create an ordered and scientific body of thought about international relations arises. The argument goes like this: "before 1914 we thought we understood the nature of international relations, but the events of 1914–1918 showed us that we did not—therefore we need to create the discipline of IR in order to fill a gap in our knowledge which we did not previously know existed."

For the purpose of this discussion, the key question is who are the "we" in this sentence? The answer is, I think, a relatively small number of thinkers most of whom were to be found in the English-speaking democracies. From the point of view of, for example, writers on the socialist left in Europe—from the German Social Democrats to the Russian Bolsheviks—the war ought not to have been, and for the most part was not, a surprise. The most important and influential pre-1914 work of socialist international political economy, Rudolf Hilferding's *Das Finanzkapital*, identified imperialism—the extension, one way or another, of the national economic territory—as the foreign policy of finance capital, and predicted that modern industrial economies would be more, rather than less conflictual in their foreign relations than the free-trade capitalist states of the mid-nineteenth century (Hilferding, 1981). What surprised socialist theorists in 1914 was not so much the outbreak of war, rather the fact that all the European socialist parties save the Serbian and the Bolshevik faction of the Russian, found themselves obliged by their working-class membership to support the national war effort. Even this shock was not inexplicable; socialist writers were well aware of the force of nationalist sentiments, even if sometimes inclined to write off this phenomenon as the product of false consciousness or of the treason of a labor aristocracy. In 1923 neither the Leninists in charge of the new Soviet Union and their followers elsewhere, nor the old Social Democratic left in Europe, had any sense that the Great War had overturned previous conceptions of international relations.

Much the same might be said of the forces of conservatism and nationalism in Europe. From the point of view of the German *ancient régime*, the Great War unfolded as expected, except that they lost. In 1918, at Brest-Litovsk they imposed a traditionally harsh peace treaty on the defeated Russian enemy. The post-1918 German government attempted to use Wilson's liberal agenda to mitigate the consequences of Germany's defeat but their commitment to the underlying principles of liberal internationalism must be doubted. The French political class in the years immediately after the war thought in pre-1914 patterns and made no secret of the contempt in which they held the new liberal internationalist thinking. God himself was satisfied with Ten Commandments, remarked Clemanceau of Wilson's Fourteen Points. There was never any question of a plebiscite deciding the fate of Alsace and Lorraine, largely because the locals could not be relied upon to vote for a return to France (partly, it should be said, because of shifts of population since 1871—but similar arguments were not accepted when they advantaged Germany). The Italian government was largely concerned with traditional territorial aggrandizement, as was the Japanese—the one time the Japanese government showed any interest in the new ideas was when their government attempted to get the League Covenant to outlaw racial discrimination; they failed, with the American and British governments leading the opposition. Opponents of colonial rule who attempted to apply the principle of "self-determination" to non-European peoples met similar resistance.

These points are well known, and, reasonably enough, are usually taken to demonstrate the lack of widespread support for liberal internationalist principles, even among those theoretically committed to the new approaches, such as Wilson and the British. But the point to stress here is a slightly different one—that it was only those who took liberal principles seriously who felt greatly in need of the new academic discipline of IR. Opponents of the new thinking, whether from the left or right, were reasonably happy with the current state of their knowledge. They believed themselves to be in possession already of more or less reliable knowledge of international relations and saw no great need to engage in a recasting of their ideas. The dissatisfaction that Webster drew upon was not as widespread as he seems to have believed it to be. Instead, it was largely confined to liberal circles in Britain and America—and whereas American leadership in liberal internationalism was initially established by a president who believed in the new ideas in a way that no British leader ever did, the failure of the United States to ratify the Versailles Treaty and the Covenant of the League of Nations meant that the torch passed, for a generation, to the British Liberal establishment. Although the study of IR as a university discipline developed in the interwar period in both Britain and the United States, it was in Britain that the new discipline had the higher profile and the greater influence, largely because Britain was, *faute de mieux* and in spite of the reluctance of the Foreign Office, the effective leader of the liberal cause in the world at large.

At this point two rather fundamental objections to the way the argument is going need to be heard. First, it might well be argued that if continental thinkers did not see the need for new ideas after the slaughter of 1914–1918, so much the worse for them; alternatively, it could be said that even if the early discipline of international relations was a one-sided affair caught up in modes of thought that were specific to a particular mind-set, the Second Foundation of the discipline—the arrival of the Realists in the 1930s and 1940s—corrected this bias. The rest of this section will examine the first of these points, asking exactly what, if anything, it was that the emerging discipline lost because of its Anglocentricity?

How did liberal internationalism differ from the conventional views on international relations prevalent on the continent? Two factors seem most important here. First, the "liberal" dimension of liberal internationalism stressed the extent to which a harmony of interests exists in world politics—there are no real conflicts of interest, the "people" always really want peace even if they are sometimes mislead into thinking otherwise, and so on. This had always been a standard liberal position whether the best expression of liberal internationalism was taken to be the Kantian project of "Perpetual Peace" or the Manchester School project of universal "Free Trade." Second, the "internationalist" side of liberal internationalism downgraded the importance of the state as a "community of fate," an affective entity, stressing instead the instrumental dimension of statehood. The liberals were, to an extent, *institutional* cosmopolitans, but they were, to an even greater extent, *moral* cosmopolitans—that is to say that although the liberal world order was populated by states, the expectation was that peoples would not identify too readily with their state and would be prepared, given time, to identify instead with a wider common interest (Beitz, 1994). The reason people would make this identification was because the state was understood to be, at root, an institution designed to solve the problems of collective action rather than an institution which was central to the constitution of the collectivity itself, and to individual personality.

To put the matter differently, liberal internationalists rejected the Hegelian—or more broadly continental—notion that the state is an institution that brings meaning into the lives of individuals, giving them a sense of their worth as equal citizens, a function that the institutions of civil society cannot perform alone. From the point of view of English speakers who take their liberalism from John Locke (or Thomas Hobbes, David Hume, Adam Ferguson, Adam Smith and Jeremy Bentham) the state is an entity which exists in civil society rather than beyond (above) it—indeed, most of the time, such liberals do not use the term "the state" at all, preferring a more administrative term such as "the government." There certainly was a neo-Hegelian tradition in the English-speaking world, attached to pragmatism in the United States and to "idealists" such as Green, Bosanquet, and Bradley in Britain, but one of the consequences of World War I was the emergence of a strong line of attack on the so-called "Hegelian theory of the god-state" (Hobhouse, 1918). In the years after the war liberals in the United States and Britain were very much attached to negative" as opposed to "positive" conceptions of liberty. In Britain the state was more or less taken for granted as a necessary social institution, even though the term itself was not much used, and patriotism was certainly not exceptional but the idea that the state ought to be the subject of an affective identification was much less prevalent—indeed, loyalty to the Crown or even the Empire was more common than overt loyalty to the British state. In the United States, then as now, metonymic patriotic symbols such as "the Flag" or "the Constitution" carried more weight than "the State," which, again, is a term rarely used in political discourse.

That the dominant political philosophy in the English-speaking world did not appear to understand the fact that elsewhere the state was capable of attracting loyalty in its own right was to prove to be a serious handicap when international politics turned rough again in the 1930s. The willingness of ordinary people to give loyalty to "their" state as opposed to the perceived "international interest" was the source of much puzzlement to liberal internationalists. This was partly because of the unwillingness of the latter to recognize similar emotions in themselves, which was, in turn, a function of the lack of a common vocabulary for expressing these emotions—thus British "patriotism" was seen as a very different matter from foreign "nationalism." They were inclined to see statism as a sign of an essentially irrational approach to the world. But is an affective attitude to the state necessarily irrational? To follow this up it may be helpful to shift the story on to the arrival of the Realist critique of liberal internationalism.

SECOND FOUNDATION

Some who would accept at least part of the story told above would argue that the "second foundation" of the discipline in the late 1930s and 1940s corrected the liberal, Anglo-American biases of the first foundation. Reinhold Niebuhr in his *Moral Man and Immoral Society* traced the theological roots of the errors of liberal internationalists, their disregard of original sin, and their heretical belief that the qualities of altruism that individuals may develop, albeit with some difficulty, can be transferred to collectivities (Niebuhr, 1932). Following on from his notion of Christian fellowship and social justice, Niebuhr stressed that "haves" and "have-nots" are bound to develop different views on matters such as the binding moral force of the rule of law, a thought developed at length from a quasi-Marxist perspective by E. H. Carr in the paradigmatic British Realist study of the period, *The Twenty Years' Crisis* (Caff, 1939). During and after the war Georg Schwartzenberger, Martin Wight, and Herbert Butterfield in Britain, Hans Morgenthau, Nicholas Spykman, George Kennan, and Arnold Wolfers in America, continued and deepened the critique. Whereas the British Realists were pushing at an open door as far as the British Foreign Office were concerned, and concentrated on educating the wider public—as with Wight's 1946 pamphlet *Power Politics*—in the United States the emerging foreign-policy elite itself required instruction, which Morgenthau and his colleagues provided (Wight, 1946; Morgenthau, 1948). As Hedley Bull later put it, American Realism provided this elite with a much needed "crib to the European diplomatic tradition" (Bull, 1972, 39).

This is nicely epigrammatic, but did the Realist critique actually provide a "crib to the European diplomatic tradition"? Were the "errors" of liberal internationalism actually corrected? Of the two defining characteristics of liberal internationalism only one was comprehensively critiqued—in the other case the critique that was developed was partial, correcting one aspect of the defective vision of the liberals, but leaving another aspect intact. The feature of liberal internationalism that was thoroughly trashed was the liberal belief in a natural harmony of interests. Someone in the 1960s remarked that contemporary social science was a conspiracy of conservatives and socialists directed against liberals. Nowadays the economists have rediscovered liberalism, and post-positivist scholars have redescribed all three doctrines as "modern" and thereby passé, but in the immediate postwar period this jibe was even more apposite than in the 1960s. The liberal faith in the essential reconcilability of human interests that had been so much a part of the "Enlightenment Project" was now characterized as facile Panglossian optimism, unsustainable in the face of the disasters of war and the death camps. The socialist heirs of the Enlightenment preserved the notion of ultimate harmony but believed it could be achieved only via planning and bureaucracy; conservative critics attempted to teach the world the inevitability of objective conflict. The assumption of a natural harmony of interests went underground, to emerge later in the work of "peace theorists" such as John Burton, who observes that "in politics we are not dealing with scarcity"—although individuals can only be expected to realize that this is so after extensive reeducation in the science of conflict resolution (Burton, 1972, 145).

But what of the liberal internationalist failure to grasp the nature of the state? Here things are rather more complicated. At one level Realism is "state-centric" both in the pragmatic sense that it is critical of those who attribute powers to nonstate international and transnational bodies that they do not, in fact, possess, and in the deeper sense that it recognizes that, as Robert Gilpin puts it,

> the essence of social reality is the group. [In conflict over scarce resources] human beings confront each other ultimately as members of

groups and not as isolated individuals. *Homo Sapiens* is a tribal species, and loyalty to the tribe for most of us ranks above all loyalties other than that of the family. In the modern world, we have given the name " nation-state" to these competing tribes and the name "nationalism" to this form of loyalty. (Gilpin, 1986, 305)

This recognition of the power of tribalism is crucial to Realism and formed a major and compelling element of its critique of liberal internationalism. Liberal internationalists who believed themselves to be more-or-less free of tribalism simply did not and could not realize that others remained in its thrall. Even more damagingly, they did not realize that their own freedom was illusory—that in denying the relevance of tribalism they were, allegedly, actually pursuing their own tribal interests.

However, the same Robert Gilpin, when actually characterizing the state, adopts an essentially liberal framework. Explicitly adopting a theory of the state in which it is seen as an organization that provides protection and welfare in return for revenue, he sees the state as "the principal mechanism by which society can provide . . . 'public goods' and overcome the free rider problem" (Gilpin, 1981, 15). Such an approach is not strictly incompatible with the notion of the state as a vehicle for the expression of the Good for a community, but it seems unlikely that individuals will give more than a highly conditional loyalty to a "mechanism." Nor should they according to Gilpin. These two quotations, taken together, tell an interesting story. Gilpin suggests that, for the purposes of Realism, the "nation-state" is simply a modern term for the tribe, but, of course, for Hegelians, neo-Hegelians and "continentals" more generally, this is not so. The "tribe" is a prepolitical affective community based on kin in which individual freedom is nonexistent. It was only when Greek tribes came together to form cities and were obliged to negotiate the terms of their association that human freedom could begin to develop. The modern state is the opposite of a tribe—it is a space wherein individuals can meet each other as political equals and free citizens rather than as members of an extended tribal family with all its attendant inequalities of age and gender. Again, Gilpin suggests that the role of the state is to resolve public goods/free rider problems—but from a Hegelian perspective this is a task performed by the institutions of civil society, the "police and the corporation" as Hegel puts it (Hegel, 1991, 259). Hegel's point is that while these problems need to be resolved, resolution will not bring reconciliation unless there is another set of institutions in which individuals experience each other as equal citizens rather than as free riders.

Gilpin, rather unusually and greatly to his credit, does actually specify a theory of the state. He is, however, associated with contemporary rational-choice modes of theorizing—on which more below—and thus it might be argued that it is not surprising that he should adopt an essentially Anglo-American liberal view of the state. Perhaps the Realists of the 1930s and 1940s, who did not think in rational-choice terms, saw things differently? To an extent they, or at least some of them, did, but not to the degree that might have been expected. Carr had little time for the continental theory of the state. For someone who professed European studies, Wight seems to have had a rather rudimentary grasp of the finer points of continental philosophy. He refers to the Nazis and Communists as the children of Hegel and Kant, and in order to prove that this is not an accidental aberration, he produced a classification of thought on IR in which Kant and Lenin are in the same category—moreover this "Kantian" (or Revolutionary) category is characterized by an ethic that the end justifies the means, which is, to the best of my knowledge, a unique reading of Kant's moral teachings (Wight, 1966, 28; Wight, 1991).

Things were very different in the United States, where a good proportion of the leading Realists were themselves continental political thinkers. Until his enforced departure from Germany for France, Switzerland and, ultimately, the University of Chicago, the greatest American Realist, Hans Morgenthau, had been steeped in the German tradition of political philosophy, and, even in America, remained in close touch with others similarly educated—Hannah Arendt, for example, was a close friend. It would be absurd to suggest that he was in any respect complicit in the kind of naiveté displayed by Wight. And yet the account of politics and the state upon which his political Realism was based is not dramatically different from that of the British thinker. Like Wight and Gilpin, Morgenthau is well aware of the power of nationalism and critical of liberal internationalism's incomprehension in the face of this power. But, also like Wight and Gilpin, he does not develop a positive account of the state along Hegelian constitutional lines, although—unlike Wight at least—he clearly was aware that such an account could be developed. What, instead, he seems to have drawn from his German educational background was, on the one hand, a Weberian concern with an "ethic of responsibility" that was combined with a Niebuhrian emphasis on human fallibility and the fragility of institutions, and, on the other, hostility to the implications of the "friend-enemy" distinction developed by Carl Schmitt in 1920s Germany (Schwab, 1996). What comes out of this mix is an emphasis on the prevalence of conflict in the world and on the significance of tribal groupings, but not an emphasis on the positive role of the community.

Perhaps this is hardly surprising given the context. Seen from the vantage point of the new millennium it is easy to see that Hegel's whole conception of politics was founded on constitutionalism and the *Rechtstaat* and that the occasional remark about the supreme authority of the state vis-à-vis the individual has to be seen in this context, just as his expressions of approval for the Prussian state of the 1820s have to be attributed to his general circumstances. Such would have been much more difficult to achieve for someone in Morgenthau's position in the 1930s and 1940s. When Morgenthau equated Hegel and Fichte and referred to them both as representatives of the nationalist philosophy of Germany in which "the national character or spirit appears as the soul, and the political organisation of the state as the body, of the national community, which needs both in order to fulfil its mission among the other national communities" (Morgenthau, 1948, 154), he was presenting an account of Hegel in particular that was partial and ultimately misleading—but, given the way in which Hegel's thought (and Fichte's for that matter) was misused by the Nazis, and German militarists generally, this is forgivable. Unless strongly Zionist, Jewish émigrés of the period tended understandably toward skepticism vis-à-vis nationalism and the nation-state, and even Zionists of this period saw Israel as a special case—in contrast to, for example, Michael Walzer who has built a strong case for self-determination and the integrity of a politics based on the community alongside and in parallel with his Zionist and socialist convictions.

To summarize the argument so far: IR was founded as an academic discipline/discourse in the immediate post-1918 world by British and American "liberal internationalists," and the liberalism upon which this position was based was of a variety that was peculiar to, or at least highly characteristic of, the English-speaking peoples. This worldview downplayed the significance of genuine conflicts of interest, and was based on an instrumental view of the state as a conflict-resolving mechanism. The Realist assault on liberal internationalism of the 1930s and 1940s corrected—perhaps overcorrected—the first of these faults but, for a variety of reasons, did little to change the second. Post-1945 Realism remained as instrumental in its view of the state as pre-1939 liberal internationalism. The center of gravity of post-1945 IR crossed the Atlantic, not for any deep ideological reason, but because of the post-war, and especially post-1947, shift in world power.

An obvious question is "what has all this to do with diversity in the discipline today?" How far can the current status of IR as an "American social science" be explained in term of the history of its two foundations as an academic discipline? To quite a considerable extent: the history of the early years can still tell us quite a lot about the modern discipline; many of the attitudes characteristic of the early years of the discipline in Britain are still present today, albeit clothed differently, in the United States.

THE PARADOXES OF PAROCHIALISM

Both post-1918 and post-1945 British and American IR were based on the time-honored disciplinary base of history, law, and philosophy—much as were parallel discourses on the European continent although the nature of the philosophical and legal (and, sometimes, historical) traditions in question were somewhat different. Liberal internationalists and Realists read the findings and wisdom of these various traditions differently but, for the most part, they deployed similar kinds of arguments; contrary to the occasional loose usage of terms like "paradigm," there was no incommensurability here, and whatever mutual incomprehension existed was a function of the ideas in question rather than of styles of reasoning.

In the year 2000, things are rather different. The intellectually powerful "rational-choice" mode of reasoning employed in American IR (and political science more generally) with its characteristic metatheories (neorealism and neoliberalism) and its characteristic problematic (anarchy and cooperation amongst egoists) is not widely employed in Britain or France, and is dominant only in those parts of Scandinavian, German, and non-European social science who are dependent on the United States for their models. In Britain, the antirational choice coalition is composed of two wings joined only by their opposition to this discourse—a wing of "traditionalists" still committed to the old project of extracting wisdom from anecdotal history, and a growing body of post-positivists for whom rational choice theory is the paradigm case of a nonhermeneutic, noncritical discourse. To the extent that U.S. scholars are able to define what the discipline is, and insofar as they use this power to define rational choice as the core of the discipline, it is unsurprising that IR remains an American social science. The "Americanness" of IR is now a matter of the legitimacy of the methods employed by the discipline. Those of us who do not employ rational choice thinking are now marginalized, whether we are American or not—in contrast to a generation or so ago when leading British and European figures such as Herbert Butterfield, Hedley Bull, or Raymond Aron found much less difficulty in establishing links with mainstream American colleagues. The issue of "diversity" today involves methods as well as cadres.

However, digging below the surface, some characteristic features of old-style Anglo-American IR can still be found exhibited by modern American rational -choicers. In many respects, new rational-choicers are but old (liberal) Realists writ large. An instrumental view of the state is, if anything, an even more pronounced feature of current IR than it was of past theories. Rational-choicers recognize the power of collective identifications—indeed a great deal of modern theorizing only makes sense if such identifications are assumed—but like their liberal and Realist (and liberal-Realist) forebears they regard such identification as essentially rather peculiar and tribal. For most modern theorists, group violence is a product of irrationality or primordial instincts, something to be explained only in terms of complex psychology. The idea that there might be some merit in individuals identifying with "their" community is not much favored. Group identification can be understood in rational choice terms—Russell Hardin's recent *One for All* shows how the trick is done—but is still a matter for profound suspicion (Hardin, 1995).

Put differently, the dominant mode of thinking in the modern discipline is profoundly *cosmopolitan*. Here is the paradox. At one level, American IR has never been more intellectually isolated than it is presently in that the only scholars in the rest of the world who are truly accepted as part of the discourse—as opposed to tolerated on the margins—are those who are trained in American methods, usually by Americans. But, at another level, the intellectual predispositions of the American discipline are universalist, committed to denying the privileging of any particular national viewpoint—indeed to denying the very idea that a *national* viewpoint could have any intellectual validity (see, for example, Porter; Crawford, this volume). What adds to the irony is that the very universalism of American IR probably contributes to its isolation. The inability of mainstream American social scientists to understand those many features of the modern world that reflect diversity and difference stems from its universalism. Because the dominant theory is universalist, because according to the model we are all potentially rational choosers—or neoliberal economic actors, to trace rational choice theory back to its roots—American social scientists often resent the suggestion that their theories are ethnocentric, and yet at least part of the inability of some American scholars—and, of course, it is important not to overgeneralize here—to get hold of such diverse phenomena as nationalism in Yugoslavia, the rise of radical Islam, Japanese trade policy, Singaporean approaches to human rights, and Somali resentment at being "helped" by outsiders, stems from the fact that the various groups involved are *not* motivated by the same things that motivate the abstract persons who inhabit rational choice models.

The real irony is that if American social science was *more* parochial it would have a better chance of getting things right. It is not American parochialism that is the problem; it is the *lack* of American parochialism that is the problem. If American social science were to be more overtly committed to promoting American values—preferably in the ironic mode of a Richard Rorty, or with the awareness of the multiple identities of the modern self of a Michael Walzer—it would have a better chance of understanding why other people who are not American are committed to promoting their own values (Cohen, 1996). The, at times deeply distasteful, waves of anti-Americanism that regularly crash over the non-American world are obviously prompted by many different factors, but are generally not set off by the overt pursuit of American interests by American governments, but by the reluctance to admit that this is what is happening, the cloaking of interest in the language of altruism. There are echoes here of attitudes toward Britain in the days of British power— *Perfidious Albion's* reputation was based on a not dissimilar unwillingness to admit that British power served British interests. The *bête noir* of continental diplomatists such as Bismarck was not a Palmerston or a Disraeli—both unapologetic wielders of British power—but the liberal Gladstone, whose every foreign policy move was covered by a miasma of moralizing rhetoric and appeals to the interests of "Europe."

It would obviously be an exaggeration to suggest that the tendency of successive U.S. governments to endow their foreign policies with sometimes inappropriate internationalist clothing is solely, or even mainly, a function of cosmopolitan tendencies in mainstream American IR. But, given the close links between the academic and government in the United States, it is not fanciful to suggest a connection here. The more general point is that the modern discipline has not yet escaped from its liberal internationalist past. The "anarchy problematic" and the assumption of "rational egoism"—whether examined from the perspective of neorealism or neoliberal institutionalism—may seem very different from the characteristic formulations of the interwar liberal internationalists or post-1945 Realists, but the same basic understanding of the relationship between the individual and society underlies all three approaches. Each regards the state in instrumental terms as a means of problem-solving rather than as an expression of the Good, and each sees politics as the pursuit of interests, however much they might disagree as to the nature of these interests. Each, essentially, is liberal in the Anglo-American sense of the term and whatever case there is to be made for this perspective when it comes to domestic social arrangements—and many of "democracy's discontents" undoubtedly spring from the liberalism of the "procedural republic" (Sandel, 1996; Sandel, 1984)—the evidence of the past century seems to be that it is singularly ill-equipped to handle the international dimension of contemporary life.

CONCLUSION

Do we need to move toward greater diversity in international thought? Certainly. Is the biggest obstacle to diversity the American domination of the discipline of IR? Partly. Is American dominance a problem because the American discipline is too "American"? No. The problem is that the American discipline is not American enough. It is dominated by a universalist, cosmopolitan worldview as was British IR in the interwar period, *as has been the "discipline" itself since its formation post-1919.* Here, at last, we may be approaching the heart of the problem. The very idea that one actually needs "a discipline" of IR may be tied up with a particular worldview. Those professors whose "duties were akin" to C. K. Webster's were, for the most part, doing the subject without working from a disciplinary base because the kind of intellectual background out of which they emerged did not need such a foundation. Hegel's *Philosophy of Right* takes the argument all the way from the family, via civil society and the state, to international relations and world history. Kant's political writings culminate in *Perpetual Peace: A Philosophical Sketch.* Green and Bosanquet incorporate the international dimension of political life into their writings as a matter of course. It is the liberals upon whom the discipline of IR has always drawn who constructed their theories on the assumption that societies were self-contained and who, therefore, once the fact that this was an unhelpful assumption could no longer be ignored, found themselves obliged to add a layer of theorizing on top of their existing ideas—a layer that we now call "International Relations." If we truly wish to promote diversity in international thought, it may be that a crucial first step will be to contribute to the work of dismantling "International Relations" as an academic discipline (see Griffiths and O'Callaghan, this volume). There are many signs that this work is under way—but that takes us beyond the scope of this paper.

NOTE

Thanks for comments on an earlier version of this chapter to all the participants in panel discussions on this volume at Toronto ISA in March 1997, especially the convenors, Robert Crawford and Darryl Jarvis, and the panel participants Mark Newfeld, John Groom, and Roger Spegele. "Fog in the Channel: Continent Isolated" is a, perhaps apocryphal, London *Times* headline of the interwar period, the significance of which will be lost on future generations now that the trip between London and Paris can be accomplished via the Tunnel without reference to surface weather conditions on the Straits of Dover.

REFERENCES

Beitz, Charles R. (1994). "Cosmopolitan Liberalism and the States System." In Chris Brown (ed.), *Political Restructuring in Europe.* London: Routledge: 114–136.

Brown, Chris. (1992). *International Relations Theory: New Normative Approaches*. Hemel Hempstead, U.K.: Harvester Wheatsheaf.

Brown, Chris. (1997). *Understanding International Relations*. London: Macmillan.

Bull, Hedley. (1972). "The Theory of International Politics 1919–69." In B. Porter (ed.), *The Aberystwyth Papers: International Politics 1919–1969*. London: Oxford University Press: 30-55.

Burton, John W. (1972). *World Society*. Cambridge: Cambridge University Press.

Carr, E. H. (1939). *The Twenty Years' Crisis*. London: Macmillan

Cohen, J. (1996). *For Love of Country: Debating the Limits of Patriotism*. (Martha C. Nussbaum with Respondents). Boston: Beacon Press.

Gilpin, Robert. (1981). *War and Change in World Politics*. Cambridge: Cambridge University Press.

Gilpin, Robert. (1986). "The Richness of the Tradition of Political Realism." In Robert O. Keohane (ed.), *Neorealism and Its Critics*. New York: Columbia University Press: 301–321.

Hardin, R. (1995). *The Logic of Group Conflict*. Princeton: Princeton University Press.

Hegel, G. W. F. (1991). *Elements of the Philosophy of Right*. Ed. Allen Wood. Cambridge: Cambridge University Press.

Hilferding, R. (1981). Finance Capital. Ed. Tom Bottomore. London: Routledge.

Hobhouse, L. T. (1918). *The Metaphysical Theory of the State*. London: George Allen & Unwin.

Morgenthau, Hans. (1948). *Politics among Nations*. New York: Knopf.

Niebuhr, Reinhold. (1932). *Moral Man and Immoral Society*. New York: Charles Scribner's Sons.

Olson, W. C. (1972). "The Growth of a Discipline." In B. Porter (ed.), *The Aberystwyth Papers: International Politics 1919–1969*. London: Oxford University Press: 3–29.

Sandel, Michael. (1984). "The Procedural Republic and the Unencumbered Self." *Political Theory* 12(1), 81–96.

Sandel, Michael. (1996). *Democracy's Discontents: America in Search of a Public Philosophy*. Cambridge, Mass.: The Belknap Press.

Schroeder, P. W. (1984). "World War I as Galloping Gertie." In H. W. Koch (ed.), *The Origins of the First World War*. 2nd ed. London: Macmillan.

Schwab, G. (1996). "Introduction and Notes to Carl Schmitt." *The Concept Of the Political*. Chicago: University of Chicago Press.

Wight, Martin. (1946). *Power Politics*. "Looking Forward." Pamphlet No. 8. London: Royal Institute of International Affairs.

Wight, Martin. (1966). "Why Is There No International Theory?" In Herbert Butterfield and Martin Wight (eds.), *Diplomatic Investigations*. London: George Allen and Unwin: 17–34.

Wight, Martin. (1991). *International Theory: The Three Traditions*. Ed. Gabriele Wight and Brian Porter. Leicester, U.K.: Leicester University Press.

CHAPTER 10

Where Have All the Theorists Gone— Gone to Britain, Every One? A Story of Two Parochialisms in International Relations

Robert M. A. Crawford

> One of the things that everyone knows but no one can quite think how to demonstrate is that a country's politics reflect the design of its culture.
>
> —Clifford Geertz

Like the world it seeks to comprehend, international relations theory remains divided between, among other things, competing nationally, communally, culturally, and ethnically derived notions of identity that are rooted in historical experiences and encounters with the world beyond the particular vantage points and boundaries of the field's primary actors. This situation makes full political and intellectual commensurability in international theory impossible, except where it is imposed artificially through totalizing constructs like *the discipline*. To date, however, parochialism in the field has manifested itself in precisely this way. Since its first awakening as an organized academic discipline in the early part of the twentieth-century International Relations (IR) has been bound up inextricably with national attitudes, priorities, and interests, first British and, from the 1940s onward, American. It has even been suggested that the "very idea that one actually needs a discipline of International Relations may be tied up with a particular worldview" (Brown, in this volume), that "the study of international relations is not an innocent profession," and that its place "in the university curriculum rests upon utility" (Wallace, 1996, 301). Small wonder then that IR is a subject of sustained interest only in countries reasonably placed to make some impact on the processes and interactions that constitute its subject matter. While all but the most autarkic countries (of which there are now very few) can be said to have a direct stake in the events and processes of world politics, only Britain and the United States, self-appointed guardians past and present of the modern liberal trading system, have had the right combination of political, economic, intellectual, and ideological resources necessary to comprehend their individual interests in terms of a global discipline of IR.

The Anglo-American origin of the subject is as well documented as the continued centrality of scholarship from the US and Britain is obvious. Though the subject matter of international relations is taught and studied theoretically in numerous other countries, these are limited largely to what K. J. Holsti calls the field's "Anglophone peripheries" (Holsti, 1985), or the established and growing tradition of international relations scholarship in continental Europe. More importantly, study in many countries is limited largely to foreign policy analyses that simply consume and apply concepts generated in the field's core or, where explicitly theoretical debates arise, to copying the latest intellectual fads in the field's primarily American-based journals. Even in ostensibly indigenous organs like Canada's *International Journal* and the *Australian Journal of International Affairs* thinking about the discipline of IR is limited mainly to the usual Anglo-American terms of debate, though these journals also reflect some measure of home-grown theoretical interest in the problem of middle powers, and a refreshingly parochial interest in the politics of "their own" part of the globe. A more telling example, perhaps, is the *European Journal of International Relations* which, despite its name, has become little more than an overseas subsidiary for the dissemination of American intellectual fads, and yet another place for well-established senior scholars to get published.[1] Even in British scholarship, which I will argue below constitutes the only viable, sustained, coherent, largely self-contained, and distinctive alternative conception to American IR, theorizing is often "remarkably derivative" of American thinking (Wallace, 1996, 304). Thus, while there is clearly an argument to be made for greater inclusiveness in international relations research, it is not clear that, under conditions of this sort, more may be better.

It is perverse that a discipline called International Relations should be so manifestly parochial, but the usual diagnosis (too little participation from other national schools) and the usual prescription (increased participation from, and acknowledgment of, IR research outside the Anglo-American core) is suspect (see for example Holsti, 1985,

102–128). Paradoxically, if IR were *more* parochial, in the sense of multiple, nationally defined, conceptions of the discipline, it would be more inclusive. If this seems like a difficult claim to substantiate, it is precisely because indigenous theoretical entrepreneurship in international relations theory tends to be stifled by the sort of universalist conception of social science that has dominated the field from its beginning, but has been all-consuming since its Americanization, bolstered as it is by a strong presumption in favor of methodological consensus and uniformity. Since ideas do not carry passports, these cannot be called strictly American influences, though they resonate strongly with the conception of social science forged in that national academic setting and have become a pillar of its support globally. Thus, while there is evidence in many national jurisdictions of an unquestioned acceptance of some generalizable set of concerns that transcend local interests and can be called international relations, it seems unlikely that any but the most powerful and happily situated countries can afford the luxury of pretending that their most cherished values and ideas will be shared with equal ardor by everyone else. Though the issues and problems posed by international relations as a phenomenon must involve actors on a global scale, the idea that these experiences are generalizable derives from a peculiarly American approach to theorizing the subject which is grounded in historically specific experiences that have been rendered invisible by a decidedly ahistorical and universalist conception of science. Like American hegemony in international politics, American hegemony in international theory masks the extent to which seemingly national policies and innovations are derivative of American interests and predilections. The illusion of universality is so complete that all national prefixes seem irrelevant or, in the case of American IR, redundant. In short, the global reach of a particular form of theoretical parochialism grounded in American experiences, expectations, and methodological assumptions has stifled the expression of *almost* all other nationally derived conceptions of international relations as an academic discipline.

An implicit assumption in this essay is that the study of international relations is, always has been, and will for the foreseeable future be, a field composed of national and other parochialisms. But the tendency for ideas about the discipline to be shaped by geographical and political location has meant that only the most powerful of countries are capable of the sort of global thinking necessary to imagine a global discipline, yielding a perversely insular variety of cosmopolitanism. Quite apart from making the field of IR unusual, this reality makes any claim about the possibility and value of inter-national diversity difficult to test. There is evidence at hand, however, that IR (even in its current state) is neither an exclusively American nor Anglo-American discipline. Rather it is *both* a distinctively American and British discipline. This essay argues that we have in British approaches to international relations, past and present, at least one broadly national orientation distinctive and different enough to allow us to question the pretensions of IR as a universally applicable social science, American or otherwise. I do not, however, wish merely to rearticulate the popular claim that there is a distinctively British place in the evolution of IR as an American social science, a view characterized by the dubious compound term Anglo-American in depictions of the growth of the discipline. On the contrary, this essay consciously resists the explicitly evolutionary logic inherent in every retrospective on the field that casts the key figures of British international relations scholarship in the role of well-meaning pioneers who didn't quite get things right. In these accounts, for example, it is simply taken for granted that a figure like E. H. Carr was trying to found the sort of science that would soon find clearer articulation, and more fertile soil, on the other side of the Atlantic. This essay argues that Carr was trying to do nothing of the sort and that he, like other British scholars past and present, exhibits a characteristically British attitude to the subject of International Relations marked by an aversion for the narrow strictures of a strictly scientific conception of the discipline, and distinctive enough to warrant inclusion under the general label of British IR. The point is not simply that IR in the United States and Britain is studied in "very different ways" (Smith, 1985, xiii), but that the source of this difference is much more profound than is generally acknowledged, and goes much deeper than contrasting national styles or methodological preferences. Rather, these differences are only external manifestations of a pronounced division emanating from conflicting assumptions about the nature and grounds of knowledge in international relations, and its limits and susceptibility to verification. It is in this largely neglected, epistemological sense, that I will explore the distinctiveness of American and British perspectives on international relations.

It should be noted that the terms American IR and British IR are used to refer to broad theoretical habits, patterns, and modes that are by no means synonymous with the particular American and British scholars who comprise most of the field's officially recognized membership. Indeed, nationality in this individual sense is largely irrelevant since American, British, Canadian, Australian, Indian or German IR scholars are as likely as anyone to conform to Americanized or Anglicized versions of the subject, though these broad styles do not, of course, preclude, so much as limit the scope for, other possibilities. In this essay the overriding objective is to establish the diversity of international relations in terms of differences in national theoretical style, rather than differences in the international political system itself, though differences in the former derive ultimately from differences in the latter (Smith, 1985, ix). In offering up only two courses, the menu of choice is, admittedly, very limited. If American and British versions of IR appear to comprise very similar disciplinary main dishes, however, it is only because of a tendency to consume them too hastily, and a sense of taste dulled to the subtleties of contrasting flavors by a bland and steady diet of universal constructs. That these are distinct conceptions of IR, rather than contrasting approaches within a single, American-dominated discipline, is thus usually overlooked.

Assuming that there can be no universal consensus about the main problems of international relations and how to study it, is there anything intrinsically valuable about a discipline fragmented between rival national approaches? Is it not more likely that "a field composed of national parochialisms" may be poorly "equipped for making sense of the new world politics that will emerge in the next century" (Kahler, 1993, 412)? The question to be asked, however, is whether it is reasonable to expect international relations to make the same sort of sense to everybody. International politics has long been described as a self-help system, marked by profoundly different cultures, ethical systems, historical experiences, and national priorities. Given the obvious relationship between practice and theory in the field, how can we realistically expect intellectual consensus? The point then is not that international diversity in international theory is inherently desirable so much as it is unavoidable. And yet there are some things to be said in its favor, at least in terms of the distinctiveness that can be discerned between the two nationally conceived IRs discussed in this essay.

First, despite the tendency of British IR to move toward a form of what Hans Morgenthau calls "nationalistic universalism" in the formative years of the interwar period (Morgenthau, 1948, 273), it has retained a healthy degree of detachment from directly political agendas, and much of its earlier conviction that IR is best understood as an interdiscipline straddling the artificial boundaries that mark its perceived autonomy from diplomatic history, political philosophy, and other cognate fields. Because this skeptical attitude toward the sufficiency of science narrowly construed closely parallels that of early figures in the growth of the American discipline as well, its survival in British IR reminds us that neither the Americanization of IR, nor its penchant for law-like generalization and scientific self-sufficiency, were inevitable. Like other fields of social inquiry the development of IR is constrained by the "essential ambiguity of human existence," and the "inherent contestability of . . . (its) . . . theories." (Brown, 1994, 221; parenthetical addition mine). Uniquely, however, the contrasting epistemological attitudes native to IR have solidified into contrasting, nationally defined, conceptions of the subject. The almost total embrace of a positivist/naturalist conception of science in American IR, where it has been dominant, has led to a stunted, self-contained, and self-replicating conception of theory that denies the basic contestability of its subject matter; encouraged us to forget that many of the theories of international relations predate the discipline that purports to explain its activities (Long, 1993, 1); stripped the field of its ability to theorize theory itself; and reduced the purpose of IR to describing, and coping with, problems rather than imagining, or trying to construct, alternative worlds. This latter idealist, emancipatory, revolutionist or similarly described impulse is an inescapable part of social theory that has been either rooted out of American IR, or demoted to the status of mere "value-judgment" by the unrelenting positivist requirement that all meaningful distinctions about knowledge be forced through its crude sieve of "facts" and "values" (de Crespigny and Minogue, 1975, xiii). Because British IR has never yielded fully to the temptations of an exclusively scientific approach to the subject, and has never insisted that all of its claims to knowledge be logically related to prescription, its existence as an alternative conception of discipline does not merely help to rectify the one-sidedness of American IR but, in an important sense, constitutes the only official disciplinary avenue for genuine, open reflection on the subject and its theories.

Second, because the American and British disciplines grew out of similar impulses, under similar circumstances, with a virtually identical substantive focus on the international system as a whole, and with similar historical and cultural experiences on which to draw, the existence of profound differences between them is of more than passing interest. If the only two bona fide national parochialisms in the field to date can exhibit decidedly different attitudes to the discipline in spite of their shared propensity to view its main issues and theories in universal terms, the diversity of international relations theory should be that much more pronounced if and when it comes finally to approximate the impressive diversity already manifest in its subject matter. This essay makes no attempt, however, to specify the myriad and subtle ways in which ostensibly international theories are affected by parochial or national political priorities, agendas, and perspectives. Rather, one of its objectives is to demonstrate that explorations of this sort are at best premature, since the dominance of American and British conceptions of the subject has denied recourse to precisely this sort of evidence.

IR THEORY VERSUS
(I)NTERNATIONAL (R)ELATIONS (T)HEORY

Chris Brown suggests that "it no longer makes much sense to ask whether scholars such as Brian Barry, Charles Beitz, Mervyn Frost,

Onora O'Neill, Terry Nardin, and Michael Walzer are political theorists, social theorists or international relations theorists." The point Brown wants to emphasize is that international relations theory is "no longer confined to its own, self-imposed, ghetto" (Brown, 1994, 213). There is little to suggest, however, that the recrudescence of international relations theory, and its alleged emancipation from the strictures of a subject described vaguely as a science, has had much impact on the conduct, teaching, and theorizing of the subject in the United States. This is not simply unusual but profoundly important, since the vast bulk of the relatively small number of scholars that constitute the officially acknowledged membership of the field, and the few of these who debate over or engage in theorizing, are American, take their disciplinary apprenticeship in the methodological trade school of American IR, or fall under the long shadow of its influence. In short, Brown's claim needs to be qualified if we are to make sense of its apparent conflict with reality. We can begin by making an important distinction between: (1) IR theory, the term used to characterize "normal" (i.e., American) activity; and (2) what Brown calls international relations theory (lowercase). The claims made on behalf of IR theory—or rather what have become its largely unexamined assumptions—is that it constitutes a set of reflections on the appropriate investigative techniques for a discipline with permanent ontological features, a distinct subject matter separate from other fields, and a subject amenable to the general propositions characteristic of natural science. What Brown calls international relations theory (and might be just as happy to call social-political theory) is much more fluid, and premised on a rejection of IR theory's hypothesized autonomy from political and social thought, philosophy, history, public law, cultural studies, and a variety of other field's whose insights may prove relevant and useful to the study of world politics. IR theory as it is defined here, and left undefined in U.S.-based journals and texts, is an essentially American preoccupation; international relations theory, and theories about these theories (or "metatheory"), is an essentially British preoccupation. With these distinctions in hand, Brown's claim could read: "it no longer makes sense to ask whether Brian Barry et. al. are political theorists, social theorists or international relations theorists, *unless one accepts* the depiction of IR as an American social science."

That Brown rejects this depiction is obvious, but his argument for what amounts to a more interdisciplinary conception of international relations and its theories is based on the assumption that we *all* feel the same way, discounting the continuing allure of the American conception of IR as a freestanding discipline, its alumni uniquely competent to engage in "IR theory." In short, Brown's characterization of IR as a "one-time" science that now, like the other discourses of modernity, is unable to muster "any degree of confidence" in its professed ability to distinguish between "theory, observation and reality" (Brown, 1994, 214–215), resonates with a distinctly British set of attitudes about the subject that has had virtually no impact on the way theory debates have been—and continue to be—conducted in the United States. Today these attitudes find expression in British-based journals like *Millennium, The Review of International Studies,* and, to a lesser extent, *International Affairs* and *Global Society.* In American-based journals like *International Studies Quarterly, International Organization,* and *World Politics* it is pretty much business as usual when it comes to IR theory and its perceived applications. The intrapositivist debates of the latter revolve around issues pertaining to the methodological application of constructs like game theory and rational choice, and are dominated by attempts to progressively modify neorealist theory, Kenneth Waltz' supposedly definitive scientific rendering of IR. While these disputes can be vigorous, they are best viewed as family squabbles that never extend to questioning basic clan values. There are of course many American scholars that do not except the legitimacy of this intellectual genealogy, some of whom are strident, even vituperative, critics of its scientific pretensions. But, while broad-brush generalizations about American IR tend to sell these rival conceptualizations short, it is American IR that is the source of their marginality. It seems reasonable to suggest, moreover, that the antiscientific invective of a Richard Ashley is itself inexorably a part of American IR in the sense that close proximity to the source of one's perceived alienation tends to magnify its effect (Ashley, 1986; Ashley and Walker, 1990). Or, to personify the discipline, the more radicalized variants of critical theory[2] in American reflections on IR seem to constitute its disciplinary alter ego. In Britain, by contrast, theoretical and metatheoretical discussion constitute an essentially normal disciplinary activity that seems decidedly less prone to the acrimony and mutual intolerance generated in American debates if, and where, real discourse occurs.

How did this state of affairs transpire? How is it possible that what counts as theory on the American side of the Atlantic is apt to be dismissed as banal, arcane, and passé in Britain, while what counts as theory on the British side of the Atlantic is apt to be perceived as self-indulgent, exotic, and digressive in America? The answer must reside in conflicting understandings of IR as a organized field of inquiry, and different assumptions about what constitutes appropriate paths to knowledge in the exploration of its main issues. Since the American attitude is as well known as it is pervasive, there is little point in rehearsing its features here, though an anecdotal example drawn from a recent, prominent American text should help to throw the distinctiveness of British IR into higher relief. The anthology *Controversies in International Relations Theory: Realism and the Neoliberal Challenge*, edited by Charles Kegley, purports to focus on the "hottest topic in international relations theory today," which it describes broadly as a set of neoliberal challenges to "the dominant" realist and, primarily, neorealist paradigm (Kegley, 1995, 1). The book introduces the "rich diversity of thought *within* both the realist/neorealist and the liberal/neoliberal perspectives" (Kegley, 1995, vii; emphasis mine), but almost entirely ignores the rich diversity of thought that has come to characterize theoretical discussion outside the self-contained boundaries of both the "neo/neo" debate and American IR. There is one passing reference to the "postmodern school" in the entire anthology which, given its deconstructive tendencies, can scarcely qualify as a "school" *within* IR. More to the point, however, it is simply not the case that the "neo/neo" debate is the hottest topic in British IR, and there are signs that it has begun to run its course in American IR as well (see Cochran, this volume), though the so-called "constructivist turn" has not freed the American discipline from its self-imposed positivist imprisonment (Crawford, 1996, 125–127). The point is not that British scholars are any less prone than their American counterparts to the neglect of contributions forged in other national intellectual jurisdictions, but that the British conception of IR makes its practitioners less prone to the sort of methodological and epistemological monism that tends to mistake a nationally flavored set of concerns for the theoretical concerns of the entire world. Far from setting the theoretical agenda for the discipline as a whole, what counts as theory in Kegley's volume, and what counts as theory in American IR, is largely devoid of critical reflection.

BRITISH IR AND *THE* AMERICAN SOCIAL SCIENCE: DISTINCT, BUT DIFFERENT?

For most chroniclers of IR, its emergence as a freestanding academic discipline is dated from the early 1940s, a period during which the allegedly scattered and unsystematic inquiries of historians, international legal experts, and would-be reformers were superseded by a concerted and explicit attempt to examine the basic and persistent forces thought to underlay international politics (Hoffmann, 1977, and in this volume). This narrow standard implied that all previous inquiry, however interesting or germane, lacked the theoretical rigor demanded of "true" science, an idea that was particularly strong in the United States. It is a widely held view that systematic study of international relations is desirable, but this notion has no necessary connection to the disciplinary issue. When thinkers as different and distant as Thucydides, Machiavelli, Hobbes, and Bentham made their respective contributions to the study of world politics, for example, they did so with neither the dubious advantage of a discipline, nor the intention of founding one. The widespread practice of treating this material as "predisciplinary" is not merely anachronistic, but close-minded and peremptory, since it fails to acknowledge, explore or to even leave room for, the possibility that meaningful international relations theory can be sustained outside an explicitly social scientific context. On this view, if IR did not exist it would have to be created. The perversity of this position is obvious, since much of international theory predates the official start of the discipline, though "the seemingly natural existence and operation of the discipline today makes it difficult to appreciate that it has only really been possible to study . . . [IR] . . . since World War I" (Cherin, 1997, 9; parenthetical addition mine).

If the American or American-influenced account of growth and progress in *the* discipline tends to go unchallenged in British IR, this is more a product of polite indifference to the disciplinary master narrative than an indication of its veracity. Despite the systematizing efforts of the "English School," British IR has never been especially concerned about the scientific treatment of international relations, or especially committed to the idea of its complete separation from other fields. As Steve Smith suggests, the evidence on this score is mixed and contradictory, with roughly equal numbers of commentators suggesting that "the subject is studied in essentially the same way" in Britain as the United States, or that "it is studied in very different ways" (Smith, 1985, xiii; see also Hollis and Smith, 1990; Jones, 1981). But it is this vacillation precisely which supports the point that the scientific status of the field in Britain is not viewed as a crucial issue, and that different assumptions about the subject, and how it should be studied, must be afoot.

To date, exploration of the similarities and differences between American and British IR has focused on conflicting attitudes toward research methods, history, and social science (Hill, 1985, 130).Whatever division exists is usually taken as a matter of degree and reduced to differences of national style or methodological preference, neither of which appear to challenge the American version of IR as a social science. As Martin Hollis and Steve Smith point out, "the social sciences thrive on two intellectual traditions"—scientific explanation and historical understanding—each of which is represented in IR by American and British approaches respectively (Hollis and Smith, 1990, 1–15). Similarly, the "English School," despite its national prefix, explores, more or less systematically, the global concept of international society, though its conception of the states system is decidedly Eurocentered (see Epp, in this volume) and, according to Barry Buzan, the school fails adequately to distinguish between international system and international society (Buzan, 1993, 327). All of these attitudes suggest that British IR, and the paradigms that originate within it, is distinctive enough from American IR to warrant its own national labels, but commensurate enough with the American version of the discipline to be considered a locally adapted extension of its overall development. This is despite the irony that most of what is distinctive and suggestive about the British discipline developed before the supposed birth of IR as an American social science.

If these attitudes cannot be supported (and this essay argues they cannot), how did they come about in the first place, and why are they so firmly entrenched? Much of the answer can be found in the essentially self-contained nature of American IR and its corresponding failure, or congenital incapacity, to: (1) notice theoretical constructs forged in different national research communities; or (2) resist the colonizer's instinct to regard all things interesting but different as candidates for inclusion within their own categories of knowledge, theory, and science. Under conditions of this sort, the idea of competing or rival perspectives to American IR, if and when they are acknowledged, becomes a polite fiction. Another part of the problem can be attributed to a marked hesitancy, itself a characteristic feature of British IR, to vigorously assert its difference in the face of American dominance, partly because theorizing in Britain is as susceptible to the lure of trend-setting American research agendas as it is anywhere else, and partly because of a curiously contradictory mix of intellectual self-righteousness and self-deprecation (Wallace, 1996, 304). Also, as noted above, state-of-the-art-type reflection is simply not a key part of British IR. Finally, at least part of the British discipline's ambivalent attitude to scientific techniques may be reducible to a simple contingency: a de-emphasis of, and dearth of training in, the quantitative methods so central to what counts as an IR education in America.[3]

Since the main obstacle to fully grasping the distinctiveness and difference of British IR is the American discipline that supposedly has superseded and assimilated it, some consideration of how this hegemonic process works is in order before turning to the issue of what precisely is characteristic about British IR, and separates its conception of the discipline from that of its American counterpart. The example of the English School[4] (Jones, 1981; Buzan, 1993), and its encounter with the essentially American enterprise of international regime theory[5] (Krasner, 1982), nicely illustrates the dynamic at work.

Despite a general propensity to share with their American counterparts the idea that IR is a self-contained and distinct subject matter, members of the English School do not feature prominently in American

IR courses, and this school (or its synonyms) seldom makes the index or glossary of major American IR textbooks. Thus, despite being part of the same intellectual tradition, and addressing virtually identical substantive phenomena, these bodies of theory exist largely independently of one another. Buzan, whose declared objective is to bring these bodies of theory together, attributes their separation, vaguely, to the "peculiarities of academic discourse" (Buzan, 1993, 328). What Buzan fails to recognize is that one of the peculiarities in question is the propensity of American IR to set the standards via which approaches like the English School will be judged worthy of attention. Paradoxically, favorable judgments of worth, like the one made by Buzan (who, incidentally, is not an American!) must spell the beginning of the end of the national distinctiveness of the English School since worth is defined in terms of eligibility for assimilation into the American science of regime analysis. The reasons for this are not overtly parochial and nationalistic, but methodological and scientific. The "problem" with the English School is not that it's British, but that it's "better developed as a historical than as a theoretical concept" (Buzan, 1993, 329). It is simply assumed that historical understanding is not a sort of theory in its own right, and we are left to admire the "pattern-seeking instincts" of an E. H. Carr or a Martin Wight, but not the "eccentricity" of their expression (Buzan, 1993, 329; see also Hoffmann, 1977, and in this volume). Seen in this light, Buzan's suggestion that regime theory and the English School have been detached from one another due to the "peculiarities of academic discourse" seems remarkably understated, since the peculiarities in question appear to have profound implications for the study of international relations, and to arise from the field's inherent propensity toward national parochialisms.

Buzan's attempt to progressively change and update the English School, and bring it into the fold of American IR is, like the synthesizing proclivities of regime theorists in general, blithely indifferent to the possibility that those theorists who comprise its membership might actually be content to understand international society as a largely historical phenomenon. This would certainly help to account for the English School's general antipathy to the investigative techniques of American IR, a dispute trivialized by Roy Jones as "little more than a family squabble" (Jones, 1981, 7). Thus, between Jone's "case for closure" of the English School (the merits of which seem dubious) and Buzan's case for its assimilation into American IR, the future of the English School (outside of Britain and Australia at least) does not look bright. It also suggests that the growth of non-American scholarship is not likely to have much significance in the discipline as it is presently conceived in American IR. Whether or not this essentially British approach should be characterized as a distinct school misses the point that, despite being a substantial literature, and a supposed part of the first major growth pole of IR in the early part of the twentieth century, it has been of marginal (or largely instrumental) value to the new American stewards of *the* discipline. That so central a body of theory should fair so badly can only make us wonder about the prospects for distinctive approaches fashioned in national settings far removed from the field's core.

The English School is reflective of, but not synonymous with, a characteristically British attitude to IR. In the face of American IR's universal aspirations, moreover, the prefix "English," and the suffix "school," can amount to a form of self-imposed incarceration within the American discipline since it alone can get by without a national prefix, and with the unspoken presumption that its criteria are alone sufficient to decide what constitutes an IR school. It is less the case that there is a distinctively British place within IR (as the idea of an "English School," perhaps inadvertently, suggests) than there is a distinctively British attitude to the subject—a distinctively British discipline of IR. It now remains only to excavate the British discipline from beneath the crushing, paradoxical cosmopolitanism of the American discipline.

"A BRITISH SOCIAL SCIENCE: INTERNATIONAL RELATIONS"

It seems a reasonable minimal requirement that anything purporting to be a theory of international relations should concern itself with the actual practices of the subject. From the beginning, however, the field's investigators have had to grapple with two basic intellectual realities: (1) "the priority of problems *within* the field" (Holsti, 1985, 11) may be contested; and (2) the way in which facts are constructed may be challenged. The first issue pertains to what is typically regarded as the "normal" business of international relations research, while the second raises problems of a philosophical or "metatheoretical" nature. In the American conception of IR as a social science, the notion of competing theoretical traditions refers exclusively to disputes internal to a discipline that cannot itself be theorized. As Immanuel Wallerstein observes "for a word so widely used, what constitutes a 'discipline' is seldom discussed" (Wallerstein, 1992). Thus, despite the tendency to understand the field as the culmination of a series of "great debates," the first serious and sustained discussion of all aspects of the theory question in international relations has only recently emerged. Ironically, with their usual determination to find continuity and meaning in even the most unpromising places, the chroniclers of the field have taken to calling these first inklings of sustained discipline-defining discussion the "Third (and sometimes Fourth!) Debate," despite its marked departure from, and explicit rejection of, the usual disciplinary story.

Prior to the arrival of critical theory, the dominant (American) inspired view of IR rested on unspoken presuppositions. The continuing, almost total, absence of metatheoretical discussion in the official channels of American IR today suggests that, here at least, disciplinary self-evaluation remains a nonstarter. The previously "alien" insights of critical theory have, however, found fertile soil in British IR which now, more than ever, seems almost entirely detached from the American discipline. This is partly because the architects of the British discipline have never been especially clear about the location of the field's boundaries, committed to their sanctity, or willing to police them with the zeal evident in American IR. But it is also because of a characteristically British view that no scientific schema, however subtle and sensitive its investigative techniques, can adequately explain all of international relations, since it is as much a subject about ideas and ideals as a subject concerned with facts (Banks, 1984, 3; Carr, 1946, 93; Hollis and Smith, 1990, 90). It is this general epistemological attitude that accounts for what Hoffmann calls the "failure" of British IR to found the scientific treatment of the subject, the intellectual atmosphere for which could only be found in America (Hoffmann, reprinted in this volume). Hoffmann's remarks are aimed primarily at E. H. Carr, whose alleged effort and failure to pioneer a scientific rendering of IR suggested that British approaches had the necessary "pattern-seeking instincts" (as Buzan puts it) but was too imbued with the historian's sensitivity to the unique. But its a funny sort of criticism that castigates Carr, and British IR generally, for failing to accomplish what he/it was not trying to accomplish. Hoffmann's evaluation of British IR is not only tendered with the clear advantage of hindsight, but from the very scientific standpoint that British versions of the discipline have tried actively to resist. The assumption that everything which fails to measure up to the American standard of disciplinarity must be "pre" or "pseudo" scientific, rather than merely different, is the product of a long-term intellectual domination that has created an academic subject international in scope, but not in complexion.

The alleged eccentricity, irresolution, or scientifically muddled character of British IR is a tired cluster of stereotypes that ought to be put to bed. Since much of this misinformed impression, and much of what is distinctive about British IR, derives from Carr's *The 20 Years' Crisis*, it is useful to explore his position, and analyses of it, in a little more depth. It is generally assumed, à la Hoffmann, that Carr was a well intentioned, but ultimately confused, would-be architect of a science of international politics. Hoffmann's position is well known and republished in this volume. Other commentators, however, have made similar claims. Martin Griffiths, for example, alleges that there is in Carr's conception of international thought an implied transcendence of its idealist/utopian and realist streams that is "frustratingly defeated" by Carr himself (Griffiths, 1992, 34). In a similar vein, Ken Booth describes *The 20 Years' Crisis* as a "flawed" work that demonstrates Carr's confusion over "where he stood in relation to utopianism and realism" (Booth, 1991, 530). As Paul Howe puts it, the general consensus on Carr's defining work is that it "offers occasional glimmers of insight but fails to provide a cogent and comprehensive theory of international relations" (Howe, 1994, 277). While Howe is certainly justified in his view that this does Carr an injury, the point to be emphasized is that Carr's critics tend to invoke an evaluative standard that is entirely at odds with the view of international theory laid out in his work: namely, that the field is composed of dual epistemological impulses—idealism/utopianism and realism—that cannot be eradicated or reconciled. Carr is explicit in his claim that utopia and reality belong to "two different planes which can never meet"; far from regarding these as barriers to theory, as would a positivist, he argues that "sound political thought must be based on elements of both utopia and reality" (Carr, 1946, 93). There is nothing muddled or ambiguous here, nor any indication that Carr envisioned himself founding a science of IR along positivist lines.

The attitude apparent in Carr's work might be called one of epistemological open-mindedness, a posture that tends to characterize British reflection on theory in general, and accounts for its relatively enthusiastic embrace of critical international theory. Where the American discipline tends to embrace or reject new approaches strictly on the basis of their ability to generate testable research programs, British IR tends to be open and receptive to anything that helps in the quest for a better theory, or better theory about theories. While there are concerns that such receptivity can go too far (Wallace, 1996, 304), Michael Banks' depiction of the debate between critical and traditional theorists as the "richest, most promising and exciting [debate] we have ever had" (Banks, 1986, 17) has no analog in American IR, where debate is a less relevant concept than "uncivil war" (Holsti, in this volume).[6] The American attitude is perhaps best summed up by Alexander Wendt's claim that "philosophies of science are not theories of international relations" (Wendt, 1992, 425).

The idea that philosophy and science—theory and ideas about theory—are entirely separate activities is treated with a justified skepticism in British IR. As Charles Reynolds suggests, it is probably impossible "to write about international politics and, at the same time, to write about writing about international politics" (Reynolds, 1973, vii). The inter-connectedness of all intellectual activities can, and probably should, be occasionally ignored for the sake of analysis, but it should never be forgotten. Because the manner in which the problems of world politics are conceptualized depends ultimately, if often implicitly, on philosophical assumptions, it is futile to pretend that issues of epistemology do not concern us. The fact/value, is/ought distinction so sacred to American IR is theoretically useful, but it is easy to forget that it is only an analytical convenience. As the viability and vitality of British IR suggests, acceptance of this reality does not preclude thinking about IR as a coherent field. Rather, it can convincingly be conceived as a special kind of science that must, on the one hand, remain focused on its facts and, on the other hand, be attentive to how these are isolated and constructed.

Ironically, a failure to respond adequately to the issues posed by the epistemological diversity of theory in international relations seems to have done more to isolate and imperil the American defined discipline than the slings and arrows of the critical theorists. This is because, while many of the issues raised in this controversy are peripheral to the purpose of international theory as traditionally defined, deeper, more basic issues related to knowing inhabit the field and are always relevant. There may be profound philosophical differences at play that may, or may not, be traceable to the numinous workings of culture and nationality. None of this makes a necessary virtue of relativism and skepticism, nor automatically undermines the shared sense of vocation that defines any scholarly community. Not if we remember that the central challenge posed by the clash of differing views over theory in international relations is to try to "transcend diversity without substituting a new orthodoxy for the old one" (Giddens, as cited in Lapid, 1989, 236). The idea of genuine and irreconcilable differences in international theory is not compatible with the sort of consensus demanded by IR as an American social science, but it is compatible with a conceptual framework capable of posing basic questions about the subject (Hoffmann, 1960, 7–10). Again it is Carr who most convincingly demonstrates that normative and empirical approaches to international theory can and must be connected to a wider prospect if the field is to be properly attuned to the ontological composition of its subject. That this is Carr's most distinctive contribution, and that this attitude is characteristic of British IR, is easy to overlook not simply because of a tendency to gauge his contribution in the afterlight of a scientific framework to which Carr may not himself have aspired, but because his most immediate purpose was to deal with a crisis of world politics. The subsequent, seemingly perpetual, crisis in international theory is entirely another matter, but Carr's notion of irreconcilable, but mutually necessary and constitutive intellectual impulses, may help here too.

Intimations of the idea that the way to knowledge in IR lays inescapably along multiple paths pervade British IR but are seldom followed to the conclusion that they may form the basis of a distinctively British discipline. It is often suggested that there is something characteristic about British IR, but the foundation for this singularity is not generally taken to be epistemological in origin. Again, attention is directed to different methodological preferences that tend to reflect the positivist logic characteristic of American IR, but little of its conviction and fervor (Hollis and Smith, 1990; Hill, 1985). As Hayward Alker suggests, however, "methodologies" (or methods) are best thought of as "applied epistemologies using particular techniques" (Alker, 1992). Despite its failure to always openly acknowledge its debts, British IR's tradition of "historical understanding," philosophical subtlety and impatience for the quick fixes of positivist science derives from a conception of the subject similar to, and influenced by, that of Carr. British IR, as Carr might have it, is "the science not only of what is, but of what ought to be" (Carr, 1946, 5); it is not exclusively realist or idealist, but "stands uniquely at the nexus of the great issues of peace and war," "theories of the good life" and "theories of survival," "ethics of responsibility" and "ethics of conviction," and political theory and governmental practice (Carr, 1946, 11–21; Booth, 1991, 528; Wight, 1966, 18). The point of British IR, Carr might add, is not to reconcile utopia and reality, so much as to realize that "sound political thought" about the subject will always endeavour to combine "purpose with observation and analysis" (Carr, 1946, 10).

The affirmation of philosophical diversity in international relations theory does not invalidate its aspirations to the status of discipline, but suggests that these should be a good deal more modest than most observers would like. The centrally described antinomy idealism-realism, for example, does not threaten the viability of IR, so much as the pervasive assumption that a discipline requires homogeneity, and convergence of belief, threatens to obscure the antinomy of idealism-realism. Full consensus is not a realistic objective, or necessary prerequisite, for international theory. Ironically, the architects of what was to become a distinctively scientific, aphilosophical American science of IR shared the idea that there was a constant, permanent interplay between normative and empirical thought in international politics, and that this derived from two distinct types of theory (Morgenthau, 1948; Hoffmann, 1960; Hoffmann, 1965). The first type of theory, writes Hoffmann, is "produced by political philosophy," while the latter is produced by modern science (Hoffmann, 1960, 8–10). And Hans Morgenthau, despite his alleged role as midwife to the birth of the American social science of IR, is still criticized by neorealists (the self-proclaimed "real" scientists of

IR) for failing to transcend the methodological individualism of political theory and its precarious reliance on the "metaphysics of fallen man" (Ashley, 1986, 261; Waltz, 1979; Waltz, 1990, 21–37). Like Carr, Morgenthau and Hoffmann view normative and empirical theory as more like a dimension of international scholarship than a sharp dichotomy. Yet each of these thinkers is now treated as a pioneer of the sort of discipline it appeared to be no part of their purpose to build. Hoffmann's account of the peculiar context in which American theorizing was disciplined is well known and compelling. Why, however, did this epistemological attitude survive the advent of IR as an organized academic discipline only in Britain?

Part of the reason is that British IR has always managed to at least partly tune out what Christopher Hill calls the "siren song of policy relevance," a distraction that can threaten the intellectual freedom necessary to the development of an academic field (Hill, 1994; Wallace, 1996; Brown, in this volume). As Wallace suggests, the danger inherent in this attitude is that theory can become "*too* detached from the world of practice . . . too fond of theory (and metatheory) . . . too self-indulgent, and . . . too self-righteous" (Wallace, 1996, 304; emphasis in original). The point, however, is that in British IR at least the appropriate role of theory and the theorist is at least a practically relevant consideration (i.e., there are no automatic assumptions about what constitutes real theory). Another part of the distinctively British tolerance—or rather simple acceptance—of epistemological diversity can be credited to its slow emergence at the juncture of cognate fields like diplomatic history, international law, and political philosophy. In many senses British IR has always remained an interdiscipline in deference to the realization that the field did not spring *ex nihilo* from the imagination of scholars in the 1920s but has, in some form or other, always existed. This has allowed British IR to eschew the progressive, hubristic logic of American IR and its depiction of cognate fields as merely primitive, exploratory paths on the road to more thorough systematic analysis and better science. In viewing these others fields as constituent elements of international relations theory as a whole, British IR has remained more attuned to its intellectual identity, more aware of its theoretical possibilities and limitations, and more open to new approaches.

That the distinctiveness of British IR is epistemologically grounded might be easier to appreciate if Carr had not so vigorously exposed and punctured the pretensions of "utopian science." Despite the perceived legacy of his argument as a sort of running dog for the new realist science of IR, Carr (and, for that matter, Morgenthau) saw in idealism an historically peculiar manifestation of a generic flaw in international thought per se: its persistent "failure to understand" that its standards are always rooted in existing reality (Carr, 1946, 14). In the case of utopianism, this failure takes the form of an undue faith in the power of progressive ideals to overcome unpleasant realities. In the case of realism, this failure takes the form on an undue pessimism that the unpleasant realities of world politics are beyond the power of amendment. Carr would have been equally troubled by what Banks describes as the "intellectual totalitarianism" of the realist school, whose chief casualty has been an "entire set of liberal-progressive ideas . . . in our own time" (Banks, 1986, 11). In their philosophical sense, then, realism and idealism are attributes of thought, or epistemological orientations, that run perpetually through discourses on international relations and transcend the distorted, dogmatic paradigms that have tended to wear these labels in the modern, Americanized version of IR (Crawford, 1996, 22–26; Berki, 1970, 84; Griffiths, 1992). What is distinctive about Carr, and British IR scholars in general, is that they tend to need no reminder of the richly contextual nature of the enterprise. Paradoxically, however, it is precisely this posture of quiet intellectual self-assurance which has helped to keep the really characteristically British aspects of the field largely out of view, thus contributing to the false impression that IR is an exclusively American social science.

CONCLUSION

The tendency for central debates in international relations theory to reflect issues of interest in American IR, and the cultural-political system in which it is based, overstates and obscures the international complexion of the subject. The objective of this essay has not been to decry the value of the many contributions of particular American scholars, or to insist that there is a deliberate conspiracy within the confines of the American "establishment" to suppress or marginalize contrasting viewpoints from outside the discipline, or outside the United States. Its purpose has been: (1) to point out the distorting effects that the hegemony of any particular version of science and theory can have on the field as a whole, whether or not it happens to coincide with national attitudes and sentiments; and (2) to make the case for a distinctively British rival account of IR as an academic field. Unlike other versions of the story, this essay has suggested that this characteristically British attitude is epistemological, not methodological, in origin, and that American and British IR are essentially separate disciplines. The hallmark of British IR is its tendency to treat the field as an interdiscipline, to accept that its paths to knowledge are multiple, and to exhibit minimal levels of anxiety that this might jeopardize a traditional concern with real world problems and their resolution. Thus, while American debates have tended to become self-contained arguments over the appropriate techniques for an unproblematically embraced and tacitly conceived version of science, it is in British IR that genuine, discipline-defining reflection is today taking place. As seen in the ready embrace of critical theory in British IR today, this disposition marks the culmination of an always present, but hitherto quiet, receptivity to theoretical diversity. This proclivity has tended to whither in the shadow of American claims to disciplinary omnipotence, but British IR now seems ready to flower into a more explicit, conscious assertion of its theoretical independence and identity. Thus, if the field remains dominated for now by American and British attitudes, the differences between them are at least pronounced enough to suggest that there is room in the study of international relations for more than one version of truth.

NOTES

1. Like elites in other peripheries the international relations literati in Canada, Australia, Europe, and elsewhere tend to consume American social science techniques and to copy American intellectual fads. The situation is somewhat analogous to the more overtly political phenomenon remarked by *dependencia* theorists in their analyses of international relationships between political and intellectual elites, where elites within the "periphery" owe their privileged status (e.g., the title of IR theorist) to cooperation and alignment with the elites of the "core."

2. Critical theory is used as a sponge term for a wide array of approaches that share a general disaffection for modernist discourse within and outside the subject of international relations.

3. I am grateful to Chris Brown for this and other insights in his comments on an earlier version of this essay.

4. Members past and present are generally believed to include Martin Wight, Charles Manning, E. H. Carr, Hedley Bull, Michael Donelan, F. S. Northedge, Adam Watson, John Vincent, and James Mayall. This school is defined broadly by its notion that the international system of states also contains strong elements of society, community, and order.

5. There have been a number of attempts to formulate a definition of regime, but none has been more widely endorsed than that offered by Stephen Krasner: "principles, norms, rules, and decision-making procedures around which actor's expectations converge in a given issue-area" (Krasner, 1979, 1).

6. I am mindful that there are many vigorous and enthusiastic supporters of critical theory (or aspects of this very diverse literature) in American international *studies*. The point I want to emphasize, however, is that argument of this sort amounts to a sort of self-imposed disciplinary exile from the American IR family.

REFERENCES

Alker, Hayward. (1992). "The Humanistic Moment in International Studies." *International Studies Quarterly 36*(4), 347–371.

Ashley, Richard K. (1986). "The Poverty of Neorealism." In Robert O. Keohane (ed.), *Neorealism and Its Critics*. New York: Columbia University Press.

Ashley, Richard K., and R. B. J. Walker. (1990). "Speaking the Language of Exile: Dissident Thought in International Studies." *International Studies Quarterly 34*(3), 259–268.

Banks, Michael (ed.). (1984). *Conflict in World Society*. Sussex, England: Harvester Press.

Berki, R. N. (1970). "On Marxian Thought and the Problem of International Relations." *World Politics 24*(1), 80–105.

Booth, Ken. (1991). "Security in Anarchy: Utopian Realism in Theory and Practice." *International Affairs 67*(3), 527–545.

Brown, Chris. (1994). "Turtles all the Way Down." *Millennium 23*(2), 213–236.

Buzan, Barry. (1993). "From International System to International Society: Structural Realism and Regime Theory Meet the English School." *International Organization 47*(3), 327–352.

Carr. E. H. (1946). *The Twenty Years Crisis*. 2nd ed. London: Macmillan.

Cherin, Ethan. (1997). "Disciplining International Studies: Post-War/Post-Cold War." Paper Presented to the International Studies Association Annual General Meeting, Toronto, Ontario, March 18–22.

Crawford, Robert M. A. (1996). *Regime Theory in the Post-Cold War World*. Aldershot, U.K.: Dartmouth.

De Crespigny, Anthony, and Kenneth Minogue. (1976). *Contemporary Political Philosophers*. London: Methuen.

Griffiths, Martin. (1992). *Realism, Idealism, and International Politics: A Reinterpretation*. London: Routledge.

Hill, Christopher, and Pamela Beshoff (eds.). (1994). *Two Worlds of International Relations: Academics, Practitioners and the Trade in Ideas*. London: Routledge.

Hill, Christopher. (1985). "History and International Relations." In Steve Smith (ed.), *International Relations: British and American Perspectives*. Oxford: Basil Blackwell: 126–145.

Hoffmann, Stanley (ed.). (1960). *Contemporary Theory in International Relations*. Englewood Cliffs, N.J.: Prentice Hall.

Hoffmann, Stanley. (1965). *The State of War*. New York: Praeger.

Hoffmann, Stanley. (1977). "An American Social Science: International Relations." *Daedalus 106*(3), 41–60.

Hollis, Martin, and Steve Smith (eds.). (1990). *Explaining and Understanding in International Relations*. Oxford: Clarendon.

Holsti, K. J. (1985). *The Dividing Discipline*. Boston: Allen and Unwin.

Howe, Paul. (1994). "The Utopian Realism of E. H. Carr." *Review of International Studies 20*.

Jones, Roy E. (1981). "The English School: A Case for Closure." *Review of International Studies*. 7, 1–13.

Kahler, Miles. (1993). "International Relations: Still an American Social Science?" In Linda B. Miller and Michael Joseph Smith (eds.), *Ideas and Ideals*. Boulder, Colo.: Westview Press.

Kegley, Charles (ed.). (1995). *Controversies in International Relations Theory: Realism and the Neoliberal Challenge*. New York: St. Martin's Press.

Krasner, Stephen, D. (ed.). (1982). *International Regimes*. Ithaca, N.Y.: Cornell University Press.

Lapid, Yosef. (1989). "The Third Debate: On the Prospects of International Theory in a Post-Positivist Era." *International Studies Quarterly 33*(3), 235–254.

Long, David. (1993). "From World Peace to International Organization: The Development of Functionalism as a Theory of International Relations." Paper Presented to the Canadian Political Science Association Annual Meeting, Carleton University, Ottawa, June 6–8: 1–25.

Morgenthau, Hans. (1948). *Politics among Nations*. New York: McGraw-Hill.

Reynolds, Charles. (1973). *Theory and Explanation in International Relations*. Oxford: Martin Robertson.

Smith, Steve. (1985). "Introduction." In Steve Smith (ed.), *International Relations: British and American Perspectives*. Oxford: Basil Blackwell.

Wallace, William. (1996). "Truth and Power, Monks and Technocrats: Theory and Practice in International Relations." *Review of International Studies 22*, 301–321.

Wallerstein, Immanuel. (1992). "Liberalism and Nation-State in Decline." *Social Justice 19*(1), 22–33.

Waltz, Kenneth N. (1990). "Realist Thought and Neorealist Theory." *Journal of International Affairs 44*(1), 21–37.

Wendt, Alexander. (1992). "Anarchy Is What States Make of It." *International Organization 46*(2), 391–425.

Yost, David. (1994). "Political Philosophy and the Theory of International Relations." *International Affairs 70*(2), 263–290.

CHAPTER 11

Above the "American Discipline": A Canadian Perspective on Epistemological and Pedagogical Diversity

Mark Neufeld
and
Teresa Healy

INTRODUCTION

The traditional view of social science is that it is a "value-neutral" enterprise concerned with capturing, in objective a fashion as is possible, the realities of the world around us. This traditional view has certainly informed much of the thinking about our discipline—International Relations (IR). Indeed, much of this we have inherited from the dominance of positivist epistemologies in IR, especially as propagated by American scholars who operate in the heartland of IR.

There is, however, another admittedly minority view that says that any effort to produce a body of knowledge is informed by normative and political interests—in the words of Robert Cox, "Theory is always for someone and for some purpose" (Cox, 1996, 87). It is this second view that forms the starting point for our reflections here.

Part of acknowledging the context-dependent nature of all knowledge claims is being explicit about the context out of which one is writing. In our case, that context is at least partly defined by the fact that we live in Canada. This has a number of significant consequences, not the least of which is the fact that we are non-Americans whose academic identities are tied up with participation in a decidedly "American social science" (Hoffmann, 1977, 41–60). At the same time, it can be argued that writing out of a location where the phrase "south of the border" means the United States coincides with a critical "thinking space" not otherwise available.[1] As Cox has noted, "Canada is not a bad place in which to pursue . . . [critical analyses] . . . because Canadians can think of themselves as on the margins of several civilizations; and because there is a now somewhat marginalized but still resilient Canadian tradition of political thought upon which to build" (Cox, 1995, 27; see also Clement, 1997).

None of this, of course, is to assert that what is offered here represents the definitive "Canadian perspective" (see, for example, the survey and discussion in the contribution by Porter in this volume). It is to affirm, however, that academics, no less than anyone else, are formed by their contexts, and that "national identities," no less than others (e.g., gender, race, and class), are relevant to understanding—and assessing—their offerings.

AN AMERICAN SOCIAL SCIENCE
IN THE PERIPHERY OF THE CORE

As was already noted, IR has, virtually from its beginnings in the early part of this century, been a quintessentially "American" social science. The United States has been the dominant actor in global politics in the twentieth century, and the global order it helped to construct can legitimately be termed "pax americana."

In this context, the question of whom and what "IR" was for is more than clear: its purpose was to produce policy-relevant knowledge for American leaders as they set to create and direct a world order consistent with the interests of America's economic and social elites.

Of course, the United States could not erect and legitimate a world order on its own. It had help from "loyal allies" like Britain and Canada, whose social and economic elites shared the worldview of their American counterparts.[2] Indeed, it can be argued that Canada played a crucial function in its "middle power" role of "helpful fixer" and "mediator," in helping to legitimize pax americana as an order which served not parochial American interests, but the common good (see Neufeld, 1995a, 7–29).

Interestingly, there are strong parallels in terms of the institutional structure of IR as an academic discipline. In most countries with a sizable IR community there is a corresponding professional-academic organization: for example, in Britain, one finds the BISA—the British International Studies Association; in Japan, the JAIR; in Mexico, the AMEI; and so on. The United States and Canada are both unique in this regard—the United States, because it has no national designation for its organization—it is called simply the "International Studies Association (ISA)"—and Canada because it has no organization of its own (that is, there is no "CISA" corresponding to Britain's "BISA").[3] Rather, Canadians are regular (not foreign) members of the American ISA, and prominent Canadian IR scholars have served as president of the ISA.

Two recent conference experiences also tell us much about the place of Canadian scholars within the ISA. On a regular basis, the ISA holds its annual convention in the "American" cities of Vancouver or—most recently—Toronto (March 18–22, 1997). At the 1997 meeting, those registering on-site were initially told that Canadian cheques drawn on Canadian banks were "not acceptable." It was only after protest that cheques drawn on Canadian banks were accepted.[4]

Even more recently, the ISA organized a joint conference with the Mexican International Studies Association (AMEI) in Manzanillo, Colima, Mexico (December 11–13, 1997). The "call for papers," posted on the ISA's website, made for interesting reading for Canadian academics. In the words of the conference organizers, the Manzanillo conference promised to provide "a prime opportunity for Latin American and U.S. scholars [sic] to exchange ideas on . . . ongoing developments in the Americas and beyond."[5]

Without too much effort, one can see here the traditional legitimizing role Canada plays in terms of pax americana (what better evidence that pax americana serves the common interest than the support for it shown by an independent-minded country like Canada?), reproduced in the legitimizing role Canadian academics play in terms of the International Studies Association: what better evidence that the ISA is a truly "International" (and not parochially "American") Studies Association than the fact that Canadians participate as regular—not foreign—members?

Given this context, it is not difficult to see that Canadian IR as an academic enterprise—from its early roots within the League of Nations Society (see Page, 1977–1978) to the program for the 1997 Annual Meeting of the Canadian Political Science Association in St. John's—has had a clear purpose as well. Put simply, the ultimate goal of mainstream IR in Canada, notwithstanding important differences between camps (for example, between "realists" and "idealists"—see below), has been and remains (1) to provide policy-relevant advice to state leaders in Ottawa on how to maximize Canada's contribution to, and interests within, pax americana, and (2) to socialize students into this enterprise so they might serve as "competent" and "responsible" state functionaries should they be called.

It is important to note, of course, that IR is not a monolith; minority currents, critical of mainstream theory and practice, can always be found.[6] This holds no less for Canada than anywhere else.[7] Indeed, consistent with its position on the margins of the core, Canadian academe has produced some of the leading figures in critical IR theory, in both its modernist and postmodernist variants.[8]

Critical IR is distinguished from its mainstream counterpart in a number of ways, ranging from epistemology to ontology. In its simplest terms, however, critical IR defines itself as follows. First, in terms of theory, critical IR is not concerned with policy relevance. It is important to stress, however, that a lack of concern with policy relevance should not be read as a lack of concern for concrete political practice. Indeed, one of the major points of criticism of the mainstream is that all questions of "practice" have been reduced to questions of "policy" carried out by authoritative state actors.

Critical IR is interested in fostering an expanded view of ethical reasoning and political practice that empowers those who have traditionally been marginalized and challenges those who have traditionally been the objects of deference. In its Canadian manifestation, that has involved a critique of the ideologies and discourses of pax americana, and a defense of alternative visions of world order, past and present. As such, critical IR in Canada is committed to providing knowledge not for policy-makers in Ottawa, but for those Canadians who constitute what Pratt has termed the "counter-consensus."[9]

Critical IR is distinguished, secondly, by its pedagogical orientation. Unlike mainstream IR, which educates students to accept established parameters of thought and action, critical IR aims to instill an attitude of "suspicion" with regard to established orthodoxies and discourses, mainstream IR discourse included. In this sense, then, critical IR contains within it a commitment to emancipatory pedagogy and an explicit rejection of education as the mastery of facts or the uncritical application of standard concepts and frameworks.[10]

Putting all of this into practice is, of course, not a simple or straightforward matter. In terms of advancing its research agenda there can be no question that critical IR in Canada has been hampered by the lack of receptivity to its general orientation in established IR journals.[11] As already noted, critical IR rejects the major shared assumption of mainstream IR—that policy relevant knowledge is the goal of academic research. This has often been enough to render it highly puzzling (when not intellectually suspect) to mainstream editors and reviewers.[12] One can also assume that the unconventional nature of critical IR does not serve applicants particularly well in peer-reviewed research grant competitions.[13]

In terms of pedagogy as well, putting critical IR into practice means confronting significant challenges. Indeed, given that critical forms of theorizing embody an "educative" notion of the relation of theory to practice (see Fay, 1987, chap. 5) teaching can never be just an adjunct to the "real" task of interpreting the world. This has led us to reflect on our role as educators and on our students as active participants in the pedagogical process.

CRITICAL IR MEETS CRITICAL PEDAGOGY: TEACHING AS POLITICAL PRACTICE

All activities take place in a context defined by time and space. We teach in a small Ontario university located outside of a major urban center. More specifically, we teach international relations in a context where undergraduate students understand the immanence of globalization. Their shoes comes from export processing zones; their salad from the hands of migrant farm workers in California; their music from the world. The students themselves may have immigrated to Canada. They may find vitality in new and shared cultural expressions.

At the same time, they may believe that all the good industrial jobs have gone to Mexico. While they may harbor secret hopes for well-paid positions in the service sector, they hear that downsizing rids the workplace of waste, inefficiencies, jobs, and, indeed, youth. The prospect of work in the public sector is rarely mentioned; the chances of finding a position in Foreign Affairs or CIDA (Canadian International Development Agency) are seen as so remote as to be laughable. But the idea that "There Is No Alternative" (TINA) to social service cutbacks is one that seems to make sense to them. Students in the year 2000 are caught within many webs of local-global relations.

If these are in fact some of the assumptions held by incoming students, then what can the major theoretical traditions offer those who wish to understand world politics?

Realism, with its emphasis on state actors in a context of international anarchy, offers students a highly structured worldview in which stability or the promise of stability may appeal. In realism they find a sense of legitimacy built upon historical precedents, actual "facts" of national borders and government appointed diplomats. In realism, IR is the preserve of those who *know*, and a hazard for those who wish. It is the underside; the world of those who look into the face of power and are forced to concede to its terrible realities. Realism offers students the authority of the status quo but cannot respond to their disenchantment with the exclusionary character of national politics that underpin it, and the uneasy feeling that elites will forever lock them out of the corridors of power.

Idealism, on the other hand, with its notions of a plurality of actors (nonstate as well as state) operating in a context of growing interdependence, suggests a more utopian future. It proposes that neoliberal hegemony will not be so bad once we get through the initial process of restructuring. In idealism, individuals can make a difference by working toward the common interest of expanded growth and modernity. It promotes the possibility of rising to the topside, the world of global civil society and "hands around the world." Idealism draws on the optimism of students who look forward to contributing their creative energies to a cooperative enterprise. Idealism is, of course, a perspective that is founded upon market relations. The real deception within it, as E. H. Carr pointed out long ago (Carr, 1946, 44), is that liberals know that the utopian market produces many expendable human lives in the service of the general interest.

These two views seem to offer students a choice, but insofar as western capitalism and a (declining) pax americana set the unquestioned limits on any possible world order, realism and idealism represent polarized aspects of a dominant/ating whole. States use the instruments of coercion at their disposal to force the expansion of market society, in our era of neoliberalism, as they have done in the past. As well, the ideology of the self-regulating market continues to obscure relations of power within and between capitalist societies. Together, these two assumptions comprise the dominant approach to the study of IR and promote the ascendancy of neoliberalism by grounding it in the realm of "legitimate ideas."

Critical IR, on the other hand, is "disruptive" of traditional views, and attempts to widen the space defining the relationship between ideas and new forms of political practice. It challenges dominant assumptions within IR, and does so without proposing an alternative based simply on individual lifestyle choices. Neither does critical IR accept the paralysis of any structuralism in which the overbearing character of global relations stifles effective intervention in the movement of human history.

Any politics of hope at the start of the new millennium must offer students more than a set of utopian fancies. The challenge for critical IR, then, is to facilitate a process through which students may interrogate the boundaries between that which is considered "domestic" and "foreign." One way to do this is by considering the social relations of class, race, and gender in an area of study that usually ignores them. Critical IR does this by framing questions of world order in terms of underlying social structures.

Following from this, critical IR asks about the possibilities for *transformative* politics in a number of different sites. In this way, struggles for democracy in the workplace and the household are linked with those of social movements acting in regional coalitions. These may be related, in turn, to broader movements that push for the democratization of the nation-state. If they are linked with movements for democracy within states, expressions of solidaristic internationalism become more substantive at the level of world order. For critical IR, there is no esoteric realm of interstate relations, nor any private sphere of intrafirm relations, that exist beyond the demands of democratic politics.

Resistance in the classroom causes us obvious concern. Teaching IR from a critical perspective means that students who assume that IR can be understood as the preserve of diplomats and generals will be rattled. (On the other hand, those who are not interested in the distant goings-on of missile counters and diplomats will be reassured that their questions have a place in the classroom.) Yet if both the instructor and the student are expected to learn from the educational experience, then the flow of discussion must depend on the students' role in shaping classroom discussions. We have found that if students can perceive their own position in relation to competing approaches, they are able to see themselves as contributors to an intellectual conversation and a political perspective that promotes specific agendas. This recognition creates a bridge between the simple assertion that "we are all members of the global village" and a deeper appreciation of the importance of *power* and *politics*. If there is more than one "truth" then they can no longer hold onto the notion that all other counterintuitive notions are wrong, or worse, promoted by people who are just plain stupid.

In ontological terms, critical theory privileges a relational view of society that many students find difficult to decipher. Alternatively, those attuned to the connections between things may need to sharpen their awareness of the discrete boundaries between different concepts. (We have sometimes noticed this as a gendered difference in the classroom.)

As argued above, making globalization link up with the lives of students is relatively easy. Their challenge is to reflect on the meaning of politics in their lives. Since undergraduate students' references tend to be so intensely individualized, talk of collectivities other than the family remains distant from their sense of reality. It is not just that they are children of the video age; more importantly, it is that they were raised in an era when political authority figures openly questioned the very possibility of human community and collective action.[14]

If, however, students can recognize some space for collective responses to social injustices, then the possibility of emancipatory politics emerges out of the interplay of structure and agency. As a result, neither the future of the planet nor their own future is perceived as a foregone conclusion. And in this regard, we have experienced successes as well.

By their senior year many have come to see politics as having a place of relevance in their lives and in a richly textured society. They are no longer convinced of the irrefutable logic of the market. TINA is out, as students begin to accept the possibility that human history moves according to the dynamics of different social forces in relation to one another. Ideas about who these social forces are, what kinds of communities they form, and for what purposes, then become the questions underlying the study of IR (see, for example, the discussion in Griffiths and O'Callaghan in this volume). And many students who are concerned with issues of social justice find in critical IR a resource for reflection that can help to sustain their active participation in oppositional movements.[15]

CONCLUSION

In closing, it is important to stress again that none of this—neither critical research nor pedagogy—corresponds to the traditional notion of "social science" as a "value-neutral" enterprise. It is consistent, however, with a reflexive orientation to knowledge production and dissemination that recognizes scholarly activity is never value-free, never politically neutral. This recognition is the first step in determining the role our discipline has played—and will play—as we move into the twenty-first century.

NOTES

1. The term "thinking space" is Jim George's (George, 1989, 269–279).

2. See, for example, Tom Keating's discussion of Bretton Woods as an "ABC" creation (Keating, 1993, chap. 1).

3. One should note the existence, of course, of the Canadian Institute of International Affairs (CIIA). This differs from largely academic associations such as BISA or ISA, however, because its focus on the discipline's traditional preoccupations with diplomacy and statecraft has tended to limit the participation of even mainstream scholars with other interests.

4. Of course, it might be countered that the very fact that registrants were given the option of paying in Canadian funds at all (converted to American prices) was a major step forward. The last time the convention was held in Toronto, payment was restricted to American funds only. This *slight* opening should, of course, be taken as further evidence of the growing nonparochialism of the organization

5. It is, of course, possible that this formulation included French-Canadians, who, given their attachment to their Romance language, might legitimately claim to be "Latin Americans" of a sort. Anglophones like ourselves, however, were, technically, interlopers at the event, though, to be fair, once there we were allowed to participate fully.

6. For an overview of critical subtraditions in International Relations, see Neufeld (Neufeld, 1995).

7. It is interesting to note that Canadian graduate students at the London School of Economics have dominated out of all proportion to their numbers in the role of editor of what is, arguably, the leading critical journal in IR theory today: *Millennium: Journal of International Studies*. It is also noteworthy that this journal is, at the time of the writing of this essay, still unavailable to students at both of Canada's "Ivy League" universities: the University of Toronto and McGill University.

8. See the work of Robert Cox (Cox, 1995) of York University, and R. B. J. Walker (Walker, 1993), of the University of Victoria, respectively. Canada has also produced one of the leading figures in the new generation of feminist IR theorists, Sandra Whitworth (Whitworth, 1997).

9. Pratt defines the "counter-consensus" as comprising "internationally minded public interest groups" generally critical of the underlying assumptions and workings of pax americana (Pratt, 1983–84, 99–135).

10. The latter would conform to the notion of "banking education," as developed in the work of Paulo Freire. For a useful introduction to Freire's critical pedagogy, see Stephen T. Leonard (Leonard, 1990, chap. 5; Gonick and Weisband, 1992).

11. For example, the *Canadian Journal of Political Science, International Journal*, and *Canadian Foreign Policy*. The exception to this rule in "Canadian" IR journals is *Études internationales*, which, due to its openness to critical as well as mainstream work, has become the world's leading French-language IR theory journal.

12. Happily, in recent times critical IR has found an increasingly sympathetic reception in the traditionally non-IR oriented publishing ventures of Canadian political economy. One finds an increasing presence of critical IR in the journal *Studies in Political Economy*, for example. Significantly, it is also represented in recent edited volumes with, for example, Laura MacDonald and Mark Neufeld and Sandra Whitworth (MacDonald, 1997; Neufeld and Whitworth, 1997).

13. For a representative—and by no means, atypical—example of the need of established figures to chastise those who deviate from mainstream norms, see the recent article by Michael Brecher (Brecher, 1995). As one colleague is fond of remarking: "They don't call IR a 'discipline' for nothing."

14. Margaret Thatcher's affirmation that there is no such thing as "society" is perhaps the clearest example. Closer to home, we have the example of the Harris government in Ontario which never speaks in terms of the "citizens" of the province, but only in terms of the atomized notion of "Ontario taxpayers." By now, we have experienced almost two decades of such rhetoric, and most of the students we teach do not know any other dominant political discourse. They

were, we must remember, only in primary school when the great "Free Trade Debate" was fought in the late 1980s.

15. Often this change in thinking is accompanied by—and, enhanced through—growing experience of collective action. For example, by their senior year, they may have participated in student campaigns in support of the demands for corporate codes of conduct in corporations like "GAP" and "Nike." Or they may have been influenced by an intensive development educational experience overseas.

REFERENCES

Brecher, Michael. (1995). "Reflections on a Life in Academe." *International Studies Notes 20*(3) (Fall), 1–8.

Carr, E. H. (1946). *The Twenty Years' Crisis, 1919–1939*. London: Macmillan.

Clement, W. (ed.). (1997). *Understanding Canada: Building on the New Canadian Political Economy*. Montreal: McGill-Queens Press.

Cox, Robert W. (1995). "Civilizations: Encounters and Transformations." *Studies in Political Economy 47* (Summer), 7–31.

Cox, Robert W. (1996). "Social Forces, States and World Orders: Beyond International Relations Theory." In Robert W. Cox and T. Sinclair (eds.), *Approaches to World Order*. Cambridge: Cambridge University Press.

Fay, B. (1987). *Critical Social Science*. Cambridge: Polity Press.

George, Jim. (1989). "International Relations and the Search for Thinking Space: Another View of the Third Debate." *International Studies Quarterly 33*(3), 269–279.

Gonick, L. S., and E. Weisband (eds.). (1992). *Teaching World Politics: Contending Pedagogies for a New World Order*. Boulder, Colo.: Westview Press.

Hoffmann, Stanley. (1977). "An American Social Science: International Relations." *Daedalus 106*(3), 41–60.

Keating, T. (1993). *Canada and World Order: The Multilateralist Tradition in Canadian Foreign Policy*. Toronto: McClelland and Stewart.

Leonard, S. T. (1990). *Critical Theory in Political Practice*. Princeton: Princeton University Press.

MacDonald, L. (1997). "Going Global: The Politics of Canada's Foreign Economic Relations." In W. Clement (ed.), *Understanding Canada: Building on the New Canadian Political Economy*. Montreal: McGill-Queens Press, 172–196.

Neufeld, Mark. (1995a). "Hegemony and Foreign Policy Analysis: The Case of Canada as Middle Power." *Studies in Political Economy 48* (Autumn), 7–29.

Neufeld, Mark. (1995b). *The Restructuring of International Relations Theory*. Cambridge: Cambridge University Press.

Neufeld, Mark, and Sandra Whitworth. (1997. "Imag(in)ing Canadian Foreign Policy." W. Clement (ed.), *Understanding Canada: Building on the New Canadian Political Economy*. Montreal: McGill-Queens Press, 197–214.

Page, D. (1977–78). "The League of Nations Society in Canada." *International Journal 33*(1), 28–65.

Pratt, C. (1983–84). "Dominant Class Theory and Canadian Foreign Policy: The Case of the Counter-Consensus." *International Journal* 39(1), 99–135.

Walker, R. B. J. (1993). *Inside/Outside: International Relations as Political Theory*. Cambridge: Cambridge University Press.

Whitworth, Sandra. (1997). *Feminism and International Relations*. London: Macmillan.

CHAPTER 12

Transcending National Identity: The Global Political Economy of Gender and Class

Jan Jindy Pettman

INTRODUCTION

International Relations (IR) is still largely an "American"[1] discipline, dominated by white, native English-speaking intellectuals, located mainly within the Anglo–North American academic.[2]

IR is also a male-dominated, and masculinist,[3] discipline, constructed out of the experiences and fears of (elite) men in or near the centers of global power. Particular understandings of masculinity infuse the discipline. Feminist scholars who have critiqued IR have revealed both women and gender power in international relations and political economy. But while women are positioned rather differently from men, they are also both united and divided in their relation to the global political economy, and in identity politics that mark the boundaries of belonging in nationalist and international politics. Attending to these differences problematizes a hegemonic IR discipline, while suggesting possibilities for both transnational feminist politics, and a gender-explicit and embodied study of international relations.

MASCULINIST IR

IR as a discipline is still remarkably masculinist, in tone, content, and personnel, especially in departments and authority structures where it matters. Mainstream IR[4] scholars appear to assume that gender is not a relevant (let alone a constitutive) aspect of IR (see, for example, Jarvis in this volume). The discipline has only been subjected recently to sustained feminist critique, decades after feminist interventions in the related fields of political science and political theory. The reasons for both the late arrival and the continuing marginalization of feminism in IR are doubtless many; but here I will take up several that are immediately relevant to issues of intellectual hegemony and diversity which are the concern of this volume.

IR and its older foundation disciplines were long dominated by men, asking questions and pursuing interests that affected them.[5] The considerable disciplinary resistance to taking gender seriously might be part of a more widespread resistance to critical perspectives and territorial challenges. It seems, however, that questions to do with sex and gender (as with race) are not only of intellectual contest, but also affect people directly. Gender is an intrinsic part of social and personal identity, which, in turn, informs the ways we perceive ourselves, others, and the world around us. The dominant group, however, has the power to name others while remaining unnamed; so gender is often seen as referring to "women," leaving "men" and masculinity unremarked upon. The passion with which feminism is rejected and most IR scholars' refusal to admit their own gender as relevant in terms of their looking positions, suggests the significance, rather than the irrelevance, of gender to identity questions—whether of the field, or of those who work within it.

Discipline content and territory also militate against feminist inquiry. IR is constructed around a definition of politics centered on public space and power, from which women were long excluded and are only now unevenly entering. The long containment of women away from politics in the classic public/private dichotomy has been critiqued by feminist theorists, revealing the statesman and the citizen as male (Grant, 1991; Peterson, 1992; Tickner, 1992). Compounding this masculinization is IR's focus on "high politics" and the prerogative state. This is especially evident in its focus on war, from which women were long officially banned, and are still subject to combat exemption rules in most state militaries.

But even in high politics, actual people are rarely evident in IR.[6] The sovereignty story upon which much of IR turns assumes a coincidence of territory, population, authority, and identity. This has had the effect of relegating differences within the state to other disciplines, like sociology and political science. Even the addition of international political economy (IPE) in the 1970s changed little in this regard. States-and-markets, structural inequalities, and world systems approaches, largely maintain the nominally ungendered but presumptively male story and cast of IR characters. In macroeconomics of different kinds "women do not appear—but neither do men" (Elston, 1992, quoted in Bakker, 1994, 8).

If "people" were displaced away from IR, "women" were doubly displaced from visibility and public space. The definition of politics in terms of public authority relations and institutions, and the contrasting definition of household, family, and sexual relations as private, nonpolitical or somehow quarantined from the state (despite the state's implication in both the construction and consequences of the public/private divide) excluded from disciplinary view much of women's politics, and the politics of gender. So too, reproductive labor (work essential to maintain and reproduce both the workforce and the citizen-body) has quite literally not counted—assumed to be naturally women's work, a labor of love, and thus not really work at all (Waring, 1988).

This extraordinary erasure of women's work, politics, and bodies has been engineered through a complicated but naturalized move from "men" to "universal," which depends for its operation on the exclusion of women from intellectual view (Cavarero, 1992). While earlier political theorists did attend to the feminine in order to exclude it, contemporary IR theorists all too often simply assume an identity or coincidence of masculinity and politics. This enables them to assume, also, that there is no place in IR for gender—or that IR is actually gender-neutral. They contribute to the situation where "men, states and wars were the basis of [IR] theory, not women" (Grant, 1991, 25).

This is a very familiar story for those who have noticed gender in IR. But even scholars critical of mainstream IR often fail to "see" women. The presumption appears to be either that women aren't in IR, that IR is men's business; or else that women and men participate in, and are affected equally by, international relations and processes. Both these presumptions are patently false (Pettman, 1993).

FEMINIST IR

Feminist IR engages in two related moves. The first is deconstructive, revealing the absences and gendered assumptions built into the field. This move demonstrates that gender *is* there, even when (especially when) women aren't. "What could be more profoundly gendered than a space said to contain nothing but men, than an activity described as performed by men only?" (Cooke, 1993, 177). Feminist IR also reveals the move from (elite?) men's experiences to universal claims, and, hence, the masculinist constructions that organize the field. Substantial feminist scholarship now documents the construction of gendered states and the masculinist politics of protection (Tickner, 1992; Peterson, 1992; Peterson and Runyan, 1993; Pettman, 1996a).

The second move (though often the two can't be neatly separated) seeks to make women visible and to demonstrate the workings of gender within both the discipline and the world it purports to explain. This currently takes different forms. It might locate significant women, who have been "lost" in national narratives and public storytelling, and retrieves them as players in significant international events and sites past (Enloe, 1990a; D'Amico and Beckman, 1994). Documenting women's roles and contributions, more generally, also involves both retrieval work historically, and analyses of contemporary movements and relations, too. These revisions trace the rise of feminist and manpower pressures to increase women's participation in the military, for example, or in the paid workforce; and reveal, too, the pressures on the institutions when "women" do start to make it within them. These studies touch directly or indirectly on fascinating and difficult debates about whether more women where it counts make a difference (Ruddick, 1983; Roberts, 1984; Epstein, 1991).

Each of these moves can be appropriated in ways that stop short of gendering by simply including or making reference to "women," and containing them as a category. But adding women in all but the most anemic ways stretches or disrupts the discipline, and so makes a space for rethinking key concepts and relations as gendered (Peterson, 1992; Whitworth, 1994). This is because "women" do not exist in isolation. Gendered identities, like any other, are relational identities. What it means to be a woman in any particular place, time, class, and so on, cannot be understood apart from what it means, there, to be a man. Femininity and masculinity are relational, often set against each other, with the most valued or rewarded characteristics still usually associated with the masculine. So too, women are rarely simply fewer or more in any site. They are usually positioned differently compared with men, a positioning that reveals gender relations, masculinity, and femininity, as key ingredients in international relations and processes. Why is masculinity (or certain kinds of masculinity) assumed intrinsic to the operation of militaries, of interstate politics? Why are debates about women in the military, and gay men in the military, so furious and emotive? Why is the preferred global assembly worker young and female? Why are some global flows, including labor migration, increasingly feminized?

Gender[7] is written on and read from the bodies of men and women: it makes a difference what body you are in. "The body"/our body is our primary location in the world, before national and global identifications. Rosi Braidotti's exploration of the notion of an embodied and *therefore* sexually differentiated subject is a useful way of considering the gendered self (Braidotti, 1994, 3). As a strategic move it emphasizes sexual difference, and can be used to visibilize other differences and associated power relations too (Pettman, 1997).[8] In IR, this encourages thinking about actual bodies and how they are impacted upon and participate in international politics.

But gender also circulates and has effects independent of particular sexed bodies. Masculinity and, in particular, notions of what it takes to be a "real man" are associated with power, aggression, and with what it takes to "do" interstate and international politics (Tickner, 1992; Cohn, 1993). A powerful woman, or a peaceable man, are seen to have crossed genders. Gendered characteristics are associated with the exercise of power, such that the reluctant warrior or socially responsible leader may be accused of being a wimp, a woman. Sexual difference and gendered discourse infuse much of the discipline, even where it has systematically removed actual or imaginary women from view or influence. The work of feminist IR writers like Carol Cohn shift our attention "away from gendered bodies toward gendered discourses," to the ways in which gendered discourse shapes how we think about, talk about and act in international relations (1993, 228).

Cohn's earlier work (1987), on the language of strategic planners and others around nuclear weapons, noted euphemisms and abstractions that disguised or distanced them from the potential human costs involved. Naming bombs "Pal" or "Bambi" appears to domesticate terror. So too, the language is often sexualized, "a bigger bang for your buck," or "orgasmic thumps," eroticizing the inherent violence and destructive capacity of megadeath weapons.

The Gulf War demonstrated the familiar "unitary masculine actor problem" in national security discourse (Cohn, 1993, 239). Then President George Bush and his officials frequently referred to Iraq or its military as "he," thereby turning complex international relations into a contest against one male competitor. In the process, "he" "functions to substitute in the mind's eye the abstraction of an implacably, impeccably evil enemy for the particular human beings, men, women and children being pounded, burned, torn, eviscerated" (Cohn, 1993, 239).

Calling up the national security romance, of the villain, the victim and the hero, facilitates the use of force, in language of sexual contest and conquest. The "rape of Kuwait" typically feminized the weak state in IR, and accused the invader of male heterosexual rape (Lerner, 1991; cf Parker, 1992). The villain is demonized and racialized. He is excessively masculine in some ways (violent, sexually aggressive), while lacking respectable, civilized masculinity (order, reason, productivity, chivalry). At the same time, the male Other in IR can be feminized, as the colonized or oriental Other so often are. Homophobic references, for example, bumper stickers in the U.S. reading "Saddam, bend over" during the Gulf War, compound sexual anxiety-high politics associations.

This heterosexist drama affirms some kinds of masculinity, and stigmatizes others. It also represents in familial language a competition between men for possession of property, including women, which is well documented in feminist or gendered analyses of nationalist rhetoric and passions. The exercise of international power is sexualized. Colonized or invaded nations are commonly represented as feminized victims of rape. These representations feed into the construction of women as dependents of men and states. "Women are the symbol of the nation, men its agents, regardless of the role women actually play in the nation" (Feminist Review 1993, 1). Women are both excluded and included as women, and especially as mothers (cf. Pateman, 1992). The nation is feminized, and the male/state must fight for her honor. In an identity shift, women are also constructed as mothers of the nation, especially in times of conflict or mobilization. Women's bodies become the territory on which national work is done. This is seen most graphically in systematic war rape, designed to demonstrate to enemy men that they are unable to defend "their" women, and to disorganize the nation by introducing "enemy seed" through forced pregnancies (Pettman, 1996c; see also Brown, 1992).

Much feminist IR work focuses on the need to demonstrate (not least of all to IR colleagues) that women *are* in international relations, that they *are* differently located and affected within them than men, that gender relations infuse, shape, and are shaped by international relations/global political economy. Admitting "women" and gender in to mainstream IR would seriously disrupt the field. Alternatively, pursuing them within a reconstructed international relations (in the anabranches) enables questions to be asked about whose experiences are to be taken seriously and used in evidence in the discipline, and about who international relations theory is for.

TRANSNATIONAL SISTERHOOD?

But an emphasis on "women" and/or gender could also give the impression that gender is *the* identity divide that matters in national and international politics. This could have the unintended consequence of reinforcing other aspects of IR intellectual hegemony, especially in terms of its English-speakingness (see Brown in this volume) and U.K.–North American centers. This reminds us how unrepresentative of "the real world" dominant IR is, and of the distorting effects of ignoring nonstate identities—race, nation, religion, ethnicity, and class, for example—which mark many a killing and dying line on the ground. National and transnational identities, and diversity, are feminist issues too—especially for white English-speaking academic feminists in the centers. So too, there are challenges to the category "women" from feminist poststructuralists and postmodern feminists. They make us think again about both who we are and who we call up in our political and intellectual work when we invoke "women" (Sylvester, 1994; 1995).

Virginia Woolf's famous declaration that "as a woman, I have no country. As a woman I want no country. As a woman my country is the whole world" ([1938] 1993,234), is one of many that assert a commonality among women and an alienation from state and patriotism. Woolf's reasons for so arguing included women's long exclusion from education, wealth, and citizenship rights, and the use of women's supposed need for men's protection as a justification for men arming themselves, to pursue both militarism and war. Her analysis of the connections between patriarchy, militarism, and fascism still makes powerful reading today, and illustrates the relevance of women and gendered explanations of the state, nationalism, and war.

Woolf urged women to make themselves "outsiders" to the state and war. Her argument is taken up, directly or indirectly, by different feminist writers on war and peace. Are women responsible for what is done in their name? Could there be war without women? For it is so often for women (and children[9]) that men supposedly fight (Elshtain, 1987; Pettman, 1996a). The symbolic uses of women as boundary markers and as vulnerable possessions—regardless of what actual women are doing—means that they must speak for themselves, or else they will be spoken for (Trinh, 1987).

Woolf also recognizes the ways in which women as dependents get locked into protection rackets that may further endanger them (see also Runyan, 1990; Tickner, 1992). They become spoils of war, possessions of "their" men and targets for violence, including systematic war rape (Peterson, 1994; Enloe, 1998). They cannot control the conditions of their protection, which may include gratitude and good behavior. Women seen as unruly, or even as independent, might also experience violence at the hands of their men.

These near-universal ways in which so many women experience identity conflicts and different kinds of violence suggest the possibility of a global identity or alliance among women, of the kind hinted at by Virginia Woolf. At the same time, they demonstrate the contributions that a gendered analysis can make to IR. Recognizing that women often experience violence from the very men who in the sovereignty-citizenship story are supposed to protect them, subverts statist and IR notions of security and danger. The protector/protected relationship takes different forms but is recognizable across the globe, not least in the difficulties women have had securing any power within the state even after they have played significant roles in the liberation armies that won the state (Tetrault, 1994). There seems to be something incongruous—and threatening—about an armed woman, or one in a position of authority.

Attending to women's experiences of insecurity and violence, and asking who or what threatens them, also allows for the possibility of a corporeal, embodied international relations. A focus on "the body," or, rather, on different kinds of bodies, makes it impossible to ignore sexual difference (Braidotti, 1994; Grosz, 1994; Jayawardena, 1996; Pettman, 1997). It also draws our attention to the irony of women invisible in a discipline whose business is to make sense of the kinds of politics and political economy that impact so directly upon actual bodies.[10]

Globally, women experience gender-specific violence, and are frequent victims of international violence. The world's most widespread crime is domestic violence against women. Globally, too, women are still severely underrepresented in terms of power and wealth, though in Nordic states their numbers in formal politics are close to equal. But while women are so often made to pay in international relations, they are not only present as victims or survivors of violence or exploitation. Many women are also players in national and international identity politics that make other people, including other women, pay too (Mazumdar, 1995). Nationality and location still matter—and women are not innocently positioned in relation to them.

WOMEN, IDENTITY, AND DIFFERENCE

Adrienne Rich (1986) responds to Virginia Woolf's giving away her country by observing that as a U.S. citizen, she (Rich) bears some responsibility for what is done in her name. Rich develops the idea of a politics of location which requires that feminists pay closer attention to foreign policy. Karen Caplan, however, has suggested that this politics might become complicit in reproducing the binary First World: Third World, or be read to suggest that a Western location necessarily makes for white women, or white feminism. "In a transnational world where cultural asymmetries and linkages continue to be mystified by economic and political interests at multiple levels, feminists need detailed, historicized maps of the circuits of power" (Kaplan, 1994, 148).

IR has long relegated culture and identities to the inside of the state, despite the implication of international processes, like colonization, in racialized and other difference (Campbell, 1992; Lapid and Kratochwil, 1996; Krause and Renwick, 1996; see also Ahluwalia and Sullivan in this volume). Yet race infuses international power relations and identities too; and the West is white, no matter how many racialized others reside within its imagined borders. But "international relations has taken as a given the identity of the West and its subjects/agents, ignoring the historical experiences and encounters with 'others' against which the identities of these subject/agents have been constituted" (Doty, 1996, 24).

"White" women are ambiguously placed in hegemonic relations that are both gendered and racialized. African American feminist Bell Hooks (1989) notes that many white women in the United States and Australia, for example, have supported white men's military and imperial adventures, and white race power structures that systematically penalize nonwhite women and men. She reminds us that identity relations must be located within (and are an aspect of) power relations. Attending to these relations can subvert any easy association of identity, community, and politics (Martin and Mohanty, 1986). Indeed, identity does depend, in part, on location and situation. Many of the one thousand African American women who attended the Nairobi International Women's Conference in 1985, for example, expected to form alliances with African women. Yet African women often regarded them as "American" women first and foremost (Hendessi, 1986).[11]

It can be argued that dominant group feminists have particular kinds of responsibilities that accompany their race, class, or national privilege, though their subordinate position within the dominant group can make this difficult and dangerous in times of war. Similarly, there are immense difficulties confronting feminists who seek to maintain solidarity across the warring identity lines, even among antinationalist feminists. Thus, Serbian feminists were attacked for their antinationalist and international feminist stand, even as some of their feminist organizations were torn apart by nationalist fears and hostilities (Mladjenovic and Litricin, 1992).

Nationality and location allocate membership in zones of peace or zones of turmoil (Cerny, 1996, 132). They load chances for escape or for entrapment in violent or otherwise desperate circumstances. They also determine priorities and demands on feminists and within feminisms in different locations. Struggles within "First World" feminisms, for example, have taught rather more white feminists than other white scholars that race, like gender, is a crucial social, political, and personal identity; that we are all "raced" as we are gendered; that our gender is racialized, and our "race" gendered; and that "white" is an international political color, too (Doty, 1993, 1996; Frankenberg, 1993; Eisenstein, 1996; Manzo, 1996; Maynard, 1996).

White South African women under apartheid were called upon to "disidentify" with the white racist project, or else recognize their complicity in its maintenance (Cock, 1994). So, too, Israeli feminists need to talk back to the state that claims to act on their behalf, and for their protection (Sharoni, 1993; Abdo, 1993). Dominant group Australian feminists are also called upon by Aboriginal and ethnic minority women to recognize and take some responsibility for dismantling white race privilege and its racist consequences (Huggins, 1992; Pettman, 1992; Lukashenko, 1994).

In Australia, as elsewhere, differences among women reflect international processes and relations. "Australia" exists in relation to, and as a consequence of, indigenous people's dispossession and displacement. Only since 1973 has immigration been nondiscriminatory in terms of race, culture, and country of origin. The legacy of "white Australia" still infects relations with neighboring states. In these times of national identity conflicts, and debates about Australia's place in the world, Australia's relations with "Asia" become a way of reflecting upon what kind of society and which international identifications its members seek. "Women" are rarely visible in these identity debates, which are usually called up in the familiar IR language of state, region, threat and alliance. But a thinking space could be forged at the intersections of national and feminist identity debates, where different women's experiences and identities would also count.

Feminists seeking or finding themselves in international relations with other women must negotiate traces of colonial and ongoing race power. So "Third World" feminists have reminded "First World" feminists of their implication in colonizing and imperial international projects, especially where their feminisms reproduce the Third World woman as passive victim and monolithic identity (Mohanty, 1988, 1991). This critique does not collude with any simple reading of politics from identity. But it does acknowledge the complex consequences of being seen as the body we are in, and the nation we are from.

Diasporic Third World feminists take up issues of power, responsibility, and representation. They labor under the familiar burden of representation, expected, on the one hand, to speak for Third World women and, on the other, allowed to speak only if they observe certain niceties—seeming to be "authentic," cultural, not too political, and not too feminist. They find themselves constrained by orientalizing moves aimed to lock them within what Rey Chow refers to as the timeless culture garden (Chow, 1990; see also Trinh, 1987, 1989; Ram, 1993; Ang, 1995).

"Feminism" is at times perceived as the property of white Western academic women; though they too are often accused of being inauthentic women,[12] unrepresentative of other, even other same-nation, women. Third World feminists can be seen as foreign-contaminated, antinational, anticulture. This is a gross denial of women's history and politics, including feminist and women's rights struggles over decades and, in some states, over centuries (Jayawardena, 1986). It is also a classic antifeminist move, attempting yet again to naturalize unequal gender relations and privatize or culturalize sexual exploitation and the surveillance of women. In the process, it denies feminists access to multiple identification and the voice with which to criticize their community, nation, or state.

Third World feminists are also often accused of being too privileged for the possibility of solidarity with poorer women of their own nation-state. Certainly, elite and middle-class women enjoy living standards (though not necessarily choices or economic independence) very different from poorer women. But there are feminist alliances across class lines in many states, though power relations and women's concerns need constant and careful negotiation. Class, along with race, ethnicity, religion, and caste divides women, including in their own estimation. Yet class is both gendered, and increasingly globalized (Grewal and Kaplan, 1994).

GLOBALIZING AND GENDERING CLASS

Class is an increasingly transnational, often global, identity and relation. Even as identity demands and conflicts bind women to territory, community, and belonging in many locations, hypermobile capital, deterritorialized communications, and transnational production mark intensifying globalization processes that cut across and undermine state borders and functions (Mittelman, 1996; Kofman and Youngs, 1996). The state is shifting from a form of civic association into an enterprise association, the competition-state (Cerny, 1996). The poorest and most indebted states, especially some African ones, are increasingly marginalized and bypassed by globalizing interests. They are left behind, and their citizens frequently move elsewhere in search of a job—or to survive.

One of the remarkable changes in recent years is the extent to which many states have willingly, or unwillingly, abandoned responsibility for the national economy. Amin (1996) notes that the "three ways"—Western managed capitalism with its safety-net welfare state; the Soviet model of state socialism; and the Bandung ("Third World") national development state—each assumed this responsibility. Neoliberalism in Western states, the demise of European state socialism, and stabilization and structural adjustment policies imposed by the World Bank and International Monetary Fund on more indebted Third World states, all make for the marketization of the state and the cancellation or truncation of states' social provisioning for their own citizens. They also intensify debate about states' responsibilities, if any, toward migrants and foreigners within their borders, including toward children born there but without citizenship rights.

The reduction of feminized aspects of state underwriting social reproduction are paralleled by a further masculinization of politics.[13] This is especially so in former state socialist Europe, where women's rights as workers made them comparatively expensive, and where growing unemployment has stimulated new traditionalist ideologies of femininity (Watson, 1993; Moghadam, 1995). There, and elsewhere, identity conflicts and exclusivist politics feed into each other, and women's rights and movements are especially targeted. These conflicts also aggravate militarism and its accompanying violence against women.

Women everywhere are greatly affected by the reduction of state provision. Women are more likely to be employed in those sectors of the state most subject to downsizing. Women, in many places, are more dependent on the state than men. As those primarily responsible universally for family and community care, they are the ones who must compensate for "tougher times" and for the withdrawal of state services or subsidies. As inequalities grow within and between states, poorer women especially experience a global crisis in reproduction (Afshar and Dennis, 1992; Brodie, 1994)

Women experience deregulation, restructuring, and the changing global division of labor differently from men. They are especially burdened by current shifts from public to private, from social to individual responsibility, because of both their double load and their already different positioning within the labor market and in relation to the state. It is no coincidence that as transnational corporations (TNCs) "prowl the globe" for cheap labor (Enloe, 1992), the proportion of women in the labor force increases. And while capital is transnationalizing, so too labor is often forced to move from poorer global locations to new centers of growth and employment. An estimated 100–125 million people are now living outside their country of birth, some half of them women. Many of them lack citizenship or even basic work rights in their places of residence (Yuval-Davis, 1991).

There is a huge difference between professional, including academic, women migrating from, for example, southeast Asian states and poorer women from those states who join labor migration flows as domestic workers, sex workers, or service workers.[14] But they are all subject to the construction of racialized, culturalized gender stereotypes that associate "Asian women" with exotic, available, submissive sex, and see those in "mixed race" marriages, often, as mail order brides. So, too, migrant or racialized women may be subjected to heightened state surveillance and face difficulties accessing social goods and services. The concerns and rights of these women are not necessarily taken up by dominant group feminists; though, for example, some European feminist forums have taken up migration and race issues in relation to the European Union (EU) as feminist issues (Brah, 1993). This is often at the insistence of black and ethnic minority feminists. They assert that migrant women workers are agents, too; not simply passive victims of global political economy forces, no matter how heavily the odds may be weighed up against many of them (Rowbotham and Mitter, 1994).

Migrant labor, whether for settlement or contract labor, is now an essential ingredient of most state labor markets, which are segmented along lines of race, ethnicity, and country of origin as well as gender and class. At the same time, many migrant workers and other poorer workers, increasingly women, do work that is badly paid, insecure, often in dangerous or unhealthy conditions. Migrant women workers may do work very similar to work their relatives are doing in their home states.[15]

There is now a global assembly line, marked by increasing casualization and feminization. In the process, there are First Worlds in the Third, and growing Third Worlds in both First and Second Worlds (Mitter, 1986; Pettman, 1996b). There are migration and employment systems that link different workers and places in transnational political economies. This fluidity does not mean that location doesn't matter (the people-flows, overwhelmingly one-way, and the large numbers of illegal workers in many states attest to this). But it does mean that it is difficult to know what we mean by "First World" and "Third World" now. The rapid growth of East and some Southeast Asian states accentuates this, and suggests possible futures and forms detached from existing Euro–North American ones (Dirlik, 1994). Old identity and dispute lines are rendered obsolete, or at least made much more complicated.

At the same time, there are women's experiences of the global political economy that cut across state and national borders. The feminization of poverty, the feminization of the global assembly line, the huge growth in international domestic and service work still associated with women, the estimated one-third of households globally that have no male breadwinner, cannot be understood without analyzing gender, and the changing global sexual division of labor. But women's experiences of the global political economy cannot be understood through gender alone; rather through its complex constitution of, and through, class, race, nationality, age, and so on, which all come together to determine how (and which) women experience the international.

TRANSNATIONAL GENDER IDENTITIES

Women are located rather differently from men in international relations and within the global political economy. Making knowledge about these relations that does not "gender" the account is only partial at best. Gender issues are increasingly transnational, often global. Women are caught up in gendered ways in both the global political economy and identity/nationalist conflicts that make up central dimensions of the post–Cold War world that IR struggles to make sense of.

Taking seriously women's experiences would also enable IR to catch up with "the real world," where women's interests enjoy a certain visibility within the "new" international agenda. This visibility is precisely the effect of women's international politics, of women as international players, in transnational campaigns and international forums, including through conferences from Nairobi and especially from Rio through Vienna and Cairo to Beijing (Krause, 1996; Otto, 1996).

These forums are testing grounds for global gender issues and women's solidarity; though there are questions to do with representation and effects on women's international participation also (Spivak, 1996). Debates about difference are played out, sometimes along First World/Third World lines, at other times cut across by political differences in understandings of gender and of women's interests. These debates are beginning to be heard in IR forums through feminist work.[16]

Taking seriously women's experiences of the international and of globalization can contribute powerfully to the discipline. It can do so, in part, by propelling IR beyond its current white, English-speaking centers and its endemic parochialism, to internationalize the discipline. This means that subordinate, minority, and noncenter men's experiences could also be included. It is no accident that their bodies, along with women's, are frequently sexualized and their masculinity both stigmatized and associated with emotion, not reason (Mercer and Julien, 1988; Connell, 1995).

"Difference" debates and transnationalizing feminisms can contribute, in turn, to feminist theory and politics, including within IR. This means paying attention to race, nationality, location, and other differences between women, and between international feminists, in the academy and outside it. This is already strongly supported by the robust and sophisticated debates about difference among feminists in other disciplinary locations (Mohanty, 1991; Grewal and Kaplan, 1994; Eisenstein, 1996). It can also be supported by the poststructural movement within IR, and by those feminist scholars who question the category "women" and interrogate the politics of IR knowledge making. They bring further insights into what is at stake in disciplinary controversies and challenges (Sylvester, 1994; Weber, 1994). They join with other critical feminist IR thinking work, urging us to ask who the constituencies are for feminist international relations, and what speaking positions are available to those of us who work as feminists within the IR academic realm.

NOTES

My thanks to Tasha Sudan for her thoughtful comments on an earlier draft of this chapter.

1. I mean here the United States of America, not the Americas.

2. There are numerous exceptions, including IR academics and rather more postgraduate students are not from English-speaking backgrounds nor from the United States, United Kingdom, or Canada. Given its relative newness, graduate students make up a significant proportion of those thinking and writing feminist IR.

3. My use of "masculinist' draws attention to social constructions of masculinity, and the association of particular characteristics and behaviors as "masculine," regardless of the sex of the actor. This distinction is pursued later in this chapter.

4. There is always the danger of homogenizing IR; but even those doing critical IR often fail to "see" gender (Sylvester, 1994; Whitworth, 1994).

5. Note the parallel with international law and, especially, traditional human rights law which "is defined in categories that reflect typical male life experiences and offers protection from actions men most fear" (Charlesworth, 1994, 125).

6. This statement sits oddly in relation to another feature of IR—that its dominant discourses personalize states, as in "going after Saddam," meaning a pursuit of Iraqi troops (Cohn, 1993).

7. Some might wish me to say "sex" here; but I do mean "gender" in the sense of the social meanings given to biological differences, and the political implications of these. Note that recent feminist writings on the body and sexual difference fault "gender constructionists" who reproduce the sex: gender and biological: cultural dichotomies (Braidotti, 1994; Grosz, 1994; for implications in IR, see Pettman, 1997).

8. But see Gedalof (1996).

9. Children are usually invisible, or subsumed within the category women, in IR—hence Cynthia Enloe's formulation of the singular "womenand-children" (1991). My file on "Children and/in IR" grows ever larger, so I regret yet another aside only, to children.

10. Women, along with boy and girl children, are the main victims of wars and intrastate violence as "civilians" and as refugees, for example; and are over-represented among those whose poverty is related, often, to uneven development and to international relations of domination and exploitation.

11. See also Dimock (1993) on links and splits among and between Nigerian, South African, and North American black feminists at a women's international conference in Nigeria in 1992.

12. Patriarchal constructions of femininity see feminist women as no longer really women, a construction nicely demonstrated by an antifeminist women's organization in Australia calling themselves "Women Who Want to Be Women." Here, feminists are seen as the gender equivalent of race or class traitors.

13. Thatcher's rage at the "nanny state" for emasculating its citizens by encouraging dependence reminds us that different functions or sites of state are gendered differently. Note, too, Ann Sisson Runyan's suggestion that in the new globalization states are feminized and seen as seeking the attention and financial support of male market forces, in gendered and sexualized metaphors (1996).

14. The vast majority of labor migrants from South/Southeast Asian states are reproductive workers, that is, those employed in care and affective jobs (Truong, 1996), which are both feminized and often occupy the vulnerable, sexualized areas of women's service work in between the public and the private. Here too the international is worked on the bodies of women (Pettman, 1996c, 1997).

15. It is very difficult to generalize across place and workplace; though much feminist work now documents this, for example, Malaysian factory workers, Lim, 1983; Thai sex workers, Truong, 1990; case studies, Blumberg et al., 1995.

16. There are suspicions voiced on occasion that feminist IR too is white and Anglo-American dominated, a suggestion made at the Feminist Theory and Gender Studies' eminent scholars' panel at the 1996 International Studies Association (ISA) meeting. But see, for example, *Alternatives* 1993; and the range of presenters and topics in ISA section panels in recent years.

REFERENCES

Abdo, N. (1993). "Middle East Politics through Feminist Lenses: Negotiating the Terms of Solidarity." *Alternatives* 18(1).

Afshar, H., and D. Carolyne (eds.). (1992). *Women and Structural Adjustment Policies in the Third World.* London: Macmillan.

Amin, S. (1996). "The Challenge of Globalization." *Review of International Political Economy* 3(2), 216–259.

Ang, I. (1995). "I'm a feminist, but. . . ." In B. Caine and R. Pringle (eds.), *Transitions: New Australian Feminisms.* Sydney: Allen & Unwin.

Bakker, I. (ed.). (1994). *The Strategic Silence: Gender and Economic Policy.* London: Zed Books.

Blumberg, R., et al. (eds.). (1995). *EnGENDERing Wealth and Well-Being: Empowerment for Global Change.* Boulder, Colo.: Westview Press.

Braidotti, R., et al. (1994). *Women, the Environment and Sustainable Development: Towards a Theoretical Synthesis.* London: Zed Books.

Brown, W. (1992). "Finding the Man in the State." *Feminist Studies* 18(1), 7–34.

Campbell, David. (1992). *Writing Security: US Foreign Policy and the Politics of Identity*. Manchester, U.K.: Manchester University Press.

Cavarero, A. (1992). "Equality and Sexual Difference: Amnesia in Political Thought." In G. Bock and S. James (eds.), *Beyond Equality and Difference: Citizenship, Feminist Politics and Female Subjectivity*. London: Routledge.

Cerny, P. (1996). "What Next for the State?" In E. Kofman and G. Youngs (eds.), *Globalization: Theory and Practice*. London: Pinter.

Charlesworth, H. (1994). "Women and International Law." *Australian Feminist Studies 19*, 115–128.

Chow, R. (1990). *Women and Chinese Modernity: The Politics of Reading between East and West*. Minneapolis: University of Minnesota Press.

Cock, J. (1994). "Women and the Military: The Implications for Demilitarization in the 1990s in South Africa." *Gender and Society 8*(2),152–169.

Cohn, C. (1987). "Sex and Death in the Rational World of Defence Intellectuals." *Signs 12*(4), 687–718.

Cohn, C. (1993). "War, Wimps and Women: Talking Gender and Thinking War." In M. Cooke and A. Woollacott (eds.), *Gendering War Talk*. Princeton, N.J.: Princeton University Press.

Connell, R. W. (1995). *Masculinities*. Sydney: Allen and Unwin.

Cooke, M. (1993). "Wo-man, Retelling the War Myth." In M. Cooke and A. Woollacott (eds.), *Gendering War Talk*. Princeton, N.J.: Princeton University Press.

D'Amico F., and P. Beckman (eds.). (1994). *Women in World Politics*. Westport, Conn.: Bergin and Garvey.

Dimock, L. (1993). "Bridges Across Activism and Academy: Conference on Women in Africa and the African Diaspora." *Australian Feminist Studies 18*, 215–227.

Dirlik, A. (1994). "The Postcolonial Aura: Third World Criticism in the Age of Global Capital." *Critical Inquiry 20*, 249–256.

Doty, R. L. (1993). "The Bounds of 'Race' in International Relations." *Millenium 22*(3), 443–462.

Doty, R. L. (1996). *Imperial Encounters: The Politics of Representation in North-South Relations*. Minneapolis: University of Minnesota Press.

Eisenstein, Z. (1996). *Hatreds*. London: Routledge.

Elshtain, J. B. (1987). *Women and War*. New York: Basic Books.

Enloe, Cynthia. (1990a). *Bananas, Bases and Beaches: Making Feminist Sense of International Politics*. London: Pandora.

Enloe, Cynthia. (1990b). "The Gulf Crisis: Making Feminist Sense of It." *Pacific Research* (November), 3–5.

Enloe, Cynthia. (1992). "Silicon Tricks and the Two Dollar Woman." *New Internationalist 227* (January), 12–14.

Enloe, Cynthia. (1998). *Does Khaki Become You?* 2nd ed. London: Pandora.

Epstein C. F. (1991). "In Praise of Women Warriors." *Dissent 38* (Summer), 421–422.

Frankenberg, R. (1993). *White Woman, Race Matters*. Minneapolis: University of Minnesota Press.

Gedalof, I. (1996). "Can Nomads Learn to Count to Four? Rosi Braidotti and the Space for Difference in Feminist Theory." *Women: a Cultural Review* 7(2): 189–202.

Grant, R. (1991). "The Sources of Gender Bias in International Relations Theory." In R. Grant and L. Newland (eds.), *Gender and International Relations*. Milton Keynes, U.K.: Open University Press: 8–26.

Grewal, I., and C. Kaplan (eds.). (1994). *Scattered Hegemonies: Postmodernity and Transnational Feminist Practices*. Minneapolis: University of Minnesota Press.

Grosz, E. (1994). *Volatile Bodies: Towards a Corporeal Feminism*. Sydney: Allen and Unwin.

Hendessi, M. (1986). "Fourteen Thousand Women Meet: Report From Nairobi." *Feminist Review* 23, 147–156.

Hooks B. (1989). *Talking Back: Thinking Feminist, Thinking Black*. Boston: South End Press.

Huggins, J. (1992). "A Contemporary View of Aboriginal Women's Relationship with the White Women's Movement." In L. Johnson, et al. (eds.). *A Woman's Place in Australia*. Geelong, Australia: Deakin University Press.

Jayawardena, K. (1986). *Feminism and Nationalism in the Third World*. London: Zed Books.

Jayawardena, K. (1996). *Embodied Violence: Communalising Women's Sexuality in South Asia*. London: Zed Books.

Kaplan, C. (1994). "The Politics of Location in Transnational Feminist Practice." In I. Grewal and K. Caren (eds.), *Scattered Hegemonies*. Minneapolis: University of Minnesota Press.

Kofman, E., and G. Youngs (eds.). (1996). *Globalization: Theory and Practice*. London: Pinter.

Krause, Jill, and N. Renwick (eds.). (1996). *Identities in International Relations*. London: Macmillan.

Lim, L. (1983). "Capitalism, Imperialism and Patriarchy: the Dilemmas of Third World Women in Multinational Companies." In J. Nash M. P. and Fernandez-Kelly (eds.), *Women and Men in the International Division of Labour*. Albany: State University of New York Press: 70–99.

Lukashenko, M. (1994). "No Other Truth? Aboriginal Women and Australian Feminism." *Social Alternatives* 12(4), 21–24.

Manzo, K. (1996). *Creating Boundaries: The Politics of Race and Nation*. Boulder, Colo.: Lynne Reinner.

Marchand, M., and J. Parpart (eds.). (1995). *Feminism/Postmodernism/Development*. London: Routledge.

Martin, B., and C. T. Mohanty. (1986). "Feminist Politics: What's Home Got to Do with It?" In T. de Lauretis (ed.), *Feminist Studies/Cultural Studies*. London: Macmillan, 191–212.

Maynard, M. (1996). "Challenging the Boundaries: Towards an Anti-racist Women's Studies." In M. Maynard and J. Purvis (eds.), *New Frontiers in Women's Studies*. London: Francis and Taylor.

Mazumdar, S. (1995). "Women on the March: Right-Wing Mobilisation in Contemporary India." *Feminist Review* 49 (Spring), 1–28.

Mercer, K., and I. Julien. (1988). "Race, Sexual Politics and Black Masculinity." In R. Chapma and J. Rutherford (eds.), *Male Order: Unwrapping Masculinity*. London: Lawrence and Wishart.

Mitter, S. (1986). *Common Fate, Common Bond: Women in the Global Economy*. London: Pluto.

Mladjenovic, L., and V. Litricin. (1993). "Belgrade Feminists 1992: Separation, Guilt and Identity Crisis." *Feminist Review 45* (Autumn), 113–119.

Mohanty, C. (1988). "Under Western Eyes: Feminist Scholarship and Colonial Discourses," *Feminist Review 30*, 61–88.

Mohanty, C. R., A. Lourdes, and T. Lourdes (eds.). (1991). *Third World Women and the Politics of Feminism*. Bloomington: Indiana University Press.

Parker, A., et al. (1992). *Nationalism and Sexualities*. London: Routledge.

Pateman, Carole. (1992). "Equality, Difference and Subordination: The Politics of Motherhood and Women's Citizenship." In G. Bock and S. James (eds.), *Beyond Equality and Difference: Citizenship, Feminist Politics and Female Subjectivity*. London: Routledge.

Peterson, V. Spike (ed.). (1992). *Gendered States: Feminist (Re)Visions of International Relations*. Boulder, Colo.: Lynne Reinner.

Peterson, V. Spike. (1994). "Gendered Nationalism." *Peace Review* 6(1), 77–83.

Peterson, V. Spike, and A. S. Runyan. (1993). *Global Gender Issues*. Minneapolis: University of Minnesota Press.

Pettman, Jan Jindy. (1992). *Living in the Margins: Racism, Sexism and Feminism in Australia*. Sydney: Allen and Unwin.

Pettman, Jan Jindy. (1993). "Gendering International Relations." *Australian Journal of International Affairs* 47(1), 47–62.

Pettman, Jan Jindy. (1996a). *Worlding Women: a Feminist International Politics*. Sydney: Allen and Unwin.

Pettman, Jan Jindy. (1996b). "Boundary Politics: Women, Nationalism and Danger." In M. Maynard and J. Purvis (eds.), *New Frontiers in Women's Studies*. London: Francis and Taylor.

Pettman, Jan Jindy. (1996c). "Women on the Move; Gender, Globalisation and the Changing International Division of Labour." Paper presented to the Globalisation seminar series, Department of International Relations, Australian National University, Canberra.

Pettman, Jan Jindy. (1997). "Body Politics: International Sex Tourism." *Third World Quarterly 18*(1).

Rich, A. (1986). *Blood, Bread and Poetry: Selected Prose, 1979–1985*. New York: Norton.

Roberts, B. (1984). "The Death of Machothink: Feminist Research and the Transformation of Peace Studies." *Women's Studies International Forum* 7(4), 195–200.

Rowbotham, S., and S. Mitter (eds.). (1994). *Dignity and Daily Bread: New Forms of Economic Organizing among Poor Women in the Third World and the First*. New York: Routledge.

Ruddick, S. (1983). "Pacifying the Forces: Drafting Women in the Interests of Peace." *Signs* 8(3), 471–489.

Runyan, A. S. (1990). "Gender Relations and the Politics of Protection." *Peace Review* 2(4).

Runyan, A. S. (1996). "Trading Places: Globalisation, Regionalism and Internationalized Feminism." In E. Kofman and G. Youngs (eds.), *Globalization: Theory and Practice*. New York: Pinter.

Sharoni, S. (1993). "Middle East Struggles through Feminist Lenses." *Alternatives* 18(1), 5–28.

Sharoni, S. (1995). *Gender and the Israeli-Palestinian Conflict: the Politics of Women's Resistance*. Syracuse: Syracuse University Press.

Smith, Steve, M. Zalewski, and J. Parpart. (1998). *The Man Question in International Relations*. Boulder, Colo.: Westview Press.

Sylvester, Christine. (1994). *Feminist Theory and International Relations in a Postmodern Era*. Cambridge: Cambridge University Press.

Sylvester, Christine. (1995). "African and Western Feminisms: World Travelling: The Tendencies and Possibilities." *Signs* 20(4), 941–969.

Tetrault, M. A. (ed.). (1994). *Women and Revolution in Africa, Asia and the New World*. Columbia: University of South Carolina Press.

Tickner, J. Anne. (1992). *Gender in International Relations*. New York: Columbia University Press.

Trinh, M. (1987). "Difference: A Special Third World Women Issue." *Feminist Review* 25, 5–22.

Trinh, M. (1989). *Woman, Native, Other: Writing Postcoloniality and Feminism*. Bloomington: Indiana University Press.

Truong, T. (1990). *Sex, Money and Morality: Prostitution and Tourism in South-East Asia*. London: Zed Books.

Truong, T. (1996). "Gender, International Migration and Social Reproduction." *Asian and Pacific Migration Journal* 5(1).

Waring, M. (1988). *Counting for Nothing*. Wellington, New Zealand: Allen and Unwin.

Watson, P. (1993). "The Rise of Masculinism in Eastern Europe." *New Left Review* 198, 71–82.

Weber, C. (1994). "Good Girls, Little Girls and Bad Girls: Male Paranoia in Robert Keohane's Critique of Feminist International Relations." *Millennium* 23(1), 377–349.

Whitworth, Sandra. (1994). *Feminism and International Relations*. New York: St. Martin's Press.

Woolf, Virginia. (1993) [1938]. *A Room of Her Own* and *Three Guineas*. Ed. Michele Barrett. London: Penguin.

Yuval-Davis, N. (1991). "The Citizenship Debate: Women, Ethnicity and the State." *Feminist Review* 39 (Winter), 58–68.

PART III

Toward Diversity in International Thought

CHAPTER 13

International Relations and Cognate Disciplines: From Economics to Historical Sociology

James L. Richardson

INTRODUCTION

International Relations (IR), whether conceived of as a field of study or a discipline, has always been open to ideas and methods from other disciplines of longer standing. This essay, endorsing such openness and even inclining toward a partial return to the conception of the subject as a field of study, will argue for a redirection of emphasis in drawing on cognate disciplines, away from economics and toward history and sociology, in particular toward that branch of inquiry which combines both disciplines, historical sociology. Stanley Hoffmann (Hoffmann, 1960) advocated this approach in his first major discussion of the discipline, unfortunately with little success; more generally, with historical approaches tending to be eclipsed by "scientific" approaches in the American social sciences for more than a century (Ross, 1991). But the present is an appropriate time to reconsider this issue with respect to International Relations. The limitations of the economic approach are becoming more evident, and a perusal of recent publications suggests that a revival of historical approaches is already under way.[1] To this extent the essay is not so much calling for a new direction as advancing reasons for welcoming and reinforcing a redirection of interest that has been taking place incrementally and relatively unremarked upon.

Borrowing from economics has extended far beyond the field of its obvious relevance, international political economy. Economics has provided analogies, as in Kenneth Waltz' (1979, 89–98) use of the market; it has provided concepts such as "free riding," "Prisoner's Dilemma," "transaction costs," and the like; and it has provided methodological criteria such as the value placed on counterintuitive explanations and on parsimony in theorizing. More generally, economics has provided a mode of analysis that calls for a high level of abstraction and universality, timeless analysis, parsimonious models and methodological individualism, and plays down historical and contextual particularities and also traditions, structures, and institutions except insofar as they can be reconstructed in terms of the choices of rational actors subject to highly general situational constraints. The more extreme version of this approach has not been taken up very much outside the United States. It can be seen as illustrating both the strength of the American discipline—its rigorous development and application of a methodology—and its weakness—its readiness to discard the baby in order to cleanse the bathwater.

On a broad understanding of historical sociology as macrohistorical studies of the *longue dureé*, the works in this genre which have begun to appear in International Relations are far more heterogeneous. They include, for example, Kal Holsti's (1991) account of institutional and normative changes bearing on peace and war in the modern states system; Hedley Bull and Adam Watson's edited work (1984) on the worldwide extension of Western norms and institutions; Robert Gilpin's (1981) and Paul Kennedy's (1988) interrelating of economic and military factors in the rise and fall of empires and great powers; and the contrasting world system and long cycle views of the development of the modern state, or global, system.[2] In an overview discussion, Richard Little (1994) draws attention to the potential relevance to IR of a wide range of work in historical sociology and world history and, in collaboration with Barry Buzan and Charles Jones (1993), proposes a radical reformulation of Waltzian neorealism to take account of the history of international systemic change.

The present essay will argue for three propositions. First, and briefly, because the issues are relatively familiar, it will claim that despite its positive contributions the economic mode of analysis in IR shows many negative features, and that the point of diminishing returns was reached some time ago. Second, it will argue that historical sociology has much to offer substantively: for example, it offers a fruitful way of approaching the central systemic issue at the present time—the nature and extent of the changes that the international system is undergoing. A *longue dureé* perspective on political organization may well provide the best approach to the question of how fundamental are the changes entailed by globalization, regionalism, new technologies, and the like. Its third and most important argument is the more general thesis, that historical sociology and, indeed, the history discipline, offers a mode of analysis that is more adequate than the economic for addressing the central questions that arise within international relations, not only at the systemic level but also at the level of decision-making. In place of a one-dimensional conceptual grid, it offers a structure that can accommodate multiple perspectives.

THE ECONOMIC MODE OF ANALYSIS

There is no disputing the intellectual and aesthetic appeal of rigorous formal deductive models, but the question is how appropriate are they in relation to the problems that are important in international relations. Formal rational choice theory, and, in particular, game theory, has been used most extensively and most fruitfully in certain areas at what may be termed the "micro" (or decision-making) level—in theories of deterrence and negotiation, for example, and on topics such as arms races where the actors are tightly constrained by the (perceived) situation. More generally, wherever strategic interaction takes place, bargaining theory is highly relevant, and the scope of strategic interaction may be greater than is commonly recognized.

However, even where the theory is on its strongest ground, three qualifications need to be made. First, even here there are countertheories, for example, psychological theories relating to deterrence, that may offer better explanations in particular cases. Second, in the broader field of decision-making there are *many* alternative conceptualizations and approaches that address aspects of the process which appear to be beyond the scope of formal theory. And third, the most fruitful applications of game theory in International Relations are heuristic, rather than fully formalized or predictive[3] (except in the loose sense that *if* a great many conditions are realized, a particular outcome will ensue, but their realization will depend on considerations beyond the scope of the theory).

These qualifications point to the major limitation of formal theory in IR. It is not just that theories which show how rational actors will choose and interact, *given* their preferences, need to be complemented by theories that explain those preferences—a point that is often conceded. It is not merely the actors' preferences (their values and goals) that are taken as given, but the actors themselves—their identities, and the processes by which these particular actors come to be selected as decision-makers—and thus the institutions, prevailing norms and beliefs, and the political, social, and economic "structures" that lie behind the actors. On the face of it, most of the questions of interest to IR arise outside the scope of formal explanations of choice and require explanations of a different kind.[5]

To say this, of course, is to discount the aspiration of certain rational choice theorists to develop game theory into a unifying theory for the whole of IR, or, indeed, of the social sciences (e.g., Snidal, 1985). The general idea is that theory will consist of testable propositions derived from specifying the interests of actors *a priori*, in accordance with certain simplifying assumptions. This aspiration, first voiced in the early 1960s, receded as major problems in applying and testing game theory in the strategic studies field became evident, but under the stimulus of theorizing on cooperation (Axelrod, 1984) it revived in the 1980s. This wave now appears to be receding, in part, as before, because of the extent to which existing game-theoretic studies fall short of the aspiration, in part because the interests that actors pursue obstinately refuse to be specified in advance by the theorist, and also because in domains such as the economic and the environmental the actors are now so numerous, heterogeneous and inter-related as to defy such specification. Arguably, international cooperation is conceptualized inadequately in terms of the choices of rational egoistic state actors, but requires more substantial theorizing on the construction of interests, and the inclusion of transnational as well as subnational actors and interests. Game-theoretic models may have heuristic value in isolating important relationships in the face of such complexity, but political contingencies of many kinds enter so strongly into complex and protracted negotiations, for example, as to render highly formal explanations largely irrelevant.

The same general approach at the macrolevel—neorealist theory— is even more contentious. Here, too, it is postulated that state actors pursue specified interests, but the focus is on the systemic structure that constrains the outcomes within certain broad parameters. For most neorealist strategic analysts, states seek to maximize security; on an alternative hypothesis, they seek to maximize influence (Zakaria, 1992); or again, their prime concern is with relative gains, which would be relevant to either.

The most valid claim here is that systemic structure constrains characteristic behavior within certain broad limits. For some purposes, this is of central importance, but for others, in particular, inquiry into specific outcomes within those limits, it is irrelevant. Other, more specific features of the system may be relevant, but these are not within the purview of neorealist theory (Richardson, 1994a, 219–235). Waltz himself allows that for inquiry into any specific outcome, systemic theory needs to be complemented by theories of foreign policy, and the kind of causal priority which he assigns to systemic influences is that, in the long run, actors who disregard these constraints will be eliminated; while other neorealists tend to ascribe casual primacy to the international system even in specific instances. Waltz does not support this.

As to the choice of maximizing assumptions—security, influence, or relative gains—the problem is that none of these is plausible as a generalization, and the assumption of maximizing is, itself, contentious. Little is gained by reformulating familiar questions in the study of foreign policy as assumptions, especially when familiar observations show that decision-makers tend to divide precisely over the priority to be accorded to these, and to other values and goals. A government may act (relatively) rationally at all times, yet its preferences may change because of changes in its decision-making personnel. The parsimony of rational choice models may screen out what is important for understanding any particular foreign policy. A case in point may be the tendency of neorealist analysts to focus on nuclear weapons as the answer to postulated regional security problems in the post–Cold War setting (most notoriously, Mearsheimer, 1990).

Similar problems arise when the economic mode of analysis is employed in historical studies: they may offer valid insights but their overall interpretations are distorted through their commitment to theoretical parsimony. To take an impressive work in this genre, Jack Snyder's *Myths of Empire* (1991), addressing the longstanding issue of the primacy of internal *versus* external causes of imperialism, usefully highlights the role of domestic coalitions but discounts other influences—international pressures, security imperatives, ideas and ideologies—not as a result of close examination of each particular case but because his parsimonious explanatory model requires him to assign primacy to one strand of causation. This frequently places him at odds with historical scholarship, with its preference for exposing multiple interrelated causes of macro (or for that matter micro) phenomena.[6]

To sum up the argument thus far: the rational choice mode of analysis, in particular game theory, has proved its value in the analysis of strategic interaction, but only if it is supplemented by other modes of theory and investigation in order to explain crucial factors that are taken as given in such studies, especially the actors' identities, goals, and preferences, and the structural contexts within which they interact. Rational choice theory has less to offer in relation to systemic or structural questions, where its weaknesses in relation to change, differentiation, and multiple chains of causality point to the need for a radically different mode of theorizing.

HISTORICAL SOCIOLOGY AND THE TRANSFORMATION OF THE INTERNATIONAL SYSTEM

If the economic mode of analysis is especially inadequate in relation to systemic change, where should we turn for more relevant theory? This section will argue that the most promising theorizing at the present time is not within international relations as at present defined, but in historical sociology, a cross-disciplinary field of study that maintained a precarious foothold for much of this century but has undergone a striking revival during the past two decades.[6] This argument will be made briefly in general terms, and will be illustrated with reference to one of the central issues in contemporary IR the extent to which the international system is being transformed. That is to say, is the five-centuries-old "Westphalian" state system undergoing fundamental change—whether through "globalization," the "end of sovereignty," new processes of integration and fragmentation, or through civilizational identity supplanting state identity, or other changes of this order of magnitude?

An alternative approach to these issues would deny the need to look outside the discipline in order to explain systemic change. Buzan and Little (1996) suggest that a modified version of neorealist theory can provide an adequate account of systemic change. They argue that the essential modification of Waltz's neorealist model is to reject his claim that there are no systemically significant functional variations among the units of the system—that is to say, the claim that all are sovereign states responsible for their own survival, systemically compelled to practice self-help and power balancing. From the perspective of world history, Buzan and Little maintain, there are significant functional variations—for example, overlapping authorities as in medieval Europe or degrees of autonomy or suzerainty in classical empires such that the subordinate unit was not fully incorporated into an imperial state yet enjoyed something less than sovereign independence. Furthermore, in their view, structural differences among units—for example, nomadic tribes, city-states, classical empires, modern nation-states—whether coexisting or succeeding one another, are also systemically significant. Recognition of these variations, they argue, opens up five millennia of world history to IR, permitting for the first time a comprehensive comparative study of international systems.

One advantage of this "structural realist" formulation of systemic change is that it builds on existing international relations theory rather than simply setting it aside and attempting an entirely new approach. And they make a persuasive case that the great political transformations studied in world history can be conceptualized in structural realist terms. However, they do not offer a theory of systemic *change*, but, rather, a typology, a framework for comparing systems, a series of snapshots or stylized maps of the international system. This appears to point toward a comparative theory of state systems rather than of systemic change. They allude to this in raising the question of how functional and structural differentiation would affect the explanatory power of realist theory, but they go on to limit themselves to causal relationships within the model: "Just how does it [such variation] fit into a generative hierarchy of structural effects that cascades from anarchy, through differentiation of units, to distribution of power?" (Buzan and Little 1996, 433). The question does not appear to offer very much purchase on systemic change.

If the modification of established international relations theory offers little promise for constructing a theory of systemic change, where might we look for such promptings?[7] Recent international relations theorizing offers some bold exploratory essays, not so much building on existing IR theory as drawing insights from a range of disciplines that might point the way to a theory of systemic change (Ruggie, 1993; Modelski, 1996), opening up vistas which are at once appealing and daunting. This essay will return briefly to Ruggie but will not pursue these particular explorations further. Rather, it will suggest that students of international relations would do well to examine one particular crossdisciplinary field of study—historical sociology. This does not offer any ready-made theory of international systemic change, but it does bring sociological theory to bear on the great processes of political, economic, social, and cultural change that form the subject matter of world history. Full discussion of these theories would require a consideration of unorthodox as well as mainstream approaches, but for present purposes it is sufficient to note the contrast between the two most influential theoretical traditions, those which stem from Marx and Weber. For the neo-Marxists, in the last analysis economic change is the driving force: changes in the mode of production, associated with technological advances and changes in class formations, provide the fundamental explanation for changes in the political and cultural "superstructure." Up to a point there can be reciprocal causation or even, in some variants, a holistic mode of analysis that departs from the primacy of the economic, but, in general, the hallmark of the Marxist approach is this primacy. This comes through clearly in Immanuel Wallerstein's monumental study of the modern world system (1979, 1980, and 1989), whereas Robert Cox (1986, 1987) may be taken as an exemplar of a more open-ended, less deterministic account of world order that nonetheless retains a characteristic neo-Marxist focus on classes and modes of production. Arguably, the exclusion of these approaches from mainstream American IR theory is one reason for that theory's weakness in relation to systemic change.

For the "neo-Weberians"—not all of whom might accept the label—the base-superstructure image of causation is fundamentally flawed. The development of modern economic and political structures, for example, is a narrative of the interaction between the two, not of the predominant influence of the one—two logics, not one (Rapkin, 1983). Historical sociologists have been concerned with "bringing the state back in," not just in its internal role but also the geopolitical dimension, traditionally neglected by sociology. Some such works highlight two dimensions, for example, Weber's classic discussion of religion and capitalism, or more recent discussions of the economic and the military. The most comprehensive attempt to interrelate all the dimensions of power traditionally regarded as essential—the economic, political, military, and ideological—is undertaken by Michael Mann (1986, 1994), for whom there is no ultimate primacy, but in different historical conjunctures any one of these may provide the principal dynamic for systemic change. In common with most structural accounts, Mann accords agency only a minor role. The current interest in cultural issues, and in "ideas," in international relations may be regarded as an attempt to remedy this gap.

The international system has not been a primary concern of historical sociology, though it receives some attention from Mann and from Anthony Giddens (1985), and the contemporary world order is a major concern for Cox and the neo-Gramscian school. On the other hand, the emergence and changing functions of the modern state have been remarkably neglected in International Relations; for theorizing about its central actor the discipline has to look outside itself, especially toward historical sociology where the state has been of major interest. The "end of sovereignty" debates would thus be enriched by a more sustained engagement with historical sociology's theoretical and institutional literature on the state. More broadly, the studies of macrohistorical change in both the Marxist and Weberian traditions provide hypotheses and modes of analysis that could serve as starting points for those seeking to identify the systemwide direction of change at the present time. For this author, the Weberian approach offers the greater promise, but the Marxist approach provides more than a corrective to dangers of the latter's lapsing into historical particularism.

This is not, to repeat, to suggest that historical sociology offers ready-made answers. Engagement with it can take the form of systematic critical examination of its theories and hypotheses, but it can also take the form of independent theoretical exercises in the same genre. A notable example is John Ruggie's (1993) essay on territoriality, which seeks to shed light on the question of the current transformation of the state by separating out some of the key ingredients in its formation, under the headings "material environment," "strategic behavior," "social epistemes," and "social empowerment." Agency and cultural change are at the center of this discussion, juxtaposed not so much with structure as with environment, an unfamiliar approach within traditional theory, but one that suggests the potential of constructivist and, indeed, postmodern theorizing in the contemporary global context. It also illustrates what I term the historical mode of analysis, the topic of the next section.

THE HISTORICAL MODE OF ANALYSIS

How is the historical mode of analysis to be characterized? Like the economic mode it is not a theory, but refers to a style of theorizing—essentially, one that articulates norms and practices characteristic of the history discipline as well as those of historical sociology[8]—just as those of the economic mode derive from the economics discipline. The economic mode includes such theories as neorealism, game theory, public choice, utility and, more broadly, the theories of neoclassical economics. It is characterized by parsimony, "thinness," mechanical models, a high level of abstraction, epistemological positivism, and the aspiration to universality and to the status of the natural sciences; its advocates tend to claim that these are necessary characteristics of theory per se. Clear-cut examples of the historical mode are not so readily obvious, but, arguably, would include classical realism, liberal theories of peace, and theories in political sociology such as class, elitist, and pluralist theories of power and decision-making. It is characterized by the relative plurality of key variables, open-ended models, contingent or time-specific generalization—thus greater concreteness and skepticism toward claims to universality—and a rejection of the traditional natural-science model and of exclusive epistemological claims.

More sharply defined alternatives to the economic mode are articulated from time to time, including hermeneutic, organic, holistic or certain "postmodern" approaches, each articulating a comprehensive alternative, developed from highlighting a specific point of difference (e.g., the epistemological, the mechanical, the abstract). What I am terming the historical mode of analysis is more open-ended, more pluralistic: from its standpoint these alternatives have something of the narrowness and one-sidedness of the economic mode, a different kind of parsimony that leads to the exclusion of much historical and social-scientific knowledge which is worth retaining. The historical mode is not a theory but a framework that permits diverse modes of theorizing to contend: it does not reject any of these *a priori* but is open to the possibility that many approaches may have something to offer, within limits that need to be specified. I see this as the working assumption of most historians who take an interest in theoretical issues; it is, perhaps, best articulated in historical sociology, from which Mann and Giddens may be taken as exemplars.

Five aspects of this framework will now be outlined, in each case drawing attention to their divergence from the economic mode. First, and most fundamental, "structured complexity" is intended to capture the most general characteristics of the social-political world, signaling a standpoint between the claims of the uniqueness of every situation which would deny all possibility of theory and the universalist claims of parsimonious theory. Second, the historical mode is not purely structural but accords an important place to agency, once again understood in a way that contrasts with the generalized abstractions of the economic mode. Third, and closely related, is the obstinate insistence of analysts in this mode on combining methodologies often regarded as opposites, in particular, the hermeneutic and the scientific. Fourth is the issue of the scope of theory, and fifth is the way in which this approach addresses differences of interpretation, steering a course between excessive claims to scientific objectivity on the one hand and an acceptance of relativism on the other. In order to illustrate and further clarify the historical mode, this general explication will be supplemented by an example, realist theorizing in both modes.

Structured Complexity

This term seeks to meet the need for a conception of theory that breaks with the economic mode's one-sided emphasis on parsimony—and the ensuing distortion and artificiality—while avoiding the opposite extreme of seeking to explain complexity in all its rich detail, or lapsing into the kind of eclecticism that sees every theory as having something to offer and avoids discriminating among them. The concept is based on the practice of historians in explaining large-scale events—wars, revolutions, and the like—as the product of multiple, interrelated causes. For example, in explaining the origins of the First World War, James Joll (1984) seeks to interrelate alliances, armaments, and military planning with economic and imperial conflicts, nationalism, attitudes to war, and domestic political pressures. The omission of any one of these strands, he claims, would leave out something essential for understanding how and why the governments and peoples of Europe came to accept the enormous costs and risks entailed in general war at that time.

In this example, as in most histories, Joll is referring to a single case and his theoretical claims are not fully spelled out. A more explicit formulation of this mode of explanation is provided by Michael Mann in his account of the changing configuration of social and political power since the earliest civilizations. For Mann, societies are constituted by multiple networks of power, the major networks being of four kinds—ideological, economic, military, and political. These are independent of one another but not separate—they overlap and interact, and each network may assume some of the functions of the others. Fundamental restructuring of power may be brought about by actors primarily within any one of the networks, often located in the interstices of established structures. No network enjoys general causal primacy in relation to the others, though in any particular case one or other may be the primary source of change (Mann, 1986, 1–33).

Mann applies this framework to the explanation of the major changes in political structures (including the geopolitical) since antiquity. Such an analysis could provide the kind of framework for explaining international systemic change, the need for which was noted above. That is to say, however, it offers what was lacking in the comparative "snapshots" of the structural realists, namely, an account of the processes through which one systemic structure breaks down and is replaced by an entirely different structure. Nor is this to endorse Mann's specific thesis concerning the four crucial networks, which could be modified without affecting his overall mode of explanation; moreover, it is evident that it would be necessary to enlarge on Mann's discussion of the geopolitical, the least theorized of his networks, in order to arrive at an explication of international systemic change. The focus here is not on the particulars but on the general character of Mann's explanatory model.

If the model encapsulates Mann's basic approach to sociological theory, its open-endedness points to one of the most striking features of his work—his combination of the scholarly commitments of the sociological theorist and the historian. His language and his determined search for patterned, structured relationships exemplify the sociologist, but his respect for the particular, his rejection of generalizations that do not fit the cases, and his acknowledgment of multiple chains of causality are hallmarks of the history discipline. Mann's struggle to bring sociological theory into accord with the recalcitrant particularity of historical experience recalls the line of thought expressed rather obliquely by Martin Wight, when he suggested that the theory of international politics should be equated with historical interpretation (Wight, 1966, 32–33).[9]

One does not have to endorse Wight's extreme position to recognize that historical sociology's explicit confronting of the tension between the general and the particular is important for international relations. Needless to say, not all historical sociologists adopt a common approach: different topics call for different explanatory models. Frequently, the inquiry is into a single one of Mann's networks, for instance, the development of the modern state, or into the relationship among two networks, for example, religion and capitalism, or Paul Kennedy's study of the economic and the military (Kennedy, 1988). Here the focus is not on the full array of variables, but on certain sectors or on certain more closely defined relationships. Even so, there should be some recognition that these are not self-contained "worlds" but are affected by other "strands" or networks. The development of the modern state will not be explained adequately in purely political terms, and an account such as Kennedy's will be open to criticism if it neglects other dimensions such as, surprisingly, the diplomatic (Richardson, 1991).

Agency

What is envisaged is not a purely structural theory but one that accords a significant place to agency, both at the level of the individual (purposive action, learning, perception and the ascription of meaning) and of the collective (cultural creativity, the mobilization of social groups, the empowering of leaders, and the like). In practice it proves difficult to keep both agent and structure in focus simultaneously. In many diplomatic histories, for example, structure tends to disappear into the background, while there seems little place for agency in most accounts of the *longue dureé*. Giddens' concept of structuration, according to which agent and structure mutually constitute and determine one another, offers a resolution of this problem at the most general level but not many signposts for resolving it in particular cases. The historical mode of analysis should be seen as one that regularly confronts this intractable problem rather than one that has achieved a particular resolution of it.

The confronting of the problem entails the acceptance of a certain kind of indeterminacy—not in an absolute sense, but the rejection of monocausal deterministic theories—not only because of the commitment to the idea of multiple chains of causality but also because agency, with its assumption of learning from experience, implies the constant possibility of new responses to otherwise comparable situations.[10] This has important implications for the character of theory: it limits the scope of prediction, which cannot be viewed, as in some versions of science, as theory's primary purpose. While prediction remains a valid goal it is always subject to limiting conditions remaining constant, and the extent to which this may reasonably be assumed depends on the context. The more general goal of theory—explanation—will typically have to be understood as explanation after the event, after the various determining strands of agency and structure have come together.

The danger implicit in this approach is that it could lapse into the atheoretical if the historian's fascination with the particular is allowed to dominate the sociologist's concern to uncover patterns, typologies, and causal processes. This is where the alternative, neo-Marxist school of historical sociology has something crucial to offer: even though those drawn to the historical mode reject the economic determinism that underlies studies such as those of Wallerstein, they pose the challenge to formulate a better theoretical analysis, not just a better narrative. If it is the neo-Weberians who best articulate the *historical* side of historical sociology, the dialectic with the neo-Marxists is integral to that subdiscipline, and thus has an essential part in any theorizing in IR that seeks to build on historical sociology.

Methodological Pluralism

Studies focusing on agency tend to employ hermeneutic methodologies, highlighting actors' understanding of situations, their intentions, frustrations, mind-sets, and the like, or the social and cultural setting that provides their normative world. Structural studies, on the other hand, tend to opt for "objective" scientific methodologies highlighting behavioral or situational regularities. The two methodologies give rise to contrasting modes of explanation, termed by Hollis and Smith (1991) explanations from the inside and from the outside, respectively. Contention between these has a long history in the social sciences, as does Hollis and Smith's view that, philosophically speaking, it is very difficult to formulate a meaningful synthesis between them. The idea of a synthesis, nonetheless, has distinguished advocates, not least Max Weber, but the present aim is not to seek to adjudicate this philosophical/methodological issue, but, rather, to elucidate the position ascribed to the historical mode of analysis.

We may begin with the practice of historians. Although emphases may differ, it can safely be said that virtually all histories combine the two modes of explanation—references to the thinking, intentions, and norms of particular actors, on the one hand, and to regularities of behavior and causality on the other. Methodologists have no difficulty in showing that even historians who disclaim all interest in generalization make general assumptions—often, in international history, along realist lines. They seek to explain both from the inside (reconstructing the thought of the actor) and from the outside (presenting commonly accepted views of normal behavior, causal relationships, and the like, assumptions which may be time-specific or deemed to hold more generally). Similar juxtapositions of actor-oriented, contextual analyses of particular situations and patterns of activity explained in terms of general causes may be found in many international relations studies. To take two examples: Kal Holsti (1991) discusses the peace settlements since 1698 mainly in terms of the key actors' intentions, but turns to variables amenable to general causal analysis when discussing the changing issues that generated wars. And the present author's study of crisis diplomacy (Richardson, 1994a) employs mainly hermeneutic methods to reconstruct individual cases but examines theories in the "scientific" genre in seeking explanations of crisis outcomes.

The basic rationale for combining methodologies is that research should be question-driven, not shaped primarily by particular techniques or methodological views. This essay will not pursue this issue further, beyond noting that writers on methodology, especially when they pay serious attention to the practice of research, continue to offer justifications for combining methodologies (e.g., Alker, 1996, especially 394–421; Bohman, 1991).

The Scope of Theory

The conception of theory implicit in the historical mode of analysis is that social science theories are context-dependent; relevant contexts might be historical, cultural, or institutional, to refer to the most familiar categories. A radical exponent of this view would claim that it is true of all social science theories, but most would be satisfied with the more modest claim that it holds for most types of theory. In either case, this would involve an extension of the view of theory as contingent generalization, which Alexander George and Richard Smoke (1974, 616–642) applied only to policy-relevant theory, to social science theory much more generally. But whereas George and Smoke did not challenge the claim that the central aim of theorizing was to achieve theory of ever greater generality, the present conception demands at least equal status for context-dependent theory.

In its less radical version, proposed here, it would allow for the possibility that theory may be able to establish some propositions that are not context dependent. This may be true of game theory, for example, insofar as it establishes the "rational" choice, given certain payoff structures. But even here certain qualifications would need to be made. First, game theory does not predict actual choices or behavior, but what the rational choice would be given certain assumptions about the actor's preferences and about the situation: any given case may not reproduce all the assumptions. Second, it is extraordinarily difficult to "apply" game-theoretic models in complex situations, as distinct from controlled experimental situations. Thus, the universal scope of the theory may be deceptive: while it has heuristic value in alerting researchers to unexpected potentialities in a complex situation, the likelihood of particular choices will depend on a variety of other considerations, requiring different kinds of theory. The same appears to be true of psychological theories. For example, the processes that affect perception may apply irrespective of context, yet in any given case the multiplicity of factors affecting an actor's perception and its consequences will render it difficult to ascertain the significance of even a well-established propensity in that particular case.

Although the conception outlined here limits the scope of social science theory with respect to its universality, it extends its scope in other respects. First, as Buzan and Little note, in place of the aspiration to construct universal, timeless theories of sovereign actors, there is an opening up of the whole of world history and of relations among more variegated political entities (Buzan and Little, 1996, 432). Second, although there is a rejection of the idea of an overarching theory or a master narrative, there is a prospect that historical experience can be illuminated by viewing it from the perspective of a plurality of social science theories and, moreover, that addressing the range of historical experience may stimulate theoretical innovation.

Differences of Interpretation

The historical mode of analysis cannot hold out the hope of the rigor and precision in testing hypotheses, nor of finality in explanation, to which the natural sciences formerly aspired and which still underpins the ambitions associated with the economic mode of analysis. Multicausal and structure-agent explanations necessarily involve a process of assessing evidence and argument. Evidence often appears superabundant but is always incomplete; analysis is necessarily selective, and is influenced by the inquirer's questions and assumptions. Differences of interpretation are a necessary feature of the historical mode, as of the history discipline—not a contingent and regrettable one. Indeed, it must be allowed that there can be different valid readings of a situation, different valid narratives; there is no single, final History. To this extent there is a certain affinity between history and postmodernism.

This, however, should not be equated with "relativism:" it does not imply that *all* interpretations are equally valid. There can be sufficient grounds for rejecting *some* interpretations. The discipline of history, like that of law, has its criteria for assessing evidence. Some readings can be shown, in the light of the available evidence, to be misleadingly selective or outright incorrect. The evidence for certain conclusions may be compelling, while, on related issues, it remains open to debate. One criterion, endorsed *inter alia* by E. H. Carr (1962, 32) is comprehensiveness: that an interpretation does justice to *all* the evidence that is perceived to be relevant. But this does not mean that these can be a final synthesis. It always remains possible that someone coming to a topic afresh may perceive it in a way which requires a new "paradigm," a thorough rethinking of established views—either because of a new theory, or because new circumstances raise new questions or prompt new insights. However alarming this may be to some methodologists, it is in accordance with the practice of IR and, indeed, of most of the social sciences.

AN ILLUSTRATION: REALIST THEORY

Neorealist theory has sought to formalize the insights of classical realism in accordance with the economic mode of analysis. A theory of timeless regularities, it not only fails to account for systemic change, but its abstractions also fail to conceptualize the characteristics of diplomatic practice in the modern states system as, for example, Paul Schroeder (1994) convincingly demonstrates. That is to say, the balance of power is not the constant preoccupation that neorealist theory suggests, but states more typically engage in a variety of practices (making "deals," evading, finessing, or "transcending" conflicts) without the disastrous consequences which the theory would suggest.[11]

But if power balancing is thus seen as something of a last resort, this does not mean that it offers security, or even predictability. If images of the balance differ radically, as at the beginning of the twentieth century, attempts to achieve a balance may exacerbate conflict in ways not clear to the participants. At that time Britain perceived Germany as a potential hegemonial threat to the traditional European balance, whereas Germany perceived itself as disadvantaged in the emerging balance among the "world powers" (Richardson, 1994a, 230–231). More generally, key realist concepts should be seen as variables, not constants of international history. To take a further example, policies are sometimes, and perhaps more often than not, guided by a reasonably coherent conception of the national interest, but this is not always the case, either because of deep international divisions or for other more adventitious reasons (Richardson, 1994a, 248–254).

As John Vasquez (1993) expresses it, realist practices are a central, but variable, constituent of modern international relations. The historical mode of analysis, with its multivariable framework and dual structure-agency focus, provides the researcher with the critical distance from realist theory that can elucidate why its injunctions sometimes appear compelling, heightening awareness of the significance of the realist conceptions of the actors themselves, and of the interaction between those realist actors and the "structures" that are at times highly constraining, and at others, such as the present, in the process of reconfiguration.

CONCLUSION

The argument has been that the attempt to remodel international relations theory along the lines of the economics discipline has amounted to a massive misdirection of effort. The struggles and antinomies that constitute the realist tradition have been reduced to a pallid abstraction, and a relatively minor branch of theorizing, the logic of choice, magnified out of all proportion to its limited potential at the expense of more fruitful lines of theoretical inquiry. One reaction, the postmodernist, has been equally extreme; its view from the margins has offered an invaluable corrective to a discipline drawn too far in the direction of idealizing the status quo, but has not offered a persuasive reconfiguration for the discipline as a whole. More recently, the constructivist school, drawing insights from the postmodernist critique, has developed an approach that highlights the importance of norms: an invitation to rethink the discipline as a whole and a new focal point for theoretical debate. These approaches are providing a much needed theoretical rejuvenation for the discipline, but structural theory appears to have receded too far. Historical sociology, and the mode of analysis that it exemplifies, can strike a better balance.[12]

What are the implications for the discipline? First, the move toward greater diversity in international thought is indeed necessary if the discipline is to do justice to the vast issues within its purview. This essay has highlighted one way in which the American discipline has been narrowing when the need is for an opening out. The historical mode, it has been suggested, is particularly concerned with the way in which answers to some of the "big" questions tend to require a combination of theories and even methodologies. But not just any combination. This points to the second implication. The essay is not calling for a "celebration of difference," diversity for diversity's sake. As the horizons open out, the criticism and delimiting of theories becomes all the more important.

Third, the claim that is being made for historical sociology is that it is more than just one more theory to be added in, along with all the rest. The claim is more ambitious: that it can offer the most promising starting point for theorizing about a core issue that the discipline has thus far been unable to address, international systemic change. Just as the discipline needs to look beyond its present boundaries for theorizing about the state, it needs to do the same with respect to systemic change.

The implications for the practice of the discipline in its research and teaching are too complex to be embarked on here. It is as if the discipline of economics were to restore economic history to the central place, which many might consider overdue, but which the rigidities of the present economics discipline preclude. International Relations, however, does not suffer from the same rigidities, and is currently in a position to reorient itself in more than one direction. This essay has argued for according a major place to historical sociology, and the historical mode of analysis, in that reorientation: they share the postmodern skepticism toward universal theoretical claims, old and new, but open to the particular strengths of theories, irrespective of their provenance.

NOTES

An earlier version of this essay was presented at a seminar in the Department of Government, University of Manchester, in February 1995. I am grateful to Richard Higgott for organizing the seminar, and to the participants for their comments. The essay has also benefited from the constructive comments of the editors.

1. Journal articles on historical topics (including historical episodes or case studies, long-term historical issues and theoretical articles drawing on historical analysis) are becoming more frequent in some of the major international relations journals, in particular, *International Organization* as well as *Review of International Studies* and *European Journal of International Relations*. They are infrequent in *International Studies Quarterly* except for a recent special issue (September 1996) on "Evolutionary Paradigms in the Social Sciences." See also the books referred to below.

2. On the world system, see Wallerstein (1974, 1980, 1989); on long cycles, see Modelski (1987), Thompson (1988), Goldstein (1988).

3. The seminal work on game theory in strategic studies (Schelling, 1960) uses game models informally, varying some standard assumptions, as do Snyder and Diesing (1977) in their study of crisis bargaining.

4. For a balanced critique of the use of game theory in international relations, see Jervis (1988). In seeking to explain the outcomes of international crises (Richardson, 1994a) I found bargaining theory essential for examining the parties' interactions, but the various "givens" required chapters on the changing international system, the choice of goals, perception and misperception and internal politics, each discussing theories other than rational choice models.

5. For example, he endorses the popular American view that Japan's policies in the 1930s were irrational, a reasonable inference from his narrowly based analysis but one that runs counter to most scholarship that examines the Japanese frame of reference. His claim that Japan's interests would have been better served by accepting the open international order advocated by the United States overlooks the economic disorder and the tariff policies actually pursued by the United States during that decade (Richardson, 1994b).

6. Interest in this side of the work of Marx and Weber was suppressed by national socialism and discouraged by the contemporary and behavioral emphases in American sociology. Reinhard Bendix, S. N. Eisenstadt, and Barrington Moore constituted exceptions during the 1960s, but historical sociology achieved greater prominence and developed a new interest in international rela-

tions from the 1970s, with the work of Theda Skocpol, Immanuel Wallerstein, Perry Anderson, Charles Tilly, and Michael Mann, to name only the most prominent. Comprehensive discussions may be found in Smith (1991) and Little (1994).

7. Mention should be made of Robert Gilpin's (1981) relatively neglected neorealist discussion of systemic change. Its primary focus is the rise and fall of hegemonial empires; in this it resembles other cyclical theories, although its scope (world history) is broader than the more familiar focus on the modern state system. These theories do not address the contemporary issue whether that state system is in the early stages of transformation into a system of a different character.

8. The term is more convenient than the alternative, "historical-sociological mode of analysis." It is also appropriate in that the contrasts with the economic mode are most clearly present in the history discipline. The concept is an ideal type: there is no claim that all historians subscribe to all its tenets, even though they would be widely shared, especially by those historians whose conception of their discipline is not wholly particularistic, that is, those who have something of the sociologist's interest in comparison and generalization.

9. Referring to "a kind of recalcitrance of international politics to being theorized about," Wight claims its essential quality and preoccupations are better "embodied and communicated" in historical writing than in political theory. It is not that history does a "different job" (presumably narrative) from theory. History, too, offers "a coherent structure of hypotheses," a "common explanation," but "with more judiciousness and modesty" (Wight, 1966, 32–33). The present chapter, taking Mann as exemplar, seeks to offer a more systematic explication of what I take to be Wight's essential point.

10. On the significance of indeterminacy in contemporary social science theory, see Bohman (1991).

11. It has been claimed by Elman and Elman that Schroeder misunderstands neorealist theory, but they concede that he shows that "balancing behavior and balances of power are not as prevalent as Waltz would have as believe" (Elman and Elman, 1995, 192). In effect, they concede that neorealist theory has little relevance to the explanation of specific international events.

12. The same may be true of some versions of feminist theory. I have not drawn on feminist theory in constructing the present argument, in part because of the literature consulted and, in part, because its central concerns appear to be elsewhere. But there is some overlap in the critique of the economic mode of analysis (e.g., Tickner 1992, 67–96), and a recent overview (Mansbridge and Okin, 1993) points to considerable affinity with the historical mode.

REFERENCES

Alker, Hayward R. (1996). *Rediscoveries and Reformulations: Humanistic Methodologies for International Studies.* Cambridge: Cambridge University Press.

Axelrod, Robert. (1984). *The Evolution of Cooperation.* New York: Basic Books.

Bohman, J. (1991). *New Philosophy of Social Science*. Cambridge, Mass.: MIT Press.

Bull, Hedley, and Adam Watson (eds.). (1984). *The Expansion of International Society*. Oxford: Clarendon Press.

Buzan, Barry, C. Jones, and Richard Little. (1993). *The Logic of Anarchy: Neorealism to Structural Realism*. New York: Columbia University Press.

Buzan, Barry, and Richard Little. (1996). "Reconceptualising Anarchy: Structural Realism Meets World History." *European Journal of International Relations 2* (December), 403–438.

Carr, E. H. (1962), *What Is History?* New York: Knopf.

Cox, Robert. (1986). "Social Forces, States and World Orders: Beyond International Relations Theory." In Robert O. Keohane (ed.), *Neorealism and Its Critics*. New York: Columbia University Press: 204–254.

Cox, Robert. (1987). *Production, Power and World Order: Social Forces in the Making of History*. New York: Columbia University Press.

Elman, C., and M. F. Elman. (1995). "History vs. Neo-realism: A Second Look." *International Security 20* (Summer), 182–193.

"Evolutionary Paradigms in the Social Sciences." (1996). *International Studies Quarterly 40* (September), special issue.

George, Alexander, and Richard Smoke. (1974). *Deterrence in American Foreign Policy: Theory and Practice*. New York: Columbia University Press.

Giddens, Anthony. (1985). *A Contemporary Critique of Historical Materialism*. Vol. 2: *The Nation-State and Violence*. Cambridge: Polity Press.

Gilpin, Robert. (1981). *War and Change in World Politics*. Cambridge: Cambridge University Press.

Goldstein, Joshua. S. (1988). *Long Cycles: Prosperity and War in the Modern Age*. New Haven: Yale University Press.

Hoffmann, Stanley. (1960). *Contemporary Theory in International Relations*. Englewood Cliffs, N.J.: Prentice Hall.

Hollis, Martin, and Steve Smith. (1991). *Explaining and Understanding International Relations*. Oxford: Clarendon Press.

Holsti, K. J. (1991). *Peace and War: Armed Conflicts and International Order 1648–1989*. Cambridge: Cambridge University Press.

Jervis, Robert. (1988). "Realism, Game Theory, and Cooperation." *World Politics 40* (April), 317–349.

Joll, J. (1984). *The Origins of the First World War*. London: Longman.

Kennedy, Paul. (1988). *The Rise and Fall of the Great Powers: Economic Change and Military Conflict from 1500 to 2000*. London: Unwin Hyman.

Little, Richard. (1994). "International Relations and Large-Scale Historical Change." In A. J. R. Groom and Margot Light (eds.), *Contemporary International Relations: A Guide to Theory*. London: Pinter.

Mann, M. (1986). *The Sources of Social Power: A History of Power from the Beginning to A.D. 1760*. Vol. 1. Cambridge: Cambridge University Press.

Mann, M. (1993). *The Sources of Social Power: The Rise of Classes and Nation-States, 1760–1914*. Vol. 2. Cambridge: Cambridge University Press.

Mansbridge, J. J., and S. M. Okin. (1993). "Feminism." In R. E. Goodin and P. Pettit (eds.), *A Companion to Contemporary Political Philosophy*. Oxford: Blackwell.

Mearsheimer, J. J. (1990). "Back to the Future: Instability in Europe after the Cold War." *International Security 15* (Summer), 5–52.

Modelski, George. (1987). *Long Cycles in World Politics*. London: Macmillan.

Modelski, George. (1996). "Evolutionary Paradigm for Global Politics." *International Studies Quarterly 40* (September), 321–342.

Rapkin, D. P. (1983). "The Inadequacy of a Single Logic: Integrating Political and Material Approaches to the World System." In W. R. Thompson (ed.), *Contending Approaches to World System Analysis*. Beverly Hills, Calif.: Sage.

Richardson, James L. (1991). "Paul Kennedy and International Relations Theory: A Comparison with Robert Gilpin." *Australian Journal of International Relations 45* (May), 70–77.

Richardson, James L. (1994a). *Crisis Diplomacy: The Great Powers Since the Mid-Nineteenth Century*. Cambridge: Cambridge University Press.

Richardson, James L. (1994b). "History Strikes Back: The State of International Relations Theory." *Australian Journal of Political Science 29* (March), 179–187.

Ross, D., (1991). *The Origins of American Social Science*. Cambridge: Cambridge University Press.

Ruggie J. G. (1993)."Territoriality and Beyond: Problematising Modernity in International Relations." *International Organization 47* (Winter), 139–174.

Schelling, Thomas C. (1960). *The Strategy of Conflict*. Cambridge, Mass.: Harvard University Press.

Schroeder, P. W. (1994). "Historical Reality vs. Neo-realist Theory." *International Security 19* (Summer), 108–148.

Smith, D. (1991). *The Rise of Historical Sociology*. Cambridge: Polity Press.

Snidal, Duncan. (1985). "The Game Theory of International Politics." *World Politics 38* (October), 25–57.

Snyder, G. H., and P. Diesing. (1977). *Conflict among Nations: Bargaining, Decision Making and System Structure in International Crises*. Princeton: Princeton University Press.

Snyder, J. (1991). *Myths of Empire: Domestic Politics and International Ambition*. Ithaca: Cornell University Press.

Thompson, W. R. (1988). *On Global War: Historical-Structural Approaches to World Politics*. Columbia: University of South Carolina Press.

Tickner, J. Anne. (1992). *Gender in International Relations: Feminist Perspectives on Achieving Global Security*. New York: Columbia University Press.

Vasquez, J. A. (1993). *The War Puzzle*. Cambridge: Cambridge University Press.

Wallerstein, Immanuel. (1974). *The Modern World-System: Capitalist Agriculture and the Origins of the World-Economy in the Sixteenth Century*. Vol. 1. New York and London: Academic Press.

Wallerstein, Immanuel. (1980). *The Modern World-System: Mercantilism and the Consolidation of the European World-Economy, 1600–1750*. Vol. 2. New York and London: Academic Press.

Wallerstein, Immanuel. (1989). *The Modern World-System: The Second Era of Great Expansion of the Capitalist World Economy, 1730–1840s*. Vol. 3. New York and London: Academic Press.

Waltz, Kenneth. (1979). *Theory of International Politics*. Reading, Mass.: Addison-Wesley.

Wight, Martin. (1966). "Why Is There No International Theory?" In Herbert Butterfield and Martin Wight (eds.), *Diplomatic Investigations: Essays in the Theory of International Politics*. London: George Allen & Unwin.

Zakaria, F. (1992). "Realism and Domestic Politics: A Review Essay." *International Security 17* (Spring), 177–198.

CHAPTER 14

At the Wood's Edge:
Toward a Theoretical Clearing
for Indigenous Diplomacies
in International Relations

Roger Epp

> One of the most perplexing ironies of American history is the fact
> that the Indian has been effectively silenced by the intricacies of
> his own speech, as it were. Linguistic diversity has been a
> formidable barrier to Indian-white diplomacy. And underlying this
> diversity is again the central dichotomy, the matter of a difference
> in ways of seeing and making sense of the world around us. . . .
> The fundamental difference in ways of looking at the world, as
> those differences are reflected in the language of diplomacy, seem
> to me to constitute the most important issue in Indian-white rela-
> tions in the past five hundred years.
> —N. Scott Momaday, "Personal Reflections"

INTRODUCTION

In the richly metaphoric, theatrical protocols of traditional Hau-
denosaunee, or Iroquois, diplomacy, it was from wood's edge that representatives of another people announced their willingness to treat, then
waited for escort from forest to clearing (Fenton, 1985, 3–36, 115–124).
The spatial metaphor is strikingly suggestive, at first glance, of the way
in which indigenous political activity stands largely outside the clearings
made by contemporary international politics. There are few welcoming
delegations of elders and packcarriers, kettles waiting, ceremonies of

condolence planned, or beaded belts of agreement to exchange; there are, to paraphrase a common metaphor for the renewal of relations, few paths to keep open. It is not for lack of indigenous activity, stretching back most notably in this century to the Iroquois' unsuccessful appeal in 1923 to the League of Nations for recognition and protection on the basis of the new legitimating norm of self-determination. In recent years, coalitions of indigenous peoples from several continents have gained observer status at the United Nations. A working group established by the UN's Human Rights Commission has produced a draft declaration of the rights of indigenous peoples in areas such as land, culture, and governance, provoking in response vigorous efforts on the part of threatened foreign ministries to soften its definitions or blunt their effect. Representatives of indigenous peoples in Canada, moreover, have engaged in international activity in European, Asian, and American capitals to block hydroelectric development; press for the settlement of outstanding land claims; lobby diplomatic opinion against recognition of a would-be secessionist Quebec; stop low-level military flight testing over traditional caribou grounds; and have fur boycotts lifted. Arctic peoples from several countries are formally linked in the Inuit Circumpolar Conference, begun in the early 1980s partly in response to the Cold War militarization of the ocean connecting them. The Miskito in Nicaragua, forced to maneuver between the centralization policies of the Sandinista regime and the indifferent cruelty of Washington's low-intensity warfare against it, and, more recently, the Mayan in Mexico's Chiapas region, resisting the implications of North American free trade for traditional land tenure, have constituted political forces impossible for governments to ignore or subordinate. Both the Miskito and the Mayan have drawn, in turn, on nascent, transnational indigenous linkages. And the list so far is drawn primarily from parts of only one continent.[1]

If this range of global political activity increasingly attracts the (sometimes irritated) attention of governments and occupies the agendas of international organizations, and is the subject of growing literatures by scholar-activists in cultural anthropology and international law, it remains relatively unacknowledged within the academic discipline of International Relations (IR).[2] What Stanley Hoffmann observed a generation ago of the American social science of IR is perhaps less valid, but it nonetheless holds some clues to this disinterest. The discipline, he wrote, is preoccupied with the present and at that with states, with the interplay of "great powers," and with scientific certainties; conversely, it lacks both historical understanding and philosophic ambition, and it neglects the experience of the "weak" and "revolutionary" (Hoffmann, 1977). It is understandable on these counts alone, then, that indigenous diplomacies should have been lost to view. There are in addition the challenges of making sense of indigenous claims to autonomy, which, though they might use familiar words such as "nation" and even "sovereignty," typically do not aspire to statehood; of the elusive but central category of culture, as that which is to be defended; of forms of power outside of conventional measures of military or economic strength. The exceptions are rare. There is Franke Wilmer's book-length start on the subject (Wilmer, 1993, 1996). There is an appendix in an undergraduate textbook by Ralph Pettman, an Australian (Pettman, 1991). There is Richard Falk's eminent warning—found in a collection of papers from a gathering of lawyers—that "the peoples of the entrapped nations are a sleeping giant in the world of power politics" (Falk, 1987, 50–68). There is Cynthia Enloe's heuristic use of the Chiapas example in a recent essay probing the discipline's inadequate conceptualizations of power (Enloe, 1996). There is greatest interest in the Iroquois, though it runs the risk, as does the metaphor that opens this essay, of perpetuating the inordinate position first assigned them by British colonial rule. There is interest specifically in the Great Law of Peace, whose study is facilitated by the uncommon provision of written text; and in relations within the historic Six Nations confederacy, the subject of a prominent article in the American flagship journal *International Organization*, whose careful, comprehensive research is diminished by the anachronistic objective of exercising the latest theories about regimes and the relationship of democracy to peace (Crawford, 1994; Bedford and Workman, 1997). Doubtless there is more. But it is scattered, marginal, and perhaps mildly exotic.

Let me be clear about my own purpose. It is not to argue that IR ought to be more territorial, even imperialistic, about subject matter rightfully belonging to it. I am not certain what it can offer in trade. While I am interested in what the neglect of indigenous peoples and practices—what I call diplomacies—says about IR as a discipline, my purpose is to rethink that neglect, and those absences, as forms of marginal presence implicated deeply in the construction of much of what is taken for granted in the discipline even at the level of its keywords: anarchy and sovereignty. Certain representations of indigenous peoples, it can be shown, have been present all along. They are front and center in the early-modern jurists' accounts of the law of nations, and in the social contract theorists' crude state-of-nature anthropologies which continue to shape IR's basic assumptions. They are participants in the complex relations, including alliances and treaties, that characterized state-building in North America and the South Pacific, where sovereignty remains problematic despite legal-military efforts to monopolize political identity, violence, and foreign relations. They are assumed to have been domesticated in the so-called expansion of international society, and continue to mark the outside limits of acceptable decolonization.

The subject is an enormous one, and this essay only preliminary in nature. Its purpose is to make present within "the clearing," and not to interpret indigenous political traditions and experiences within it. Such a task demands diverse linguistic-cultural competencies.[3] My forays are meant to be suggestive, not exhaustive. Out of many possible points of departure, I would identify two. One is philosophical hermeneutics. Its insistence that all understanding, all being-in-the-world, is language-bound is highly appropriate to any discussion of diplomacy, whose pivotal figure is the interpreter; and its stress on reflexivity, on thinking through the horizons of the inquirer, asks what cannot be avoided in this essay (Gadamer, 1976, 3–17). What does it mean to think about indigenous political activity from within the horizons that constitute IR? What does it mean to recognize the chasm of languages, across the worlds and ways of knowing from which they derive? What kinds of openness are required? Who is theorizing?

The second point of departure is the work of Martin Wight and, secondarily, the "classical," "English," or "international society" school in IR associated with him. Here my reasons are partly strategic, since it seems necessary to begin on familiar ground to preempt the charge of faddishness in a discipline whose long-time practitioners lament the loss of a common subject. But, more than that, my reasons are intellectual. First, Wight's work—attentive to language, refusing to reduce the subject to ahistorical mechanics, or to fence it in at all—bears none of the limitations catalogued by Hoffmann. It tells multiple narratives about international relations. Second, it takes seriously the spheres of law, international organization, and diplomacy, in which the terms of indigenous dispossession have been worked out and in which a good deal of contemporary indigenous activity is deployed. Third, there are critical openings yet to be explored in Wight's often caricatured, scarcely read work, especially his posthumously published lectures that made such a mark on IR in Britain in the 1950s. Long before it could be fashionable, Wight's lectures put the problem of relations with the "other," the outsider, the barbarian, at the ontological-moral center of international theory and held Western rationalism accountable for the tutelary "humbug" of colonialism. The lectures are strikingly preoccupied with, and unusually passionate about, the "fit of world-conquering fanaticism" that describes "the West since 1500" (Wight, 1991, chap. 4)—the period roughly coincident with the emergence of a European state-system. They are particularly, if episodically, attentive to aboriginal peoples, whose presence seemingly should not have to be read back into the discipline if the lectures were as influential for a generation of British IR as is often claimed. Moreover, in their richness of detail more than their triadic architecture, these lectures evoke the critical posture recommended by Edward Said: that is, a "'relentless erudition,' scouring alternative sources, exhuming buried documents, reviving forgotten (or abandoned) histories" (Said, 1994, xv; see also Ahluwalia and Sullivan in this volume). This essay proceeds in that same enterprise.

PLACING IR: A VIEW FROM THE CANADIAN PRAIRIES

Place

Aristotle proposes that philosophy was not merely the greatest of goods, but the most readily accessible. Philosophers needed "no tools or places for their work." They could take it up "wherever in the world one sets one's thought to work," for they did not so much claim a particular home in the world as feel "at home" in the pursuit of truth (Ross, 1952, 33–34). There is, I submit, a similarly profound placelessness about IR. This will seem an odd comment in light of the common and valid complaints about American predominance in the field and the parochiality of its literature's thinly veiled preoccupation with what are often U.S. policy problems. But I am thinking of place in a more particular, self-conscious sense. Richard Ashley, with a purpose more metaphorical than mine, captures something of what I mean when he describes IR as a "field of strangers," each like a lone horseman on the open plains, or better yet an itinerant late-Renaissance condottiere, "a stranger to every place and faith, knowing that he can never be at home among the people who dwell there," searching paradoxically for places where "his strategic art" can be performed (Ashley, 1996, 240–253). The reasons for this intellectual nomadism are varied and reinforcing. They include the actual exile experience—like Aristotle's—of many of IR's postwar stalwarts in the United States, Hoffmann among them; the pervasive influence of social-scientific positivism with its search for universally replicable knowledge; the caprices and conforming imperatives of a difficult job market; the incursions of postmodern claims whose point is precisely to unsettle, if not in a strictly geographic sense, then in a way that problematizes categories of space and belonging; and, not least, the built-in pretense of a discipline whose scope is properly global. As a result, IR research—mainstream and critical—has an overwhelmingly placeless appearance. It could as easily originate in Aberystwyth, mid-Wales, as in New York City; it is probably important to its reception that it should appear so.

One of the risks underlying this paper is that it arises deliberately, if unsurely, out of the context of what the essayist Wendell Berry calls a "beloved country" (Berry, 1990), that is, out of a local ecology and the problems of people struggling to live well within it. In my case that means the Canadian prairie West, where I was born and where I now teach in a rural setting. This region is not defined by fixed territorial borders, but by what might be called an aesthetic of light, color, landform, and by the distinctive imprints made by human cultures in response to it. From this vantage point, 600 kilometers from the nearest border crossing, 3,000 kilometers from Ottawa, IR denotes, especially to my students, an abstract, distant, and distinctly metropolitan world of connected capitals: political, financial, intellectual, cultural. This sense of distance is more than the inevitable collision of life world and the attempt to conceptualize it in a classroom. It is compounded by an additional kind of alienation, subtle but profound, and derived from the reality that "most social theory in the West . . . has been generated in urban, highly industrialized environments . . . where the only trees and plants available to human observation are products of hyper-cultivation, and the only visible animals are profoundly domesticated" (Smith, 1994, 50–51).

There are few IR horsemen on these northern plains. There is little to territorialize. Even war is experienced vicariously on television, or through the stories of an older generation that fought fascism abroad, or, in my case, through the experience of a student back from a United Nations mission in the former Yugoslavia. War happens elsewhere. These plains are unscarred by modern war, save for the few battlesites of the short-lived Metis and Cree uprising of spring 1885 and, in sparsely populated areas, preparations for war that include weapons testing, training exercises, and proximity to the American missile silos and air bases situated in the "empty" spaces between large urban centers.

Treaties are a different matter. Treaties we have strong opinions about. Not Westphalia, Utrecht, Versailles: the placename markers of European international history. Treaties. The ones we live with.

Story

Fort Pitt in 1876 was scarcely a fort at all. Having neither a stockade nor soldiery, it had been a lonely outpost of the mercantile, Hudson's Bay Company branch of the British Empire, midway on the North Saskatchewan River between two more significant posts hundreds of miles in either direction. Bands of Plains Cree who lived off the buffalo had traded provisions for supplies there. In early September 1876 the flats surrounding the fort were ringed with more than a hundred Cree lodges. On the top of the hill a tent had been pitched for ceremony and

protection from the weather. Young Cree riders criss-crossed in dangerous patterns on horseback—colliding at one point and requiring medi-
cal attention—in front of the band chiefs advancing up the hill. The
chiefs took their places in a large semicircle, with perhaps three hundred
listeners behind them; this would be public diplomacy. A Royal North-
West Mounted Police band had bumped across the plains with instruments for the occasion to play God Save the Queen. Pipes were presented, smoked, and placed in front of the Lieutenant-Governor
Alexander Morris. He read out the terms. They were identical to those
already accepted by bands at Fort Carlton to the east. There could be,
he said, no changes. But Morris promised his "Indian brothers"—the
Queen's "children"—that they would be cared for and taught the "cun-
ning of the white man." In exchange for 121, 000 square miles, and a
promise to obey the law and keep order among themselves, reserves
would be set aside for them, annuities paid, schools and a "medicine
chest" provided, and farm implements ("four hoes for every family cul-
tivating") and livestock distributed (see Morris, 1971, chap. 9; Price,
1979). After several days of deliberation, there were few dissident chiefs.
The buffalo were disappearing; the decisive technologies of steel and
steam were moving west, and the gatling gun north, to claim this land
for Canada.

The land that was once Fort Pitt now keeps its silences. It was
ploughed under in the first wave of European homesteading but no
longer farmed. Treaty Six is inscribed in its particulars on the appropriate parchments, and inscribed equally over a domain extending far
beyond Fort Pitt. The lines it drew are real and the interpretations it
evokes are fresh as argument: a pledge of peaceful coexistence and
mutual sharing, as the elders recall it described, or a real estate deal, perhaps even a cynical one, justified at the time by the march of civilization
and in retrospect by the productive use made of the land by its settlers.

When in 1995 the Treaty Six bands were threatened with cuts to
health services they appealed collectively to the UN Commission on
Human Rights under the terms of the draft declaration. The UN, they
acknowledged, was tedious and bureaucratic, but it "was one forum
that we can use to have Canada honour and fulfill the obligations and
sacred trust" of what was "an international nation-to-nation treaty."

Family

If I inquire into indigenous diplomacies, I do so with all the ambivalences of a settler. Most of us are settlers here even after a century. We
are either, in Fanon's dichotomy, settlers or natives. My family has lived
for four generations on lands designated in Treaty Six. I have read

Machiavelli with a classroom of Cree students, and will not forget their uniformly strong recognitions at book 5 of *The Prince*, which describes three options ("each one has happened to us!") for conquering a people accustomed to liberty: devastation, settlement, or proxy rule through a friendly, tribute-paying oligarchy. I cannot disentangle the story of who I am from the complex set of interactions, cultural codes, and government policies that have also defined the Indian. Something of the same is true, I want to show, for international relations.

DIPLOMATIC INVESTIGATIONS (i): (S)WORDS INTO PLOUGHSHARES

There is in Wight's work the suggestion of a subtle, gradual, but fundamental transition from medieval to modern Europe, this side of which is found the state and state-system. While the transition can be probed geographically and chronologically, its expression is a new political vocabulary typically of power in place of right (Wight, 1946). Wight does not pursue this idea in relation to European colonial encounters in the sixteenth century. But his lectures mark the centrality and the ambivalences of the Spanish debate over the moral status of the Indians and, therefore, of the conquest. Wight proposes that it is out of this debate, "this problem of the barbarians," rather than out of intra-European requirements related to the demise of Christendom, or war, or resident embassies, that modern international law can be said to emerge for a world of multiple sovereigns. Its first great treatise is Vitoria's *De Indes* (Wight, 1991, 69–70). This point of origin is no mere accident, for the Indians constitute an extreme test case for the more general principle. In a passage that calls to mind Hobbes' state of nature, Vitoria can anticipate the objections of his opponents: the Indians, even putting aside their "mortal sin" of human sacrifice, are without "proper laws or magistrates . . . literature or arts; . . . they have no careful agriculture and no artisans; and they lack many other conveniences." Nonetheless, Vitoria puts the Indians inside the law of nations, with a rightful claim to dominion over their territory and therefore to self-defense against Spanish attack and papal presumption. But his achievement is a two-sided one. Its price is a reciprocal right of outsiders to travel, trade, and preach unharmed within that same territory, one that can be asserted lawfully by force should "reason and persuasion" fail or should the Spanish ambassadors, "by the law of nations inviolable," be denied a "friendly hearing" (Victoria, 1964, 154–156). Its price is the Indians' redefinition as potential Europeans. It is to cast European-Indian relations in the discoverers' terms of rights and the capacity for reason.

Vitoria's argument, as Wight puts it, effectively and unilaterally "condemns the hermit-kingdoms" (Wight, 1991, 70–71; see also Terpul, 1989–90, 3–45). It also preserves the idea, found equally in Grotius, that within an inclusive law of nations there is an inner circle of European, Christian nations, whose primacy implies a paternalism that in its stronger, subsequent mediations becomes a right of empire and a duty of trusteeship, in which "wards" have rights they can neither claim nor formulate (Wight, 1991, 79).

There are elaborations of Wight's reading in Tzetvan Todorov's *The Conquest of America*. Todorov links the Spanish voyages of discovery and wars with the development of a new instrumental attitude to language symbolized by publication of the grammar cited above. Language was flexible, a means of manipulation as well as veneration. For the Aztec, meanwhile—literally, "people who explain themselves and speak clearly"—it denoted a highly-ritualized, rigorously inculcated set of verbal practices that provided both exchange with the gods and a materialization of "social memory" (Todorov, 1984, 87); it was less capable of improvisation. Vitoria is no nominalist but even he is not immune to the instrumentalization of language: "the seizure and occupations of those lands of the barbarians whom we style Indians can best, it seems, be defended under the law of war" (Victoria, 1964, 165). In his treatise, too, Europeans speak and Indians must give a friendly hearing. In the prolonged Spanish debate over the conquest and particularly in the mid-century councils at Valladolid, the latter were not even present in such a passive role. Todorov captures this irony nicely: "in the best of cases, the Spanish authors speak well of the Indians, but with very few exceptions they do not speak to the Indians" (Todorov, 1984, 132). Aboriginal admission to the law of nations apparently comes with neither voice nor vote.

There is arguably a more crucial representation, more constitutive of IR, in that early-modern international theory for which the Indians are no longer the real, if voiceless, inhabitants of self-governing nations whose rights must be worked out. They are rather the stylized American savages—uncultivated and uncultivating—who dwell in the fictional states of nature from which seventeenth-century social contract theorists cast arguments about authority and property. Hobbes' description is the most notorious and graphic. His state of nature a state of war pitting all against all, is approximated by jealous, well-armed European sovereigns, but is lived out in a suitably "brutish manner by the "savage people in many places of America" (Hobbes, 1962, 13, 101). The latter "proof" is readily skipped while reading Hobbes. The former, Wight argues, has been accepted since his own time by so-called realists and rationalists alike, as describing the precontractual, state-of-nature anarchy of relations among European sovereigns (Wight, 1991, 30). It collects, among others, Grotius, Hobbes, Locke, and Pufendorf, who between them not only confound Wight's categorizations but also accomplish the recasting of natural law expressed in terms of rights, not right, and grounded in nothing nobler than the primacy of self-preservation. This basic assumption is, in broad terms, the source of IR's domestic analogy in which states are likened to persons, with similar motives of self-preservation, and the private property appropriable toward that end is, beginning with Grotius, likened to territorial sovereignty. The degree of state sociability under conditions of anarchy is the stuff of secondary argument. But there is more to interrogate for IR in state-of-nature images of the world as a source of powerful reasons for dispossession of aboriginal lands and nonrecognition of aboriginal governance.

Locke's *Two Treatises* provide the fullest expression of the contractarian position for my purposes. It is possible to credit Grotius, whose first "classic" of international law, *De Jure Praedae*, was also occasioned by a colonial problem, with having already produced a "useful ideology for competition over material resources in the non-European world" with his account of self-preservation through property acquired by labor (Tuck, 1979, 62).[4] It was Locke, however, who developed that position for an English-American readership, and who embellished and located its crude anthropology to suit their imaginations. "Thus in the beginning," he writes, "all the world was America" (Locke, 1960, Book II). It was, in other words, a blank slate against which to trace the evolution of property (from common to private) and government (from patriarchal to contractual). Defoe's *Robinson Crusoe* is his fictional counterpart, set somewhere off the mainland in the western hemisphere. Where Locke's arguments can be given a radical reading in an English context they suggest a rather different, no less consequential one in a colonial context. Locke, associating liberty with property, and property in the first instance with appropriation from nature, can allow even the "wild Indian" ownership of "the fruit or venison which nourishes him" (Locke, 1960). But he moves quickly to the claim that cultivation of the "earth itself" is the "chief matter of property." The Lockean standard of "civilization" and "progress" rests on relative efficiencies in the use of land: "For I ask whether the wild woods and uncultivated waste of America left to Nature, without any improvement, tillage or husbandry, a thousand acres will yield the needy and wretched inhabitants as many conveniences of life as ten acres equally fertile land doe [sic] in Devonshire where they are well cultivated. . . . And a king of a large and fruitful territory there feeds, lodges, and is clad worse than a day labourer in England" (Locke, 1960, Book II). For Locke, loading his case with adjectives like "wild," "wasted," and "wretched," the absence of cultivation is definitive of a primitive state of nature, though he conveniently neglects all the aboriginal assistance that settlers received in growing suitable crops, some of which fruit was introduced in Europe as well.

The colonial implications in Locke's point about cultivation as the measure of efficient occupation were reiterated more plainly by Emmerich Vattel, the most eminent diplomatist of the next century. His *Law of Nations* begins from the familiar contractarian premise that the earth belongs to all in common, but that at some stage of population growth cultivation was required of every nation as a matter of natural duty, since hunting or herding were no longer acceptable: "Those who still pursue this idle mode of life occupy more land than they would have need of under a system of honest labor, and they may not complain if other more industrious Nations, too confined at home, should come and occupy part of their lands" (Vattel, 1964, 7, 81). Vattel was careful to disavow the deplorable Spanish "usurpation" of Mexico and Peru. By contrast, the establishment of colonies in North America—whose "vast tracts of land" were "roamed over," rather than inhabited, by "small numbers" of "wandering tribes"—could be considered "entirely lawful." For "the savage tribes of North America had no right to keep to themselves the whole of that vast continent; and provided sufficient land were left to the Indians, others might, without injustice to them, settle in certain parts of a region, the whole of which the Indians were unable to occupy." It was not against nature to confine them within narrower bounds (Vattel, 1964, 7, 81, 207–209).

Vattel is more commonly remembered for his insistence that membership in international society was exclusive to states on the European model. This position, too, can be rooted in the contractarian position, from which emerges a sense of properly constituted government. Locke's *First Treatise* and parts of the second are concerned, of course, to rebut the patriarchal justification for absolutist kingship identified with Robert Filmer. Locke carefully separates a political society from other forms of association, above all the family, on grounds that it alone is fully consensual and possesses the authority to punish to the point of death. In effect, he helps to write the family out of modern political thought. There is a point in the *First Treatise* where Locke challenges Filmer with examples of patriarchal rule outside the privileged evidence of the Old Testament, specifically the tribes of America, though he doubts that, even in these "little independent societies," there is reason to infer fatherly authority derived from Adam (Locke, 1960, Book I) Locke himself professes to know nothing of their political arrangements, but cannot imagine that they left the state of nature by the only possible means: a compact to make a body politick.

This standard of governance would judge the Indian unruly and, in warfare, wild and undisciplined.[5] It also involves the international diplomatic collision of contract-based and kinship-based politics. Contract-based governance is a matter of human artifice, conceptualized territorially and in a separation of limited state and atomistic society. It is an answer to the problem of authority, as the right to punish, which preoccupied early-modern Europe. Its creation myth begins in an original state of alienation from others, or nonhuman nature, or both, then determines which rights and forms of property are alienable. Kinship-based governance typically is described as a gift of the creator, an answer to the problem of harmony not justice, and conceptualized in networks of kinship extending across families, generations, and even nations commonly organized by confederation in all parts of North America. In the Mikmaq legal-political-diplomatic tradition, for example, confederation means "many families living in one house." The Georgian-era treaties, adds James Youngblood Henderson translates (again made by tribal more than by European protocols) were understood to create a "living kinship" or "living relations rather than mere contracts" (Henderson, 1991, 18, 23). Likewise Iroquois society is described in terms of "a body of relatives," and relations beyond of symbolic kinship, into which the stranger—not least the British Crown at a crucial point in eighteenth-century diplomacy—is adopted (Fenton, 1985, 13).[6] The general features of such a kinship-based understanding of politics and international relations can be found in tribal traditions across the continent.[7]

Clearly, then, early European diplomatic encounters of necessity involved the adoption of metaphoric kinship language and aboriginal ritual forms, a theme returned to in the next section of the paper. Fraternal terms permeate sincere reports of those encounters. Sir William Johnson at the Onandaga conference of 1748 recalled to his "brethren" of the Five Nations their "first brothership" and "first Friendship."[8] The British Crown, of course, never capitulated wholesale to Lockean principles, and does not appear to have minded turning kinship metaphors in its favor. The 1730 treaty of alliance and commerce with the Cherokee, for example, its English text duly reproduced in the Consolidated Treaty Series, identifies the king repeatedly as "father," who in his "tenderness" would have "the Indians and the English live together like children of one and the same family"—as "brothers" (Parry, 1969, V.33, 279–282). This treaty is perhaps uncharacteristically patronizing for the time in its use of kinship language, and disingenuous, too, in what would have been a contested representation of monarchical authority in Britain and most of the colonies. There is a similar tone in Lt.-Gov. Morris' familial metaphors at Fort Pitt in 1876. But, as Russel Barsh suggests, persistent use of such metaphors, especially the later European and American preference for claiming the title of father, did not mean shared understanding; for fathership implied "a change in role from partner to peacemaker." In obligations, moreover, "there were important conceptual distinctions between the indigenous role of 'father' and 'sovereign' in European law" (Barsh, 1986, 194–195).There is, in short, a recurring aboriginal domestic analogy embedded in familial understandings of international relations, but it is unrecognizable from within the antikinship assumptions imported into IR from contractarian political images. Contrary to Hobbes, metaphors are scarcely the least dangerous, because least precise, form of speech.

DIPLOMATIC INVESTIGATIONS (ii): THE EXPANSION OF INTERNATIONAL SOCIETY?

International society, in Wight's most-cited definition, refers to "the habitual intercourse of independent communities, beginning in the Christendom of Western Europe and gradually extending throughout the world. It is manifest in the diplomatic system; in the conscious maintenance of the balance of power to preserve the independence of the member-communities; in the regular operations of international law. . . . All these presuppose an international social consciousness, a world-wide community sentiment" (Wight, 1966, 96–97). This is Wight's narrower, Grotian definition, not the contested one he presents across three traditions in his lectures. Even here he is careful not to restrict it to states alone and to identify the restriction itself as an ideological one, proposed in eighteenth-century texts and later established as diplomatic convention. He remains willing, for example, not only to recall the important balancing role played by the Iroquois in British-French relations but also to wonder, *pace* the orthodox response, whether the Six Nations could be counted inside the state-system on the evidence of regular diplomatic relations (Wight, 1946). But his qualifications are those of a historian. When his definition is projected forward under the editorship of Hedley Bull and Adam Watson in *The Expansion of International Society*, the resulting collection is a curious landmark in the kind of reflective re-engagement of IR on which I have embarked—this despite Bull's evident interest in the Third World case against Western domination and in the future of diplomacy without cultural commonalities. In the first place, it evinces scant interest even historically in aboriginal communities. The "preliterate peoples" of North America and Australia are dispatched in the introduction. They evidently dealt with their neighbors according to codes of conduct, but their "geographical awareness did not extend very far" (Bull and Watson, 1984, 2–3). In the second, the evolutionary narrative of international society unfolding in time, enlarged as regional puzzle-pieces are added, made universal by imperialism and revolt, is seductively simple; its very inclusiveness suggests completion. As Bull puts it, the growing together of diverse political entities to form a single international society presupposes that they should come to resemble each other as forms of rule. Accordingly, the emergence of "new states in the Americas" is presented retrospectively as an unfolding of a latent sovereignty by either revolution or devolution from European masters (Bull, 1984, 121).

It is equally plausible, however, to read the same history as one of exclusion. The so-called expansion of international society is at the same time its homogenization. The settler states' claims to admission on grounds of territorial sovereignty are at the same time a repudiation of other modes of coexistence and a domestication of the aboriginal peoples. On these points Wight's memory is commendably better, and his lectures taut, bitingly critical. They recall exterminations in Australia, Indian Wars and scalp bounties in the American West, resettlement everywhere on reserves where lives are regulated and "the brighter specimens get presented to the Queen if she comes around" (Wight, 1991, 52–53). Wight calls this the Anglo-Saxon realist encounter with the barbarian, aboriginal or Celtic, and the philosophy of its frontier societies. His lectures trace a story encompassing a number of related points: the British Crown's open colonization charters for land "not occupied by any Christian prince"; the concentration of treaty-making powers before the Seven Years' War; the inconsistent pretense of the 1763 Royal Proclamation; the American inheritance of the same pretense at independence; the Cherokee cases of the 1820s and 1830s;[9] the forced removal west of the Cherokee notwithstanding even those rights; the suspension of treaty-making in the West by 1871; the chipping away at tribal jurisdiction over major crimes in the late nineteenth century; individual allotment of tribal lands; full assimilation into U.S. citizenship (Wight, 1991, 60–61).

The story of domestication is impressively told, unusual as it is in an IR text of any vintage. Broadly similar stories could be told for Canada, New Zealand, and perhaps Australia, albeit with less violence, less recognition of aboriginal independence, and less opportunity for resistance through the courts than in the United States.[10] In the Canadian case, the British law authorizing confederation in 1867 assigned responsibility for "Indians and lands reserved for Indians" to the federal parliament—obviously a domestic matter, since control of foreign affairs was retained in London. Before the treaties had been signed in the west to facilitate agricultural settlement and sovereign occupation against U.S. designs, the government had consolidated an Indian Act, defining membership, promising elected councils with limited powers to "advanced" bands, and imposing paternalistic regulations on everyday life. The underlying purpose is widely described as assimilation, but it can be viewed alternatively as the suppression of independent tribal governance. The Indian Act in its subsequent versions would ban such ceremonies of leadership, cohesion, and culture as the sundance and potlach, and it forbade all dancing and wearing of traditional costume off-reserve without consent of the Indian Agent (see Boldt, 1993; Pettipas, 1994). The courts participated in the struggle to control the meaning of treaties, defining them as domestic legal documents that could be abrogated by federal legislation. They backdated to time immemorial the Crown's sovereignty in land, against which aboriginal peoples had only an extinguishable right of use. Like the Spanish debates, the pivotal case was decided in the absence of any speaking by either the Ojibway most immediately affected by it or other aboriginal representatives.[11]

Such stories can and should be told. But the troubling thing about them (Wight's or mine) is that they can be made too clean, too inevitable, too willing to consign aboriginal peoples to the dustbin of international history. Stories of atrocities, fraud, and injustice still risk casting the perpetrators as their only active protagonists. They can overlook points of resistance or alternative tellings. They risk an interest in aboriginal diplomacies only where they fit into an extended European treaty system and not the other way around, from which perspective diplomatic relations with colonial powers are but another link in a covenant chain, grapevine, or symbolic kinship network, and engaged reluctantly, as "part of a continuous struggle to stay neutral" in their exported conflicts or to find a way of coexistence with the immigrants (Henderson, 1991, 22; see also Milloy, 1991, 67). The expansion of international society, sovereigns all, is a story that is particularly susceptible to the temptations of making its conclusion inevitable and now universal, and therefore finished. So is the parallel story of sovereignty as domestication within a territory of exclusive domain.

One point of resistance came in 1923 when the Six Nations brought a complaint against the government of Canada and the British Empire to the League of Nations, though it remains unmentioned in prominent studies (see Zimmern, 1936; Walters, 1952; Manning, 1932), and the foremost history of Canada's involvement devotes a chapter to it that is couched in adjectives such as "bizarre" and "absurd" (Veatch, 1975, chap. 7). They appealed for a hearing by two different avenues provided under the League covenant: their own eligibility for membership as a state, on grounds of recognition implicit in the historical treaties; and the existence of a threat to international peace, which required an existing member's sponsorship. The complaint struck at the heart of contention over entitlement to membership under the self-determination principle. At the time, the question of membership for Canada and the other British imperial dominions had itself scarcely been settled; none of them was independent in foreign policy. Canada and New Zealand had been embarrassed earlier in the century by Nishga and Maori appeals, respectively, made directly to London. New Zealand had spoken for other white dominions in its concern over the possibility of compulsory arbitration in the League's covenant, in thinly disguised reference to its aboriginal policy: "there is great danger that the Court of International Justice at The Hague, consisting mainly of foreigners, might hold that the New Zealand law is contrary to the comity of nations, and that the New Zealand system is not a question of merely domestic jurisdiction" (quoted in Manning, 1932, 50). That the Iroquois should have found a sponsor in 1923 will have given no reassurance. First it was the Dutch, who were subjected to considerable British diplomatic pressure not to "interfere," then Panama, Persia, Ireland, and Estonia, each of which had another grievance against Canada: its attempt to win by resolution a narrow interpretation of article 10, which committed members to come to the aid of others in the event of a threat to its territorial integrity or political independence. The Six Nations' chief Deskaheh became a popular figure in Geneva, winning public sympathy—some of it, alas, of the noble-savage variety. Iroquois and Canadian briefs were filed and published in the League's *Official Journal*. The former accused the Canadian government of misappropriating funds and invading Iroquois territory, guaranteed by treaty, in order to impose Canadian law. The Canadian government argued that the matter was properly a domestic one.[12] To press the point, with Deskaheh still in Geneva, Canada exercised its authority under the Indian Act to dissolve the hereditary council of chiefs for which he spoke and replace it with an elected band council.

While British and Canadian diplomatic acuity managed to keep the issue off the floor of the Assembly, both governments had been pushed to speak to what could not be taken for granted. The League, too, had been pushed to show itself, to draw a line of membership short of aboriginal peoples, a line the United Nations would redraw in 1960 as the "blue-water" definition of colonial territory to be relinquished (i.e. overseas possessions). The distinction served to preempt criticisms of western hemispheric states for having colonized indigenous peoples, while the UN resolution's strictures against the disruption of national unity or territorial integrity satisfied the legitimation needs of the fragile, newly independent states (Brownlie, 1995, 307–309).

DIPLOMATIC INVESTIGATIONS (iii):
"THE INTIMATE ENEMY"

There are at least two types of contemporary international indigenous political activity. First, there is a "politics of embarrassment,"[13] whose tactical purpose is expressed as bringing external pressure to bear on a government where domestic avenues of appeal are either exhausted or do not exist (this rational is also stressed in Morris and Churchil, 1987, 10). By itself this type does not challenge the domestication of indigenous peoples in international relations, though it exploits the opening created against the doctrine of noninterference in a state's "internal affairs" by the condemnation of white-minority regimes in South Africa and the former Rhodesia. Governments that trade internationally on their moral standing, such as Canada, New Zealand, and Australia, are perhaps most susceptible to the tactics, and most inclined to dispatch senior foreign officers for purposes of damage control after indigenous successes abroad.

The second type of indigenous political activity might be called a politics of self-representation that identifies in international activity the prospect of recovering "nation-to-nation" traditions (and therefore contesting the dominant meaning of treaties where they exist). It also consists of legitimizing indigenous governments, and expressing "Fourth-World" solidarity with indigenous peoples worldwide. In this spirit Canada's Assembly of First Nations has called on "indigenous peoples to begin to represent themselves and their interests and perspectives more directly," and in support of each other's quests for self-determination.[14] The politics of self-representation involve a sense both of distinct position and a distinct path of historical experience as entrapped peoples in a world of territorial states and economic modernization. The solemn declaration agreed upon at the founding conference of the World Council of Indigenous Peoples in 1975 refers to "a consciousness of culture and peoplehood on the edge of each country's borders and marginal to each country's citizenship" (quoted in Jhappan, 1992, 66). That distinct path of experience is reflected transparently in the kind of rights specified in the UN draft declaration. They include: the right to self-determination in political status; to participate fully in wider decision-making that affects them; to maintain a "distinctive spiritual and material relationship" with lands traditionally owned or occupied; to secure "recognition, observance and enforcement" of historic treaties and other agreements; to practice, revitalize, and teach traditional cultural customs; to have artifacts restored; to determine rules of internal membership according to tradition; to maintain contact with members separated by international borders; to invoke special international protection, in the event of armed conflict, against both forced recruitment and removal; to demilitarization of indigenous lands; and to maintain distinctive juridical practices in keeping with international human rights standards.

The two types of politics are not mutually exclusive. The Grand Council of the Crees of James Bay, for example, distributed from its Ottawa "embassy" a 500–page interpretation of international law in advance of the 1995 Quebec referendum on sovereignty. In it, the Grand Council asserted a right of self-determination against the prospect of forcible inclusion of the Cree and their lands in any unilateral declaration of independence. It noted the growing recognition of indigenous communities' distinct international-legal personality, and it chided the Canadian government for acknowledging "aboriginal rights" in its own constitution, while resisting them at the international level. At the same time, the Grand Council proposed that this unqualified right of self-determination be used in order to remain in Canada. It called on the Canadian government to fulfil its fiduciary responsibilities—to the point of being ready to defend Cree territory by force—and called on the international community not to sanction what would be "an acceptable act of colonialism" whereby Quebec could secede, boundaries intact, on a mere pledge to assume all obligations to indigenous peoples.[15]

The Cree position reflected neither naiveté nor loss of nerve. Following a skilful, sophisticated lobby and international coalition-building campaign against the Great Whale hydroelectric project, it could not be dismissed, though it was taken on behalf of only twelve thousand people. Accompanied by a parallel referendum whose result was decisively against separation, it represented the most fundamental challenge in everyday political language not only to the idea that Quebec as a legal-territorial entity could secede uncomplicatedly from the rest of Canada, but also to commonplace assumptions about a clear domestic-international distinction and sovereignty as an all-or-nothing exclusive domain. In this respect the Cree position already lives out the autonomy to which it aspires, quite apart from formal recognition. It is indicative of much of the global indigenous movement in its desire not for statehood but for a transformed relationship with states, in which, as a Maori told the UN General Assembly in 1992, the "prestige of our people and land remains sacrosanct" (Ewen, 1994, 90). The sentiment was echoed by indigenous representatives from the Americas, the Arctic, and southeast Asia on the occasion held to mark a "new partnership" with the UN and inaugurate 1993 as the Year—since extended to the Decade—of the World's Indigenous People.

Clearings for diplomatic speech, however, can signify risk as well as hospitality; they guarantee neither attentiveness nor a friendly hearing. The General Assembly was sparsely attended on the day in question.

The draft declaration will meet with stronger resistance from many of its member-states the closer it gets to the floor. Words matter. The International Labor Organization's Indigenous and Tribal Population Convention (169), adopted in 1989, refers in its text but not its title to the self-determination of peoples, but, because of pressure from member-states, carefully qualifies the word's meaning within the terms of international law and the UN Charter. The UN Decade likewise is one of people rather than peoples. Self-determination is often conflated with full political independence in light of the Third World experience of decolonization. Indigenous is itself a contentious word. Governments in central and south Asia have resisted its applicability to tribal peoples within their borders. And so the limits of international standard-setting exercises are readily acknowledged, and are magnified when juxtaposed against fresh reports of massacre and dispossession from, say, the Brazilian Amazon. Michael Dodson, an Australian indigenous leader, observes: "The hard reality is that states decide what will and will not be recognized and incorporated into international law . . . ; self-determination . . . is seen as a potential 'nation-wrecker'" (Dodson, 1994, 25).

There are risks greater than futility or inattentiveness, however, in contemporary indigenous diplomacies, particularly where they attempt to put their case in the openings provided by international law and thereby transform it from an instrument of subjugation and dispossession to one of recognition and protection. Success does not alleviate the risk. James Der Derian, for example, suggests that modernist diplomacy is not about dialogue so much as about incorporation into a dominant discourse that allows passage across cultural frontiers (see Der Derian, 1996, 86; 1987). If diplomacy emerges in the West, in his phrase, as the mediation of estrangement, what is striking is the extent to which the estrangement of the colonial encounter has been recreated within indigenous communities and those who would speak for them, not between them and the member-states of international society. The enemy is very much an intimate one (Nandy, 1993). In other words, the most difficult work of negotiation and maneuver falls to the indigenous side in at least two related ways.

First, international activity—conferences, lobby trips—takes place at a distance from indigenous communities, and its use of the legal-diplomatic idiom, however subversive and tactical the purpose, necessarily puts the discussion into the realm of technical expertise. The clearings are doubly marked by an absence of many listeners. While foreign policy, even in liberal democratic states, is among the most secretive domains and most insulated from public scrutiny, those characteristics exacerbate tensions within indigenous communities in which the legacy of colonial paternalism can be a clientelist politics or else what is framed imprecisely as a struggle between "accommodationist" and "traditionalist" factions, modes of authority, and approaches to economic development (see Deloria and Lytle, 1984; Dyck, 1985). The nature of nation-to-nation talk and the places where it happens together can invite charges of elitism and suspicions of either personal benefit or co-optation. They can leave indigenous speakers vulnerable, rightly or wrongly, to claims from home communities, government, or even rival organizations that they are not representative and have no authority to speak.

Second, and more fundamentally, it is left largely to indigenous participants to mediate between languages, modes of speech, and ways of looking at the world. They must negotiate within themselves between an instrumental and a venerative politics. They must negotiate between the insistence upon precise, justiciable definitions of rights and the preference for the symbolic, the metaphoric, the oral, the gestural, the narrative. They must negotiate between plain speaking and the appropriate protocols (Lyons, 1994, 119–124), and, in some cases, between the dominant, noun-based languages and verb-based languages, in which diplomacy may be a "standing-between" (as in the Cheyenne peace-chief tradition), treaties a form of sharing, autonomy a "nesting" within a state, and sovereignty a leading of the hunt.[16] These mediations necessarily fall to indigenous speakers. No one else can or will perform them. And if there is no longer any estrangement, there is nothing distinctive for indigenous diplomatic activity to preserve.

The discourse of indigenous rights has been described as both the means of legal-definitional confinement and the promise of something more, something unknown and therefore threatening, "just over the horizon of established property relations." This is potentially the point of negotiation based on mutuality, the "fluid line of contact between two social orders" (Kulchyski, 1994). The description is one of diplomacy in the widest sense. While this appears as a familiar subject to IR, it resists the impulse, heightened in a climate of multicultural sensibilities, merely to territorialize emerging and reemerging forms of indigenous political activity by explanations and theoretical models.

SETTLING WELL: BEYOND MERE TOLERATION OF DIVERSITY IN IR THOUGHT

This paper has proposed two preparatory tasks having to do with the hospitality of IR's clearings or, more appropriately for prairies (and outback), the openness of its horizons. The first is to rethink the stories the discipline tells in which indigenous peoples are rendered silent, uncultivated, and domesticated out of sight. Such representations are betrayed by contemporary politics alone. The work of the international society tradition, or at least Wight, is helpful in this kind of rethinking, because of its historical memory; its attentiveness (and, in places, resistance) to the transformations of modernity; its interest in cultural-political frontiers; and its reflexive potential. Where that tradition identifies most closely with Grotius and natural-law rationalism so implicated in colonial dispossession, however, and where its focus narrows through Vattel to a society of states, the juxtaposition of indigenous experience is a critical mirror on that same society. What it reflects back is more than a melioration of *raison d'état*, more than a middle way defined by its extremes, but also a powerful, culturally anchored ideological position of its own—what Bull in a candid moment called "the perspective of the international establishment" (Bull, 1991, xv).

The second task is to remain attentive to the complex mediations embedded in indigenous diplomacies; they, too, constitute a critical mirror on international practices. This task, in turn, requires more than facilitating the entry of indigenous voices—as numerous book titles put it—into the technologically aided cacophony of contemporary political argument, and more too than a Wightian reimagination of international theory as a dialogue among distinct positions or traditions. What bears rethinking is precisely that which makes it hard, not to tolerate a plurality of voices, but to hear any one of them (Smith, 1994, 42). Mere talking has become the equivalent of the "incessant scribbling" that once irritated the Iroquois about colonial treaty makers. The measure of IR's ability to settle well in the localities from which indigenous activity is undertaken may well be a reciprocality manifested in respect for what cannot be known, attentiveness to alternate modes of speaking, and a willingness to listen.

NOTES

1. On various aspects of this recent activity, see, *inter alia*, Alexander Ewen, Franke Wilmer, C. Radha Jhappan, and Frances Abele (Ewen, 1994; Wilmer, 1993; Jhappan, 1992, 1990). On the Miskito case as a problem for indigenous statecraft, see Glenn T. Morris and Ward Churchill, Douglas Sanders, and Klaudine Ohland and Robin Schneider (Morris and Churchil, 1987; Sanders, 1985; Ohland and Schneider, 1983).

2. See in particular the *Documents* series published by the Copenhagen-based International Working Group for Indigenous Affairs and the journal *Cultural Survival Quarterly* published in the United States. See also James Anaya, Russel Lawrence Barsh, and the work of Howard R. Berman (Anaya, 1996; Barsh, 1994, 33–86; Berman, 1993, 313–324).

3. A wonderfully instructive and provocative example is James Young-blood Henderson, who registers his concern that to understand any particular indigenous worldview requires both a knowledge of language and a living in that world. Otherwise the result is to give indigenous thought an abstractness or a "contrived uniformity" (Henderson, 1991, 14, n. 52). Henderson also alludes to a hunter's methodology in international relations.

4. Richard Tuck skillfully shows the links between the social contract theorists and their debts to Grotius in particular. He describes Locke's position on property and the natural right to punish as the "most faithfully Grotian political theory available from the presses of the late seventeenth century" (Tuck, 1979, 173). On the Grotian lineage of Hobbes and Locke, see also Deborah Baumgold (Baumgold, 1993, 6–27). Suffice to say, Wight's realist-rationalist distinction is more useful in describing the differences between Machiavelli and Vitoria in the sixteenth century than in categorizing the social contract theorists.

5. See Russel Lawrence Barsh (Barsh, 1986, 196). "Europeans, reacting to a history of oppression, always assumed that power must be lodged somewhere and concentrated on sharing, transferring, or otherwise *limiting* it. . . . Plains Indians viewed U.S. soldiers with contempt because they followed orders!" On the U.S. and Canadian frontiers, nonetheless, chiefs typically were held responsible for the conduct of young males over whom they had no formal authority.

6. Truce-making as a form of adoption was also practiced by Cree and Blackfoot in the prairie West as late as the mid-nineteenth century. See Edward Ahenakew (Ahenakew, 1995, chap. 10).

7. Russel Barsh writes: "Diplomatic relations among North America's original nations were established according to the norms of kinship, with each nation assuming the role of a kinsman within a confederation. Once that role was defined or named, it was complete. No further detail or precise contract was necessary. . . . Referring to European ambassadors as 'brothers' did not reflect naive awe. It was a deliberate choice of words with grave international significance" (Barsh, 1986, 194)

8. See the account of Conrad Weiser, sent on behalf of the colonies of Virginia and Pennsylvania, to a council at Onandaga in 1743, and reprinted in Francis Jennings (Jennings, 1984). Weiser's account also records his presence as an observer at an intra-indigenous council, a useful reminder lest it be thought that it was European arrival that hastened the need of diplomacy.

9. In these cases the U.S. Supreme Court introduced the phrase "domestic dependent nations" to define tribes as "distinct, independent political communities" with rights to land and self-government but under U.S. guardianship—and lacking jurisdiction, significantly, in foreign relations (Shattuck and Norgren, 1991).

10. The fact that the U.S. Bureau of Indian Affairs was located in the War Department, or that hostilities were not punished as treason, is ironic indication of such recognition, and of the historical messiness of domestic-foreign distinctions.

11. The case in question is the St. Catherine's Milling case (1888), which is reprinted and introduced in Peter Kulchyski (1994).

12. The Canadian government reply, which incorporates the widely circu-

lated Iroquois claim, is found in the League's *Official Journal* (1924, V.5, 29–42). For accounts of the episode, see Veatch (1975).

13. This phrase is now fairly common; it can be found, for example, in Robert Paine (1985, 55) and also in Pettman (1991, 227–228).

14. Assembly of First Nations (1993), *Reclaiming Our Nationhood, Strengthening Our Heritage: Report to the Royal Commission on Aboriginal People*, pp. 151–159.

15. *Sovereign Injustice: Forcible Inclusion of the James Bay Crees and Cree Territory into a Sovereign Quebec* (Nemaska: Grand Council of the Crees, 1995), 13–14, 62, 162, 285, 370–371. The document quotes liberally from Grand Chief Matthew Coon-Come's addresses in Washington and elsewhere, and from statements of support issued by such ad hoc bodies as the Arctic Leaders' Summit.

16. Matthew Coon-Come, Grand Chief of the James Bay Cree, explains this last concept: "Otsimaw, that is what my people call the leader of a Cree hunting camp. He is the one who decides where the group will go. He presides over feasts and, following our traditions, determines the way the camp will operate. Otsimawin is Cree leadership and authority. It surpasses government, Tibeytachewin, because it sets the rules for good government. It is with our term otsimaw that we translate European concepts referring to leadership and sovereignty" (Matthew Coon-Come, 1990, 114).

REFERENCES

Abele, A. (1990). "Confronting 'Harsh and Inescapable Facts': Indigenous Peoples and the Militarization of the Circumpolar Region." In E. Dosman (ed.), *Sovereignty and Security in the Arctic*. London: Routledge.

Anaya, S. J. (1996). *Indigenous Peoples in International Law*. New York : Oxford University Press.

Ashley, Richard K. (1996). "The Achievements of Post-Structuralism." In Steve Smith, Ken Booth, and M. Zalewski (eds.), *International Theory: Positivism and Beyond*. Cambridge: Cambridge University Press: 240–253.

Assembly of First Nations. (1993). *Reclaiming our Nationhood, Strengthening our Heritage*. Report to the Royal Commission on Aboriginal People.

Barsh, Russell L. (1986). "The Nature and Spirit of North American Political Systems." *American Indian Quarterly* 10(3), 181–198.

Barsh, Russell L. (1994). "Indigenous Peoples in the 1990s: From Object to Subject of International Law?" *Harvard Human Rights Journal* 7, pp. 33–86.

Baumgold, D. (1993). "Pacifying Politics: Resistance, Violence, and Accountability in Seventheenth-Century Contract Theory." *Political Theory* 21(1), 6–27.

Bedford, D., and T. Workman. (1997). "The Great Law of Peace: Alternative Inter-Nation(al) Practices and the Iroquoian Confederacy." *Alternatives* 22, 87–111.

Berman, H. R. (1993). "The Development of International Recognition of the Rights of Indigenous Peoples." In *IWGIA Document 74*, pp. 313–324.

Berry, W. (1990). *What Are People For?* New York: North Point Press.

Boldt, M. (1993). *Surviving as Indians: The Challenge of Self-Government.* Toronto: University of Toronto Press.

Brownlie, I. (ed.). (1995). *Basic Documents in International Law.* 4th ed. Oxford: Clarendon Press.

Bull, Hedley. (1984). "The Emergence of a Universal International Society." In Hedley Bull and Adam Watson (eds.), *The Expansion of International Society.* Oxford: Oxford University Press: 117–126.

Bull, Hedley. (1991). "Martin Wight and the Theory of International Relations." In Martin Wight, *International Theory: The Three Traditions.* Ed. Gabriele Wight and Brian Porter. London: Leicester University Press/Royal Institute of International Affairs: ix–xxiii.

Bull, Hedley and Adam Watson (eds.). (1984). *The Expansion of International Society.* Oxford: Oxford University Press.

Coon-Come, M. (1990). "Untitled Address." In Frank Cassidy (ed.), *Aboriginal Self-Government.* Montreal: Institute for Research in Public Policy.

Crawford, N. C. (1994). "A Security Regime among Democracies: Cooperation among Iroquois Nations." *International Organization* 48, 345–385.

Deloria Jr., V., and C. Lytle. (1984). *The Nations Within: The Past and Future of American Indian Sovereignty.* New York: Pantheon.

Der Derian, James. (1987). *On Diplomacy: A Genealogy of Western Estrangement.* Oxford: Basil Blackwell.

Der Derian, James. (1996). "Hedley Bull and the Idea of Diplomatic Culture." In R. Fawn and J. Larkins (eds.), *International Society after the Cold War: Anarchy and Order Reconsidered.* London: Macmillan: 84–100.

Dodson, M. (1994). "Voice of the People—Voices of the Earth; Indigenous Peoples—Subjugation or Self-Determination?" In L. van der Vliest (ed.), *Voices of the Earth: Indigenous Peoples, New Partners, and the Right to Self-Determination in Practice.* Utrecht: International Books/Netherlands Centre for Indigenous Peoples: 80–88.

Dyck, N. (1985). "Indigenous Peoples and the Nation-State: Fourth-World Politics in Canada, Australia, and Norway." *Indigenous Peoples and the Nation-State: An Introduction to Analytical Issues.* (Working Paper no. 14) Institute of Social and Economic Research, Memorial University of Newfoundland: 1–26.

Enloe, Cynthia. (1996). "Margins, Silences and Bottom Rungs: How to Overcome the Underestimation of Power in the Study of International Relations." In Steve Smith, Ken Booth, and M. Zalewski (eds.), *International Theory: Positivism and Beyond.* Cambridge: Cambridge University Press.

Ewen, A. (ed.). (1994). *Voice of Indigenous Peoples: Native People Address the United Nations.* Sante Fe, N.M.: Clear Light Publishers.

Falk, Richard. (1987) "The Struggle of Indigenous Peoples and the Promise of Natural Political Communities." In R. Thompson (ed.), *The Rights of Indigeous Peoples in International Law: Selected Essays in Self-Determination.* Saskatoon: University of Saskatchewan Native Law Centre: 50–68.

Fenton, W. (1985). "Structure, Continuity, and Change in the Process of Iroquois Treaty-Making." In F. Jennings (ed.), *The History and Culture of Iroquois Diplomacy.* Syracuse: Syracuse University Press: 3–36.

Gadamer, H. G. (1976). *Philosophical Hermeneutics*. Berkeley: University of California Press.

Henderson, J. (1991). "First Nations' Legal Inheritance." *Working Paper 91/5*, Canadian Legal History Project, University of Manitoba Faculty of Law.

Hobbes, Thomas. (1962). *Leviathan*. Ed. Michael Oakeshott. London: Macmillan.

Hoffmann, Stanley. (1977). "An American Social Science: International Relations." *Daedalus 106*(3), 41–60.

Jennings, F. (1984). *The Ambiguous Iroquois Empire*. New York: W. W. Norton.

Jhappan, C. R. (1992). "Global Community? Supranational Strategies of Canada's Aboriginal Peoples." *Journal of Indigenous Studies 3*, 59–97.

Kulchyski, P. (ed.). (1994). *Unjust Relations: Aboriginal Rights in Canadian Courts*. Toronto: Oxford University Press.

Locke, John. (1960). *Two Treatises of Government*. Ed. Peter Laslett. Cambridge: Cambridge University Press.

Lyons, O. (1994). "Epilogue." In A. Ewen (ed.), *Voice of Indigenous Peoples: Native People Address the United Nations*. Sante Fe, N.M.: Clear Light Publishers: 31–36.

Manning, C. (1932). *The Policies of the British Dominions in the League of Nations*. London: Oxford University Press.

Milloy, J. (1991). "'Our Country': The Significance of the Buffalo Resource for a Plains Cree Sense of Territory." In K. Abel and J. Friesen (eds.), *Aboriginal Resource Use in Canada*. Winnipeg: University of Manitoba Press.

Momaday, N. Scott. (1987). "Personal Reflections." In C. Martin (ed.), *The American Indian and the Problem of History*. New York: Oxford University Press: 156–161.

Morris, A. (1971). *The Treaties of Canada with the Indians of Manitoba and the North-West Territories*. Toronto: Bedfords, Clarke & Co.

Morris, G. T., and W. Churchill. (1987). "Between a Rock and a Hard Place— Left-Wing Revolution, Right-Wing Reaction and the Destruction of Indigenous People." *Cultural Survival Quarterly 11*(3), 17–24.

Nandy, A. (1993). *The Intimate Enemy: Loss and Recovery of Self under Colonialism*. Delhi: Oxford University Press.

Ohland, K., and R. Schneider (eds.). (1983). *National Revolution and Indigenous Identity: The Conflict between the Sandinistas and Miskito Indians on Nicaragua's Atlantic Coast*. Copenhagen: International Working Group for Indigenous Affairs, Document 47.

Paine, R. (1985). "The Claim of the Fourth World." In J. Brostad et al. (eds.), *Native Power: The Quest for Autonomy and Nationhood of Aboriginal Peoples*. Bergen. Norway: Universitetsforlaget.

Parry, C. (ed.). (1969). *Consolidated Treaty Series, 1648–1918*. Vol. 31, Dobbs Ferry, N.Y.: Oceana Publications.

Pettipas, K. (1994). *Severing the Ties that Bind: Government Repression of Indigenous Religious Ceremonies on the Prairies*. Winnipeg: University of Manitoba Press.

Pettman, R. (1991). *International Politics: Balance of Power, Balance of Productivity, Balance of Ideologies*. Melbourne: Longman.

Price, R. (ed.). (1979). *The Spirit of the Alberta Indian Treaties*. Montreal: Institute for Research on Public Policy.

Ross, D. (ed.). (1952). *The Works of Aristotle: Selected Fragments*. Vol. 12. Oxford: Clarendon Press.

Said, Edward. (1994). *Representations of the Intellectual*. London: Vintage.

Sanders, D. (1985). "Mosquitia and Nicaragua: An Incomplete Revolution." In J. Brostad et al. (eds.), *Native Power: The Quest for Autonomy and Nationhood of Aboriginal Peoples*. Bergen, Norway: Universitetsforlaget: 77–102.

Shattuck, P., and J. Norgren, J. (1991). *Partial Justice: Federal Indian Law in a Liberal Constitutional System*. New York: Berg.

Smith, D. (1994). "On Discursivity and Neurosis: Conditions of Possibility for (West) Discourse with Others." *Dianoia* 3, 50–51.

Todorov, T. (1984). *The Conquest of America*. New York: Harper & Row.

Tuck, R. (1979). *Natural Rights Theories: Their Origin and Development*. Cambridge: Cambridge University Press.

Turpel's, M. E. (1989–90). "Aboriginal Peoples and the Canadian Charter: Interpretive Monopolies, Cultural Differences," *The Canadian Human Rights Yearbook*. Number 6.

Vattel, E. (1964). *The Law of Nations, or the Principles of Natural Law*. Trans. Charles Fennick. New York: Oceana Publications.

Veatch, R. (1975). *Canada and the League of Nations*. Toronto: University of Toronto Press.

Vitoria, F. (1964). *De Indes et De Jure Belli Relectiones*. New York: Oceana Publications.

Walters, F. P. (1952). *A History of the League of Nations*. 2 vols. London: Oxford University Press.

Wight, Martin. (1946). *Power Politics*. London: Royal Institute of International Affairs.

Wight, Martin. (1966). "Western Values in International Relations." In Martin Wight and Herbert Butterfield (eds.), *Diplomatic Investigations*. London: George Allen and Unwin

Wight, Martin. (1991). *International Theory: The Three Traditions*. Ed. Gabriele Wight and Brian Porter. London: Leicester University Press/Royal Institute of International Affairs.

Williams, R. (1983). *Keywords: A Vocabulary of Culture and Society*. London: Fontana.

Wilmer, F. (1993). *The Indigenous Voice in World Politics*. Newbury Park, Calif.: Sage.

Wilmer, F. (1996). "Indigenous Peoples and the Discourse of Modernization." In F. Beer and R. Hariman (eds.), *Post-Realism: The Rhetorical Turn in International Relations*. East Lansing: Michigan State University Press.

Zimmern, A. (1936). *The League of Nations and the Rule of Law, 1918–1935*. London: Macmillan.

CHAPTER 15

Out with Theory—
In with Practical Reflection:
Toward a New Understanding
of Realist Moral Skepticism

Roger D. Spegele

INTRODUCTION

Diversity in international relations theory conjures up images of competing perspectives in, or about, an increasingly fragmented discipline. Many of the contributors to this volume address diversity in this outward sense, exploring and pushing beyond the limits of standard, usually American, interpretations. This paper is no less concerned with these issues but takes a different tack, searching for a viable and fresh perspective on International Relations (IR) not in its allegedly new approaches, but in its oldest conception: political realism. Despite its venerable status there is much *within* political realism that remains to be mined, and numerous misperceptions about it that need to be put to bed. For my purposes, therefore, diversity refers to the inner richness of a long-standing theoretical tradition rendered unfamiliar and uniform by crude caricature.

My particular interest is the problem of ethics in international relations, and my primary purpose to refute the oft-stated claim that political realism is a form of moral skepticism. In the usual story, political realism is portrayed as wedded unequivocally to moral skepticism and—in another version of the "shoot the messenger" syndrome—is held virtually accountable for "the history of selfishness and brutality . . . spying, deceit, bribery, disloyalty, ingratitude, betrayal, exploitation, plunder, regression, subjection, and genocide" it describes (Cohen, 1984, 299). The key point here is not to deny a certain realist tendency to moral skepticism but to suggest that the commitment is not as straightforward as critics of political realism seem to think. The most prominent and influential of these critics today constitute a position that can be called "neo-Kantianism" or "neo-Kantian international relations" (NKIR). Some representatives of this position are: Mervyn Frost, Morris Cohen, Onora O'Neill, Thomas Pogge, Charles Beitz, and Friedrich Kratochwil. I shall argue that, paradoxically enough, NKIR proponents are just as likely to wear moral skepticism as their realist rivals. My objective, however, is not to *disprove* NKIR but to fight my way to a distinctively different, but nonetheless realist, conception of ethics for international relations. I shall call this rival understanding of morality "soft moral realism" (SMR) since, among other things, it offers certain possibilities of putting moral skepticism out of harm's way.

MORAL SKEPTICISM

A Definition

Moral skepticism comes in many varieties and it may at first appear impossible to capture it in a definition. We do however have some notion of what, in general, it consists of and can characterize it adequately enough for our purposes. It is the theory, position, or attitude that maintains that there can be no such thing as moral knowledge; or that there are no valid moral arguments; or that ultimate moral principles cannot be determined; that morality has no rational basis; or that the difference between right and wrong is merely a matter of taste, opinion, feeling, or convention. However, in international relations theory moral skepticism sometimes comes into the picture via a somewhat different route, namely, a neo-Kantian presupposition that there is a split between the normative and the non-normative, the world of theory and the world of fact, the world of norms, rules, and principles and the domain of empirical description. Once we accept this NKIR split, then two problems come into play: (1) on what basis do we say that normative statements have truth values in the way that descriptive statements do? and (2) how do we match up one sort of statement with the other sort? Both of these problems bring skepticism onto the turf: the first by holding that norms are not part of the objectivity of the world; the second by implying that we have no basis for saying how the two kinds of statement can be made to cohere.

Its Consequences

Why should international relations theorists care about whether people are moral skeptics? One reason is this: if the world is dominated by people who refuse to accept the idea that moral positions can be argued and rationally resolved, then one apparent consequence is that the scope for the forceful resolution of disagreements is expanded. If our moral judgements are *au fond* arbitrary, how could we think to resolve our conflicts by appealing to reasoned moral judgments?

The issue of whether states are morally justified in intervening in the affairs of other states is a case in point. While some claim that intervention ought never to take place (Mill, 1873), others say that it should occur whenever certain democratic principles or rights are violated (Doppelt, 1978).[1] Each protagonist tends to believe that their point of view is grounded on something self-evident, yet neither position can be adjudicated from initial intuitions. Once one accepts one position and refuses to accept the possibility of a middle ground, the following disjunctive prescription comes into play: always intervene when rights are being violated or never intervene no matter how compelling the grounds. There seems to be here no basis to prefer one conflicting option to the other since reason appears impotent to resolve such deep differences.

Is reason powerless before people with whom we have deep differences? Clearly, we are in no position to *disprove* or to *demonstrate* that those who hold values we regard as rebarbative *are* wrong. Notions of logical demonstration reach their limit here. To say the least, there is not always complete agreement among all the members of the world community, but does this make moral skepticism correct? The answer is no, since skepticism in ethics cannot be shown to be true on the basis of continued disagreement. It is only when we give up the inappropriate model of *showing* derived from models in the natural sciences, and contend that showing is equivalent to deliberative reason in the Aristotelian sense (in which assumptions and presuppositions are assumed to be shared by one's opponent) that showing may indeed be possible. Moral skepticism is thus often the result of a failure to distinguish knowledge and science. If one holds that not everything that counts as knowledge is scientific knowledge, then we may be able, if not to refute moral skepticism, to deflect its hold on us so that we can trust our human capacity to make moral judgments and to do so, in particular, in certain cases of interest to international relationists.

It is this view of practical reason that I call soft moral realism. By this I mean a view that resists naturalistic models of practical reason and focuses on our *actual* practices of moral deliberation, debate, and understanding, and accepts (in principle at least) that there are certain moral values that have a claim on us and that our moral reasoning can discover. SMRers are committed to three claims: (1) that ethics is not well construed as a subject that lends itself to certain kinds of theorizing; (2) that there are no strict boundaries between the ethical and the political;

and (3) that we must give up universalism and take up a particularistic perspective on ethics-politics. As I shall indicate below, these commitments tend to deflate moral skepticism. Before further elucidating SMR, however, we need to demonstrate as wrong the popular view that all versions of political realism articulate, imply, or otherwise fall into, the clutches of moral skepticism.

IS POLITICAL REALISM A FORM OF MORAL SKEPTICISM?

Many in the discipline of IR hold it as self-evidently true that political realism cannot provide an adequate understanding of morality or ethics. Michael Walzer, for example, admits that it may be *conceptually* possible for us to act as realists have recommended, but doubts whether this can be done in practice:

> If we had all become realists like the Athenian generals or like Hobbists in a state of war, there would be an end alike to both morality and hypocrisy. We would simple tell one another, brutally and directly, what we wanted to do or have done. But the truth is that one of the things most of us want, even in war, is to act or seem to act morally. (Walzer, 1977, 20)

Realists like the Athenian generals and Hobbes would have no difficulty in agreeing with the claim that most of us want to *seem* to act morally. But for these realists the issue is not whether we want to seem to act morally, but whether we in fact do.[2] A key distinction has to be made between the way in which individuals and states represent their actions and what those actions really are. The question is a pointed one: is political realism a form of skepticism? Certainly Marshall Cohen, in a well-known article, believes it to be (Cohen, 1984).

In a sustained attack, Cohen claims that political realism is historically, and right down to our own time, committed to moral skepticism. However, his argument is overgeneralized. While some of the things that realists say might lead us to infer a general commitment to moral skepticism, the charge fails to do justice to the expressed views of the "older" realists, that is, Hans Morgenthau, Reinhold Niebuhr, George Kennan, Henry Kissinger, Martin Wight, Raymond Aron, and others. We have, for example, Morgenthau's explicit statement that we can "know that nations are subject to the moral law" (Morgenthau, 1973, 11); Niebuhr, though pessimistic about human nature, still held that power could be "answered by morality," that what we require is "an ethic of responsibility based on consequences" (Diggins, 1992, 142); and Kennan recommended a foreign policy for the United States that would "distinguish at all times between the true substance and the mere appearance of moral behavior" (Kennan, 1985/86, 218). If moral skepticism is the view that there can be no such thing as moral knowledge or that the difference between right and wrong is merely a matter of opinion, then it is hard to see it as an adequate representation of the views of these "older" political realists.

Moreover, as Cohen himself points out, it is not political realism that has caused moral skepticism; moral skepticism is bound up with, and seemingly inseparable from, international relations. Since the immoral activities of world politics, chronicled in my introduction, preceded the construction of political realism as an idea, political realism should not be held causally responsible for them. Nor can it be held responsible for describing what is there to be observed in the world as we perceive it even though one may deplore what we see.

But there is more to Cohen's argument. First, he claims that international conduct is open to moral assessment, a proposition that only realists who are also moral nihilists would be prepared to deny.[3] In a second proposition that is of dubious truth value, Cohen argues that "these [moral] assessments rest on principles that govern every domain of human conduct and govern them with equal rigour" (Cohen 1984, 302). This marks a blank refusal to make certain distinctions, namely, a distinction between an impersonal and personal domain, a distinction between obligations which are apolitical and those that are political and, most importantly for our present concerns, a distinction between what the representatives of leaders have to do by virtue of representing their constituency and what the private citizen is obligated to do.[4]

The latter distinction is quite a plausible one. As Kennan points out: "Government is an agent, not a principal. Its primary obligation is to the *interests* of the national society it represents, not to the moral impulses that individual elements of that society may experience" (Kennan, 1985/86, 206). Since there is a very large literature in democratic theory sustaining the idea that representation of the sort identified by Kennan and an ethic of responsibility are intertwined, Cohen's failure to argue against this point is question-begging.

It may also be a feature of politics itself that those of us who engage in commonsense moral judging, and in taking political action, should want a special class of people to make the hard and morally disagreeable choices that we are too squeamish to make ourselves. As Bernard Williams has remarked "it is a predictable and probable hazard of public life that there will be . . . situations in which something morally disagreeable is clearly required. To refuse on moral grounds ever to do anything of that sort is more than likely to mean that one cannot seriously pursue even the moral ends of politics" (Williams, 1981, 60). By this I take Williams to mean that treating the political realm as equivalent to realms in which *only* moral judgments are appropriate may deprive us of the ability to make moral judgments in the political realm altogether. For example, if one is forced to preemptively destroy a chemical warfare factory in a country known for its propensity to deploy toxic agents against its "enemies," one may have committed a moral wrong, but also a political act with good moral consequences. It is acts of this sort that we expect self-conscious political leaders who are deeply informed by a sense of morality to commit as representatives on our behalf.

But can a position that is both realist and not skeptical be reconstructed from the rubble of refuted and partially refuted moral theories to which realists might have been committed in the past? It is my view that this is possible, and that the possibility hinges on the capacity of SMR to present an attractive account of itself. Though a full-blown account of SMR is beyond the scope of this essay, we can at least adumbrate some of its features and show how they differ from rival neo-Kantian understandings of morality as these relate in particular to international relations. The strategy will be twofold: first, to show that political realism's strongest challenger—neo-Kantianism—falls victim to even more robust forms of moral skepticism than that alleged to be true of political realism; and second, to argue that whatever difficulties older political realists may have had in avoiding moral skepticism, SMR holds out the promise of resisting its blandishments.

NEO-KANTIAN INTERNATIONAL ETHICS VERSUS SOFT MORAL REALISM: WILL THE REAL MORAL SKEPTIC PLEASE STAND UP?

According to NKIR, international relations should be guided by a set of universal moral principles understood as a theory of obligation, justice, peace, some kind of normative theory, or some other aspect of Immanuel Kant's general project of developing a moral-theoretical foundation for international relations. These theories are *Kantian* insofar as they retain Kant's project of constructing moral principles that validate the idea of a world ethical community grounded in human agency; and they may be considered *neo*-Kantian insofar as they are prepared to hive off certain features of Kant's thought such as his rigorism, his excessive "abstractionism," and, in particular, his appeal to metaphysics.

For our purposes here, NKIR may be construed as a commitment to at least three ideas, each of which constitutes a point of comparison with SMR (see table 15.1). Let us now consider each of these features of NKIR more closely, as well as the SMR response.

TABLE 15.1

Neo-Kantian International Relations vs. Soft Moral Realism: Key Differences

Ideas	NKIR	SMR
Theory	• committed to "normative theory" • committed to showing the underlying unity of disparate phenomena (whether part of the natural or human realm) • holds that there is a single account true for all moral considerations	• diversity and complexity of moral phenomena thwart any single normative account • skeptical about NKIR project but not morality as such
Ethics over Politics	• morality has a privileged position over politics: (the political should always fall in line with ethical principles in order to avoid moral skepticism) • moral skepticism defeated when every morally required act has a reason that grounds it and does not require any reference to the political	• NKIR cannot defeat moral skepticism because it cannot demonstrate the rationality of being a moral person (moral standards must be more than rational: they must motivate agents)
Rationalist Universalism vs. Moral Particularism	• dominated by the search for universal laws, rules, and norms • commits to rationalist-universalist understanding of morality • expresses a "thin" conception of morality (i.e., an ethics that appeals to abstract general notions such as *rights*, *justice* and *equality*). • rationalist universalism	• NKIR's "thin" conception of morality cannot yield specific practical principles, thus opening the way to moral skepticism • SMR avoids moral skepticism by providing a "thick" conception of morality (i.e., it gives *real* agents moral reasons that are particular, practical, and rooted in a *real* community) • moral particularism

Theory

NKIR is committed to the discovery or construction of a normative theory that systematizes the intuitive knowledge of our moral practices.
Normative theory claims explicitly, or simply presupposes, that moral
phenomena exhibit a unity that can be adequately represented by the
ordering of norms. In international relations theory this idea is well
represented by Mervyn Frost in *Ethics in International Relations: A
Constitutive Theory* (Frost, 1996). Normative theory, on this view, has
the form of a natural scientific theory in the sense that if the generalizations articulated in the theory are correct, we should be able, *ceteris
paribus*, to derive deductive consequences in particular cases. Perhaps
for this reason NKIR is optimistic about what normative theory in
international relations can accomplish. By contrast, there are a group
of thinkers, many of them self-described realists, who are skeptical
about the capacity of normative theory (or indeed any moral theory) to
accomplish what it purports to be able to accomplish. In their analyses
of morality and statecraft, this group of theorists eschews "abstract
moral propositions or the construction of theoretical models" (Nolan,
1995, 1). So there is a sense in which political realism is skeptical about
something, but it is not (or not generally) about morality as such.
Rather, political realism is skeptical about whether "theory" can
deliver on its promise of unifying our moral intuitions with a view to
enabling us to make adequate practical judgments and deliberative
choices. Let us call this form of skepticism "theory skepticism" and distinguish it from "moral skepticism," as described in the third para-
graph of this essay.

According to Mervyn Frost, normative theory is involved in the task
of "explaining the meaning of, setting out the relationships which hold
between, and seeking to evaluate different comprehensive patterns of
core normative concepts such as liberty, equality, justice, human rights,
political obligation . . . and so on" (Frost, 1994, 110).

On such an understanding, the task of normative theory is so monumental that it is implausible to believe that it can perform it adequately. I shall now suggest why I believe theory skepticism is warranted
and why it need not slide into moral skepticism.

Three arguments against normative theory are adduced, all of which
suggest that international relationists would be well advised to seek
reflective understanding of our actual practices over a normative theory
for the subject. The arguments are: (1) the diversity argument, (2) the
uncodifiability argument, and (3) the tension argument. These arguments, adopted by SMR, display considerable theory skepticism, but
none of them entails moral skepticism.

Diversity. It is a commonplace that diversity in international society is pervasive. International society is divided into numerous states each with its own laws, traditions, history, customs, norms, cultures, and ways of going on. In our commonsense understanding of what international relations materially consists of, SMR recognizes the extent to which these diverse ways of going on produce moral attitudes and beliefs that are distinctively different. To be sure, SMR grants that there are some universal claims that are common to all people, but it suggests that actual local moralities are more pertinent in shaping our moral beliefs. Annette Baier points out that when one considers the religious and cultural dimensions of our actual moralities it seems unreasonable to think that some theory could unify these moralities by reducing them, for example, to a set of transparent principles or to a hierarchy of norms of some kind (Baier, 1985). In attempting to systematize norms, one would be tearing them out of contexts in which they could actually guide our practices and placing them in a *constructed*, noncontextual domain in which the relation of the theoretical postulates to what we should actually do is obscure. Such contexts are assembly points for the collection of real traditions that people can refer to for guidance when they engage with moral problems. As Baier says, the difference between normative theory and these traditions is that "actual moral traditions . . . do address directly the question of what one should do now, and do not retreat into accounts of what one should do in hypothetical conditions" (Baier, 1985, 210). Frost's account of settled norms is what Baier would call a "full compliance account," that is, an account (theory) which assumes that by postulating an ideal world in which everyone does her duty, in which aggressors are always punished, and in which noncoercion and nondeception are the rule we can determine what norms should apply in specific situations. Normative theory in this idealized sense not only fails to tell us what people ought to do in real situations of conflict, it is also harmful when it implies that there ought to be fundamental agreement, and even perhaps convergence, on these idealized norms.[5] Such a view obscures the reality of conflict both within and between states.

SMR holds, on the other hand, that the widespread diversity in ways of going on in the international arena is a primary feature of human existence on this planet. Given the pervasiveness of the differences, it is hard to believe that some theory could explain the meaning of, and set out the relations that hold between, concepts that cut across all these differences in the way that Frost's normative theory would require. If, contrary to Frost, there must always be moral conflicts which cannot be resolved by a theoretically identifiable and consistent method, then perhaps we need not theorize about morals at all; we should perhaps engage in practical reflections, as I shall argue below.

Uncodifiability. A second argument against theory is the idea that moral principles cannot be codified without losing their action guiding capacity. According to John McDowell:

> If one attempted to reduce one's conception of what virtue requires to a set of rules, then, however subtle and thoughtful one was in drawing up the code, cases would inevitably turn up in which mechanical application of the rules would strike one as wrong—and not necessarily because one had changed one's mind; rather, one's mind on the matter was not susceptible of capture in any universal formula. (McDowell, 1989, 93)

Moral situations are just too complex to be captured in universal norms of behavior. Instead, various substantive virtues such as honesty, integrity, and generosity may each be seen as embodying a form of responsiveness to some range of moral considerations about truth telling, helping others, and so on. Virtues like sensitivity and empathy may be present to ensure that one does not overlook relevant considerations in particular cases. On this view, there are no fixed rules or decision procedures that will tell one how to weigh relevant competing considerations once they have been identified. As Aristotle says, our generalizations about behavior hold only for the most part and this implies certain constraints on theorizing," "for what is itself indefinite can only be measured by an indefinite standard" (*Nichomachean Ethics* 1137b31–32).

What makes an action right in these circumstances is not whether it derives from some normative (or other kind of) theory; rather, an action is right (if it is) because it is validated by thoughtful judgment or practical wisdom, informed by virtuous concern. No theory is likely to recapitulate or reconstruct the situation which the person of practical wisdom sees as appropriate for moral deliberation; for such a person will collect up the greatest number of genuinely relevant concerns that suit the situation which is ripe for deliberation. But since these concerns will arise from the situation and situations will differ, the person of practical wisdom (almost by definition) will have no basis for appealing to any rule, norm, or principle in making a moral choice about the situation at hand.

Suppose a stateswoman is faced with a crisis in which a revolutionary group has taken over an embassy and is threatening to kill hostages if the group's comrades are not released from jail. Suppose the stateswoman refuses to negotiate the release of the prisoners, notwithstanding the credibility of the hostage-killing threats. Such a determination by someone who is practically wise involves both sensitivity to the feelings of those who are urging negotiation with the revolutionaries and also sensitivity to facts about what constitutes the right thing to do under the circumstances. Since there are no limits either to the number of facts that would be relevant to deciding this case nor to how much consideration one needs to give to the sensitivities of others, it is hard to see how the practically wise person's moral choice can be assisted by theoretical knowledge of some sort. If it is implausible to think that moral judgments can be codified in rules, principles, and norms, then we may need to give up the idea that theory will be able to help us in the burdensome task of making correct moral choices.

Tension. A third argument that tends to undermine the possibility of a normative moral theory in international relations is what I call "the tension argument." This is the idea that we are unlikely to eliminate the tension that arises from taking up an impartial perspective of the sort that normative theorists presuppose, on the one hand, and a partial personal perspective that normative theory ignores or distorts, on the other.

NKIR advances normative theories that presuppose that there is only one point of view to have on morality, that is, the impartial point of view, according to which we ought not to give special weight to the desires, needs, and interests of our own selves, special groups, or nation-states. SMR, by contrast, holds that we ought, sometimes at least, to give special weight to such desires, needs, and interests. There is no good reason to think that theory can resolve this tension. Let us consider why.

In taking up the impartial viewpoint, the individual is trying to set aside her particular desires, concerns, and projects and look at herself as just one person among many who have a moral stake in an issue. She is looking from "the outside in" and trying to abstract from situations in which she has a special concern, desire, or interest. Nonetheless, in viewing herself in this way she is not leaving the partial point of view behind (Nagel, 1991). The moral conflicts with which she is involved matter to her in a way that is not given sufficient weight in the impartial perspective of normative theory. The partial standpoint involves strong allegiance to particular communities and, by extension, to ethnic groupings, nations, and states. It is significant that we cannot maintain an indifference to our projects, concerns, desires, and interests. To be sure, these allegiances are partially bound up with our identities; we cannot just give them up as if the self were, to use Michael Sandel's phrase, "unencumbered" (Sandel, 1984).

Now normative theory presupposes that the tension between the personal and the impersonal viewpoints can be either ignored altogether or resolved in terms of the impartial viewpoint. But both of these options pose difficulties. For ignoring the personal point of view risks falling into dogmatism while claiming to resolve it risks utopianism in insisting that the personal point of view lacks genuine substance. Since the point about dogmatism seems obvious, let us consider the danger of utopianism. A proposal is utopian if it is not politically viable, where political viability identifies those components of a society—national or international—the recognition of which contributes to consensus and mutual cooperation. Utopianism arises when, in failing to give sufficient weight to people's projects, one proposes a social transformation that reasonable people would not be sufficiently motivated to accept (Nagel, 1991).

Normative theory runs a particularly acute risk of utopianism in so far as it gives no weight to political viability since it is based on an hypothesized, idealized situation of some kind. As Baier points out, this is not what we require.

> The real moral guidance comes when we are told not how the law of an ideal community would apply to a concrete case in that ideal world, but when we are told what we should therefore do, in this nonideal world. (Baier, 1985, 210)

If we are to avoid both dogmatism and utopianism, it seems that we must make a place for both the impersonal and personal viewpoint. But the problem with doing so is that it is unclear just how these two viewpoints can be integrated into a general principle and made ready for theoretical cogitation. For example, consider the morally deplorable gap between the rich countries and the very poor countries of the world. Any general principle that is meant to deal with this problem by deploying an impartial theory of some kind will discover that from the impersonal point of view of the poor anything the rich countries are likely to do to relieve their distress will be insufficient, whereas from the rich countries' personal perspective anything that the poor countries are likely to request will be too demanding (Nagel, 1994, 173–174). There is a tension here between two perspectives that cannot be integrated into one another in a way which preserves the legitimacy and integrity of each position.

If we have no basis for resolving these tensions and we hold that any morally and politically viable understanding of the world requires both these viewpoints, it is hard to see how theorizing about justice (and other normative concepts) could be of much use to us. In the face of such tensions what we seem to require, once again, is the practically wise person who deliberates well and offers reasons of a practical sort.

We have seen why reasonable individuals might take up a position of theory skepticism but does such a stance lead to moral skepticism? Not as far as SMR is concerned. And the main reason for this lies in SMR's reliance on "practical reflections" to replace the neo-Kantian craving for theory. The idea of practical reflections is derived from Aristotle's understanding of *phronesis*, usually translated as "practical wisdom." The central idea behind it is that none of our theorizing about ethics will assist human beings to escape the burden of reflective thought (i.e., the sort of thought that requires people faced with a political-moral problem to weigh, by the best lights they have, the reasonable course/s of action/inaction). A person engaged in practical reflection will try to perceive how things stand, morally and politically, within a particular context. Since the relevant features of the situation may not come immediately into her conceptual framework, she may have to rely upon imagination to activate deliberative thought about what needs to be done. When thus engaged, the agent does not treat the concerns which she brings to a situation calling for a moral-political decision as forming a closed system. Since practical reflection does not deal with situations fixed in advance, it may not even be clear to her just what the relevant concerns are. The situation that practical reflection engages has an indeterminate character to it that makes it more suitable than theorizing for imaginative understanding of the moral-political issues at stake.

Normative theory makes an explicit distinction between what is and what ought to be; between the descriptive world of hard data, facts, and empirical knowledge, on the one side, and the norms, principles, rules, and values that normative theory is designed to capture on the other. But this opens up a gap into which moral skepticism can enter (Thomson, 1996). The idea of practical reflection circumvents this distinction by partially collapsing theory into practice. Practical reflection is construed neither as theoretical knowledge nor as craft knowledge: it is concerned with action and what comes about as a result of deliberation and choice (*Nichomachean Ethics* 1140a31–b4). Since it avoids positing the two worlds of norms and descriptions, practical reflection provides a basis for circumventing moral skepticism.

Ethics over Politics

For NKIR, ethical considerations always dominate nonethical ones. NKIR holds that politics is often conceived of, particularly in realist understandings, as that which results from the actions of self-interested agents and, by outward extension from that, from states acting in their national interests. When politics is understood in these terms, there is, according to NKIR, insufficient space for morality and justice. What is needed, on this view, is a conception of ethics that will override and restrain, the political, paradigmatically conceived as directed by self-interest. Insofar as we are unable to achieve this, we will be forced into moral skepticism.

This view is found in Charles Beitz's lucid work *Political Theory and International Relations* (Beitz, 1979). Beitz describes his aim as the attempt to distinguish "international skepticism" from the sounder idea of a theory that he characterizes as "cosmopolitan (in Kant's sense)" (Beitz, 1979, 9). For Beitz, the only valid reasons for moral action are those that can be derived from a detached, neutral, and impersonal viewpoint. Moral judgments have to do with obligations that are impartial.

What is fundamental to morality, Beitz holds, is to give an appropriate answer to the question: "how can anyone have a reason to do particular actions or subscribe to a general position that cannot be shown to work to his advantage when a more advantageous alternative is available? In other words, how is ethics possible" (Beitz, 1979, 56)? The alternatives Beitz presents here are clear enough: either we admit the idea that there is a moral point of view, acceptance of which effectively eliminates self-interest, or we renounce the possibility of ethics altogether and succumb to moral skepticism. Not surprisingly, Beitz chooses the first alternative.

Here the going gets pretty rough, since Beitz is attempting to define the very possibility of a moral point of view that precludes an agent's self-interest. The leading assumption behind this thought is that the only alternative to ethics is self-interest and this is clearly inadequate. It would mean, for example, that racists, whose proponents eschew self-interest, would find a place in the moral point of view, whereas Aristotelians, whose self-defined task is precisely to reconcile self-interest and altruism, would not. Such an outcome is counterintuitive and unacceptable.

Beitz's attempt to define morality so as to exclude self-interest from the realm of reason and morality is far too quick and easy. Certainly, someone who acts in his self-interest may be, as Philippa Foot says, "convicted of villainy but not inconsistency" or irrationality (Foot, 1978, 161). But, contrary to Foot, perhaps he should not necessarily be convicted of villainy either. Think of a statesperson who establishes an arms-control agreement: he may be covered with glory, thus satisfying his self-interest, namely, achieving renown; but his actions may nonetheless be good insofar as they benefit the common interest in reducing the likelihood of nuclear war. His actions would not, on any neo-Kantian view, count as "moral" since his motives are selfish; nonetheless they may, on some commonsense understanding anyway, be considered good actions because they benefit the common good. It would not, in any event, seem appropriate to classify him as a villain.

These critical considerations are not simply a response to Beitz as a particular neo-Kantian thinker. Let us, for example, consider how another such philosopher develops a notion of obligation that is intended to override the political and to defeat skepticism.

After providing us with incontrovertible facts about the miserable plight of the needy, and criticizing alternative rights-based and consequentialist accounts, Onora O'Neill (in *Faces of Hunger*) says that the "solution" lies in accepting a Kantian account of morality, that is, one grounded in the concept of obligation (O'Neill, 1986).

But what is an obligation? According to O'Neill, moral obligations are expressed in one especially important kind of deliberative conclusion, namely, a conclusion that is directed to what to do. Not every conclusion of a particular moral deliberation expresses an obligation. Some moral conclusions merely announce that you may do something and, as such, do not refer to an obligation. What tell us which moral conclusions are obligations is the human capacity to be rational. So O'Neill draws a tight connection between rationality and what morality requires; but this will not in itself defeat moral skepticism. For even if we succeed in showing that morally required acts are bound up with rationally required acts, this does not begin to show that it is rational *to be* moral and this is what would be required to defeat this more comprehensive form of skepticism.

O'Neill does not speak to this issue, evidently because she assumes that skepticism is defeated once one shows that rationality requires acting morally. Motives do not matter because reasons can guide moral action independently of desire or interest. But is this so? It is one thing to draw an intimate connection, as O'Neill does, between what is rational and acting to alleviate people's hunger; but if one does not really care about the people whose hunger is to be alleviated, then is not one morally remiss, indeed a moral skeptic? Does not avoiding moral skepticism involve being the sort of person who cares about others rather than, say, someone who merely goes through the motions of caring? And does not caring imply that notwithstanding our official obligations we actually have to be in a position to care about them? It would appear that obligation backed by rationality is impotent to defeat the kind of skepticism that arises from an absence of motive to care about others.

But what does SMR want to put in the place of a neo-Kantian understanding of obligation? According to SMR, one way to show that it is rational to be moral, and defeat skepticism, is by locating the reasons for an agent's actions in her motivational set (Williams, 1981, 102).Though lots of things may be in the set, in talking of political events, it would presumably be a common experience for actors to appeal to their interests. Let us suppose that actors are motivated to act to satisfy their interests, where doing so involves caring about others.[6] The person who acts in her interest has a reason to act which is located in her existing motivations; she is not reaching outside her motivational set to appeal to some external standard, such as an obligation, as a reason for acting. If she did, it would be unclear how, in the absence of an appropriate motive, obligation alone could move her to action. To explain an agent's actions, we need a perspective internal to the agent that picks out something that motivates her to act. From her internal perspective, external standards—for example, rights, justice, goodness, and so on—will be arbitrary at best; only standards that motivate the person to act—internal standards that, roughly, refer to what people want—will have the chance of being nonarbitrary.

What SMR objects to in the neo-Kantian view is the idea that moral judgments concerning obligations are considered overriding in character so that consideration of interests—political and moral—cannot find undistorted space in the space of internal reasons. On the SMR view, then, O'Neill is mistaken to think that our obligations to the hungry can be derived from external reasons in which motives are independent of interests. O'Neill wants our obligations to be binding on agents regardless of their motives. She evidently believes that reasons alone provide sufficient guides to action. What is left out, according to SMR, is that something can be a guide to action only if it is capable of motivating an agent; and an agent's interest has been a prevalent, time-honored source of agent motivation. Something can be good only if a person can be motivated to seek it. To say that something must motivate to be part of a person's good is to say that it must be something that can matter to her or be an object of concern. That something is in a person's interest—in the larger sense of interest which includes a person's interest in the welfare of others—satisfies that requirement. So if we think of politics as an activity that seeks to satisfy interests, as SMR suggests, then we have a way of bringing ethics and politics into closer connection with one another than they would be on any NKIR account.

Rationalist-Universalism vs. Commonsense Particularism

According to SMR, NKIR is a form of rationalist-universalism and on these grounds alone it should be resisted (Morgenthau, 1946; see also Rorty, 1982; Putnam, 1995). The central thrust of rationalist-universalism is to make "claims to universal truth, or claims about the essential nature and identity of persons" (Rawls, 1987, 6–7). A particularly powerful form of rationalist-universalism thus understood is to be found in some of the recent writings of Thomas Pogge who defines human beings as universally equal and free persons (Pogge, 1992, 48–49). I shall now argue that Pogge's failure to make rationalist-universalism work leads to the very skepticism it is designed to overcome.

Pogge explicitly endorses a conception of justice based on a metaphysical conception of the self—persons as universally autonomous and equal—that, in Rawls' terms, embodies a "comprehensive moral ideal," which may or may not be true but which, given the long-standing controversies concerning such ideals, we have good reason to think of as metaphysical in the pejorative sense—that is, metaphysical accounts of justice cannot meaningfully be said to be true or false and hence should be abandoned in favor of a political conception of justice (Rawls, 1985, 233; Rawls, 1995, 132–142).[7] In the absence of such abandonment, the appropriate response to comprehensive systems of the rationalist-universalist sort would be a thoroughgoing skepticism.

Pogge's strategy is to dismiss out of hand all *antiliberal* conceptions of the good. But then Pogge's commitment to liberalism becomes a form of dogmatism. For example, Pogge argues that

> if my neighbour wants the U.S. to be organised like the Catholic Church and I want it to be a liberal state, then we can *not* both have our way. There is no room for accommodation, and, if I really believe in egalitarian liberal principles, I should politically support them and the institutions they favour against their opponents. . . . My rational is the analogue of this: While the world can contain societies that are structured in a variety of ways, some liberal and some not, it cannot itself be structured in a variety of ways. If the Algerians want their society to be organised as a religious state consistent with a just global order and . . . organised according to the Koran, and we want it to accord with liberal principles, then we can *not* both have our way. There is no room for accommodation here, and if we really believe in egalitarian liberal principles . . . we should politically support these principles, and the global institutions they favour, against their opponents. (Pogge, 1994, 217)

But to rule out societies, especially international ones, which do not accept egalitarian liberal principles grounded in a metaphysical conception of moral personality is, in effect, to label such societies as unreasonable, without explaining why we should accept the appropriateness of the label. That conceptions of the good such as fundamental Islam are nonliberal is, of course, clear but that is surely no argument against their reasonableness. What would be the attitude of nonliberals if they did not succeed in blocking the egalitarianism of the most powerful liberal states in the community of states? It might well be that they failed because there were not enough of the nonliberals with enough power to prevent the more powerful liberal states from erecting a legal order reflecting *their* values and requiring us to live by them in a legal order that we could not change except by resort to force. Would that not come down to a Hobbesian condition of the sort which Pogge is attempting to escape? And would not that Hobbesian condition be one that is endorsed by the very moral skepticism which Pogge officially deplores? The fallout of Pogge's neo-Kantian international relations is a structure of power articulating a kind of liberal order ruled in the name of liberal values, irrespective of the views about the global order to be found in other cultures and communities. But this is dogmatic rationalist-universalism, an ideology that, given its implausibility, will tend to generate a skeptical response.

By contrast SMR adopts moral particularism, an idea that denies the rationalist-universalist assumption that what any one person ought or ought not to do in a given situation is what any similarly placed person ought or ought not to do. It is important to be clear about the meaning of "similarly placed." According to the rationalist-universalist, Situation B is "similarly placed" if it shares with Situation A all the properties that were reasons why Situation A was right or wrong. The particularist denies this on the grounds that what may have been a sufficient reason for making certain moral judgments in one case may not be in another case (see Dancy, 1993, 61).

One way to support particularism is to develop examples where a consideration that served intuitively as a reason in one case could not do so in another similar case (Dancy, 1993, 60). For example, let us say that country A is a poor country deserving of foreign aid from rich country B and country B provides it. Soon after country B discovers that the leaders of country A have diverted foreign aid funds into secret bank accounts abroad and that they have no intention of distributing the funds to develop the country. Here country A's poverty—the original reason for providing aid—is no longer a reason for country B to provide country A with foreign aid. What was once a reason is no longer a reason even though the condition of the country has not changed.

Here is a nonfictional example. Moral philosophers, historians, and political scientists have often praised President Kennedy's actions in the Cuban Missile Crisis as admirable, courageous, conscientious, and so forth. However, of those who have made generally positive assessments, some have tended to condemn Kennedy for not immediately accepting Khrushchev's offer to trade off the withdrawal of Soviet missiles from Cuba for the withdrawal of U.S. missiles from Turkey and a pledge not to invade Cuba.[8] For example, although Stephen Nathanson grants that Kennedy's actions in the Cuban Missile Crisis were "admirable," he also holds that he ran unnecessary risks of nuclear war (Nathanson, 1991, 95). My interest here lies not so much in criticizing Nathanson's assessment but in bringing out the difference between universalism and particularism.

An important part of Nathanson's "case" against Kennedy concerns what he says was Kennedy's opinion about the removal of U.S. missiles from Turkey. As a universalist, Nathanson sees no difference between Soviet missiles in Cuba and U.S. missiles in Turkey: they both have the property of being nuclear missiles very near the territories of the two superpowers constituting a threat to their respective nations. According to the principle of universalizability to which Nathanson implicitly appeals, political leaders, insofar as they are moral agents, are morally committed to making the same moral judgments in situations which are similar in the required way. But President Kennedy did not do this and his failure so to act, according to Nathanson, increased the risks of nuclear war. The particularist may (although she is hardly logically compelled to) be prepared to accept the conclusion but would not be disposed to do so on the basis of the reasoning that the universalist uses. For the particularist, what the United States did previously with respect to deploying missiles near the territory of the Soviet Union may be a reason for what the Soviet Union did in Cuba, but it could have been a reason for doing something different. Examining these general reasons is not, according to the particularist, to the point; for, moral judgment does not lie in the move from what happened in one case to what happened in another. Reasons function in different ways because, quite obviously, they have been importantly affected by other considerations, paradigmatically of a political nature, which may have been present. The key point is that there is no ground for the hope that we can find out in new cases how older considerations in similar cases should now function, nor for the hope that we can move in any automatic fashion to the way they will function in future cases. The major task of the particularist is to eschew universalism and to examine the moral issues that each case invokes.

In the case of the Cuban Missile Crisis this might involve analyzing Kennedy's response to the news that the Soviets had lied about putting only defensive weapons into Cuba. According to Theodore Sorensen, Kennedy was angry at Khrushchev's attempts "to deceive him and immediately aware of their significance" (Sorensen, 1965, 673). Moreover, Kennedy was not opposed, in general, to the Soviet Union's making agreements to transfer nuclear weapons to other countries to improve its deterrent posture. "But," according to Sorensen, "those agreements had always been reached in public and announced to the world. He [President Kennedy] felt very strongly that the transfer of nuclear missiles to Cuba in an atmosphere of secrecy and deception made a tremendous difference in terms of the United States' reaction" (Allyn, 1989, 19). The strict universalist, however, would give no weight to this judgment on Kennedy's part unless it could be put into some universal schema like: "All political leaders in Kennedy's situation ought to have been angry and immediately aware of the significance of an adversary's efforts to deceive other nations about its deployments of nuclear weapons." But attempts to discover what is universal here is to fail to give any weight to the fact that Kennedy may have developed a moral character during the course of the crisis such that we can now see his actions not as similar to anyone similarly placed, but as particular to that situation itself, and what was morally required there.

One could say about Kennedy's particular moral judgments that they were undertakings, promises, or pledges to do certain things and that these can be explained by alluding to Kennedy's character. For example, President Kennedy undertook, according to Robert Kennedy, not to be "the Tojo of the 1960s" (cited in Thompson, 1992, 202). By this he evidently meant to commit himself not to use U.S. military forces to engage in a surprise attack. Kennedy also made an undertaking to disclose the facts that he would discover to "the people of the United States" (Sorensen, 1965, 690).President Kennedy never lost sight of his important undertaking to avoid actions that would result in killing other human beings (Thompson, 1992, 338). In making these particular commitments, there does not appear to be any implication that all similar individuals who are similarly placed ought to have done the same thing. The moral particularist is not interested in discovering what later cases have in common with earlier cases but rather with finding out as much as possible about the case at hand. While comparison with previous cases may assist in finding out what is going on, the moral diagnosis (always bound up, as previously argued, with political diagnosis) is meant to be particular. Previous cases are simply meant to sharpen one's sensibilities as to what is at stake morally and politically in the case now at hand.

Does particularism embody or lead to moral skepticism? I see no reason why it should. What leads to skepticism, so far as SMR is concerned, is commitment to abstract, general principles that we have good reason to believe cannot serve as guides to particular moral decisions because of the gap between the principles and the real world in which human beings act and morally reflect on their actions. Since the idea of general principles is de-emphasized in SMR, the gap between moral principle and moral action is, if not closed altogether, insufficiently wide to permit moral skepticism.

CONCLUSION

Despite the currently fashionable view among IR commentators that political realism is susceptible to moral skepticism, there is no evidence that this is true in any unequivocal sense. There is no basis for saying that political realism maintains that moral claims have no truth value, that their truth or validity are relative to moral frameworks, or that it is not possible to find out about any moral claims that they are objectively true or valid. On the contrary, when SMR says that something is in someone's interest, we can construe that as saying that it conduces to someone's welfare, or that someone would be in better condition having that something than she would otherwise be. So, if anything, SMR is claiming a connection between interest and moral goodness of a sort that would, if established, nullify moral skepticism.

What SMR encourages, we have argued, is theory skepticism. For NKIR, theory's task is to generalize the principles, rules, and norms that putatively apply to a large range of moral situations in which decisions are required. NKIR transforms what are essentially commonsense maxims into formalistic axioms and postulates that are remote from the commonsense morality of real societies. This provides the groundwork for a distinction between theory and the real world, that is, between one kind of statement—theoretical—and another kind of statement—factual—in character. This split in the universe of discourse creates the problem of how (and on what basis) these different discourses are to be matched up with one another. Skepticism is a natural response to this split.

By contrast, SMR focuses not on theory but on our reflective practices. Here it might be useful to make a distinction between theoretical reflection and practical reflection. Theoretical reflection involves taking up a critical attitude toward abstract ethical concepts that are intended to apply universally—concepts such as right, justice, and the good. Williams calls them thin concepts, perhaps because they are meant to stretch beyond local communities and apply everywhere (Williams, 1985, 140–145). Thin ethical concepts are susceptible to being split between factual and evaluative components and the evaluative component cannot maintain its objectivity in the face of critical theoretical reflection on the application of these terms to particular cases. Hence, skepticism would come into play. By contrast, concerning thick ethical concepts, that is, those that apply to specific cultural situations such as *coward*, *lie*, and *brutality*, the factual and evaluative components cannot be separated and therefore the split which encourages skepticism would not arise. Propositions employing thick concepts have the possibility of being true. To understand how a thick concept can be applied to a new situation and have the possibility of being true, one would have to grasp the evaluative point of the concept and this would presumably be done by grasping the cultural circumstances in which such concepts would be used. Only within specified cultural contexts would it be possible to say that in correctly applying such concepts one had moral knowledge. So here is the paradox: moral knowledge may be obtainable at the local level but not necessarily at the universal level. At the universal level, given the split between factual and evaluative statements, there is the ever present danger of moral skepticism, whereas at the local level—the level, say, of communities, nations, and nation-states—there is the possibility of the kind of knowledge that arises from practical reflection on thick concepts. Thick ethical concepts may survive theoretical reflection because these concepts apply to concrete situations in which appliers of the concepts are intent upon finding a solution to a problem of choice and action within a particular context.

But there is more. Since thick concepts are those deployed at the local level, it is plausible to think that these are the concepts that give content to the ethics of nation-states. The thin vocabulary that we use in global relations—notions of justice, right, and good—are external concepts that do not have the power to motivate agents in the way that thick internal concepts do. Since thick ethical concepts, on this view, not only motivate agents but also hold out the promise of ethical knowledge, it is easy to see why the institutional envelope in which they flourish, for example, the nation-state, may not be thought to be as morally undesirable as certain theorists think. Thus, rather than rooting around for alternatives to political realism and the skepticism it is believed widely, and wrongly, to create, the route to genuine, meaningful, and practical moral reflection in IR is right under our nose.

NOTES

1. Tony Smith argues that "the Clinton administration needs to articulate a clear definition of the American self-interest served by defending human rights and democracy in a place like Haiti." And again, we are told that "leadership is called for to articulate the American interest in fostering democracy abroad in terms the American public will accept." Clearly, political realists would be opposed to any foreign policy constructed on this basis (Smith, 1994, 36, 45).

2. Remember Hamlet's appropriately aggressive remark, "Seems, madam! "Nay, it is; I know not 'seems'." *Hamlet*, act I, scene ii.

3. There seems to be an unfortunate tendency among neorealists to a kind of nihilism that traditional political realists were not vulnerable.

4. Cohen says that "the standards of morality . . . apply with equal force to princes and private persons, in the domestic and in the international arenas." He is objecting to Hume's claim "that there is a system of morals calculated for princes, much more free than that which ought to govern private persons" (Cohen, 1984, 330).

5. Frost's concept of "settled norms" is a version of idealized norms (Frost, 1994, 104–112).

6. I am assuming, of course, that acting in one's own interests does not preclude acting in the interests of others.

7. Such a metaphysical account of justice is one among many possible accounts that have as their common root the fact of long-standing, intractable disagreements between disputants and the comprehensive systems which their discourse expresses.

8. According to Robert Smith Thompson, in a book based on archival material released in the late 1980s, President Kennedy did, during the course of negotiations, give a pledge to the Soviet leaders not to invade Cuba and to remove U.S. missiles from Turkey. But there is an important difference between a secret undertaking made in private during the course of negotiations and a decision to do the same thing at the beginning of a crisis. This difference is obscured by many, including Thompson himself (Thompson, 1992).

REFERENCES

Allyn, B. J., J. G. Blight, and D. A. Welch. (1992). *Back to the Brink*. Proceedings of the Moscow Conference on the Cuban Missile Crisis, January 27–28.

Baier, A. (1985). *Postures of the Mind: Essays on Mind and Morals*. London: Metheun.

Barry, Brian. (1986). "Can States Be Moral? International Morality and the Compliance Problem." In A. Ellis (ed.), *Ethics and International Relations*. Manchester, U.K.: Manchester University Press.

Beitz, Charles R. (1979). *Political Theory and International Relations*. Princeton: Princeton University Press.

Cohen, M. (1984). "Moral Scepticism and International Relations." *Philosophy and Public Affairs* 13 (Fall), 299–346.

Dancy, J. (1993). *Moral Reasons*. Oxford: Blackwell.

Diggins, J. P. (1992). "Power and Suspicion: The Perspectives of Reinhold Niebuhr." *Ethics and International Affairs* 6, 141– 61.

Doppelt, G. (1978). "Walzer's Theory of Morality in International Relations," *Philosophy and Public Affairs* 8(1), 3–26.

Foot, P. (1978). *Virtues and Vices Other Essays in Moral Philosophy*. Oxford: Basil Blackwell.

Frost, M. (1994). "The Role of Normative Theory in IR." *Millennium: Jounral of International Studies* 23(1), 109–118.

Frost, M. (1996). *Ethics in International Relations: A Constitutive Theory*. Cambridge: Cambridge University Press.

Kennan, G. (1985/86). "Morality and Foreign Policy." *Foreign Affairs* 64(2), 205–218.

McDowell, J. (1989). "Virtue and Reason." In S. G. Clarke and E. Simpson (eds.), *Anti-Theory in Ethics and Moral Conservatism*. New York: The State University of New York Press: 87–109.

Mill, John Stuart. (1873). "A Few Words on Nonintervention." In *Dissertations and Discussions*. Vol. 3. London: Longmans: 111–24.

Morgenthau, Hans J. (1946). *Scientific Man vs Power Politics*. Chicago: The University of Chicago Press.

Morgenthau, Hans J. (1973). *Politics among Nations*. New York: Alfred Knopf.

Nagel, T. (1991). *Equality and Partiality*. New York: Oxford University Press.

Nathanson, S. (1991). "Kennedy and the Cuban Missile Crisis: On the Role of Moral Reasons in Explaining and Evaluating Political Decision-Making." *Journal of Social Philosophy* 22 (Fall), 94–108.

Nolan, Cathal J. (1995). "Introduction." In Cathal J. Nolan (ed.), *Ethics and Statecraft: The Moral Dimension of International Affairs*. Westport, Conn.: Greenwood.

O'Neill, Onora. (1986). *Faces of Hunger: An Essay on Poverty, Justice and Development*. London: G. Allen & Unwin.

Pogge, T. W. (1989). *Realizing Rawls*. Ithaca: Cornell University Press.

Pogge, T. W. (1992). "Cosmopolitanism and Sovereignty." *Ethics* 103 (October), 48–79.

Pogge, T. W. (1994). "An Egalitarian Law of Peoples." *Philosophy and Public Affairs* 23(3), 195–224.

Putnam, H. (1995). *Pragmatism: An Open Question*. Oxford: Blackwell.

Rawls, John. (1985). "Justice as Fairness: Political not Metaphysical." *Philosophy and Public Affairs* 14(3), 223–251.

Rawls, John. (1987). "The Idea of an Overlapping Consensus." *Oxford Journal of Legal Studies* 7(1), 1–27.

Rawls, John. (1995). "Reply to Habermas." *Journal of Philosophy* 92 (March), 132–180.

Rorty, Richard. (1982). *Consequences of Pragmatism*. Brighton, U.K.: Harvester.

Sandel, Michael. (1984). "The Procedural Republic and the Unencumbered Self." *Political Theory* 12(1).

Smith, T. (1994). "In Defence of Intervention." *Foreign Affairs* 73(6), 34–46.

Sorensen, T. C. (1965). *Kennedy*. London: Hodder and Stoughton.

Thompson, R. S. (1992). *The Missiles of October*. New York: Simon & Schuster.

Harman, G., and J. J. Thomson (eds.). (1996). *Moral Relativism and Moral Objectivity*. Cambridge, Mass.: Blackwell.

Walzer, Michael. (1977). *Just and Unjust Wars: A Moral Argument with Historical Illustrations*. New York: Basic Books.

Williams, Bernard. (1981). "Politics and Moral Character." In B. Williams (ed.), *Moral Luck: Philosophical Papers 1973–1980*. Cambridge: Cambridge University Press: 54–70.

Williams, Bernard. (1985). *Ethics and the Limits of Philosophy*. London: Fontana.

Williams, Bernard. (1995). "Replies." In J. E. J. Altham and R. Harrison (eds.), *World, Mind, and Ethics: Essays on the Ethical Philosophy of Bernard Williams*. Cambridge: Cambridge University Press: 185–224.

CHAPTER 16

Beyond International Relations: Edward Said and the World

Pal Ahluwalia
and
Michael Sullivan

INTRODUCTION

Although Edward Said is a preeminent public intellectual, his work is little studied in mainstream American social science outside the discipline of English and comparative literature. Said's pioneering theoretical work, especially his efforts to bring together power/knowledge, text/context, intellectual and political history; his attack on reifying theories of culture and attention to the interplay between cultural patterning and individual creativity; and finally, his concern for literature and the arts and their relationship with the social sciences, form a legacy of interdisciplinary scholarship that is particularly compelling at a time when the social and human sciences are being challenged to consider alternatives to traditional, Western political theory. But it is not only in this domain that Said's voice is heard. He is a well-known social and political critic in the United States and an ardent supporter of the Palestinian cause. In the best traditions of a public intellectual, he has carved out a large and diverse audience, yet his work and the critical debate it has inspired in a number of fields[1] figure rarely in International Relations (IR).

The aim of this essay is to undertake the up until now neglected task of assessing critically the contributions of Edward Said to IR as a way of understanding the world. To this end, the essay consists of four sections. The first considers the extent to which the production and policing of "truth" about the world in IR after the Cold War reflects the hegemony of the discipline as an "American social science." By "hegemony" we mean that the American discipline of IR speaks authoritatively for humanity, transcending the sectarian and representing as "universal" Western discourses on human rights, sovereignty, democracy, and the market. While we recognize that the "hegemony" of the American discipline is always highly contested in debates within IR, and that the "Third Debate" has problematized the discipline in ways that students of IR find unsettling, for us such debates remain a predominantly *Western* intellectual enterprise, despite their critical, postmodern interrogations (see George, 1994). This, we argue, extends to, and is represented by, the way in which the authoritative voice of the American discipline of IR imagines a "normal" world and the existence of threatening "others." During the Cold War, for example, the enemy was "international communism," against which the defense of the "free world" was undertaken in the form of America's national security state. While in the post–Cold War era external enemies have become more difficult to imagine, the American discipline has nonetheless managed to settle on some non-Western "other" as the new nemesis. We explore this in relation to the much celebrated writings of Samuel Huntington and, to a lesser degree, Francis Fukuyama.

The second section discusses the challenges to IR posed by Said's reimagination of the world. This introduces the student of IR to the field of *postcolonial studies*, which reestablishes the centrality of local identities, places, and meanings in understanding the world (see Ashcroft, Griffiths, and Tiffin, 1995; Childs and Williams, 1997). The power to erase meaning and impose a new reality on the landscape, to deny the "other" its memory, was the awful truth of Western imperialism. Postcolonialism expresses resistance to that power and seeks to transcend it, reincorporating marginal identities, places, and spaces into theoretical discourse and exploring them in terms of their suppressed meaning.

The third section then introduces students of IR to the possibilities of postcolonial studies in the post–Cold War era through the application of Said's insights to Samuel Huntington's discussion of the "Clash of Civilizations" (1993; see also Huntington, 1996a, 1996b). In a sense, our choice of Huntington was made for us, since this work was described by the editors of *Foreign Affairs* as the most widely discussed article in IR since George Kennan's "X" article was published in the late 1940s. This comparison gives some idea of the desired impact of Huntington's claim that he has established *the* "paradigm" for "viewing global politics" that "will be meaningful to scholars and useful to policy makers" (Huntington, 1993, 13). Huntington, we suggest, "alerts" the American discipline and national security state to the existence of post–Cold War enemies, defined as the non-Western "other" and thus reinvents the "enemy" so endemic to American IR. Interestingly, Huntington's emphasis on "culture" and the "geopolitics" of intercivilizational conflict is usually presented as an alternative paradigm to Francis Fukuyama's earlier, triumphant equation of the end of the Cold War with the "end of history" (Fukuyama, 1992). We argue, instead, however, that Huntington imagines the post–Cold War era in much the same hegemonic manner as IR has always "imagined" non-American "others." Indeed, it is our contention that both Huntington and Fukuyama, while claiming to speak for "humanity," in fact speak in defense of the "universal" interests of *Western culture.*

The final section of the essay explores the challenge to students of IR issued by Said's understanding of the role of the intellectual. We conclude that the responsibility of students of IR is to "speak truth to power" about the many local, imagined worlds that comprise global politics and that hitherto now have been all but expunged from the American discourse.

INTERNATIONAL RELATIONS: AN AMERICAN SOCIAL SCIENCE?

The question of whether the discipline of IR remains "an American social science" is, perhaps, only answerable from perspectives beyond its disciplinary boundaries. This, in turn, presupposes that we are able to peg precisely where the boundary fence lies between IR and other disciplines and agree on what to include within "our" enclosed discipline. More fundamentally, the question presupposes that the words "discipline," "IR," and "American" have fixed meanings that we already know and accept.

If the answer to the question of whether IR is an American discipline is to come from beyond its boundaries, must it follow that it will come from a different discipline, or from IR with a different national prefix—English or Australian, for example? We wish to answer this question by challenging the assumptions upon which it rests; that is, by not only questioning where disciplinary boundaries are fixed, but also the exercise of boundary fixing itself. Thus, we wish to question boundaries beyond identifying them as simply "inside/outside" markers in Western political theory (see Walker, 1993). The questions, therefore, are twofold.

First, many heterogeneous communities with different cultures—white, Afro-American, Hispanic, indigenous, migrant, urban, rural, rich, poor, north, south, East, West, and so on—comprise the United States of America. The nation is imagined differently by different citizens. We ask, therefore, which America does the national prefix privilege in IR? For whom can the discipline and the national security state speak?

Second, in what sense does and should IR exist as a discipline?

In answer to the first question, it is pertinent to question the relevance of the very prefix "American." What is the purpose behind naming the discipline as such? What interests are served? Although there are numerous claims made about the world from within the hegemonic American discipline of IR, we argue that there is no peculiarly American knowledge of the world, nor knowledge that can be attributed exclusively to any nation. While IR posits the only alternative to state-based knowledge as a more idealistic cosmopolitanism, one does not have to aspire to universal knowledge. The alternative to the "grand narrative" about global politics may be found in the voices of "local narratives." Nevertheless, there is a body of knowledge in America that draws on Western traditions of political thinking. It conflates the two claims to knowledge, national, and universal, and engages in debates over their precise meaning and policy implications. Despite cultural heterogeneity, this is the "American" discipline of IR.

In answer to the second question, IR exists as a discipline in two senses. First, as it defines itself and, second, in terms of what it excludes. The discipline's exclusionary and discursive practices discipline knowledge of the world in such a way that IR is an imitation of what it claims to be: it is reflective only of its self-defined parameters and constituted by knowledge deemed "legitimate" in terms of self-definition. In this sense, the discipline is self-referential and self-serving, interested in "truth" only to the extent that this conforms to the interests of the "American state" and the "American discipline." As David Campbell and Michael Dillon note, this makes IR "little more than a cheer-leader for modernity" (Campbell and Dillon, 1993, 43). Yet knowledge of the world can also be found beyond the disciplinary boundaries, in what IR excludes. Perhaps, ironically, then, once the boundaries are removed, such knowledge will also include that which is currently fenced in/out by the discipline. IR will finally *be* when it no longer *is* a discipline.

In the meantime, boundaries are policed, but against what? It is not against what is "outside" the discipline, because what is "out there" is largely unknown. Fear is shaped largely by what is "in here." "In here" is familiar and normal. Rather, the American discipline of IR protects itself against those who claim to be on the "right side" of the boundary at the same time as they challenge the exclusion of the "other." This is not the voice of the "other" "speaking international relations," but the voice of the discipline itself. Despite attacks by many "critical" IR scholars of different theoretical and political persuasions, the discipline remains American and "Us-Them" in its voice and conceptualization of the "issues" and "problems" of international politics. Furthermore, despite the efforts of those who have been co-joined in what, from certain vantage points in IR—not that of journals like *Foreign Affairs*, but *Millennium* and *Alternatives*—is called the "Third Debate"—authors as diverse as Rob Walker, David Campbell, Michael Dillon, Simon Dalby, Bradley Klein, James Der Derian, Michael Schapiro, Jim George, and Christine Sylvester, for example (see Smith, 1995, 1–37)—the discipline, with all its theoretical heterogeneity and development of ethical and emancipatory voices, continues to reproduce discourses on world order with a predominantly Western voice.[2] For some, this is a desirable return to "normative theory" in IR. Nicholas Rengger, for example, is even more explicit in contextualizing this as (a question, answered affirmatively); "The Fall and Rise of 'Anglo-American' Political Theory"? (Rengger, 1995, 2–9).

John Macmillan and Andrew Linklater's recent *Boundaries in Question* (1995) is a case in point. For them, "Global Politics should replace IR," and the solution to the current crisis in theoretical discourse is for the "academic study of IR . . . to overcome its peculiar separation from Political Theory" (Macmillan and Linklater, 1995, 4, 14). While clearly challenging the utility of traditional boundaries, the diagnosis they offer leads simply to different "problem solving theories." "Who" identifies "problems" does not change. It is "our" interests that are served. But this simply replicates the problem of "global politics" being constructed as the intellectual realm of Western theoretical discourse. While embracing "emancipatory politics," it amounts to a call for the hegemony of Western political discourse to be better reflected in IR.

Mark Neufeld's recent writings also replicate this problem. Despite his emphasis on "theoretical reflexivity" and its admirable "antipositivist" sentiments, this also is an example of Western reflection upon Western theorizing (Neufeld, 1995, 40). There is no room for postcolonial reflection on postcolonial theorizing. Neufeld, for example, identifies three "minority traditions in the discipline"—"neo-Gramscian," "postmodern," and "feminist" (Neufeld, 1995, 58–66)—yet the silencing of the voice of the "other" here is just as total as anywhere else in IR. Consequently, whether for Macmillan and Linklater, or for Neufeld, the "solution" they advocate ends up being merely a "corrective" to Western discourses, not their transcendence. Instead, the "insight" they offer is reduced to the observation that "traditional boundaries of the discipline were not carved out in isolation from features of the world 'out there'" and that IR theorists should be cognizant of this (Macmillan and Linklater, 1995, 2). But as Said points out, such an approach repeats the error of separating "theory" from "reality," an error that constitutes the elemental problem in contemporary theoretical discourse. In Said's estimation, boundaries are imaginative and discursive features that *become* the world "out there." Rather than redrawing boundaries to better fit a changed reality "out there," the challenge thus becomes to reimagine the world: thinking otherwise is constitutive of social change.

Perhaps more surreptitiously, we also witness the conflation of the "Western" to the "American," with the tension between the aspirations to identify true "national" and true "transcendental" knowledge, a penchant characteristic of American IR. As Justin Rosenberg concludes, "the US has found in the modern clerisy of this 'American social science' a rather more serviceable ideologue than Charles V was able to command in the Dominican Order of his day" (Rosenberg, 1994, 173). Not that this close association of "imagining the world" and foreign policy is peculiar to the United States. It is a feature of *all* states. What is peculiar about the relationship in the American academy is the hegemony of its conflation of the "national" with the "universal," which frames the discipline to such an extent that American foreign policy analysis and interest *become* IR. Its voice is *Foreign Affairs*. The rest of us can only respond and critique an agenda, set of interests, "legitimate" knowledge and theories, devised, defined, and perpetuated by the "American" discipline writ "universal."

This has three consequences. First, the American discipline can never be exclusively American, because the "national" is also the "universal." While speaking for itself, its speaks for others, but not necessarily for the many "other" Americas—Chicanos, African Americans, women, and the *imarginatti* (Spivak, 1996, 29–52)—and most certainly not for those in the world beyond the discipline's boundaries. The "others" that American discourse speaks for are states and interests that imagine the world through similar exclusionary, Western eyes. They take this world as their given. They desire an American discipline of IR to universalize their "normal" world. It is an imperialist discourse that colonizes through Western conceptions of meaning.

Second, the discipline of IR can never be exclusively "Western" either. Regardless of whatever intellectual content we choose to give the "West" as a concept, it is always defined by what it is *not* as well. This is one of the major thrusts of Said's work (Said, 1993) and a starting point for how critical scholars should move *beyond* the discipline. "Exile," Said concludes, "becomes something closer to a norm, an experience of crossing boundaries and charting new territories in defiance of the classic canonic closures" (Said, 1993, 384). It entails "the contrapuntal lines of global analysis, in which texts and worldly institutions are seen working together" (Said, 1993, 385–386). This requires, at the very least, a critical reexamination of the way physical space is delineated in the Western tradition and comes to be imposed on the world, whether it be through, for example, Gearoid Ó Tuathail's "Critical Geopolitics" (Ó Tuathail, 1996; see also the special issue of *Environment and Planning D: Society and Space*, 1994), or McKenzie Wark's "Virtual Geography" (Wark, 1994) among others. This emerging trans—or post—disciplinary genre (Soja, 1989; Pickles, 1985; Rose, 1993; Agnew and Corbridge, 1995; Darby, 1997; Shapiro, 1997; Shapiro and Alker, 1996) of recentring discursive constructions and obliterations of local landscape, identity, and meaning in understanding world politics, owes explicit debts to Said's "imagining place" as central to both imperialist and resistance discourses (Said, 1995a). We would also do well in this context, and that of the limited nature of *Boundaries in Question*, to reflect upon Partha Chatterjee's critical question of Benedict Anderson's "Imagined Communities"—whose imagination? (Chatterjee, 1993, 3–13). Defending "Us-them" does not give expression to the world.

The third consequence of what it means for IR to be a discipline, and a predominantly American one, is that the heterogeneity of American foreign policy is taken to exhaust all possible, or at least "rational," "normal" or "realistic," avenues of inquiry about the world and how best to proceed in it. A cursory examination of the debates that fill the pages of *Foreign Affairs* illustrates how the centrality of American foreign policy is framed, and how others ought to proceed with American foreign policy interests in mind. By refracting the world through the lens of American foreign policy interests, *we* "are subjected to the production of truth through power and we cannot exercise power except through the production of truth" (Foucault, 1980, 93).

Perhaps readers of *Foreign Affairs* are unaware that boundaries are under challenge, and that theoretical life beyond "neorealism" and "neoliberalism" is both alive, vibrant, and informative (see, for example, Baldwin, 1993; Kegley, 1995). Similarly, perhaps they are unaware that questions affecting global politics are not exhausted by the choice between Paul Kennedy's "Decline of America" or Joe Nye's "Bound to Lead." As we have argued elsewhere, despite much heat and noise these debates occur within a common framework that function not to destroy it but most often to identify how best to protect and enhance it. Thus, the "neo-realist wolf in neo-liberal sheep's clothing is reformist, but is not about to challenge the current order" (Sullivan, 1996). Despite their differences, Robert Keohane saw his task as unifying neoliberalism with the neorealism of Kenneth Waltz. Keohane accepted "Waltz's emphasis on system level theory and his acceptance of the rationality assumption as starting points for theory," but added that neorealism could be "improved upon." This was a matter of incorporating "Waltz's notion of structure" not rejecting it outright (Keohane, 1986, 17–18). While we recognize that this had lead to a confusing proliferation of prefixes within the American discipline, and has contributed to its heterogeneous nature, it is also evident that such debates are largely variations around a state-centric, power-politics—for example, variations on an essentially realist theme.

Realist theory and its variations thus continue to inform the conceptual parameters of how we have imagined the world even in the post–Cold War era. However, debate and controversy have arisen within this framework. The work of Huntington, for example, on the surface appears to mark a radical break from IR because of its emphasis on the importance of "culture" in world politics, and because it promises to move us beyond the fatuous celebration of the "end of history" celebrated in the writings of Fukuyama. Through an analysis of how Said challenges us to "reimagine" the world we conclude that the "debate" between Huntington and Fukuyama is, however, a chimera. Both are committed to a Western discourse on the world, simply varying the imagined implications of their discursive constructions for America's defense of the West after the Cold War. Huntington's "culture" is simply a Western stereotype which re-empowers orientalism.

INVENTING ENEMIES: THE CLASH OF CIVILIZATIONS AND THE NEW ORIENTALISM

The end of the Cold War raised hopes for a "New World Order"—a new sense of history. For international relations it signaled the end of a bipolar era and a period of assessment and critique. In the United States, however, even before the anticipated "peace dividend" began disappearing into the oil fields of the Persian Gulf (Campbell, 1993), Western political discourse was mobilized (no pun intended) in order to reposition Western interests. This occurred in two different, but related, ways: (1) the celebration of "the end of history" and the associated "triumphialism" in the wake of the collapse of the Communist bloc; and (2) the emergence of a discourse that sought to reinvent an enemy by focusing on the threat from "other" civilizations. As Campbell argues, while "the objects of established post-1945 strategies of otherness may no longer be plausible candidates for enmity, their transformation has not by itself altered the entailments of identity which they satisfied" (Campbell, 1992, 195).

There is no simple cause and effect relationship between the end of the Cold War and the emergence of these two particular American concerns. Nevertheless, the displacement of Cold War rhetoric is a convenient way to highlight what is at stake in the post–Cold War era.

Although the positions staked out by Fukuyama and Huntington appear to be diametrically opposed, they nonetheless share common ground with realism in IR, which invariably plays the role of soothsayer when the world appears uncertain or threatening. Realism offers a chance to predict the future and protect American interests (see Gaddis, 1992/93, 5–58). But Huntington is no more describing a real world than imagining a threat, in which the category "civilization" replaces the privileged role reserved previously for (communist) states. The realist game does not alter. He simply redraws the "world" map.[3]

Huntington's "clash of civilizations" is a discourse that seeks to invent an "other." In this context, it is possible to draw on Said's pioneering work *Orientalism* (Said, 1979), a study of how Western academia has represented the Orient over the last two centuries. Said establishes that the modern discipline of Oriental studies is indebted to traditional representations of the Orient (especially the Middle East) that were forged in the Occident (historically Western Europe but now inclusive of the United States). By examining Orientalism as a discourse, Said is able to argue that Western academia is responsible for the creation of the "other," the Orientals, who are significantly different from those in the Occident. Through this process, IR "Orientalizes" different regions and places, expunging local meaning and identity. IR also plays on imaginative fears, investing the "other" with exotic differences that are threatening to our "normal" way of life.

Orientalism, in short, is a Eurocentric discourse that constructs the "Orient" by the accumulated knowledge of generations of scholars and writers who are secure in the power of their "superior" wisdom. The charge that Said makes about Orientalist discourse applies equally as well to the American discipline of IR, since it too has tended to treat non-Western societies as "alien" entities, and revolves around a central juxtaposition of "us" and "them" (in which knowledge about "them" is accumulated and reported by "us"). This juxtaposition, central to Said's critique, is instructive when we examine the manner in which Huntington has chosen to characterize and represent civilizations.

The need to reinvent an "enemy" highlights the importance of the "other" in American discourse. Huntington's intervention needs to be seen as an attempt, first, to reimagine America and the world after the Cold War and, second, to recenter American foreign policy in the discipline of IR. Hence, it should not be too surprising that Huntington and his colleagues feel that it is time to act before "other" cultures identify their place in history—before the Subaltern speaks and *Imaginary Maps* decolonize our minds (Spivak, 1996, 276–286).

The urgency of Huntington's warning about the "other" to scholars and policy-makers was directed as a corrective to Fukuyama. But neither dispute that the end of the Cold War was a "triumph" for Western interests and values as defined by IR. For Fukuyama, the triumph of Western economic and political liberalism has seen off all challenges. He denies the "other" a chance to regain its histories by pronouncing history at an end. What does not come to an end here, however, is IR's representation of the "other" in the West's history.

Fukuyama's faith in the West is shared by Huntington who is simply more cautious about the world America "ought" to be imagining. In his critique of "the end of history" thesis, Huntington asserts: "To hope for the benign end of history is human. To expect it to happen is unrealistic. To plan on it happening is disastrous" (Huntington, 1996a, 32). This is simply to say to Fukuyama that, though you are wrong because more work than you envisage needs to be done, *our* frame for viewing the world remains unaltered.

Unlike IR, which treats the positions of Huntington and Fukuyama as highlighting the theoretical richness and openness of Western debate, for us both transpose the same American disciplinary worldview into claims about the unique, universal nature of the Western imagination. Despite their differing conclusions about the "other," the "debate" between them highlights the closed, limited nature of IR.

For Huntington, then, the end of the Cold War represented an opportunity to create a "new" global order that addresses problems of American national security by continuing to marginalize the "other." The invention of a new enemy, a new "other," is epitomized in Huntington's vision of the future, where the "clash of civilizations will dominate global politics." In his role as soothsayer, he predicts that "conflict between civilizations will be the latest phase in the evolution of conflict in the modern world" (Huntington, 1996a, 32). Huntington's argument is that until the end of the Cold War conflict was predominantly *within* Western civilization. In the post–Cold War period, however, conflict "moves out of its Western phase. Its centerpiece is interaction *between* the West and non-Western civilizations and among non-Western civilizations" (emphasis added, Huntington, 1996a, 24).

Huntington's hypothesis is based on five propositions (Huntington, 1996a, 25–27):

1. There are basic differences between civilizations.
2. The world is becoming smaller and as people interact more with each other, their sense of identification with particular civilizations is heightened.
3. As a result of global economic and political changes, people identify less with the nation state—consequently, the vacuum that is created is filled by religion.

4. The West at the peak of its power not only enhances civilizational identification, but also fosters a "return to our roots phenomenon" among non-Western civilizations.

5. Civilizational differences are difficult to reconcile and, consequently, override political and economic factors.

The implication of identifying with civilizational aspects such as "religion" and "ethnicity" is that people are apt "to see an 'us' versus 'them' relation existing between themselves and people of different ethnicity and religion" (Huntington, 1996a, 29).

In raising the possibility of such threats to "us," Huntington remains true to the modernization school of comparative politics and its unilinear view of history. Imperialism and the ravages of colonization are not confronted. This is precisely what Said sees as central to international relations when he reveals the interplay between culture and imperialism. In Jane Austin's *Mansfield Park* (1814), for example, the health of the Bertram estate in Antingua is central to that of Mansfield Park, yet the estate is only in the background, never central to the novel. It is "both incidental, referred to only in passing, and absolutely crucial to the action" (Said, 1993, 106). Through such embodiment in the novel, the study of which is central to postcolonialism, indigenous peoples are subsumed by the pervasiveness of European culture (see, for example, Ashcroft, Griffiths and Tiffen, 1989; Tiffen and Lawson, 1994; Azim, 1993). The "other" non-Western is rendered simply irrelevant, while resistance to imperialism and colonialism is rendered a threat to Western civilization (Kiberd, 1995).

The place of the "novel" in the dominance of Western culture, as described by Said, expresses the way legitimate interactions between individuals and communities in world politics are established and described discursively in IR. Despite "Western" culture permeating virtually all parts of the globe, there is a refusal to recognize the effects of global capitalism and cultural imperialism on the identity of the "other." Resistance to globalization is seen as confirmation of the enemy. There is little attempt to understand the "civilization," if such a concept has any validity, as a product of the interactions between different societies. As Fouad Ajami argues, "in making itself over the centuries, the West helped make the others as well" (Ajami, 1993, 3). The "other" also made the West. Hence, when Huntington speaks of an African civilization, it immediately conjures up images that are textually created. These creations are reinforced further by global communications and media events. Said, for example, notes that "one aspect of the electronic, postmodern world is that there has been a reinforcement of the stereotypes by which the Orient is viewed" (quoted in Wark,

1994, 26). The myth of the "dark continent" takes on real meaning.

Huntington's observation that politics around the globe is changing and non-Western civilizations, or the peoples and places he labels as such, are becoming actors, rather than objects of history, is accurate. However, this change is more about the manner in which the world is *perceived* by IR. First, history and the world are not merely European and North American. *All* other locations have vibrant and dynamic histories. Second, modernity is a legacy of the "West." It has penetrated virtually every corner of the globe. This means that the "West" and the "rest" are mutually constitutive. They come into existence in our discourses only through their interactions. The "rest" object to the "West," not merely because of the lasting legacy of imperialism and colonization, but also because of the "West's" chauvinistic exertion of hegemonic power.

More fundamentally, we might object to the concept of "civilizations" which is also fraught with difficulties. In this case, the mere substitution of "civilization" for "nation-state" does not solve the deeper problems endemic to international relations. The root of the problem lies in a discourse that has to play the role of soothsayer because of its dependence on the notion of the "other." For too long, IR has privileged a Eurocentric worldview and thus, by default, the division of human kind via either "nation-states" or more recently "civilizations." Thus, the charge that Said levels against anthropology applies equally to IR. For Said, the discipline of anthropology "can continue on one side of the imperial divide, there to remain as a partner in domination and hegemony" (Said, 1989, 225), or in the case of American IR, it can start to break out of the tyranny of its discursive structures and embrace the richness and diversity of local and global outlooks. To seek salvation among the "clash of civilizations" is not the answer. American IR needs to move beyond the disciplinary boundaries and end the process of policing its intellectual frontiers. Moving beyond boundaries, occupying in-between spaces, and escaping from the straitjacket of imposed identities are major themes of Said's work that, if addressed, promise to re-invent and reimagine the world in more fruitful and meaningful ways. These themes offer IR much to mine, and are exemplified in Said's *Representations of the Intellectual.*

REPRESENTATIONS OF THE
INTELLECTUAL AND THE "WORLD"

The 1993 Reith Lectures, *Representations of the Intellectual,* are a continuum of themes that have preoccupied Said since *Orientalism*: authorial creativity, the manner in which the Orient has been represented by the Occident, and questions about the role of the intellectual. And while the Reith Lectures are concerned with questions of how the "other" is represented and the nexus between power and knowledge, at the heart of his project is the responsibility of the intellectual. They also reflect Said's own position, location, and identity. Importantly, Said demonstrates how the politics of location and identity provide insight into how the world is imagined differently by each individual. This problematizes the manner, and disrupts the assurity, by which IR sees the "world." In doing so, Said seeks to demonstrate how the personal is political. In this context, the overarching theme of the lectures is "the public role of the intellectual as outsider, 'amateur, ' and disturber of the status quo" (Said, 1994a, x). This is Said's attempt, by example, of trying to speak the truth to power (Said, 1994a, xiv).

Said's identification with organic intellectuals in a Gramscian sense is clear when we look at the distinction he makes between the potentate and the traveler in his writing on the role of the academic. Said urges intellectuals to adopt the identity of the traveler because they "suspend the claim of customary routine in order to live in new rhythms and rituals." Unlike the potentate "who must guard only one place and defend its frontiers, the traveler crosses over, traverses territory, and abandons fixed positions, all the time" (Said, 1991, 18). The identity and location of each intellectual means that they need to be contextualized within their own cultural specificity. At the same time, globalization has important implications for the individual intellectual who seems to embody more "than strictly local application" (Said, 1994a, 20).

There remains, however, the thorny question of nationality and nationalism. Said again reminds us of the prevailing bias of Western academics who "speak reductively and . . . irresponsibly of something called 'Islam'" (Said, 1994a, 23). These representations are repeated in order to maintain national identity. He argues that the creation of the "other" consolidates "our" identity as "beleaguered and at risk" (Said, 1994a, 24). The questions that most concern Said are as follows:

> Does the fact of nationality commit the individual intellectual, who is for my purposes here the center of attention, to the public mood for reasons of solidarity, primordial loyalty, or national patriotism? Or can a better case be made for the intellectual as a dissenter from the corporate ensemble? (Said, 1994a, 24)

The short answer for Said is "never solidarity before criticism." It is here that one has to be the outsider, the amateur, and disturber. The intellectual makes political choices to follow the difficult path. The modern intellectual's role, then, is to disrupt prevailing norms because "dominant norms are today so intimately connected . . . to the nation, which is always triumphalist, always in a position of authority, always exacting loyalty and subservience rather than intellectual investigation and reexamination" (Said, 1994a, 27).

The question of exile has long preoccupied Said. He captures its fate in perhaps his most insightful lecture, "Intellectual Exile: Expatriates and Marginals." Exile is like the "mind of winter."[4] It embodies notions of "decentering," "dislocation," and "displacement." While the idea of the exile seems to enjoy an exalted status in the West, Said is well aware that, in the late twentieth century, it is also "a cruel punishment of whole communities and peoples, often the inadvertent result of impersonal forces such as war, famine and disease" (Said, 1994a, 35). His concern is with largely unaccommodated exiles, like the Palestinians, "whose presence complicates the presumed homogeneity of the new societies in which they live" (Said, 1994a, 36).

Said focuses on the exilic intellectual who is unwilling to make adjustments as an outsider, "unaccommodated, un-coopted and resistant" (Said, 1994a, 36). This allows him to argue that exile is not only an *actual*, but also a *metaphoric*, condition. It is, for intellectuals in such a state, unsettling with little chance of ever being at home. Said urges the intellectual to push boundaries and reconcile identity with recognition of the other. He points out that, despite a proliferation of the liberal rhetoric of equality and justice, injustices continue to proliferate and intensify in various parts of the globe. The task for the intellectual is to bring one's reconciliation with the other to "bear on actual situations" (Said, 1994a, 71). In Said's own case, his consistent campaigning on behalf of the Palestinian peoples and his calls for peace did not preclude him from speaking out against the Oslo peace accord at a time when there was considerable euphoria (Said, 1994b). He continues to play the difficult public intellectual role of defender of a cause and critic of a process that falls short of a solution (Said, 1995b). It is this role and responsibility of the intellectual that the IR scholar needs to emulate. For too long, they have operated from within the confines of the hegemonic discipline. For those who have tried to break out, as in the case of the "Third Debate," constraints remain as we have argued above. The task is to adopt a position on the margins, to consider and reimagine another world, to speak truth to power.

CONCLUSION

The discipline of IR has been accepted over time as part of American social science, and its legitimacy stems from its alleged ability to speak authoritatvely on questions of American foreign policy and interests. In order to gain legitimacy, the discipline has drawn boundaries and conflated particular American interests with supposed "universal values." In this essay, we have examined the manner in which, since the Cold War, a certain conception of the world has been constructed in the discourse on the "clash of civilizations." It highlights the manner in which worldviews in the American discipline of IR are constructed and policed. By way of contrast, the work of Edward Said problematizes IR. He breaks down the tyranny of structures and disciplinary boundaries that deploy exclusionary discursive practices. By examining such practices, it is easy to see why American IR remains entrapped in a type of Orientalist discourse.

What, then, is the solution? How can we avoid the traps of the kind of scholarship that Said exposes in his work? How can the discipline of IR aspire to such ideals? Here the notion of "worldliness" may be construed as the beginning of a solution to the problem. According to Said, texts are "worldly" in that they adopt a circumstantial setting that requires contexts. This places them within the public domain where they are open to interpretation (see Said, 1983). Said describes worldliness as the un- —or non- —neglect of other ideologies and experiences. He argues that it is predominantly a twentieth century phenomenon that requires the existence of an emerging global community. However, worldliness is more than physical accessibility to global communication vectors. It is the ability to communicate on an intersectional plane after the dismantlement of imagined geographical barriers. Said's notion of worldliness implies an awareness of the effects that researchers and their knowledge have on the subjects of their study.

It is here that postcolonial theory, which has grown out of the pioneering work of Said, may well prove poignantly instructive for the American discipline of IR. As Gyan Prakash argues:

> Based on the belief that we do not have the option of saying no to the determinate conditions of history—capitalist modernity, discourses of liberty, citizenship, individual rights, nation-state—postcolonial criticism attempts to identify in the displaced historical functioning in these discourses the basis for other articulations. . . . [I]t directs attention to those relocations of dominant discourses that emerge from elsewhere— not from the space of the nation state . . . but from contingent, contentious, and heterogeneous subaltern positions. (Prakash, 1996, 201)

It deploys, in other words, a discursive approach that seeks to disrupt traditional academic boundaries. It is through such an approach that the processes of globalization and hybridity that are ignored by American IR can be understood and appreciated. We are thus left to conclude with Said that "a faltering and outdated concept of a single national identity lords it over the true variety of human life. . . . A single overmastering identity at the core . . . whether Western, African or Asian is a confinement, a deprivation" (Said, 1991, 11).

NOTES

1. Critical debates surrounding Said's work figure prominently in and across a number of disciplines—indeed, in most places except International Relations! For an excellent recent discussion, see Kasbarian, Young, Ahmed, Ahluwalia and Ashcroft (Kasbarian, 1996; Young, 1990; Ahmed, 1993; Ahluwalia and Ashcroft, 1999).

2. On "ethics" in IR, see Mervyn Frost (Frost, 1996). For a different approach to the question of ethics, see the work by Daniel Warner and Jim George (Warner, 1996; George, 1995).

3. This point, however, does not discount Fouad Ajami's point that "civilizations do not control states, states control civilizations." See Fouad Ajami (1993). See also Ahluwalia and Mayer (1994).

4. The phrase "mind of winter," Said points out, is one used by Wallace Stevens. See Edward Said, "The Mind of Winter: Reflections on Life in Exile," *Harpers*, no. 269, p. 49.

REFERENCES

Agnew, J., and S. Corbridge. (1995). *Mastering Space: Hegemony, Territory and International Political Economy.* London and New York: Routledge.

Ahluwalia, P., and B. Ashcroft. (1999). *Edward Said: The Paradox of Identity.* London: Routledge.

Ahluwalia, P., and P. Mayer. (1994). "Clash of Civilizations or Balderdash of Scholars?" *Asian Studies Review* 18(1), 21–30.

Ahmed, A. (1993). *In Theory: Classes, Nations, Literature.* London: Verso.

Ajami, F. (1993). "The Summoning." *Foreign Affairs* 72(4), 2–9.

Ashcroft, B., G. Griffiths, and H. Tiffen. (1989). *The Empire Writes Back: Theory and Practice in Post-Colonial Literatures.* London and New York: Routledge.

Ashcroft, B., G. Griffiths, and H. Tiffen. (1995). *The Post-Colonial Studies Reader.* London: Routledge.

Azim, F. (1993). *The Colonial Rise of the Novel.* London and New York: Routledge.

Baldwin, David (ed.). (1993). *Neorealism and Neoliberalism: The Contemporary Debate.* New York: Columbia University Press.

Campbell, David. (1992). *Writing Security.* Manchester, U.K.: Manchester University Press.

Campbell, David. (1993). *Politics without Principle: Sovereignty, Ethics, and the Narratives of the Gulf War.* Boulder, Colo.: Lynne Reinner.

Campbell, David. (1996). "The Politics of Radical Interdependence: A Rejoinder to Daniel Warner." *Millennium* 25(1), 111–128.

Campbell, David, and M. Dillon. (1993). "The End of Philosophy and the End of International Relations." In David Campbell and M. Dillon (eds.), *The Political Subject of Violence*, Manchester, U.K.: Manchester University Press: 1–47.

Chatterjee, P. (1993). *The Nation and its Fragments: Colonial and Post-colonial Histories*. Princeton: Princeton University Press.

Childs, P., and P. Williams. (1997). *An Introduction to Post-Colonial Theory*. London: Prentice Hall.

"Critical Geopolitics: Unfolding Spaces For Thought in Geography and Global Politics." (1994). *Environment and Planning D: Society and Space* 4(5) (Special Issue).

Darby, D. (ed.). (1997). *At the Edge of International Relations: Post-colonialism, Gender and Dependency*. London and New York: Pinter.

Foucault, Michel. (1980). *Power/Knowledge: Selected Interviews and Other Writings 1972–77*. London: Harvester Press.

Frost, Mervyn. (1996). *Ethics in International Relations: A Constitutive Theory*. Cambridge: Cambridge University Press.

Fukuyama, Francis. (1992). *The End of History and the Last Man*. London: Hamish Hamilton.

Gaddis, John Lewis. (1992/93). "International Relations Theory and the End of the Cold War." *International Security* 17(3), 5–58.

George, Jim. (1994). *Discourses of Global Politics: A Critical (Re)Introduction to International Relations*. Boulder, Colo.: Lynne Rienner.

George, Jim. (1995). "Realist 'Ethics, ' International Relations and postmodernism: Thinking Beyond the Egoism-Anarchy Thematic." *Millennium* 24(2), 195–223.

Hollis, Martin, and Steve Smith. (1991). *Explaining and Understanding International Relations*. Oxford: Clarendon Press.

Huntington, Samuel P. (1993). "The Clash of Civilizations?" *Foreign Affairs* (Summer): 22–49.

Huntington, Samuel P. (1996a) "The West Unique, Not Universal." *Foreign Affairs* (November/December), 28–46

Huntington, Samuel P. (1996b). *The Clash of Civilizations and the Remaking of World Order*. New York: Simon & Schuster.

Kasbarian, J. A. (1996). "Mapping Edward Said: Geography, Identity, and the Politics of Location." *Environment and Planning D: Society and Space* 14(5), 529–557.

Kegley Jr., Charles W. (ed.). (1995). *Controversies in International Relations Theory: Realism and the Neoliberal Challenge*. New York: St. Martin's Press.

Keohane, Robert O. (ed.). (1986). *Neorealism and Its Critics*. New York: Columbia University Press.

Kiberd, D. (1995). *Inventing Ireland: The Literature of the Modern Nation*. London: Random House.

Macmillan, J., and A. Linklater. (1995). "Introduction: Boundaries in Question." In J. Macmillan and A. Linklater (eds.), *Boundaries in Question: New Directions in International Relations*. London and New York: Pinter.

Neufeld, Mark. (1995). *The Restructuring of International Relations Theory.* Cambridge: Cambridge University Press.

Ó Tuathail, G. (1996). *Critical Geopolitics.* Minneapolis: University of Minnesota Press.

Pickles, J. (1985). *Phenomenology, Science and Geography: Spatiality and the Human Sciences.* Cambridge: Cambridge University Press.

Prakash, G. (1996). "Who's Afraid of Postcoloniality?" *Social Text 14*(4)< 187–203.

Rengger, Nicholas J. (1995). *Political Theory, Modernity and Postmodernity.* Oxford: Blackwell Publishers.

Rose, G. (1993). *Feminism and Geography: The Limits of Geographical Knowledge.* Cambridge: Polity Press.

Rosenberg, J. (1994). *The Empire of Civil Society: A Critique of the Realist Theory of International Relations.* London: Verso.

Said, Edward. (1979). *Orientalism.* New York: Vintage Books.

Said, Edward. (1983). *The World the Text and the Critic.* Cambridge, Mass.: Harvard University Press.

Said, Edward. (1989). "Representing the Colonized: Anthropology's Interlocutors." *Critical Inquiry 15* (Winter), 205–225.

Said, Edward. (1991). "Identity, Authority, and Freedom: The Potentate and the Traveler." *Transition 54.*

Said, Edward. (1993). *Culture and Imperialism.* London: Chatto and Windus.

Said, Edward. (1994a). *Representations of the Intellectual.* London: Vintage.

Said, Edward. (1994b). *The Politics of Dispossession: The Struggle for Palestinian Self-Determination, 1969–1994.* London: Chatto and Windus.

Said, Edward. (1995a). "Secular Interpretation, the Geographical Element, and the Methodology of Imperialism." In G. Prakash (ed.), *After Colonialism: Imperial Histories and Postcolonial Displacements.* Princeton: Princeton University Press, 21–39.

Said, Edward. (1995b). *Peace and Its Discontents: Gaza–Jericho 1993–1995.* London: Vintage.

Shapiro, Michael. (1997). *Violent Cartographies: Mapping Cultures of War.* Minneapolis: University of Minnesota Press.

Shapiro, Michael, and Hayward Alker (eds.). (1996). *Challenging Boundaries: Global Flows, Territorial Identities.* Minneapolis: University of Minnesota Press.

Smith, Steve. (1995). "The Self-Images of a Discipline: A Genealogy of International Relations Theory." In Ken Booth and Steve Smith (eds.), *International Relations Theory Today.* Cambridge: Polity Press, 1–37.

Soja, E. (1989). *Postmodern Geographies: The Reassertion of Space in Critical Social Theory.* London, New York: Verso.

Spivak, G. (1996). "Explaining and Culture: Marginalia (1979)." In D. Landry and G. Maclean (eds.), *Selected Works of Gayatri Chakravorty Spivak.* New York and London: Routledge, 29–52.

Sullivan, Michael. (1996). "Australia's Regional Peacekeeping Discourse: Policing the Asia-Pacific." In G. Cheesman and R. Bruce (eds.), *Discourses of Danger and Dread Frontiers.* St. Leonards, Australia: Allen and Unwin, 221–222.

Tiffin, C., and A. Lawson (eds.). (1994). *De-Scribing Empire*. London and New York: Routledge.

Walker, R. B. T. (1993). *Inside/Outside: International Relations as Political Theory*. Cambridge: Cambridge University Press.

Wark, M. (1994). *Virtual Geography*. Bloomington: Indiana University Press.

Warner, D. (1996). "Levinas, Buber and the Concept of Otherness in International Relations: A Reply to David Campbell." *Millennium* 25(1), 129–141.

Young, R. (1990). *White Mythologies: Writing History and the West*. London: Routledge.

CONCLUSION

International Relations: An International Discipline?

D. S. L. Jarvis

In bygone eras it was not unusual for scholars to travel from the "periphery" to the "core" to peruse the repositories of knowledge and undertake their academic apprenticeships. Academic channels of communication tended to rotate around a few imperial enclaves that acted as the epicenters of knowledge production and the educational training grounds for the colonized, acculturating them into the ways of the imperial power. British hegemony, for example, was accompanied by educational imperialism that saw elites from colonized countries transplanted into the lecture halls of Oxford and Cambridge to receive a "formal" education in subjects defined by the history, culture, and imperial interests of the British Empire. Intellectual hegemony in this context was overt, albeit disguised as a benign liberalism promoting the pursuit of truth and bringing knowledge to those otherwise thought bereft of it. The publishing industry too tended to be highly concentrated, coalesced around a few centers reflecting the costs of printing and the highly concentrated markets for these products. Knowledge production and consumption was an elite activity, confined to a few privileged institutions and exported to the far-flung corners of empire. Much of this reflected the limited means of communication and the impediments to travel, making for a concentration of intellectual activity in centers where ideas could be freely exchanged, critically examined, and tested. So too was it a reflection of the absolute power of the hegemon, power that manifested itself not just in military and economic affairs, but in the ability to sanction the production of certain types of knowledge whose subject categories were often functional to the extension or legitimization of the hegemon's interests.

Much, of course, has changed since the days of European imperialism and British hegemony. Not least has been the reaction against imperial orders and the emergence of a postcolonial sensibility, celebrating the hitherto expunged indigenous knowledges and subjects of inquiry that now blossom in university curricula throughout the world and that appear to displace the "core-periphery" relationship so indicative of academic apprenticeships in the past. More generally, many if not most of the structural conditions that made for the imperial concentration of knowledge production have evaporated. Real-time data communications links, email and the Internet, as well as telecommunications have all contributed to an information explosion, allowing for the cost-effective transmission of data and knowledge in ways that only a decade ago would have seemed fanciful. Ease of communication and information retrieval, especially through the increasing availability of full-text delivery systems of a vast array of scholarly publications appear indicative of a kind of intellectual diaspora. External influences beyond the confines of discreetly defined national scholarly communities would appear to be the order of the day, obviating the ability of anyone national or hegemonic interest to dictate the parameters of intellectual inquiry. Few can now avoid the "international," "global," or "transnationalized" milieu that informs our political and social consciousness. Parochialism, it might reasonably be assumed, is an endangered trait, banished to the margins as things "global" subsume the "national" not only in terms of the production of goods and services, trade, travel, and communications, but intellectual inquiry too.

It seems reasonable to assume that International Relations (IR), a discipline concerned with events and processes that occur between national borders, must thus itself be undergoing some degree of internationalization in terms of the locus of those who produce and consume knowledge? And this, we might also expect, portends to a diversification in our political and social acumen as revolutions in communications and "globalization" make us less parochial, less bordered geographically and culturally, and less defined by the cultural proclivities and interests of any one great power. The intercultural transmission of ideas and values, mass intercontinental migration, and the mass transmission of intercultural taste preferences through food, music, and fashion, all appear to be on the increase and resulting in a kind of intercultural fusion. So too, the sheer growth in the number of universities and IR departments around the world, the burgeoning expansion of the international conference circuit precipitated by the declining costs of international travel, and the absolute increase in the number of individuals who now count themselves as students of international politics, must surely be disingenuous to the idea of American intellectual hegemony in IR? All these developments, and there are many more, suggest increasing diversity, the cross-national/cross-cultural production and fertilization of ideas, theories, methods, and epistemologies used in the study of international relations. On this interpretation, diversity should thus be on the rise, and hegemony, at least in the crude sense of the geographic concentration of persons who do IR, should be declining. Borders everywhere are "tumbling down," so why not those of abstracted "national" scholarly communities traditionally bordered by the tyranny of distance and that often conspired for an inward, parochial focus?

RECENT HISTORY

Recent disciplinary history, unfortunately, does not support this interpretation. In 1977 Stanley Hoffmann (Hoffmann, this volume) infamously described IR as "An American Social Science," while Kalevi J. Holsti some years later in 1985 reported much the same when he identified "a British-American intellectual condominium." Hierarchy, he noted, seemed to be a "hallmark of international politics and theory," with only two countries out of the 155 surveyed producing the overwhelming "mutually acknowledged literature" in the field (Holsti, 1985, 102–103). For Holsti, the patterns of international exchange of scholarly knowledge remained "far from an ideal model of an international community of scholars, and that over time parochialism in reading habits, publication for national audiences, and mutual [intranational] reference" was increasing (Holsti, 1985, 148). International Relations as a professional activity appeared to be bucking trends apparent elsewhere in the social, political, and economic world, turning increasingly inward as everything else turned outward. But has much changed since Hoffmann and Holsti made these observations? One would expect so judging from the tumultuous changes in communications technologies, and the dramatic changes in the global political landscape in the last decade alone: the fall of the Berlin Wall, the end of the Soviet Empire and with it the Cold War, bipolarity, and the fear of nuclear annihilation. Change is emblematic of what we study, so why not also of how we study it, and of who studies it? Things must surely be different now?

HEGEMONY OR DIVERSITY?

Seemingly so simple a set of questions as those posed above generate contradictory responses as witnessed by the contributors to this volume. Part of this might be explained by the fact that "hegemony" and "diversity" are interpreted differently depending on what one counts as the currency specific to these categories. Holsti, for example, used national prefix and mutual reference as a medium to assess diversity much like Hoffmann who explained the growth of the discipline as a function of American hegemonic interests. Both saw a diminution in "diversity" as so defined.

The conclusions reached in this volume, however, tend to be more disparate. On one measure, for instance, "diversity" might be assessed to be on the rise if by diversity we mean the breakdown in the three-centuries-long intellectual consensus which has traditionally organized "philosophical speculation, guided empirical research, and provided at least hypothetical answers to the critical questions about international politics" (Holsti, 1985, 1). As the essays in this volume suggest, diversity is all about us, whether characterized by the "interparadigm debate," or simply by observations of the expanding number of research projects, methodologies, and epistemologies now endemic to the discipline. Realism and positivist-based epistemologies no longer dominate the field to the exclusion of other approaches. Students may now select from a veritable panoply of competing theoretical and epistemological frameworks to guide them in their research. In this volume alone, Jan Jindy Pettman suggests the centrality of feminist and gendered perspectives for understanding global political relations, James Richardson of the methods contained in historical sociology, Roger Spegele of the need to return to the fold of political theory and mine classical realism for its insights, and Roger Epp of the utility of indigenous vistas, specifically those that deconstruct the culturally specific European diplomatic discourses adopted unproblematically as the universal subterfuge of our disciplinary history. Indeed, the extent of methodological diversity, or the umbrage of what has previously been characterized as the "dividing discipline," is demonstrated by the now strident reactions that it generates. D. S. L. Jarvis and Kalevi J. Holsti both fear what they perceive as the decentering of the discipline, and are perturbed at the loss of disciplinary focus, purpose, and a corpus of concrete method. Both are reacting to the advent of the "Third Great Debate" that has allegorized the numerous methodological ruptures now evident in the discipline as theorists are urged to explore post-positivist, postrationalist, and postmodernist formulations. On this measure, then, we might assume diversity the very life blood of our professional activities, and the unitary rigidity of a predominately positivist discipline something long since gone.

Such an interpretation, however, would be only half-true. The promotion of, and resistance to, methodological diversity itself reflects the predominance of a singular epistemological motif—positivism. Despite the increasing array of formulations advanced to challenge this, positivist-rationalist-empirical approaches still tend to predominate. A perusal of the pages of the discipline's leading journals, for example—measured in terms of circulation—(*International Organization, International Studies Quarterly, International Security, World Politics*, etc.—all

American journals incidentally), display an affinity for methodological conformity evidenced by how few articles feel the need to even problematize the issue of method or epistemology. Most telling of all, though, is that the would-be challengers to positivist-rationalist–based epistemologies derive almost universally from non-American pedigrees. British, European, Canadian, and Australian theorists have been the originators and driving force of most of these alternative perspectives, only subsequently adopted by American theorists—if at all. Poststructural and postmodern innovations, for example, have emanated typically from French theorists (Foucault, Derrida, Baudrillard) and then been imported by theorists like R. B. J. Walker (Canadian), Richard Ashley (American), and promulgated predominately by non-Americans like Steve Smith (British), Jim George (Australian), Mark Neufeld (Canadian), and David Campbell (Australian). Most, if not all, of these discourses arose as a reaction against the positivist-realist nexus prevalent throughout the discipline, and attempt to explore metatheoretical avenues beyond an explicitly American understanding of purpose, theory, and method in IR. Similarly, critical theoretic perspectives have typically entered the discipline from outside America through theorists like Robert Cox and Stephen Gill (Canadian), Andrew Linklater (Australian-British), Roger Tooze (British), and Mark Hoffman (British). All tend to explore a variant of neo-marxist theory, especially Gramscian method historically marginalized in "American IR." Even the current proclivity for historical sociological and constructivist approaches has a European pedigree, especially in British social theorists like Anthony Giddens' and his pioneering work on structuration theory, and before him in the pivotal writings of Max Weber (German), both of which provided the cornerstone for a British-German condominium prior to its importation in the United States. Functionalist and neofunctionalist theory too is more properly associated with European theorists, in the first instance with the writings of David Mitrany (French), and subsequently with Ernst Haas, a European émigré to the United States.

While by no means a comprehensive survey of the field, what these few examples illustrate is a tendency toward external assault of a national-American-intellectual edifice seen by those from the "outside" as the preponderant power in the production of knowledge, theory, and method. Measured in the context of the geographic locals from which these alternative approaches have been generated, diversity might thus appear to be increasing, but measured in the context of the geographic local of the knowledge system(s) these alternative approaches are attempting to displace, hegemony appears preponderant, if not reminiscent of a core-periphery type relationship many might have assumed long since vanished.

For those of us on the "outside looking in" there is, of course, no great mystery to this parable. The United States remains the sole uncontested hegemon at the close of the twentieth century, indeed its hegemonic status ensured well into the first half of the twenty-first century. It alone accounts for one-quarter of global gross national product, remains the preeminent military power, consumes a disproportionate amount of global resources relative to population size, is pivotal in controlling the global financial architecture not least through the influence it exerts on global currencies referenced against the greenback, controls the vast proportion of the world's patents and patented technologies, supplies most of the world's leading software applications for business and commerce, dominates the world's pharmaceutical industry, is the leading producer of military technology, commercial aircraft, and heavy machinery, and is paramount in orchestrating a global liberal trade regime. Why, then, should we assume the contrary true of knowledge production in the social sciences and humanities? As much as the communications revolution has been touted as a diffusionist mechanism, in reality it might be just as facilitative of greater wealth, power, and knowledge concentration. And, arguably, this is what Hoffmann and Holsti each recognized, and what we here must again observe at the close of the millennium.

While, then, in the strict sense of the word it might be inappropriate to hark back to an imperial model of tutelage and agenda setting, it remains the case that the United States commands influence beyond what is often acknowledged. Most of us who "do IR," for example, tend to have been acculturated to its ways, methods, and theories in one of the hegemonic (teaching) centers, the United States or the United Kingdom. The spatial dimensions of IR in this sense do appear to comprise only a few, discrete geographic locals, suggesting less rather than more diversity. As A. J. R. Groom and Peter Mandaville observed, only until very recently was it the case that students in continental Europe wishing to pursue graduate studies in IR were forced to do so exclusively in the United Kingdom or the United States. And, to the extent that a few graduate schools have now opened up outside of the United Kingdom and the United States, it remains the case that these two centers alone still act as the instructional heartland for those of us who "do IR," reaffirming the hegemony of place at least in terms of official accreditation and training. In Australia, for example, 70 percent of all recent appointments to that country's seven leading research universities received their doctorates from North America and the United Kingdom. In Canada, also, the proclivity to "travel south" and be trained in an American institution is often viewed as the path better suited to the "more talented" student. "Cultural cringe," despite strong evidence of robust and equally talented indigenous intellectual communities, still makes for a "brain drain," and not just in International Relations. Across the humanities and social sciences generally, "American degrees" and an "American education" are still highly prized. Casual observations about the number of Asian students who travel to North America for their academic training, for example, or to Britain in the case of students from Singapore and Hong Kong, continues to suggest that the lure of accreditation from American and English universities retains social and economic prestige.

This apparent educational duopoly might account for the alleged "homogenization" of those who "do IR" if only because so many of us receive our formal training, and thus socialization, at institutions in the "hegemonic center" where we are versed in similar methodologies, taught the major lines of intellectual rupture embodied in the "great debates," and instructed in the canonical texts. And while the question of "diversity" as canvassed in this volume has been done so largely in relation to epistemological and methodological considerations, all of us who "do IR" recognize the disproportionate number of voices that resonate from American enclaves. It will not have escaped the reader of this volume, for example, that our forum for this dialogue occurs in an American university press, conforms to American spelling, and that the series editor is an American. Undoubtedly, this is testimony to the great openness of "American IR" for critical self-examination, and a sign of its strengths, not weaknesses. But still, it points to the tendency for IR to be filtered through American lenses, and for the discipline's subjects of inquiry, issues, and concerns to be those that resonate with American audiences. The discipline's research agendas and debates tend to be defined by interests and concerns that are "American," of questions concerning its global hegemony, and perhaps of its relative decline. "The debate" at any given moment in "the discipline" refers implicitly to "American" definitions and understandings, not those of Australian, Canadian, or British scholars.

Evidence for this is not hard to find. Ole Wæver (Wæver, 1998) in a recent article, for example, surveyed the national composition of authorship among eight leading American and European International Relations journals. His findings were not encouraging. Figures for 1995 (the latest available), show that American authorship dominates, comprising 85.7% of the articles published in *International Organization* (*IO*), 83.3% of the articles published in *International Studies Quarterly* (*ISQ*), 96% of the articles published in *International Security* (*IS*), and in *World Politics* (*WP*) 91.7% of the articles published. Even among the European journals surveyed, American authorship was strongly represented, comprising 43.3% of the articles published in the *Review of*

International Studies (RIS), 30.8% of the articles published in the *European Journal of International Relations (EJIR)*, 46.7% of those published in *Millennium: Journal of International Studies (MILL)*, and 43.8% of those published in the *Journal of Peace Research (JPR)*. And, much like Holsti discovered back in 1985, the remaining authorship was overwhelmingly accounted for by British authors. Outside of Europe and the United States, authorship from the "rest of the world" among all the journals surveyed for 1995 averaged a mere 3.9% (Wæver, 1998, 698). Hegemony, at least in terms of the overwhelming predominance of American authors, and to some degree British, is still the order of the day, and represented starkly in figure C.1.

In and of itself, however, is this concentration of authorship among American and British nationals a problem for IR? Does it simply tell us that a lot of Americans and Britons think and write about international politics? Does the national origin of authors matter when they write about international relations? The answers to these questions comes in two parts. First, it tells us that there *are* "national" IR disciplines and that these quite naturally tend to be concerned with their own national interests. American scholars can hardly be faulted for a preoccupation with their country's international affairs, and for less concern with the international affairs of Bangladesh, Ethiopia, or France. This is not the problem. Rather, the problem arises when national discipline's extrapolate their interests, and assume (or justify) their worldviews to be universal views. As Mark Neufeld and Teresa Healy and A.J.R. Groom and Peter Mandaville highlight in their contributions, it matters from where one views the world, national contexts frame questions, issues, and concerns differently in Canada, Britain, or Germany than they do in the United States. Unavoidably, theory is a function of location, or at least viewing position, and attempts to universalize international theory is a highly problematic task. Steve Smith long ago noted that the world looks sufficiently different from, "say, Calcutta than it does from Moscow, Kabal, Tehran or Kansas" so that "people in different countries will have contrasting views of what the most important issues are, and of how these are to be dealt with" (Smith, 1985, ix). Nationality matters, and international relations remains a game between discretely defined national communities regardless of the euphemisms surrounding revolutions in communications technologies or "globalization." This harbors implications for theory construction, of the questions asked, the facts focused on, and of the interests that are promoted or defended. The problem, then, might not be one of parochialism in the context of American IR but, as Chris Brown and Robert Crawford suggest in this volume, the fact that American IR is not parochial enough. Were it more so, the hegemon's interests expressed via its national but overwhelm-

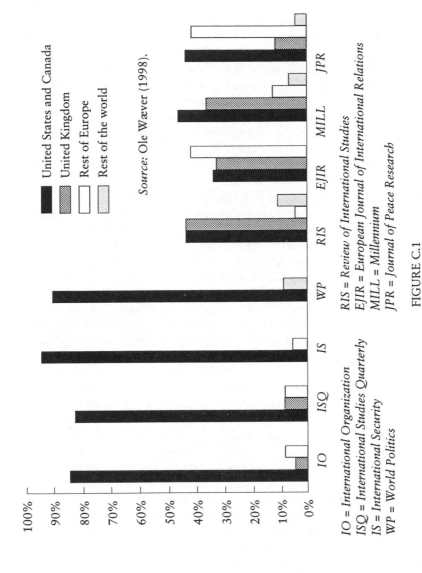

IO = International Organization   RIS = Review of International Studies
ISQ = International Studies Quarterly   EJIR = European Journal of International Relations
IS = International Security   MILL = Millennium
WP = World Politics   JPR = Journal of Peace Research

FIGURE C.1

Distribution of Authors by Country of Residence in International Journals, 1995 ingly predominant discipline might abate its tendency to universal aspirations.

Not all contributors to this volume have been convinced by such arguments, or that the issue of nationality and national identity are even important in the first instance. Tony Porter in his contribution, for example, was suspect of such an interpretation, suggesting that the lines of rupture we observe within IR tend to be structured not along "national" divides but ideological ones, and defined not by "national" outlook but the epistemological framework into which our respective research agendas fit. Porter's point is well made when he asks, for example, "What do Kenneth Waltz, Richard Ashley, Cynthia Enloe, and Craig Murphy have in common?" All, he observes, are American. But beyond this observation it would be impossible to suggest a shared outlook, ideological disposition, methodological proclivity, or common set of values and research interests, that could be inferred as distinctly "American." The differences between feminist, Gramscian, structural realist, and postmodern approaches, are so diverse as to render a notional "American" approach highly suspect. These same observations might also be made of the British, Australians, Canadians, and New Zealanders, whose own epistemological and methodological diversity renders national prefixes problematic devices for inferring a particular theoretical inclination, approach, or outlook.

There is much to what Porter suggests, especially since national prefixes are themselves less than revealing of the ethnic composition of those who write about international relations. More often than not, national prefixes mask the diversity inherent not just in the authorship of this volume, but likely also the discipline more generally. Pal Ahluwalia, for example, while born in Kenya, is a Canadian citizen now teaching in Australia who has an ethnic background descended from the Indian subcontinent. Likewise, Molly Cochran, while positioned in England, hails from the south of the United States, and D. S. L. Jarvis, while born in England of Welsh ancestry, also holds Australian and Canadian passports. These same observations could be made of other contributors to the volume and countless others who "do IR" throughout the world. National prefixes no longer delineate discrete lines of ethnicity in an age of hypermobility and mass migration, and might not be good indicators of the extent of diversity apparent in the discipline. But if Porter's arguments are to have lasting value they need to counter what remains a stinging rebuke of American disciplinary images of global politics that tend to predominate. Kim Richard Nossal, for example, sees too little "diversity" and a tendency to a omnipresent American representation of non-American people and places. Canvassing the pages of recently published American IR textbooks, Nossal finds not just erroneous images of the world that lie beyond American shores, but, as a consequence, an endemic parochialism that seems destined to reproduce jaundiced images of peoples and places beyond the immediate purview of our American colleagues. Mark Neufeld and Teresa Healy likewise see a pedagogical approach that is largely ubiquitous in its tendency to replicate current social and political orders by assuming a "value-free" and uncritical pedagogical posture. For them, challenging hegemony means involving students in a broader project, one that allows them to connect political and international events amid the context of power relations and globalization. On these appraisals, IR remains dominated by the views, concerns, and methods of the hegemon.

There is reason to suppose, however, that American hegemony might be breaking down. The "issues" now canvassed as apposite to IR, for example, are increasingly variegated: gender, the diplomacies of indigenous peoples, sexuality, ethnicity, migration, trade and money, identity politics, regionalism, and environmental issues, to name but a few, are now standard additives to the ever growing list of "issues" in IR. In this sense, IR might well start to outgrow its American centeredness, in part by challenging its sense of "discipline" and making redundant its previously restrictive catalogue of "war and peace" as ordering categories for "legitimate" research subjects. Many would welcome this. Jan Jindy Pettman, for example, berates IR for its masculinized and biased research agendas, extending IR questions to include how international politics are gendered, and how the study of such has been influenced by predominately white, privileged, male practitioners who have pursued questions and research issues that interest and affect them. The strictures that otherwise defined the outer parameters of the discipline as traditionally conceived, Pettman rejects, and in doing so renders void previous approaches, and the previous subjects and objects of inquiry. The "American discipline," in other words, is put to rest by breaking down its self-imposed boundaries and extending them into broader concepts like gender and identity. The same is true of Pal Ahluwalia and Michael Sullivan's contribution, which obliterates the boundaries of conventional scholarship and understanding in the discipline by highlighting how contingent and flawed was the knowledge it produced. Enmity, they are able to demonstrate, derives from the cultural and linguistic construction of "otherness" as with the construction of "the Red Menace" or the cultural antipathy personified in Samuel Huntingon's construction of an alien "Eastern" civilization opposed to Western interests. The parameters of IR are thus judged to be culturally suspect, rendering moot the subcultural issues of national identity in the context of "American IR." Likewise, James Richardson sees the parameters of IR moving beyond the essentially economistic mediums of theorizing that have been so indicative of IR theory in the last few decades, and incorporating a more historically focused research agenda. What each is suggesting is that the disciplinary parameters of "American IR" are now likely threatened by the expansion in the number of issues theorists must now confront, diminishing the utility of "discipline" to our scholarship, and with it likely the predominance of "American IR" as a conduit via which so much of our scholarship has been funneled. Add to this the expansion in the series of methods now seen as pertinent to our area of study (and demonstrated in the remaining essays presented here), and the disciplinary parameters of IR seem increasingly precarious. However, as with all forms of social, political, and economic transformation, change must be measured in the longer term, not within generations but between them. This is also true of those factors that have until now conspired for the predominance of American values and interests within IR. Transformation might well be afoot, but for the present it would be naive to suppose that those dynamics which made for the prevalence of American images, understandings, and methods in IR have been transcended.

REFERENCES

Smith, S. (1985). "Introduction." In S. Smith (ed.), *International Relations: British and American Perspectives*. Oxford: Basil Blackwell.

Holsti, K. J. (1985). *The Dividing Discipline: Hegemony and Diversity in International Theory*. Boston: Unwin Hyman.

Wæver, O. (1998). "The Sociology of a Not So International Discipline: American and European Developments in International Relations." *International Organization* 52(4) (Autumn), 687–727.

CONTRIBUTORS

D. Pal Aluwahlia is Senior Lecturer in the Department of Politics at the University of Adelaide, Australia, where he teaches courses on comparative politics and the politics of trade and development. His research interests are concerned with comparative politics, the politics of Africa, cultural criticism and critical theory, global trade policy and international political economy. He is author, with Paul Nursey-Bray, of *African Politics: A Critical Assessment* (Nova Science, 1995), and with Paul Nursey-Bray, Doug McEachern and Carol Johnson, of *A Guide to Contemporary 'Isms* (Longman Cheshire, 1995). He has also contributed articles to the *Journal of Modern African Studies*, *Caribbean Issues*, *Asian Studies Review*, *Current Affairs Bulletin*, and the *Australian Journal of Political Science*.

Chris Brown is Professor of International Relations, London School of Economics, England, where he teaches courses on international relations and political theory. His research interests concern ethics and theoretical debates in international relations. He has published numerous articles in *Millennium: Journal of International Studies*, *Review of International Studies*, and recently published *Understanding International Relations* (Macmillan, 1997). He is also editor of the volume *Political Restructuring in Europe: Ethical Perspectives* (Routledge, 1994).

Molly Cochran is Lecturer in the Department of Politics, the University of Bristol, England, where she teaches international politics and ethics. Her publications include *Normative Theory in International Relations: A Pragmatist Approach* (1998), articles in *Millennium: Journal of International Studies*, *Review of International Studies* and contributions in the edited volumes *Boundaries in Question: New Directions in International Relations* (1995), and *Richard Rorty and Political Theory* (1998). Her current research concerns issues surrounding cosmopolitan and communitarian debates in international relations and feminist international relations theory.

Robert M. A. Crawford is Lecturer of introductory humanities and social sciences in the Arts One Programme, Faculty of Arts, at the University of British Columbia, Vancouver, Canada. His publications include *Regime Theory and the Post–Cold War World: Rethinking Neoliberal Approaches to International Relations* (Dartmouth, 1996) and *Idealism and Realism in International Relations: Beyond 'the' Discipline* (Routledge, 2000).

Roger Epp is a Professor in the Department of Political Studies at Augustana University College, Alberta, Canada, where he teaches international relations, political philosophy, and aboriginal politics. He has recently published articles and book chapters on aboriginal diplomacies, the idea of moral responsibility, the "English School" in international thought, and Canadian Foreign Policy. He was a recent visiting fellow at the Department of International Politics, the University of Wales, Aberystwyth. His current research is concerned with globalization, democracy, community, and the political economy of rural Alberta.

Martin Griffiths is Senior Lecturer in the School of Political and International Studies at the Flinders University of South Australia. His publications include *Realism, Idealism and International Politics* (Routledge, 1992), and *Fifty Key Thinkers in International Relations* (Routledge, 1999). He has also contributed articles to the *Review of International Studies*, the *Australian Journal of Politics and History*, and chapters to the volume *Middling, Meddling, Muddling: Australian Foreign Policy Under Labour* (Allen and Unwin, 1997). His current research is concerned with debates over nationalism and the state in international politics, and a book project dealing with the politics of the Cold War.

A. J. R. Groom is Professor of International Relations and Head of the Department of Politics and International Relations at the University of Kent at Canterbury, England. He currently serves as Director of the Centre for Conflict Analysis and is founder and Chair of the Standing Group on International Relations of the European Consortium for Political Research. He has held numerous visiting appointments and has served as Vice-President of the International Studies Association in the United States. His research interests are concerned with international relations theory, international organization, conflict studies, and European international relations. He has written or edited nearly twenty books, and has authored or co-authored over a hundred articles and chapters. Among his recent works are *Frameworks for International Cooperation* (Pinter, 1995, edited with Paul Taylor); *International Relations: Then and Now* (HarperCollins, 1991, edited with Williams C

Olson); *The European Community in Context* (1992); *Contemporary International Relations: A Guide to Theory* (Pinter, 1994, edited with Margot Light); *Burdensome Victory: the UN and Iraq* (edited with Edward Newman and Paul Taylor).

Teresa Healy is a graduate of the Department of Political Science at Carleton University. She has taught international relations and international political economy at Carleton and Trent Universities. Her current research focuses on gender and counterhegemonic movements in the context of globalization.

Kalevi J. Holsti is a distinguished Professor of International Relations in the Department of Political Science, Faculty of Arts, at the University of British Columbia, Canada. He has been past President of both the Canadian Political Science Association and the International Studies Association, is a member of the Royal Society of Canada, and has recently been named a Killam University Professor, only the seventh faculty member of UBC to be so named. His numerous publications include *The State, War, and the State of War* (Cambridge, 1996), *Peace and War: Armed Conflicts and International Order, 1648–1989* (Cambridge, 1991), and *The Dividing Discipline: Hegemony and Diversity in International Theory* (Allen and Unwin, 1985). His well-known textbook *International Relations: Framework for Analysis*, now in its seventh edition, has appeared in English, Chinese, Japanese, Korean and Indonesian language editions.

Darryl S. L. Jarvis is Lecturer in the Department of Government and International Relations, Faculty of Economics and Business, at the University of Sydney, Australia. His research interests include international relations theory, The politics of global money and finance, and international political economy. He is author of *International Relations and the Challenge of Postmodernism: Defending the Discipline* (University of South Carolina Press, 2000) and editor of the volume *Post-modernism and Its Critics: International Relations and the Third Debate* (Preager, forthcoming). He has contributed articles to *Politics and Society* and is currently researching a book on the politics of money, credit, and finance in the Asia-Pacific.

Peter G. Mandaville is Lecturer in the Department of Politics and International Relations at the University of Kent at Canterbury, England. His research interests include cultural globalization, transnational social theory and the international relations of the Islamic world. He is currently completing a project on transnational Muslim identities.

Mark Neufeld is Associate Professor in the Department of Political Studies at Trent University, Ontario, Canada, where he teaches in the field of global politics. He has taught previously at Carleton University as well as at York University, where he remains an External Associate of the Centre for International and Strategic Studies. His primary research interests concern critical approaches to globalization and world order. He has published articles and chapters in books dealing with international relations (meta)theory, ethics, and world politics, religion and politics, Canadian foreign policy, and critical pedagogy. He is the author of *The Restructuring of International Relations Theory* (Cambridge University Press, 1995), and currently holds a Social Sciences and Humanities Research Council research grant to explore the relationship between globalization and democracy in contemporary world politics.

Kim Richard Nossal is Professor in the Department of Political Science at McMaster University, Hamilton, Ontario, Canada. His publications include *The Patterns of World Politics* (Prentice Hall Canada, 1998); *The Politics of Canadian Foreign Policy*, 3rd ed. (Prentice Hall Canada, 1997); *Relocating Middle Powers: Australia and Canada in a Changing World Order* (University of British Columbia Press, 1993, with Andrew F. Cooper and Richard A. Higgott); and *Rain Dancing: Sanctions in Canadian and Australian Foreign Policy* (University of Toronto Press, 1994).

Terry O'Callaghan is Lecturer in International Relations at the University of South Australia, Adelaide, where he teaches courses on global politics and peace and conflict. His research interests are concerned with normative international theory and international security. He is currently working on a book with Martin Griffiths on key concepts in international relations to be published by Routledge in 2001.

Jan Jindy Pettman is Reader in Global Politics and Director of the Centre for Women's Studies at the Australian National University, Canberra. Her publications include *Living in the Margins: Racism, Sexism and Feminism in Australia* (Allen and Unwin, 1992), and *Worlding Women: A Feminist International Politics* (Routledge, 1996). She is also the author of numerous articles and chapters in edited books. Her current research interests include the gendered politics of nationalism, the international politics of feminism, and the international political economy of sex.

Tony Porter is Associate Professor of Political Science at McMaster University in Hamilton, Canada. He is the author of *States, Markets and*

Regimes in Global Finance (Basingstoke, U.K.: Macmillan, 1993) and has co-edited, with A. Claire Cutler and Virginia Haufler, *Private Authority in International Affairs*, (Albany: State University of New York Press, 1999).

James L. Richardson is Professor in the Department of International Relations, Research School of Pacific and Asian Studies, at the Australian National University, Canberra. He has held the posts of Research Associate at the Center for International Affairs at Harvard University, was a member of the Arms Control and Disarmament Unit in the British Foreign Office, Associate Professor in the Department of Government at the University of Sydney, Australia, and has served previously as Professor of Political Science in the Faculty of Arts at the Australian National University, Canberra. He has written on German and European security, the Cold War and détente, Australia's foreign relations, arms control and crisis diplomacy. He is author and co-author of numerous books and articles and has contributed to many edited volumes. His current research concerns theories of long-term historical change and the problems confronting liberalism in post–Cold War international relations.

Roger Spegele is Senior Lecturer in the Department of Politics, Monash University, Melbourne, Australia. He has held teaching appointments at Wesleyan University and the Universities of Nairobi, Witwatersrand, and Bophuthatswana. He is the author (with Alastair Davidson) of *Rights, Justice and Democracy in Australia* (1991), *Political Realism in International Theory* (Cambridge, 1996), and has contributed articles to the *Review of International Studies*, *Millennium: Journal of International Studies*, *American Political Science Review*, *Political Studies* and *Review of Politics*. His research interests are concerned with the theory of international relations with special reference to critiques of realism; international political economy, historical and contemporary, including Australia's current trading problems; ethics and politics; globalism; political theory and aspects of literary studies.

Michael Sullivan teaches courses on international relations with special focus on Asian and Chinese politics in the Departments of Politics and Asian studies at the University of Adelaide, South Australia. He has recently published "Australia's regional Peacekeeping Discourse: Policing the Asia-Pacific," in the edited volume *Discourses of Danger and Dread Frontiers* (Allen and Unwin, 1996). His research interests are concerned with international relations in the Asia-Pacific region and Australian foreign policy.

INDEX

387

SUNY series in Global Politics
James N. Rosenau, Editor

List of Titles